Grail Knights of North America

For my friend and companion, Joelle Lauriol,
and for Winifred Eva Czulinski (Winnie Jr.),
Rob Iveson, Rae Thurston, and Delayne Coleman
of the Prince Henry Sinclair Society of North America.
And, as always and forever, for my son Jason.

Grail Knights of North America
On the Trail of the Grail Legacy in Canada and the United States

Michael Bradley

HOUNSLOW PRESS
TORONTO · OXFORD

Hounslow Press
A Member of the Dundurn Group

Publisher: Anthony Hawke
Editor: Wendy Thomas
Design: Scott Reid
Printer: Transcontinental Printing Inc.

Canadian Cataloguing in Publication Data

Bradley, Michael, 1944-
Grail knights of North America: on the trail of the grail legacy in Canada and the United States

ISBN 0-88882-203-0
1. America — Discovery and exploration — Pre-Columbian. 2. Grail.
3. Templars. I. Title

E103.B72 1998   970.01'1   C98-931581-9

1   2   3   4   5   02   01   00   99   98

THE CANADA COUNCIL | LE CONSEIL DES ARTS
FOR THE ARTS | DU CANADA
SINCE 1957 | DEPUIS 1957

We acknowledge the support of the **Canada Council for the Arts** for our publishing program. We also acknowledge the support of the **Ontario Arts Council** and the **Book Publishing Industry Development Program** of the **Department of Canadian Heritage.**

Care has been taken to trace the ownership of copyright material used in this book. The author and the publisher welcome any information enabling them to rectify any references or credit in subsequent editions.

Printed and bound in Canada.

Printed on recycled paper.

Hounslow Press
8 Market Street
Suite 200
Toronto, Ontario, Canada,
M5E 1M6

Hounslow Press
73 Lime Walk
Headington, Oxford,
England
OX3 7AD

Hounslow Press
2250 Military Road
Tonawanda NY
U.S.A 14150

Contents

"Kyot, the master of high renown,
Found, in confused pagan writing,
The Legend which reaches back to the
prime source of all legends."

From *Parzival* by Wolfram von Eschenbach

1

Et in Arcadia Ego
("And I am in Arcadia")

The pale sunlight of mid-November Pennsylvania slanted tentatively through trees that were mostly bare. A shy late afternoon sun cast hard shadows and soft rays through an intricate filigree of branches onto the twin ruts of the logging road.

It was a cuculoris, or "cookie" (as film people call it), effect that created a pattern all the more interesting and intricate because it was animated. Bare branches swirled, nodded, and curtseyed to the cold northwest wind that gusted over the abrupt rocky perimeter of Mason Mountain. The few remaining leaves would suddenly flutter like desperate rag-flags of parley, but judging from the knife slashes of cold wind, the oncoming winter scorned mercy, negotiation, postponement.

This road seemed almost as tentative as the sunlight, because, on the rocky outcrops, which were frequent, the twin ruts disappeared altogether. And, at this season, even when tire marks of man's activity had tried to assert themselves in softer ground, the resulting ruts had filled with defeated leaves.

And yes, I thought to myself, our mission was just as tentative, just as elusive, and yet just as real as the logging road and the pale swirling and flickering sunlight. The four of us were on a quest for the Holy Grail.

But it hadn't started out that way.

We were just enthusiastic amateurs — amateur historians, archaeologists, and linguists. Over the years we had each come upon evidence that challenged history as it is written in school books...but only gradually had we arrived at the realization that some of this evidence formed a consistent, cohesive pattern in the

weave of conventional history. And only reluctantly, with a sense of
nostalgic and unbelieving wonder, had we begun to recognize this
pattern as a tracery of shining gilt thread woven into the shabby and
time-tattered cloak of western culture by the Grail.

I, Michael Bradley, sometime university lecturer in history,
ancient land migrations, and voyages of discovery, and author of
several books on these subjects, brought up the rear of our small
procession. Immediately ahead of me, the small wiry form of Mike
Twose, an audio-visual technician at the University of Toronto's
Faculty of Music, whose occupation and age (sixty-three years)
belied his sure-footed balance and seemingly inexhaustible stamina,
walked the humped and jagged spine of the logging road between
the deep ruts. Mike and I formed the Canadian contribution.

Ahead of Mike, tall and stolid Don Eckler of Houghton, New
York, professional microscope technician and amateur historian,
plodded onwards with unstoppable enthusiasm. And in front of
Don, heading the vanguard of our small historical commando force,
was our lean and weathered Pennsylvania guide, Bob Williams, from
the nearby town of Emporium. Don and Bob were the American
contingent of our allied effort.

Bob, a former State Police officer and more recently a retired
prison guard, also moonlighted as an amateur historian and
archaeologist. He was, quite naturally, interested in the Indian and
colonial history of his part of central Pennsylvania, where he'd lived
all his life. He knew the ancient Indian trails and village sites, and
early colonial roads, hamlets, and farmsteads as few living men
know them. Rugged mountains and gorges of swift streams, which
modern people and modern roads shunned, were not strangers to
him, for he was also an avid hunter and naturalist.

And it was Bob who had inspired our modest invasion of Mason
Mountain. In the course of his hunting and historical expeditions
over this northeastern extension of the mighty Appalachian
Mountains, expeditions that concentrated in, and on, his own local
area of the Allegheny-Susquehanna watershed, he'd come across
things that didn't fit into either Indian or colonial culture...and he
knew both very well.

Bob had found the ruins of what looked like ancient, jumbled
stone citadels on mountain tops. Or, maybe, some were ancient
villages that had once been protected by massive stone palisades,
walls composed of large stone blocks. Most of the walls had been
tumbled down in confusion, but here and there a length of wall still

stood for several yards or metres, a still-formidable bastion of large, square stone blocks each weighing several hundred pounds.

And sometimes, but usually on mountain summits, Bob had found inscribed stones. He'd always supposed these "inscriptions" to be of Indian origin, although he well knew that no North American Indians were supposed to possess true writing before the coming of Europeans.

Not often on mountains, but on protected cliff shelters along the courses of many waterways, Bob had come across curious carvings, "in low relief" as he described them, depicting symbols and mythical creatures redolent of Masonic lore (and perhaps I should make it clear that, as far as I was able to find out, Mason Mountain was not named because of anything Freemasonic, but was named in honour of a farmer of the 1790s).

In the meticulous way of policemen, trackers, and naturalists, Bob Williams had recorded his discoveries in personal notebooks. His descriptions of ruins and inscriptions, preserved in his large and somewhat laborious-looking longhand, were sometimes augmented with sketches and pictures of the mysteries he'd seen. His sketches were stunning. They revealed a considerable artistic talent that had never had opportunity for much development or expression; a natural eye for composition, scale, perspective, texture, and lighting that argued strongly that Bob could have had a career other than his lifelong fight against crime.

It is at least possible that the discoveries of Bob Williams would never have escaped the covers of his schoolboy copybooks if Don Eckler, a decades-long friend of Bob, had not bought a copy of *Holy Grail Across the Atlantic* while on a visit to Canada. This book, the first of two I wrote on the general subject of the "Holy Grail," was published by Hounslow Press of Toronto in 1988 and has been available only in Canada. But many visitors bought copies while on vacation or business in Canada, and returned home with them.

Don Eckler was one such American visitor and, as soon as he opened *Holy Grail Across the Atlantic*, he saw Norse and North Scottish architecture that resembled stonework that Bob Williams had found during forty years of excursions into his beloved Pennsylvania mountains. And he also saw inscriptions, and curious carvings, attributed to the Knights Templar. In other books listed in my bibliography, Don saw yet more stone sculpture, stone carvings, and stone inscriptions from the Knights Templar memorial chapel at Rosslyn, Scotland. Some of these seemed very similar to stone carvings that Bob had seen along the Allegheny and Susquehanna rivers and their Pennsylvania tributaries. Don Eckler contacted with me, and he called Bob Williams. Eventually, several outings were arranged so that I could see what Bob had found.

Mike Twose accompanied me on these visits to New York State and Pennsylvania, as he had also been one of my companions on visits to Quebec City and Magog in the province of Quebec, and to Peterborough in the province of Ontario, to see intriguing ruins and artefacts on the Canadian side of the huge Great Lakes and St. Lawrence waterway. I'd learned to appreciate Mike's photographic skills and his iconoclastic perspective.

Sometimes we travelled in my old and much-abused Dodge B200 factory camper van, a vehicle as reliable as it was battered, which I had driven to Nova Scotia, New Brunswick, Vermont, New Hampshire, and Connecticut on the trail of Grail evidence in remote places reached by broken roads; but for shorter trips I much preferred riding in Mike's British-made vintage 1962 Rover 100. His car's tasteful external styling, estate-car suspension, and walnut-and-red-leather interior not only provided comfortable travelling, but seemed to attract a truly inordinate amount of attention in a North American culture acclimatized to plastic.

I've compared our little four-man procession along the Mason Mountain logging road to a historical commando force, and perhaps I should clarify this. We had set out to see one of Bob's discoveries that particularly intrigued me. If it was just as Bob had described it, and if it were genuine, then the artefact was a small datum that could be lobbed against the high and solid wall of conventional history. Presented properly (along with a lot more related data), it might have enough impact to nudge too-complacent conventional academics into at least semi-wakefulness. They might then start to look at some awkward facts of western history, *and especially facts about the geographical discovery, colonization, and socio-political development of Canada and the United States — **but particularly the United States** — which argued a much different impetus to, and perspective on, western civilization than has been presented in orthodox textbooks.

So I want to make it clear that academics were not *within* our commando force, for none of us could claim any impressive academic credentials, but the reverse. Conventional history was the *target* of our November assault on Pennsylvania's Mason Mountain. To over-stress this militant metaphor, perhaps, I was then (and remain) doubtful that our small guerrilla raid on Mason Mountain in 1995 would make much of a dent in the formidable citadel of conventional history and complacent wisdom (which is, of course, the most popular kind of each). But we could unnerve the garrison a bit more. Barraclough Fell of Harvard (*America B.C.*, *Saga America* and *Bronze Age America*), Dr. Michael Salvatore Trento (*The Search for Lost America*), Dr. George Carter of Texas A&M in various publications, my own *Holy Grail Across the Atlantic* and *The Columbus Conspiracy*, many of Frederick Pohl's books (*The Lost Discovery*, *Prince Henry Sinclair*, *The New Columbus*, etc.), not to mention Laurence Gardner's *Bloodline of the Holy Grail* , *The Hiram Key* by Christopher Knight and Robert Lomas, and many more — all had thrown up new facts and interpretations that had already chipped the walls of the great fortress.

Some nervous academics had started to venture out, in secret, to learn the increasing strength of our data. But it would still take many more facts thrown against those imposing battlements before the conventional academic establishment would consider any sincere reassessment of their basic historical construct.

Perhaps it was the bright red caps and criss-crossed fluorescent orange reflectors, worn bandolier-style over Don's and Bob's duffle coats, that put me in this military mind mode. They had insisted that bright red was necessary in autumn Pennsylvania woods as protection against itchy-fingered deer hunters. This was always a wise precaution in the northeast hunting season, but in the past few years the danger of getting shot had greatly increased.

Another, and more insidious, danger lurked in these woods. The very real possibility of getting shot, combined with the knowledge that a much grimmer fate could await us because of the little monsters in the underbrush, made me associate our excursion with a commando-style penetration into unwelcoming, forbidden, and besieged territory.

Don and Bob had insisted that Mike Twose and I wear high boots and even higher thick socks into which we could tuck our jeans. This was necessary, we were told, to protect ourselves against the *Ixodes dammini* tick which now, it seemed, infested all the bushland in the northeastern United States. This tick, in turn, carried the *Borrelia burdorferi* bacteria that caused the dreaded Lyme disease. Our high boots and higher socks were not absolute protection against the ticks because the creatures were adept at entering seams and wrinkles in clothing, just as bright orange caps and bandoliers could not be considered absolute protection against eager bounty hunters. But the precautions were better than nothing...if the risk was considered worthwhile.

First identified in the mid-1970s when fifty-one residents of Lyme, Connecticut, caught a mysterious disorder with symptoms similar to acute rheumatoid arthritis, by 1995 Lyme disease had been reported from all northeastern states. New York led the northeast in the number of diagnosed cases (6.09 of every 100,000 people), with Pennsylvania a close second. "Untreated, the ailment could be lifelong, leading to a range of neurological disorders, amnesia, behavioral changes, serious pain syndromes in the bones and muscles, even fatal heart disease or respiratory failure."[1]

Like so many of the newly emerging viruses and bacteria that currently threaten humanity's very future, Lyme disease has become a troublesome problem because of man's destruction of the environment. The *Borrelia* bacterium has existed for millions of years, and so has the *Ixodes dammini* tick. The tick was a parasite on a common northeastern woodland mouse, *Peromyscus leucopus*, which naturally and formerly inhabited the depths of the primeval American forest. Man in the form of Native Americans or early Puritans could never have had much contact with these mice because both Indians and early colonists lived on the fringes of the great forest, not in it.

But as this magnificent virgin forest was cut down, to be replaced by the open bushland and secondary growth that now blankets all of the northeast United States, the forest mice had to make a new home in the bushland. This is perfect habitat for deer, which formerly grazed on the edges of the forest and not in the depths of it, and, because all the deer predators had long been exterminated, there are now many more deer in the northeast than there could have been when the Pilgrims landed in 1620.

The mice, driven from their natural forest habitat, adapted to the bush, where the ticks they carried began to infect the deer. The size of the deer population soon began to explode so that they now graze on suburban lawns and azaleas in a desperate bid to fend off starvation due to over-population.

And, of course, in their new, man-made, and greatly expanded habitat, tick-infected deer began to infect people, dogs and cats in suburban villages like Lyme, Connecticut.

The story of Lyme disease is not much different from the recent and tragic emergence of much deadlier diseases: Machupo in

Bolivia; Ebola, Lassa, Marburg and HIV in Africa (all viruses). Mankind has penetrated, usually by clearing forests to make way for agriculture, into remote areas where people can come into frequent contact with rare or retiring animals that are natural carriers of microbes. The microbes are harmless to the natural, preferred host (usually termed the microbes' "reservoir" by epidemiologists); it does not make any evolutionary sense, from the microbe's point of view, for it to kill its natural host but it may prove deadly if it is transferred into any other species, including *Homo sapiens*.

The natural reservoir of Bolivia's terrible Machupo hemorrhagic *virus* turned out to be, as with Lyme disease's *bacterium*, a retiring forest rat, *Calomys*. Clearing the forests along the Machupo River for cattle-raising grassland brought *Calomys* into contact with haciendas and railhead cattle towns. The rat population soared in the new environment. Natural forest predators had died out with the trees, and new frontier towns had not yet acquired the usual quota of dogs and cats. The deadly virus that *Calomys* carried began to infect people. Thousands of Bolivians died before an effective treatment was discovered by American virologists. But the real, long-term cure was the airlift of thousands of cats, collected from the slums and gutters of major South American cities (in what must surely be one of the strangest emergency-aid airlifts on record) into the catless cattle-towns of northeast Bolivia. *Calomys* once again has "natural" predators. Machupo still claims a few victims each year, but it is no longer epidemic.

It is known that some African monkeys are *intermediate carriers* (like the eastern white-tailed deer with the Lyme disease *bacterium*) of Ebola, Lassa, Marburg, and HIV *viruses*, but many experts doubt that monkeys can be the real "natural reservoirs" for these microbes. African monkeys have been pushed, by human destruction of the natural environment, into dwindling pockets of forest where they have picked up microbes from whatever creature, probably some sort of blood parasite or blood-eater, that actually hosts these viruses. The search is on for some kind of tick, leech, or spider, rare mouse or rat, bat or other scrabbling hider that's truly the "reservoir" where Ebola, Lassa, Marburg, and HIV viruses can live and evolve. Is it too fanciful to think that if we delve too deeply into our earth's substance we will be stricken? Too fanciful to wonder if our planet has its own natural defences against excessive human rapacity?

But it is no wonder that townships and regions throughout the northeastern United States have embarked on serious strategies to stop Lyme disease by reducing the deer population. As in Bolivia with Machupo some thirty years earlier, the idea was to introduce artificial predators to replace the natural ones that had long been exterminated. Bounty hunting was thought to be the best and fastest answer for some areas. On our drive from Canada to New York State and Pennsylvania, Mike Twose and I had noticed a surprising number of deer carcasses along the roadside, but we didn't realize the cause until Don and Bob explained that truly serious bounty hunting was a reality in New York State and Pennsylvania. Hunters would take proof of the kill needed for payment and leave the rest of the carcass conveniently beside the highway for road maintenance crews to pick up. The regional population, sensitized to the dangers of Lyme disease, would not touch these dead deer. We'd counted at least one dead deer every twenty miles or so (32 kilometres) beside the highway on our drive through western New York State into Pennsylvania. That's why Don and Bob had insisted on precautions against deer hunters and ticks. I got the feeling that both the intellectual and the physical environments seemed hostile to our foray to see Bob's discovery on Mason Mountain.

In a way, our environmental rapacity has loosed new microbial threats to our survival because we have lost the psychological and cultural balance once conferred by belief in the Grail. This statement is not at all exaggerated or romanticized. The Holy Grail was, and remains in an increasing "underground" resurgence, a religion. It is partly a heretical and aberrant form of Christianity, partly the preserved knowledge and tradition from much, much earlier non-Christian sources. Together, these two streams of ethics, principles, and life-knowledge offered believers a practical guide for balancing human psychology and activity on several different levels.

And while it is true (as we shall see) that the founding practical principles of North American democracy were based on Holy Grail political philosophy, it is also true that in consigning the Grail to myth, and in consigning its principles to sentimental romanticism fit only for poetry, our conventional historians and religious leaders have disguised and obscured the core spirituality of the Holy Grail. It is this living spiritual balance of Grail belief that, had it been openly acknowledged as a foundation of our culture, might have weighed human need and greed against environmental endurance. And this might have prevented the breakout of microbial terrors from their remote preserves. Had the Grail openly and principally guided our values, instead of merely influencing them through filters of purposeful obscuration, deliberate denial, and synthetic spirituality, then diseases like Lyme, Machupo, Lassa, Ebola, Marburg, and HIV *might* not have been loosed upon us. There is actual, medieval evidence to support this suggestion, as we will learn.

Or, at the very least, if the Holy Grail principles had been the guiding and dominant ones in our western culture, these new diseases might have only gradually trickled into our world giving us time to deal with them. Guided by a Grail ethic and knowledge, small groups of trained people would have penetrated remote areas, like tropical rain forests, to assess carefully the resource exploitation that these areas could withstand, balanced against human need. A few of these people might have contracted the new diseases, but that would have been an occupational hazard with contingency planning for isolation of the victims and study to find a cure.

As it has been, the world has witnessed hordes of farmers and foresters invading remote areas, clearing the rain forests with fire and bulldozers, with hundreds of people suddenly and simultaneously contracting new viruses and new bacterial infection. Although many die in the remote areas, many travel out before the disease has taken a fatal grip. Since modern travel is so efficient, the disease may spread to other continents before medical people even have a chance to know that a new plague has been unleashed. It may take weeks (or months) to identify its geographical origin in order to make an attempt at containment until some cure or treatment can be developed. By then, the disease may have spread by human transcontinental travel past any hope of containment.

Marburg virus, almost as deadly as Lassa, is named after a town in Germany where the first victims died. It comes, though, from Central Africa, the same area where HIV leaped on us like a ravening beast. With our behaviour, new diseases have no chance of "trickling out" of remote areas leaving time for us to deal with them. They explode outwards in epidemics. With Grail-impelled values about life and the world, this *might* not have been the case.

Up ahead, Bob stopped just where the road topped a gentle hummock in the woods. As the rest of us came up to him and gathered around, Bob (a man of few words) pointed downwards and to our right with his pipe stem. Following this direction, we looked that way down the curving breast of the knoll and saw, not so far away down in a dell, a pale and angular shape not yet covered by drifting leaves. It was one corner of a stone block shimmering grey-white in the capricious light filtering through disturbed branches. We knew that both Bob and Don had been here before and were theatrically leaving a rediscovery to us, so Mike and I scrambled down into the leaf-drowned dell to the stone.

"Make lots of noise in the leaves," called Bob.

"Why?" I shouted back with the wind's help.

"Copperheads."

"Oh." Copperhead moccasins are a three-to-four-foot-long kind of venomous snake indigenous to eastern North America. They are of a mottled red-brown colour and live in the humus of fallen leaves, which disguises them effectively. Very effectively.

So Michael and I more or less goose-stepped our way down to the stone, heaving cascades of leaves before us with every step. Apparently we made enough noise to give any snakes sufficient warning. We weren't bitten. After a few minutes of this, and of fighting our way through tangled, leafless bushes that boasted thorns and the strength of steel springs, we cascaded our way to the centre of the dell.

I knelt down and brushed the stone free of leaves, and Mike began to brush more energetically with his leather glove in order to clear away ingrained, accumulated leaf mould and humus. Soon it became apparent that we were looking at a tombstone, a slab of granite about three feet long, perhaps two feet wide and about ten inches thick (1 by .66 by .25 metres). It bore a brief and crudely incised inscription. We could not make this out at the time because of the weathering on the letters and the attached humus and lichens, but something stood out very clearly — two boldly cut Latin letters: AE. Mike and I looked at each other across the stone, because this was not the first time we'd seen this enigmatic AE in improbable places, and then we both automatically glanced around to gauge available light and time. Mike pointed to the curious tumble of large, squarish-looking boulders that lay beyond the protected dell. They looked like a jumbled, ruined building.

"You go have a look at that," Mike offered, "and I'll try to get some pictures of this while the light lasts."

I nodded, stood up, and began to clamber out of the dell. As I duly kicked leaves every so often for the benefit of the copperheads, I was aware of Mike calling up to Don and Bob, and then their scuffling down into the dell. Thereafter, from time to

Tombstone found in north central Pennsylvania in 1992. The faint dark lines along the middle of some letters indicate where the blunted end of the chalk did not completely fill the actual V-shaped incisions in the stone. Is AE a short form of the Latin phrase *Et in Arcadia Ego*? Photo by author.

time, flaws in the wind brought snatches of their activity and conversation around the tombstone.

They had planted him well, I thought. The little dell would be a sun-dappled tiny glade in the summer, no doubt adorned with honeysuckle and wild roses on the branches that had impeded us. But in winter, the small hollow would nestle his body and protect his spirit from the cold and lonely winds that gusted over the edge of the mountain. And his spirit might well be lonely for he had been buried far from home. And yet, in a way, he *was* in Arcadia....

Arcadia.

In very ancient Greek myth, Arcadia had been the first home of humankind. It was remembered as a kind of pastoral paradise of perpetual spring-summer where people lived in a natural and peaceful state. According to Hesiod, possibly the first Greek poet, and certainly the first one of ongoing and remembered respect, Arcadia had been the home of the "Proselenes" — the people who had lived before the moon was in the sky. Modern experts identify these Proselenes with the Pelasgians, an ancient and probably Neolithic people who lived in the Greek peninsula before the "Greek" invaders from the Indo-European steppes of Russia invaded their preserve.

Very little is known about the Pelasgians, and less actually

survives. There are no ruins, no artefacts, only words. Some
Pelasgian words survive in the Greek language. We have always
tended to regard Greeks as a seafaring people, but they were not
originally so. They came from the common Indo-European steppes
of Russia and the Ukraine in the distant past. They were such
landlubbers that they did not even have a word for the sea or the
ocean. When they invaded Greece, and saw salt water for the first
time, they had to borrow the Pelasgian word for it. The present
"Greek" word for sea is not Greek at all. *Thalassa* is Pelasgian, and
this word is one of a very few words in the ancient, classical and
modern Greek languages that indicate the former existence of the
Pelasgians, or Arcadians.

Later, Arcadia became a synonym for any sort of haven or refuge.
But it did not *quite* convey the modern idea of a geographic region
of safety, a preserve against identifiable contemporary enemies.
Arcadia was seen more as a refuge against *time*. The ancient and
classical Greeks, who conquered Arcadia and more or less
exterminated the Arcadians, did not believe in "progress," as we do,
but the reverse. The Greeks believed that human culture, wisdom,
and knowledge had gone *downhill* since Arcadia — and that they
themselves, the conquerors of Arcadia, represented a *lesser* breed of
humankind. According to Hesiod, the poet, the gods had walked on
earth with the Arcadians during a "Golden Age" and things had got
worse since then.

Therefore, the idea of Arcadia gradually evolved into the notion
of a refuge or haven, true enough, but one safe from people who
were enemies because they were deficient, or degenerate, in wisdom,
knowledge, and the secret of human love. The AE on the
tombstone signified, I was starting to learn, that the individual had
passed on into a realm where it was possible to find a refuge from a
degenerate and distorted world. The AE epitaph had begun to
establish itself, from southern France to Pennsylvania, as an
indication that Grail-believing people had been buried under the
AE stones. But...in the middle of Pennsylvania? Then, I did some
hard thinking about this, trying to pretend that a twentieth-century
education in a major North American university would
approximate the everyday cultural knowledge that supposedly more
ignorant fourteenth- to seventeenth-century "educated" people
always carried in their hearts and heads.

It was the bare trunks of all the trees that made me see the
Medieval-Renaissance light. Penn*sylvania*, Penn's woodland, named

after both William Penn and the Roman god of the forest, *Sylvanus*. And who was *Sylvanus* if not the Roman version of ancient Greek *Pan*? And where was Pan the chief deity? Only in Arcadia. Elsewhere, rustic Pan was but a minor godling. They had buried him well, and the AE was more than a reverent hope. Yes, he had been in Arcadia and he would remain there. But I was aware of a curious, almost uncanny, *synchronicity* (as C.G. Jung would have it) that continually intrudes upon the story of the Holy Grail. I had encountered it many times, from the start of my investigations in Nova Scotia three decades earlier to this latest example at the tomb on Mason Mountain. The AE on the stone had been true, not only symbolically but also literally (in translation from Roman to Greek); the man had been laid to rest in *one* Arcadia.

And yet, of course, if my investigations could claim any credibility, the inscription had been cut at least two centuries before William Penn had gained proprietary rights over this tract of the New World, two hundred years before he had named it Pennsylvania because of the still-virgin forest that then clothed the rugged land. The man who had died here, and his companions who had laid him to rest in the dell and who had cut the rough inscription for him, could not have known that one day in the future the place would be called *sylvania*, a synonym for *Arcadia*. But they had cut the AE...and it had happened. It was just one more instance of "coincidence" that hinted at some force at work behind the scenes of history.

There was certainly nothing nebulous or elusive about the force behind the jumbled stone blocks, however. They had once been arranged with brute force and sweat. As I approached this curious construction, I could see that the builders had made use of a long, rocky ridge that rose four feet (1.3 metres) above the level of the ground. It seemed to be an outcropping of the precipitous edge of the mountain itself. The upper surface of this ridge had either been naturally flat and level or had been made so by the hand of man, and on it had been laid blocks of stone that were all roughly squared. Most of these stones were about three feet long, and about two feet thick and wide (1 by .66 by .66 metres) and enough had been laid to form a wall about five feet high (1.6 metres) above the foundation ridge. Thus, one might say, a stone battlement rose about nine feet or a little more (3 metres) above the very edge of Mason Mountain. The width of the ridge foundation left a "walkway" about two feet (.66 metres) wide inside the entire length of the wall. There, a man might stand and look over the crude crenellation into the sudden and awesome drop of almost two thousand feet (600 metres) into a valley cut by the West Branch of the Susquehanna River. Before enjoying this view myself, I decided to take a close look at the entire complex.

Some of these laid, squared blocks had been thrown down, some to land on the expanse of mountain summit, but others had gone over the edge into the abyss. I examined the tumbled blocks perched on the ridge-foundation and looked carefully at the few that had fallen off the ridge and onto the ground. So far as I could tell, there seemed to be traces of mortar on some faces of the blocks, but it had been poor-quality stuff. Most of it had weathered away leaving a thin layer of residue that would crumble when rubbed between thumb and forefinger. Gypsum mortar, perhaps, that had been made with a conglomerate of too-coarse sand. I had come across the same bad mortar before, from Nova Scotia to Pennsylvania, and usually on mountain ruins. It was too hard to haul fine river sand up to the top. The builders tried to find some sand nearer to hand, on the mountain closer to their activities, and this sand was generally coarse; it had not been made finer by water action.

Other blocks and boulders, some roughly squared, lay in some confusion—but a confusion suggesting that they had once formed walls at right angles to the precipice "battlement." There was no firm indication that there had ever been a fourth wall facing the plateau of the mountain's rather flat and expansive top, although there were quite a few rocks scattered around and radiating in a sort of fan-shaped pattern from the battlement and its side walls (if they had truly *been* side walls). A few of these scattered rocks and blocks seemed to have been purposefully squared.

Some of the blocks of this curious construction were large, but none was so massive that three or four strong men, perhaps with the aid of levers of wood, could not have lifted or shoved the stones into place. The site was not truly "megalithic" in the European sense, like some I had seen in other parts of Pennsylvania, in New York State, and particularly in Ontario, Canada. And, indeed, as a mysterious site, except for the AE tombstone, this one wasn't as impressive as many others I'd seen. Finally, I could find no evidence of fire on the stones themselves or in the general tumble of them. No charred beams or branches. No scorched stones. Not even the remains of a hiking fire in a crude hearth of rocks. This rather surprised me since Mason Mountain was not all *that* inaccessible. Serious hikers or hunters must sometimes have come here, and the windbreak made an obvious place for a camp.

I looked around the construction as carefully as the time and light permitted, but saw no evidence of inscriptions, symbols, or petroglyphs. That was an advantage of visiting interesting sites in the autumn. The lack of summer foliage made examination easier. What foliage there was was mostly dead and fallen and could be brushed away from the base of stone blocks. When I had finished my rapid but careful examination, I was pretty certain that no one had incised any information on this structure. The top of the ridge showed both fine and coarse scratches and abrasions, evidence that it had been chipped and rubbed flat by the hand of man and had been levelled with a careful eye and a lot of grinding.

My major puzzlement was that this site did not seem to make much sense. As I climbed onto the foundation's walkway to look over the battlement, I did immediately appreciate that the wall above the precipice would give protection against the wind for those below and "within" the structure. But why place the strongest wall above a cliff that could not be climbed anyway? Yes, it was a good and necessary place for a windbreak, and the ridge formed a convenient and ready-made foundation for it, though to level it might have required much effort, but surely the stoutest wall of any fortification should have faced the vast and sloping expanse of the mountain's summit? This plateau, almost flat at the very top, gradually descended in a series of folds, steps, and ramps all the long way down to the level of the river a few miles away. It was *this* approach that had always given access to the summit, just as it did now. Our logging road wended its way from the main highway near the base of the mountain up to the top in a series of serpentine curves and switchbacks using the slope's natural ramps and steps and folds. Potential enemies would have come that way, just as loggers and amateur historians did today.

Yet the perimeter of this apparent structure that faced the accessible slope was the "side" with the least robust stonework. But if there were no potential enemies to worry about, why go to the trouble of erecting a stone battlement at all? Why not just camp in the lee of the natural ridge, or improve it a bit by piling a few more stones on top of it and filling in the chinks with mud or wood? Why the careful levelling of the ridge, and then the careful placement of *squared* blocks to make a crudely crenellated battlement with a superb view?

And the view was breathtaking. Resting my hand atop the battlement but (remembering the crumbly mortar) being careful not actually to lean against it, I looked down onto the earth-toned pastoral patchwork of autumnal Pennsylvania. The river curved around the stolid buttress of Mason Mountain like a thin stream of molten copper cast by the westering sun. Across the river, where there was some arable land on the gentle rolling foothills of the next ridge of mountains, tiny cubes of houses, some brick, some grey fieldstone, and some startling white-painted wood, dominated much larger neat rectangles of fallow, ochre fields. Between, behind, and above the fields, irregular remnants of woods seemed to retreat upward towards the stone-bare crests and ridges of what must be, I thought, the Allegheny Mountains. The tiny, twisted trunks and branches seemed to stumble upward and away from the lowlands like a defeated powder-blackened rabble wearing sienna and russet tatters of stubbornly loyal, rearguard leaves.

The sun was poised to drop behind western peaks, which is why dusk comes so soon and so suddenly in mountainous country, and a fine drizzle began to ride on the wind, prickling the skin and misting my glasses. Thus muted, the pastoral *sylvanus*, or Arcadia, far below gave the illusion of still being whole, healthy, and natural. From the height of the battlements in that misty soft light, the vista seemed to be the whole world and there was no hint of soil poisoning by acid rain and dumped chemical waste, no hint of air pollution produced just over the southern horizon in Pittsburgh, no hint of lingering nuclear radiation from the Three Mile Island disaster at the confluence of the Allegheny, Monongahela and Ohio rivers. There was no hint that this Arcadia, the sylvania of our whole planet, was in serious trouble. No indication that in the nearly ruined environments below diseases like Lyme disease, Ebola, Lassa, Marburg, HIV, and Machupo were lurking and ready to strike back on behalf of Arcadia.

AE.

As I clambered down from the curious, jumbled ruin, I thought about the significance of these two letters. These two conjoined letters suddenly appeared in western civilization about the year A.D. 1500. They meant something to somebody, but what? And to whom?

Their first manifestation seems to have been on the famous series of "Unicorn Tapestries" now in The Cloisters of New York City's Metropolitan Museum. All seven of the existing tapestries bear these two letters woven in gold thread into the fabric. Generations of art experts have wondered what this mysterious AE means, and many theories have been offered without any single one earning general acceptance.[2]

I saw an AE carved into the back of an antique Elizabethan settee, part of the furniture of Exploration House, an upscale cartographic and antiquities shop in Toronto. This shop was the location chosen for me to appear in a film called *It's in the Genes*, produced by the National Film Board of Canada, a documentary about the widespread Leblanc family from Acadia.[3] My contribution to the film was the observation that many Acadian genealogies seemed "too long," to have too many generations, for some families to have come to Canada with the official French Acadian colonization of 1634–35. By my count, some of the families must have been in Canada since about 1400.

I didn't notice this settee with its carved AE. Perhaps I was too preoccupied with trying to remember what I was going to say on camera (and too worried about my thinning hair on film). A friend familiar with my research, fellow-writer Winifred Czulinski of Toronto, who had come along to lend moral support, pointed it out just before I was subjected to the last of many audio and lighting checks. Winnie smiled and said that the AE must certainly mean good luck for the filming. To me, it was just one more instance of Carl Jung's principle of *synchronicity*.

My filmed pontification was all within the context of the Holy Grail and its relationship to the Sinclair voyage to Nova Scotia of A.D. 1398.

Aside from the Unicorn Tapestries, the settee, and the tombstone we'd just seen, this AE turns up on the title pages of several books published during Elizabethan times, it is prominent in at least two of the most famous and enigmatic paintings of European art history, and it turns up, in the reversed form of "EA" (which would not alter the meaning), on the now infamous tombstone of Marie de Blanchefort at Rennes-le-Château. It is coyly reversed, but it heads both columns of an inscription that reads "Et in Arcadia Ego,", in mixed Latin and Greek letters, and the words are strangely broken so that the E *can* head one column of letters, and A *can* head the other. In short, this reversed AE was purposefully worked into the inscription of Marie de Blanchefort's tombstone. Moreover, it was purposefully worked into the phrase "Et in Arcadia Ego."

So, to me, the cryptic meaning of this AE is quite transparent. It stands for "Arcadia Ego." It's just a shorthand code for the longer phrase. All well and good, but even if it is true that AE was a shorthand code for the longer phrase, what significance does "Et in Arcadia Ego" have? For whom did it have significance? Why was any sort of cipher message necessary?

Now, for the first time (but not the last), I will ask readers of this book to bear with me in the trust that, eventually, everything will come together to make a coherent and understandable whole. The story we are dealing with is not only of immense importance to western history, *present society*, and entire western civilization, it is one of immense complexity. In fact, this story *is nothing less than an alternative version of western history for the past two thousand years*.

It is the story of the Holy Grail.

Not a cup or a chalice, the Holy Grail is the most elusive and evocative secret of the western world. I do not know whether this secret conceals the truth, and I make no claim one way or another. I can only state that there is a great deal of evidence that the Holy Grail may conceal a momentous truth. But the reality and validity of the Holy Grail is not really the issue. The important thing is that many men and women during the past two thousand years, some obscure in history and others very famous, *believed in* the truth and validity of the Holy Grail. Their *belief* motivated their actions, whether that belief was justified or misguided. And their activities have moulded the western world to a degree that mocks the construct of textbook history, that shocks our everyday concepts of society.

Belief in the Holy Grail was behind the American Revolution and the establishment of a republic with a democratic form of government. The Holy Grail even motivated the earliest voyages from medieval Europe that discovered America and the New World. The Holy Grail preserved the principle of religious freedom that, in the course of time, evolved into all the other forms of social freedoms that the West presently cherishes. The Holy Grail was largely responsible for the "rebirth" of Europe, the Renaissance, with its cultural progress. Earlier, during medieval times, the Holy Grail had been instrumental in introducing into Europe basic medical and financial knowledge, and it kindled a special kind of spiritual awareness that at least partly ameliorated the brutality of the age. Even further back, after the Fall of Rome, the Holy Grail played a larger role than has ever been suspected in the preservation of some western continuity of history and identity.

Belief in the Holy Grail is a *fact* that has created and moulded western history even more, perhaps, than the *fact* of orthodox Christianity and the Roman Catholic Church. This statement may seem an absurd exaggeration but, I think, later pages will show that it is no exaggeration at all.

The nature of the Holy Grail, and belief in it, was a closely guarded secret. Secrecy was necessary because of dreadful persecution. Activities of Grail believers have intruded into the fabric of visible, orthodox, and conventional society through all of the past two thousand years. But their disguised belief and organizational methods have left only curious and puzzling traces on the pattern of western history that conventional academics have tried so desperately to weave. The AE and the significance of "Et in Arcadia Ego" are part of just one such curious and puzzling thread that gleams unexpectedly on the conventional fabric, just as the AE glows golden within the weave of the Unicorn Tapestries. It is a hint of the secret, a glint of the Grail.

This book is really just a record of tugging at the AE thread. Other threads could have been chosen, but the AE one will serve to unravel the story. When we hold at least the outline of the Grail Knights of North America story in our hands and minds, we will grasp a strand of gold that leads all the way back to Jesus. It is a strand that can lead us to new social and spiritual insights as we approach the year 2000, just as it once bound special men and women to a New Covenant. The secret of the Holy Grail can lead us to a wider understanding of Christianity, a new reason for reverence, and a new form of reverence, perhaps much better suited to twentieth-century realities — and this is precisely what I argued when I was invited to address the Maafa Commemoration in September 1997 at the St. Paul Community Baptist Church in New York City.[4] As Bishop John Spong of Newark, New Jersey, has said: "Orthodoxy is orthodoxy because it won, not because it is true."[5]

Tugging at the AE strand will reveal most of what the Grail is all about — and also why America was discovered and why American democracy was created. The Grail and its works will largely be revealed, and we can each judge for ourselves whether it seems a truer version than orthodoxy. Americans, particularly, may appreciate how valuable their republic and democracy really are...and also, perhaps, realize more fully the dangers that threaten both.

So let's tug at the AE thread and see what unravels.

"Et in Arcadia Ego" sounds like it comes from some Latin poem.

And, like many others who have been intrigued with the origin of the phrase, I combed Virgil and Catullus. This was a task I never thought to repeat after high school (which, in fact, I once *swore* never to repeat *when* in high school). Virgil wrote a lot about Arcadia, but he didn't write "Et in Arcadia Ego." Finally, I found a book that confirmed what I hadn't been able to find, but which I feared I might have missed somewhere in the thousands of lines of too many Roman poets.

In his *Death and Rebirth in Virgil's Arcadia* [6], M. Owen Lee writes: "Virgil did not write the haunting, elusive line '*Et in Arcadia ego*,' though many people suppose that it is to be found somewhere in the *Eclogues*.....We first meet the phrase...in a painting done in about 1621 by Guercino (Giovanni Francesco Barbieri)...." This painting depicts shepherds beside a stone tomb. A skull rests on the tomb, and a bumble-bee rests on the skull. The tomb is painted with the words "Et in Arcadia Ego" inscribed into the stone.

This enigmatic work by "il Guercino," painted 1618-21, is the first known work of the "shepherds of Arcadia" series. Note that the phrase *Et in Arcadia Ego* is painted as if inscribed into the stone of the tomb, and note also the skull (with a bee on it) resting on the tomb.

As Owen Lee states, there is something "haunting, elusive" about this phrase, though it is not immediately obvious in English. In Latin, "*Et*" means simply "*and*" in ordinary usage, but this word doesn't occur in an ordinary way in "Et in Arcadia Ego." There's really no reason for it to be included in the phrase at all, so it could, perhaps *should*, have more force and meaning than a mere "and." Owen Lee himself suggests that a better translation might be "Yet I am in Arcadia" or "Even I am in Arcadia." Because of the skull on the tomb in Guercino's painting, Owen Lee writes (incorrectly, I think) that the skull represents Death, and that Death is meant to speak the "Et in Arcadia Ego" inscribed on the tomb. Owen Lee's idea is that even though Arcadia was a primal sort of unspoiled pastoral paradise, Death exists *even* there.

The problem with Owen Lee's idea of Death intoning this grim reminder of human mortality is that other references suggest that this skull isn't just any old cranium that could represent Death, but, on the contrary, is the very specific skull of one individual whose identity is known. Identification of this *corpus delicti* will have to wait.

I would accept a slightly stronger "Yes, I am in Arcadia" — but my own favourite rendering of the phrase is "Behold! I am in Arcadia." This is probably too much for Owen Lee, but it is at least a long fly (into linguistic left field?) within the ballpark of allowing "Et" some greater emphasis.

The next known appearances of the phrase occur in two more paintings, this time by the French master, Nicholas Poussin (1594–1665). His first painting of the type, painted sometime around 1630, was actually called *Et in Arcadia Ego*. It shows the now-familiar shepherds gathered around a tomb inscribed with the now-familiar phrase. There's a skull on top of the tomb and a bee on the skull. Poussin's second painting on this theme, *Les Bergers d'Arcadie* ("The Shepherds of Arcadia"), painted between 1640 and 1642, is accounted a true masterpiece of form, composition, colour, texture and light. Moreover, in spite of the lifelike fluidity that actually seems to animate the shepherds, the trees, the clouds, and the light and shadow playing over a large background landscape, Professor Christopher Cornford of the Royal College of Art (London) has demonstrated that the painting was created according to a strict canon of geometric, *pentagonal* structure. Cornford has said that the fluidity of the painting, a painting also containing a rigid and perfect geometric structure, represented "an extraordinary feat of virtuosity."[7]

The Shepherds of Arcadia, painted during 1640-42 by Nicholas Poussin, is a painting incorporating many mysteries.

Les Bergers d'Arcadie has always enjoyed a certain notoriety. Mystery swirled around it even before the astonishing affair of Rennes-le-Château burst upon the English-speaking world in the 1970s and 80s with three BBC television specials by Henry Lincoln, and two bestselling books by Michael Baigent, Richard Leigh and Henry Lincoln — *The Holy Blood and the Holy Grail* (1982), *The Messianic Legacy* (1986)[8]; *The Temple and the Lodge* (1989)[9] was written without Henry Lincoln's collaboration. It has never been explained, for instance, why King Louis XIV of France tried so hard to obtain this particular painting and, when at last he did, then hid it away in his private apartments so that viewing it was highly restricted. What secret did the painting depict?

A partial answer to this question came in the mid-1980s when Henry Lincoln was advised by a mysterious source that there existed in France *a real tomb* identical to the one in Poussin's painting. Lincoln went to the spot with a BBC crew and was astounded. It was immediately obvious that the existing tomb, near the castle of Arques in southern France, was absolutely identical to the one featured in *Les Bergers d'Arcadie*. But more mysterious yet, Lincoln noticed and then confirmed by photographic comparison that the landscape's skyline in the painting conformed absolutely to reality...and the reality was unnerving. Poussin had accurately painted the heights of Mount Cardou, the hilltop castle of Blanchefort — *and the hill on which the village of Rennes-le-Château still perches.*

We will recall that the tombstone of Marie de Blanchefort, *in the churchyard of Rennes-le- Château*, bore not only a reversed AE inscription, but also the entire phrase "Et in Arcadia Ego" — and *Les Bergers d'Arcadie* depicted this same Latin epigraph on the painting's tomb. If this were not an overdose of coincidence, Henry Lincoln and many researchers had long suspected that something very important was going on. The village of Rennes-le-Château seemed to be involved, and involved in several intriguing ways, but it was pretty clear that people like Guercino and Poussin had been in on the secret. Indeed, one of the most delicious (alleged) discoveries from Rennes-le-Château was a parchment in code. Deciphered, the parchment advised the reader that "Poussin, Teniers, hold the key...."

The Teniers (father and son) were painters roughly contemporary with Nicholas Poussin. Researchers and adventurers cannot agree on which of the Teniers' works may be relevant as part of the "key."

Almost incredibly, Henry Lincoln discovered that Rennes-le-Château, which is a village on a hill, forms a *perfect pentagon* with four other hilltop constructions and natural elevations: the Castle of Blanchefort, the old Templar castle at Bézu, and the natural elevations of La Soulane and Serre de Lauzet. This can be checked on maps published by the Institut Géographique National of France (1:25,000 scale, the largest scale). But use a pen or pencil with an extremely fine point. The pentagon is absolutely perfect, *within a matter of feet*, from height to height. But the towns are two and a half miles apart side by side, and four miles "across" the pentagon from each other! And yes, although these places are clustered together in a small area of Languedoc in southern France, the measurements are in English miles.

Henry Lincoln recounted all this, with diagrams, in *The Holy Place*[10], but I imagine that few readers (and fewer "experts") bothered to substantiate and duplicate Lincoln's claims on the appropriate maps. Once he had discovered the pentagon figure linking these towns and places, Lincoln naturally wondered if the pentagonal geometry of Poussin's *Les Bergers d'Arcadie* was a sophisticated clue pointing to the importance of Rennes-le-Château.

And what *is* the importance of this small village?

Well, for one thing, it had long been known that a truly vast treasure must be buried somewhere nearby. It is a matter of historical record that when Alaric's Visigoths sacked Rome in A.D. 410, and then made off with most of the accumulated wealth of an acquisitive empire, they came to rest and settled in Languedoc. Rennes-le-Château was the Visigothic capital for a while. It was then called Rhedae or Reddis (and other variants). Most of this loot must still be cached in the area, although there are excellent reasons for thinking that some of it has been recovered. The area is pockmarked by excavations undertaken by the Knights Templar of the region, for example. Centuries later, some curious activities and constructions undertaken by a village priest of Rennes-le-Château, Bérenger Saunière, suggest very strongly that he found several million francs' worth of treasure around 1898.

But because Henry Lincoln found that builders of medieval churches in the region had gone to incredible trouble to construct churches that were in exact mathematical relationships to the "Rennes-le-Château pentagon" (Lincoln's work can be verified on maps), he felt there was more to the story than mere metallic wealth. He felt that there was, in addition to whatever uncollected Visigothic loot might linger around, some sort of powerful religious importance attached to Rennes-le-Château and its immediate neighbourhood. Just from the number of old Knights Templar ruins in the area, he reasoned that the Templars must have been in on the secret and maybe the loot.

Richard Andrews and Paul Schellenberger claim to have finally discovered the secret of Rennes-le-Château. In *The Tomb of God* [11], by relying a great deal on Henry Lincoln's research, but being somewhat churlish in their appreciation of it, they conclude that the body of Jesus is buried inside Mount Cardou. This is certainly a provocative theory, as the authors themselves modestly acknowledge, contradicting as it does the Christian dogma of the Resurrection. Unfortunately, though, the proof or disproof of this notion requires the removal of several hundred thousand tons of Mount Cardou. Since the affected landowners would probably have objections to such a massive excavation, this theory will not be put to the test for a long time — not until long after the authors have made their money, spent it, and died. And that's by far the best kind of provocative theory. It appeals to the kind of mind that yearns to contribute to James Redfield's *Celestine Solvency*.

In all this welter of complexity, one of the thankfully obvious things is that the phrase "*Et in Arcadia Ego*" is significant in some way. It started to become significant, say, around 1480–1500 when the Unicorn Tapestries were woven, was still important in 1621 (when Guercino created his painting), and remained important when Poussin created his final masterpiece on the Arcadia theme (1640–42, according to all art authorities). This cryptic message may have retained its importance even longer. At Shugborough Hall in Staffordshire, England, there's a curious carving called "The Shepherds' Monument." This is basically a rendition, *in reverse* and carved in low relief on a stone block, of Poussin's *Les Bergers d'Arcadie* painting. The carving was created by the commission of the powerful Anson family between 1761 and 1767. The most famous Anson was Baron George Anson (1697–1762) who was First Lord of the Admiralty during what Americans call the "French and Indian Wars" (1689–1763).

Later, we will suggest an explanation for "The Shepherd's Monument" that has much to do with the transfer of New France to Great Britain by the Treaty of Paris (1763), but more to do with the Battle of Quebec City (1759). This conflict marked the last usefulness of the phrase for the people concerned. Thereafter, it was merely a "haunting, elusive" line that some novelists used in order to invoke an ambience for their work (for example, *Brideshead Revisited* by Evelyn Waugh, 1945).

The "Shepherds' Monument" at Shugborough Hall in Staffordshire, England. It is a marble relief of Poussin's painting reversed. The monument was commissioned by the Anson family in 1761. Baron George Anson was the architect of Britain's victory in the French and Indian War. An encoded inscription beneath the marble sculpture has never been deciphered.

The light was growing distinctly pearlescent by the time I rejoined Mike, Don, and Bob at the tombstone. They had cleaned the inscription carefully with brushes and then had chalked the inscription so that it would show up well in the iffy light. Mike had not thought there was enough sunlight, especially in the dell with its trees and branches, to get good enough contrast on the inscription. In places, the letters were too weathered to cast much of a shadow, though they could be followed easily enough with a sensitive finger and chalk.

Mike had already taken a number of photographs, and he and Don were already hoisting their camera bags to their shoulders. I could read, now that it was clearly chalked, the single word above the bold AE. It must have been the man's family name, Iotigolo. An Italian, perhaps, or a Spaniard, or a Portuguese. Someone who had once known sunnier climes. Yes, he'd been laid to rest far from home. And yes, his spirit would have been thankful for shelter from chilling winds. I knelt down beside the stone again to check if the chalking had faithfully and accurately followed the old, weathered grooves. My companions had done their job well, but now that I knew the dead man's name, I felt some obligation to take my own photograph. So, while the others waited a few minutes, hiding their impatience with conversation and some foot-stamping in the lowering temperature, I unlimbered my faithful Pentax and snapped a memento of Iotigolo's grave.

Later, I was able to verify that "Iotigolo" was actually a Mediterranean surname. Phone books for Italy, Sicily, Corsica, and the Costa Brava coast of Spain list many Iotigolos. An interesting aspect of this inscription, though, is that the form of the letter "g," which looks much like the number "9," is not a southern European style of calligraphy. Research, much later (1996–97), indicated that this form of the letter derived from the northern European runic "g." And, further, that it was a lower-case form of the runic "G" that came into usage about A.D. 1300 in Scandinavia, Germany, and parts of Scotland for the purpose of writing Latin. Our modern "printing" form of the lower case "g," in schooldays' handwriting, developed from this evolution.

Therefore, although Iotigolo's name itself was patently of Mediterranean origin, whoever carved the inscription was not. Iotigolo's companions had been from a more north European tradition and culture. As we shall see, this fits very well with the construct that will gradually be presented in this book.

At last (it must have seemed to them) I was done. Bob produced a powerful flashlight from his backpack. Since the temperature had dropped with the sun, we did little talking as we clambered up out of the dell and back onto the logging road, beginning the trek back to Don Eckler's car. It was parked some way down the mountain on a more gentle stretch of the logging road.

AE. Et In Arcadia Ego. It is interesting that "A" is the first letter of the alphabet, and that "E" is the fifth. AE can thus be a way of writing "15." Is it mere coincidence that fifteen is the fewest number of Freemasons that can form a Lodge? Is it mere coincidence that Freemasonry was born in Scotland? And can it be mere coincidence that the oldest (publicly acknowledged) Freemasonic document specifies the Sinclair family as the hereditary heads of the organization? These may seem nonsensical and irrelevant questions, but we will see, as the story of the Grail Knights of North America unfolds, that these questions make a great deal of sense and are anything but irrelevant to our world on the brink of the twenty-first century. Having realized this, though, we still have to explain why Templar-Masonic symbols are carved into rock faces all along river banks as far south as central Pennsylvania, but at least we will have some inkling of the AE and 15 inscriptions on these petroglyphs.[12]

Et in Arcadia Ego.

Strangely enough, there *was* an Arcadia that had been important in Europe, and particularly important to France, during the lifetimes of Guercino, Poussin, Marie de Blanchefort, and Baron George Anson. This Arcadia was the Atlantic coast of New France. By internationally recognized claim, it extended from the latitude of present-day New York City north to the latitude of the middle of Cape Breton in Canada. It extended westward...well...who knew how far? When "l'Arcadia" or "l'Arcadie" first appears on Atlantic maps, about 1534, no one knew how far westward the New World extended.

By the geographical concepts, and claims, of that time, Mason Mountain was well within the territory of Arcadia. That was just another instance of Jung's *synchronicity*. The man in the mountain tomb had been buried in an Arcadia defined by maps and claims, and not just an Arcadia suggested by cross-reference to Sylvanus through Greek-to-Roman mythology. In the course of time, "Arcadia" on the maps became corrupted into "Acadia."

Acadia has always been associated with the French. It was a part of New France. And this is only right because since medieval times the region has been populated mostly by French people.

This may be so, but their first leader was a Scot.

We will now trace the evidence indicating that believers in the Holy Grail, and protectors of the Holy Grail, fled from religious persecution in Europe. Their refugee trail led from France to Scotland, then from Scotland across the Atlantic to Nova Scotia in Canada, then along the St. Lawrence and Great Lakes waterway as far as New York State and Pennsylvania.

The Grail Knights of North America represented the ideals embodied in the Holy Grail. They sought a haven in the western continents, but they also strived to preserve values of freedom that would, eventually, inspire the creation of a new world and a "new world order" — the western democracies. They died all along their refugee route as they explored inland from the Atlantic, and that enigmatic AE marks the fallen.

The Grail Knights of North America died, one by one, in the wilderness. But their ideals did not perish.

2

Merika and Iargalon

Although the mere phrase "Holy Grail" has a remarkable power to evoke a romantic and nostalgic response in people, there is really nothing mystical, mythical or spiritual about the basic facts.

These facts constitute a secret that has been known to a few conspirators for a long time. More recently, these facts began to be rediscovered and revealed by modern writers in widely available books. Mysteriously, the first clues seem to have been anonymously placed in France's national library, the Bibliothèque Nationale, and are usually called the *dossiers secrets* ("secret files") by most Grail enthusiasts — but even now no one knows what individuals or organization deposited the articles and genealogies that led researchers to begin unravelling the facts. Originally, back in the 1950s, this was a French rediscovery and the principal writers were Gérard de Sède, Maurice Magre, Fernand Neil, and Jean-Marie Angebert. But their books were naturally written in French and were seldom or never translated into English or other languages, and so the secret had limited public circulation for a generation.

In the late1960s a British researcher and writer named Henry Lincoln happened to pick up one of Gérard de Sède's paperbacks while on vacation in southern France. He became utterly fascinated with de Sède's perspective on a number of curious things about the village of Rennes-le-Château. By pure chance, Lincoln happened to be vacationing near this village and was in a position to verify the alleged facts in Gérard de Sède's book. He found the situation in this village to be both enigmatic and incredible, and he began to do wider research. Gradually, an amazing story emerged. Lincoln had excellent contacts within the British Broadcasting Corporation, and some BBC producers became just as fascinated as Henry Lincoln. Eventually, during the 1970s, three BBC documentaries were produced in co-operation with Lincoln. They fascinated British television audiences, too, and the story of the "Holy Grail" (as it related to the small southern French town of Rennes-le-Château) was at last introduced to English-speaking people. But, as yet, only in Britain itself.

Then, in 1982, Henry Lincoln teamed up with two other British writers, Michael Baigent and Richard Leigh, to publish *The Holy Blood and the Holy Grail.* This book was an instant international bestseller and was co-published by Warner Books in the United States, so a much wider English-speaking audience was introduced to the Holy Grail story. By now, the basic Holy Grail history is part of popular culture again. The British trio of Baigent, Leigh, and Lincoln (an alphabetical listing of authorship which did scant justice to Henry Lincoln's contribution) followed up their 1982 bestseller with a sequel. Baigent and Leigh wrote a second sequel. Other authors, who had either been legitimately working on similar research or who simply jumped on a bandwagon, were able to get many more "Grail books" published.

The basic story, which we will cover briefly in Chapter 6, is that the "Holy Grail" is *another* religion. As noted in passing in the last chapter, the Grail religion is an amalgam of two fundamental components. First, it incorporates a stream of ancient tradition and knowledge from a pre-Christian source going back to Pharaonic Egypt and earlier. Second, the Grail religion is an alternative version of "Christianity" — another version of the life and legacy of Jesus. In the religion of the Holy Grail, Jesus is not only the point where the ancient pre-Christian tradition merges into a New Covenant, Jesus is presented as a much different person than in orthodox Catholicism, which is essentially the same historical perspective as orthodox Protestantism.[1]

In writing that the Grail religion is partly an alternative version of "Christianity" and a different perspective on the life of the historical Jesus, I am, I think, being literally correct and literally accurate. But the words do not convey the emotional gulf separating "Grail Christianity" from orthodox Roman Catholic and Protestant Christianity. Nowadays, Jesus and "Christ" have become synonymous. But the two words did not stand for the same thing in first-century Judea, or earlier in Hebrew history.

"Jesus," or "Yeshua" in Hebrew, is just a Romanized version of the Hebrew name better known as Joshua. The historical Jesus was named Yeshua ben Joseph — Joshua, son of Joseph.

Christos, or "Christ," is a Hellenistic Greek word meaning "the anointed one" in a ritual recognizing legitimatized kingship. *Christos* is absolutely cognate with the Hebrew word *Messiah*. They mean precisely the same thing: an officially recognized and anointed king. There were many Messiahs in Hebrew history, more than thirty counting the kingdoms of Israel and Judah. There were even more Christoses in Greek history, and here one would hesitate to guess at even an approximate number. Certainly hundreds.

Now, it is true that in Roman-ruled first-century Judea, the idea of the Messiah had, to some extent, evolved from its original and ancient meaning. For some radical Jews influenced by Greek thought, a Messiah could be a kind of "people's leader" whose primary purpose was to overthrow Roman rule, to re-establish the line of Jewish kingship begun with the unfortunate Saul and continued with the much more successful reigns of David and his son, Solomon. For yet other Jews, even more radical but representing a much smaller percentage of the Jewish population, a Messiah could be a "spiritual leader" — the idea being that since the Romans were so solidly in control of earthly affairs, a reconstituted Jewish kingship would have to relate to God's heavenly territory, which was beyond Rome's power. But, among Jews in the time of Jesus, the idea was never fully abandoned that the Messiah had to come from the legitimate lineage of David. Jesus was of the lineage of David and had this going for him.

But another man had sprung from the same lineage at about the same time, born six months earlier than Jesus — John, called "the Baptist" by modern Christians. Since there was no one around to anoint him with oil in the appropriate kingly fashion, he decided to anoint himself in God's liquid, water. Modern Christians view John as a precursor of the "true Christ," Jesus. But Roman-hating Jews of first-century Judea were not so sure. And, indeed, even two of the so-called synoptic (i.e., "the same viewpoint" — Matthew, Mark, and Luke — as opposed to John) Gospels of both Luke and Mark, begin and continue with the idea that John the Baptist was the principal Messiah, and that Jesus was a back-up contingency. Although the Gospels of Luke and Mark were edited to obscure this interpretation as much as possible, the words that still remain (even in the King James Version), if read very carefully, can support this view. Then there's the Gospel fact that Jesus began his brief ministry only when he had definite news that John had perished at King Herod's hands.

The Grail religion thus embodied the perspective that John was the first *Christos* or *Messiah*, and that Jesus took over only when John was known to have been killed. Indeed, when St. Paul travelled to the (now) Turkish town of Ephesus to preach the new Christianity, he found that there were already Christian churches there. But the Ephesian *Christos* wasn't Jesus. It was John. Thus, along with many other departures from Nicean orthodoxy levelled against it, the Grail religion was also accused of harbouring the despised "Ionnite heresy" — the belief that John, not Jesus, had been the true and original Messiah.

There's yet another complication in grasping the Grail religion. This was once merely a cultural, domestic, and obstetrical complication, but it became *the* departure from Roman orthodoxy with which there could be no reconciliation, no negotiation...and for which there could be no mercy. This was the crux of the *medieval* conflict between the Grail believers and Roman Catholic orthodoxy. We will deal with this in Chapter 6.

Although the orthodox Christian churches are vehement in denying it, the Grail version of Jesus was the most serious threat to dominance that orthodoxy ever faced. The Grail tradition competed for supremacy against the Catholic Church's official version, "ratified" in A.D. 324 at the Council of Nicea, for almost a thousand years. Even today, in modern Turkey, there are so-called "Christian" churches that consider John, not Jesus, to have been the true Messiah. These scattered denominations and churches persist and survive only because the Roman Church never gained absolute supremacy over the Eastern Orthodox Church ("Greek" Orthodox Church) during the time of the Crusades. And the Greek Orthodox Church itself survived only because of the tolerance of Islamic conquerors who shrugged at squabbles between "Christians" and "Jews" (and sects in between) but forcibly kept peace among them.

But very frequently during the centuries after the Council of Nicea, over large areas of Europe itself, the Grail religion had more power and more followers than Rome. Official Church history naturally plays this down. Struggles against other "heresies," like Arianism, are stressed in order to disguise the fact that the Grail religion truly challenged the very supremacy of

Roman dogma. This was a situation that could not be tolerated by the Roman Church in its own sphere of otherwise unchallenged religious-military influence.

Finally, the issue was settled in one of the most savage religious wars ever fought in Europe, the so-called Albigensian Crusade (A.D. 1209–44), which devastated most of southern France and large parts of northern Italy. The Church of Rome won a decisive military victory. The Grail tradition was all but crushed. The infamous Inquisition was established during this war for the sole purpose of rooting out, and destroying, believers in the Grail religion. The Grail religion's spiritual leaders were almost exterminated, being burned at the stake *en masse*, or dying individually and hideously on the Inquisition's torture racks. Although the Inquisition later turned its attention to other dissidents from Roman orthodoxy, the Grail religion was labelled as the most monstrous heresy. The victory of Nicean orthodoxy was so complete that real knowledge of the Holy Grail tradition was all but forgotten. French historian Maurice Magre has called the outcome of the Albigensian Crusade "the greatest single turning point in the religious history of Mankind." This may, in retrospect from the twenty-first century, prove to be no exaggeration at all.

All that survived from the wreckage of the Grail religion were distorted and romantic ballads and stories, mostly about King Arthur, Parsival, Galahad, Elaine, The Lady of Shalott, and the Holy Grail (whatever *that* had been). The Church tried to eradicate even these songs and stories, but they were too entrenched in folk mind and memory. The Church had no choice but to let these songs and stories live, and finally the Church even encouraged creation of the literature so long as poetic elaboration and exaggeration substituted harmless sentimental romanticism as an obscuring cloak under which real history was concealed. The Church-approved and tacitly encouraged Grail became a tangible object of some sort, usually the Cup of the Last Supper, in all the romances. It had vaguely awesome spiritual and mystical power that, however, did not threaten any specific Roman Catholic doctrine. And that's how the "Legend of the Holy Grail" has reached us, until very recently, and remains the way that most of us are prepared to understand it.

Although believers in the Grail religion were decisively defeated in the war, and were very nearly exterminated, some survived...and so did their real history, although it was kept carefully secret for almost exactly seven hundred years.

If I have made any original contribution to an understanding of the Holy Grail, it is merely to point out that although most of the Grail's history and conflicts took place in Europe, there was a crucial North American chapter in the story. Grail-believing religious refugees fled from their defeat in southern France and northern Italy to the very fringes of Europe, principally to Scotland and Portugal. And from these two places, by about A.D. 1325, they began a desperate search for a secure haven across the Atlantic. As we shall see, a North American refugee settlement was established in A.D. 1398, roughly a century before Columbus and Cabot supposedly "discovered" America. The evidence for a Grail haven in North America before Columbus was the subject of *Holy Grail Across the Atlantic*, published in 1988. I followed this up in 1991 with *The Columbus Conspiracy*, showing that even the celebrated project of Christopher Columbus, when examined closely, had definite Grail-related overtones.

From 1398 until about 1600, a period of two hundred years, Grail-believing Europeans lived in North America, primarily in the Great Lakes–St. Lawrence River region. Eventually, I think, they simply melded into the frontier life of New France, and they did so with the help of some officials who distorted their reports about the interior of the continent and who patently falsified census figures of French colonists.[2] These Grail refugees left traces, however, of their existence before Columbus and before official French colonization. Discovering this evidence is what this book is all about.

The story of these religious refugees will gradually unfold as we visit sites where their constructions and inscriptions have been located. But right now we must deal with another aspect of this complex history. How did the refugees *know* that there was land across the Atlantic that might serve them as a haven from the Inquisition?

It would be perfectly justifiable to assume that they *didn't* know, to accept that they just set sail upon the ocean in the certain knowledge that whatever fate awaited them at the mercy of the waves would be much kinder than what they could expect at the hands of the Inquisition. Refugees pursued by cruel and implacable enemies have made this choice before and have been lucky.

For example, Thor Heyerdahl has presented convincing evidence that this sort of desperate choice was made at least twice in the history of Pacific Ocean colonization. Around A.D. 500 a group of defeated people under a leader named Viracocha fled from coastal Peru out into the unknown Pacific to escape further massacre and torment at the hands of South American Indians. A few raft-loads of these refugees reached Polynesia. Seven centuries later, a group of British Columbia natives from Bella Coola Inlet fled out into the Pacific to escape their Salish enemies. They set out in their huge dugout canoes, and some of them reached Hawaii. Some of the Polynesian population claimed these two groups of refugees as ancestors.[3]

So it is not at all implausible that Grail refugees might have considered that the Atlantic at its worst would be better than the Inquisition at its best. But, unfortunately for simplicity in an already complex story, the actual evidence indicates that Holy Grail sages and navigators *knew* of land across the Atlantic to the west. And more, the available evidence argues that they had known about it for a very long time. Further, the evidence argues that they knew this land was not Asia, and did not confuse it with Asia, as Columbus supposedly did more than a century later.

In order to tell the story of the Grail Knights of North America as completely as possible, it is necessary to cover, as briefly as possible, the history of navigation on the Atlantic. Only in this way can we get an idea of how the Grail refugees came to learn about the western lands — how and why they knew about "America" long before Christopher Columbus. Indeed, we will see that there is good evidence that Columbus himself actually learned of the New World from the descendant of a Grail voyager.

There is another reason to review the history of transatlantic navigation. It will become apparent that many seafaring European and African peoples visited "America" from the earliest times of what might be called western civilization. It will become just as obvious that European and African colonies were planted in "America" when Rome was no more than a collection of huts. Some of these colonists raised stone buildings and left inscriptions of their own. By having a grasp of transatlantic contact and colonization, we have some hope of distinguishing between the works of "non-Grail" colonists and the works of medieval Holy Grail refugees.

All ruins and inscriptions in North America are not evidence of Grail Knights. By the same token, not every ruin or inscription was left by "Ancient Celts," Carthagenians, or Egyptians.

How did Grail refugees know that there was land westward across the Atlantic at least two centuries before Columbus? The answer to this question will lead us into realms that may be considered legendary, fanciful, and ridiculous by some people. One part of the Grail religion was a body of ancient knowledge and tradition. And it seems that this ancient knowledge demonstrated to medieval Grail refugees that there was land across the Atlantic. Ancient traditions suggested to them that it might provide the geographic haven they so desperately required.

But, unfortunately for easy emotional acceptance of the credibility of this book by "informed readers," the ancient knowledge and tradition embodied in the Grail religion must lead us all the way back to...

Atlantis and "Merika"

I can only try to assure "too informed readers" — those with good, conventional twentieth-century educations — that cold, hard twentieth-century facts will lead us to Atlantis. I refuse to be led, and would not presume to lead anyone else, by intuitive and wistful New Age interpretations of old myths and legends. Bear with me.

Yes, I had to swallow Atlantis, and I must ask readers to swallow it too. But surprisingly I found it to be the meat of solid scientific data, not any ephemeral savour redolent of nostalgic sentimentality. Most of this evidence is very recent. It not only challenges, but makes a mockery of, conventional academic complacency — most of this evidence is so new that it may not have come to the attention of the informed "layperson." I promise that we will fork it in digestible pieces.

In 1967, Dr. Manson Valentine of the University of Miami, and his small team of diving history enthusiasts and amateur archaeologists, claimed to have discovered an underwater "wall" around the island of Bimini in the Bahamas.[4] What was first visible to divers was the top of the alleged wall, which appeared to be constructed of large rectangular blocks of coral rock, called *coquina* by the early Spanish. From above, it looked like a road on the shallow seabed, a road composed of huge cut stones. However, divers examining the structure more closely could see that in places where sand had been scoured away by the currents, the sides of the blocks extended an unknown depth into the bottom of the coastal sea.

Now, this discovery was immediately interpreted by Valentine and his people as *solid* (in no uncertain terms) evidence of Atlantis. More specifically, it was taken to be evidence of "Poseidia," supposedly the most southerly part of Atlantis that had not, perhaps, immediately sunk with the larger mainland mass of the lost continent.[5] The idea was that Poseidia might have experienced gradual sinking after the great cataclysm that destroyed Atlantis, and that the surviving Atlantean outpost had tried to construct a wall to preserve all or part of Poseidia. This had proved futile, because the sea level overtopped the retaining wall. What had been an outpost of Atlantis, and possibly one of sizable land area, became fragmented into the scattered islands of the present Bahamas. Cultural cohesion had been lost, and perhaps much agricultural land had been submerged. At some point, civilization was abandoned. But ruins of it had been discovered near Bimini.

This assumed and reconstructed scenario was automatic and almost obligatory because there had been an admittedly mystic component of the expedition from the start. Valentine and his associates had been inspired by Edgar Cayce's psychic prophecy that part of Atlantis would be discovered in 1967. The expedition to Bimini was, at least in part, an attempt to make this prophecy come true.

The "Establishment" of conventional academia responded immediately that this structure was not man-made, but was merely a formation of "beach rock."[6] The notion of Atlantis was ridiculed. Unfortunately, most major newspapers dropped the story after the academic verdict had been delivered, in thundering broadsides, by several so-called experts. At the time, I was willing to accept the "beach rock" verdict tentatively, but with serious reservations, since I had been learning that the knowledge "Establishment" was not above indulging in conscious and outright dishonesty in order to protect its world view.

Over the years, other news trickled out from Bimini. There was an alleged discovery of temples and pyramids beneath the sea nearby. A lake that exists on the island of Bimini had been artificially shaped into the outline of an obvious shark — a lake large enough so that it was hard to credit that the artificial shaping could have been done only from ground level; the work must have been directed from a higher vantage point. A natural spring on the island fed a pool that had rectangular sides of large cut and laid stones. This pool also had an artificially cut and stone-sided exit to the sea. It was said that this spring had powerful curative properties because of the minerals carried upward with the current. It was speculated that this spring and pool were Ponce de Leon's Fountain of Youth, which had once been merely a physiotherapy facility of Poseidia, Atlantis.

In due course, *The Stones of Atlantis*,[7] was published and was illustrated with rather unnerving photographs of all this. Looking at the so-called Bimini Wall from various angles in good underwater photos, it was very difficult to accept that this construction was any sort of natural "beach rock" formation. And what about the shark-shaped lake and the stone-lined pool? When university academics replied to this book, they conceded that some of the underwater constructions were obviously man-made, but were stone pens, made between 1900 and 1930, for the collection and containment of living turtles intended for future sale.[8]

Who would (or could) make *turtle pens* composed of stone blocks weighing twenty to thirty tons? Then there's the further consideration that these "turtle pens" are covered by two to six fathoms of water. Now, the turtles in question are sea turtles. They can swim. What was to keep them in these turtle pens? It was pretty clear that the Establishment was getting so nervous about the Bimini ruins that it was starting to gibber. But worse was to come.

Between June 21 and August 2, 1997, the Egyptology Society, affiliated with the Miami Museum of Science, issued a series of press releases concerning the discovery of temples and pyramids "near Bimini."[9] The pyramids were smaller than, but otherwise identical to, the pyramids at Giza in Egypt. The casing stones of some Bimini pyramids have the same angle of ascent as the Great Pyramid at Giza, an angle that allows the proportions of the whole structure to incorporate numerous mathematical relationships. According to the last press release, the one of August 2, 1997, hermetically sealed "organic remains" were discovered in the temple structure. The statement didn't say what these "organic remains" were (a mummy?), but the release was postponed until the remains could be radiocarbon dated. Their age was 12,500 years before the present.

Keep this date in mind, 10,500 B.C., because of other relevant dates that have been associated with the Giza complex.

But one further little snippet of information especially intrigued me because it dovetailed with a notion I've developed over the past few years, and because it may have much relevance to the importance and mysteries of Rennes-le-Château. An early July press release put out by the museum noted that glyphs and symbols had been carved into some of the stones of a temple found off Bimini. These symbols consisted, for the most part, of "chequerboard" patterns used for calculation in Celtiberia and Central America. Other glyphs were outlines of animals, some now extinct, which are identical with Magdalenian cave art of France and Spain.

If anyone is wondering how a "chequerboard" pattern can be used for calculation, I must admit that I don't know the specifics of the technique. I only know that our modern word "exchequer" originally derived from a word referring to payments calculated on a cloth arranged in squares of two colours (usually green and white). Ministers of the Exchequer, acting for a king or noble, paid off state debts from the exchequer, including payments to mercenary soldiers. Crusader mercenaries were paid by such "exchequer" calculations, and the process is described in several Crusader diaries. The modern word "cheque" (in Britain, Canada, and France) and "check" (in the American dialect of English), meaning a promise or token of monetary payment, also derives from this ancient chequerboard method of record-keeping.

As for the animal glyphs similar to the cave art of southern France and Spain, we will get to those a little later.

Very little further information about the new Bimini-area discoveries has been released by the Miami Museum of Science as of this writing (March 1998). Both the museum and the affiliated Egyptological Society are keeping the exact locations of the sites secret for the moment, a completely understandable decision. They may have located one of the greatest archaeological discoveries of human history. From the rather vague locations given, some sites could arguably be in international waters, and rather shallow water in some instances. Pirates in the form of artefact hunters and treasure hunters, not to mention much more ruthless buccaneers — competing academic organizations wanting to get in on the Atlantis bandwagon — would swarm to the sites like flies if exact coordinates were given out.

With the Bimini finds, we are faced with choices of varying appeal. Either we can accept the existence of some localized and unsuspected Caribbean civilization more than 12,500 years ago that had contact with Egypt, Celtiberia and Central America and that seems to have been called "Aztlan" if Aztec and Maya traditions are any guide or we can gulp and finally accept that a real Atlantis was remembered by faithful, if confused, legends.

Now, doubtless, some "experts" will prefer the first option and create another culture called Aztlan, which was certainly not the Atlantis of myth, but which was the same age, with nearly the same name, and with the same cultural contacts that were once attributed to the mythical Atlantis. The similarities are merely coincidence, the experts will say, and they will gladly take credit for clearing up the confusion that lamentably befuddles laymen. Academics have always been adept at creating complexity so that they can explain it, and they make their livings doing it. Heinrich Schliemann, for example, did not find the Troy of Paris, Agamemnon, and Helen in his woeful ignorance, according to conventional archaeologists — he just found another city, in the same place, the same size, with the same artefacts (including Agamemnon's death golden mask and Helen's jewellery) as described by Homer.[10] But to imagine that he found Homeric Troy is preposterous.

Or, with the Bimini finds, we can just honestly throw in the towel and admit that there was an Atlantis, of which Plato's tale, told in the *Timaeus* and *Critias* dialogues, is a genuine if garbled memory preserved in Egypt and recounted to a very distinguished Greek visitor named Solon. If we take this intellectual option, then the Aztec and Mayan memories of Aztlan become only the New World's version of Plato's story, a priceless corroboration of the Greco-Egyptian story. If we choose this option, we might as well accept the Bimini finds as evidence that Poseidia had been a southerly outpost of Atlantis. And, in this case, we are obligated to look for the main portion of the now-sunken lost continent.

It is not hard to find. Remnants of it have always been in plain view. It is precisely where Plato said it was. Indeed, after oceanic surveying had attained the status of a science in the 1920s and 1930s, it is difficult to see how there could have been such vehemently expressed denial and controversy, or so many wild theories, about the reality and location of lost Atlantis.[11] It is, and was, the Azores Plateau. The nine existing Azores Islands are really the peaks of Atlantean mountains, most of them volcanic, which had sufficient height to remain above sea level when the rest of the land mass sank. By 1935, the German research ship *Meteor* had sonar-sounded the entire Azores Plateau with the new Behm transducer and had found it to be at least some 154,144 square miles (400,000 square kilometres) in extent...about the size of France. This undersea plateau, still some 20,000 feet above the actual floor of the Atlantic, extended southward from the Azores Islands in an elongated, irregular triangular shape.

This undersea plateau was fully large enough to have been Plato's Atlantis. And there were probably other, much smaller islands stretching away from the southern tip of Atlantis that curved towards the New World and Bimini. Seamounts and irregularities in the floor of the Atlantic Ocean have indicated this since the ships *Porcupine*, *Dolphin*, *Challenger*, and many others took systematic soundings and seabed samples starting in 1880. All of these national research ships recovered *tektites* from the raised sections of the Atlantic Ocean's floor.

Tektites are small pebbles, or nodules, of volcanic glass that were ejected from volcanoes into the atmosphere in the form of molten silicon compounds and that cooled into a kind of glass in the air before falling into water. Once hitting water, no longer molten but still hot, the pebbles cooled very rapidly with characteristic fractures in their structure. In some places, the *Challenger* (1887) and *Meteor* surveys of the 1930s brought up, not only tektites, but fine sand typical of beaches that had long been battered by surf. But in most other mid-Atlantic places, probes brought up diatomaceous ooze that had never known sea level. There had once been a large land mass, and many smaller islands, in the middle of the Atlantic, and not so long ago. Now, there are only the nine abrupt peaks of the Azores.

The fairly recent existence of a very large mid-Atlantic island or sub-continent is not a matter of an *if* or a *maybe*. Such a land mass *must* have been there, and it *must* have been precisely where the underwater Azores Plateau is today. These statements are not based on the authority of old Platonic dialogues, or on psychic visions of Edgar Cayce. They are firmly based on fact that was first, so far as I know, brought to the world's attention by a distinguished German scientist with the unfortunate name of Dr. Otto Muck.

It is now agreed that the last so-called Ice Age ended rather abruptly in both Europe and North America about 12,500 years ago, in about 10,500 B.C. But during the 80,000 previous years of the Wurm-Wisconsin glacial period it is known that the climates of northeastern North America and northwestern Europe were virtually identical. Terminal moraines left by Ice Age glaciers show that the ice cover extended southward to about the same latitude in both Europe and America. Since ice melts above the freezing point, 32° Fahrenheit or 0° Celsius, we can state with a fair degree of confidence that the Wurm-Wisconsin ice sheet extended southward to the "32F degree isotherm" — just as Arctic glaciers do today. That is, the ice extended southward until the line where the mean annual temperature of the air exceeded 32°F (0°C).

At that time, this line was in about the same latitude in both Europe and North America until 12,500 years ago, but that is not the situation today. Northwest Europe is currently much warmer than similar latitudes in northeast North America. The line of the 32F degree isotherm now incorporates a huge northerly bulge in Europe that embraces most of Scandinavia, Iceland, and all of the British Isles. There is only one reason for this: the Gulf Stream. This warm ocean current carries millions of cubic miles of tropical Caribbean water from Florida, across the Atlantic, to the coasts and islands of northwest Europe. It is a huge warm-water radiator that keeps northwest Europe far above the average temperature of similar latitudes in northeastern North America. The Gulf Stream is the only reason Britain does not have the climate of Labrador and Norway does not have the climate of Ungava. The Gulf Stream is the only reason northwest Europe can support agriculture, civilization, and a population of millions.

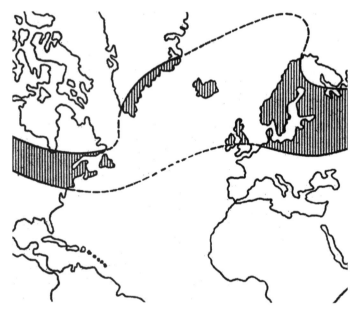

The "32 degree (F) isotherm" about 10,500 B.C. (bottom line) and the same isotherm today (top line), the southern limit of Arctic glaciation. The Gulf Stream, bringing warmth from the tropics, is responsible for northwest Europe's relatively mild climate today compared with Europe's bitter cold during the last Ice Age. Otto Muck suggests that during the Ice Age, the continent of Atlantis, now represented by the nine Azores islands and the sunken Azores Plateau, turned the Gulf Stream back towards the Caribbean before it could reach Europe.

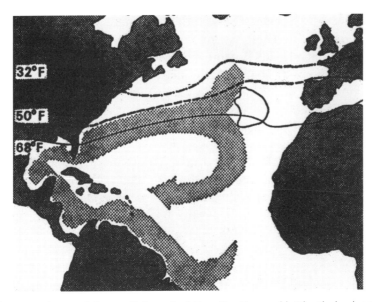

The now-submerged Azores Plateau depicting Atantis, a mid-Atlantic land mass about 10,500 B.C. deflecting the Gulf Stream before it could reach Europe during the last so-called Ice Age. This deflection of warm Caribbean water before it could reach Europe accounted for the position of the 32-degree isotherm, or the southern limit of glaciation, across the middle of Europe during the last phase of Wurm glaciation. On the other hand, the Gulf Stream would have given Atlantis a much milder climate during the Ice Age than its latitude would suggest. If Plato's description of Atlantis is correct — high mountains in the north (the present nine above-water peaks that make up the Azores islands) and the more central parts of Atlantis being a plateau sloping down to lowlands in the extreme south — then Atlantis would truly have exhibited the geographic and biological diversity that Plato claimed for it. High, cold, and arctic conditions in the north (especially during the Ice Age) moderating to a temperate central plateau and tropical lowlands in the south (warmed by the Gulf Stream) would have provided a range of suitable environments from bears in the north to elephants in the south. The mountains would have provided the fabled *orichalcum* ("mountain copper") of Atlantis.

But before the end of the Ice Age 12,500 years ago, glacial terminal moraines show that northwest Europe and northeastern North America had a similar climate. This can mean only that the Gulf Stream did not reach northwest Europe before 12,500 years ago. Something prevented the warm water from crossing the Atlantic to Europe. That "something" could only have been a mid-Atlantic land mass large enough to deflect the Gulf Stream back towards the Caribbean before it could reach Europe.

As it happens, the Gulf Stream currently crosses the Mid Atlantic Ridge just at the Azores Islands and the submerged Azores Plateau. Today, the scattered nine Azores islands are not sufficient to deflect the Stream. The warm water simply flows around them (accounting, by the way, for their near-tropical climate) and continues on towards Britain. But, before 12,500 years ago, a very large land mass *around the Azores* must have existed to account for the European climate during the Wurm-Wisconsin glacial epoch.

This is just where Plato's dialogues place Atlantis. Dr. Otto Muck covered this climatological proof for Atlantis in great and pedantic detail and also presented a biological proof for the recent existence of a large mid-Atlantic land mass (the breeding behaviour of European and Americal eels) in his 1976 book, *Alles uber Atlantis*.[12] Since *Grail Knights of North America* is not intended to be a book about Atlantis, I refer readers to this book instead of rehashing more of Muck's work — which is, to me, the most scientific and convincing book about Atlantis I've ever read. However, the bibliography on Atlantis consists of more than 25,000 titles, and I haven't read all of them. Perhaps some other writer has equalled Otto Muck's scientific approach, instead of amassing the usual compendium of transatlantic cultural similarities. Maybe it is justifiable to comment that Otto Muck's work has not been read widely in the non-German world. Dr. Otto Muck was an enthusiastic Nazi, one of Nazi Germany's premier scientists, and the inventor of the submarine snorkel, which greatly increased the number of Allied ships sunk by U-boats during World War II. In short, Otto Muck would win no popularity contests in western Europe or North America, and publishers have not rushed to translate his works into English, French, Dutch, or Scandinavian reprint editions.

Readers may now concede that Atlantis did once exist; that the main part of it perished in the same cataclysm that ended the Wurm-Wisconsin glacial period somewhat abruptly about 10,500 B.C.; that smaller islands may have remained above water for some time thereafter, but eventually sank below sea level; that, judging from the Bimini ruins, a sophisticated culture or civilization existed on Atlantis and its islands before 12,500 years ago. These concessions are based on facts. But in order to speculate about the cultural level of Atlantis, we must rely on literary tradition like Plato's dialogues and Aztecan and Mayan traditions.

Psychics and theosophists have generally agreed that Atlantis had an extremely advanced technology, equalling our own in many ways and surpassing it in many others. This belief awaits evidence and verification. And, except in one relatively minor area, it is irrelevant to the *Grail Knights of North America*.

A civilized people on an insular domain are almost certain to be a maritime people. Plato stresses that Atlantis had many ships and a far-flung commerce. The following factual evidence will indicate that Atlanteans had at least reached a level of technology in which they possessed accurate shipboard chronometers; had refined mathematics so that they were capable of drawing maps with exact, accurate, and complex projections for various purposes; knew that the earth was a sphere; knew the size of it as precisely as we do; had explored the earth so that they had a grasp of its geography at least as good as our own before the advent of satellites; had an excellent knowledge of navigational astronomy; and had refined naval architecture to the point where they had seaworthy, sturdy, and speedy ships capable of carrying a lot of cargo.

I will not speculate further on the level of Atlantean civilization. For my limited purpose, there is no need or obligation to do so.

In 1929, a map of inexplicable accuracy was discovered in the old Imperial archives of Constantinople. It had been drawn, in 1519, by a man known as Piri Re'is, once a pirate and then an admiral in the Turkish navy. It showed the eastern side of the New World with amazing accuracy just twenty-seven years after the first voyage of Christopher Columbus. In fact, it showed places that the Spanish had supposedly not seen in 1519. Piri Re'is had made many notations on his map, and one of them stated that he had based his map "on the map of Christopher Columbus, and on maps dating from before the time of Alexander the Great."[13]

The discovery of this map caused great excitement in the United States because of the possibility that a map drawn by Columbus himself might still be filed away somewhere within the dusty archives. The American secretary of state, Henry Stimson, officially requested the Turkish government to conduct a careful search for other old maps, and correspondence went back and forth during much of the 1930s, but the Turks found no other similar maps.

The United States government acquired the Piri Re'is Map (it is now in the Smithsonian) and turned it over to cartographic experts for study. In 1935, Captain Arlington Mallory of the U.S. Naval Observatory announced the astounding discovery that the Piri Re'is map had been drawn according to "Azimuthal Equidistant Projection." Other cartographers confirmed Mallory's verdict.

I've found, and not particularly to my surprise, that modern people boasting fine university educations can seldom grasp azimuthal equidistant projection. When I was testing these same

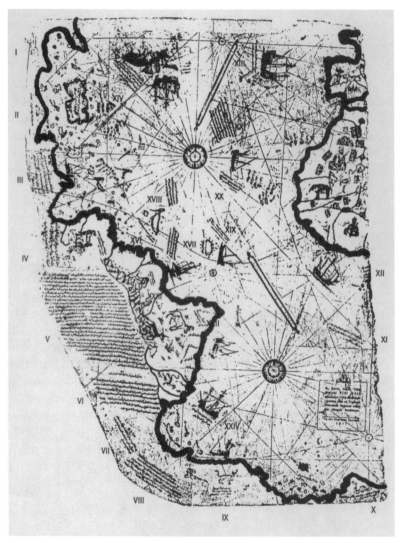

Surviving fragment of the Piri Re'is Map discovered in 1929 in the archives in Constantinople. To the left is the American continent. Compare Piri Re'is American geography with the shape of the American continent derived by Equidistant Projection based on Cairo. Coastal outlines emphasized by the author.

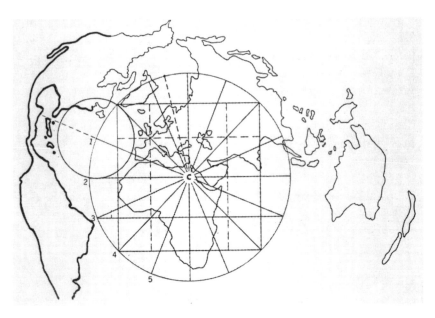

The Piri Re'is shape of North America and South America imposed on an "Azimuthal Equidistant Projection" of the world. This is not really as difficult as it sounds! *Azimuth* is an Arabic astronomical and navigational term meaning the angular distance between the horizon and the observer's zenith. *Zenith* is another Arabic astronomical and navigational term meaning a point directly over the observer's head. Therefore, in "Azimuthal Equidistant Projection" simply pretend that you're suspended high above some convenient point on earth and that the horizon is equally distant from you all around. Then, pretend that, somehow, the surface of the whole earth has been miraculously split open and spread flat so that you can see even land masses that were on the other side of the earth. The most convenient point for doing this happens to be directly above the Great Pyramid near Cairo in Egypt. The reason for this is that the Great Pyramid happens to be located at the centre of the earth's land masses and the earth's surface can be "split and flattened" with the least amount of distortion if viewed from this point. If you are successful in imagining this projection, you will immediately see that the coastline of North and South America of the Piri Re'is map, which I have emphasized to make it clearer, is remarkably similar to the same coastline shown in a modern Strategic Air Command "Azimuthal Equidistant Projection" of the world. It is this similarity of the Piri Re'is map to modern ones that raises the question of how the Piri Re'is projection appears on a map drawn in 1519, but based on even earlier ones. At some time in the past was the earth surveyed from space? Whatever the answer, experts have concluded that the Piri Re'is map must have been based on aerial photography of some sort to present so accurate a representation of the American coast as seen from a great distance.

illustrations for publication in *Holy Grail Across the Atlantic*, one of
the worst visualizers turned out to be a Toronto film-producing
friend of mine who had been a university Woodrow Wilson Scholar.
His business is supposedly visualizing film scenes, locations, stage
sets, and so on from written descriptions, scripts, drawings, and
storyboards — and he could make nothing of azimuthal equidistant
projection. Garage mechanics, building contractors, and salmon-
boat skippers have no problem. For what it is worth, I have
described the projection to the best of my ability in the
accompanying illustrations, have reproduced the Piri Re'is map
(coastal outline only, to keep things simple), and have also
reproduced a modern United States Air Force Strategic Air
Command map of the world on the same projection. Compare the
Piri Re'is coast of the New World with the same coast depicted on
the modern U.S.A.F. map. If you're not *too* educated, you'll see why
Captain Arlington Mallory was so astounded.

Modern U.S. Air Force
Equidistant Projection
map of the world
centred "near Cairo"
(i.e. centred on the
Great Pyramid). Note
that the shape of the
American continent is
almost identical with
the geography of the
Piri Re'is map.

The problem with the Piri Re'is map is that azimuthal equidistant projection was not invented until the late nineteenth century, and it was not refined, perfected, or used until the twentieth. Its primary usefulness is to aircraft. A bomber's navigator can tell at a glance which targets, for example, are equidistant at any given point in the plane's course so that an alternative target can be chosen, using the same amount of fuel, if the preferred target is unreachable for any reason. That, indeed, is the projection's primary value to the Strategic Air Command. Or, if an aircraft is in distress over water, for instance, the navigator can tell which lands are equidistant from his present position. The projection has the same application for ships, of course, but because of speed and time factors the projection is not so critical for maritime situations.

The Piri Re'is map was drawn in 1519, and the old pirate certainly didn't know about azimuthal equidistant projection. Neither did Columbus twenty-seven years earlier. It was obvious to Captain Mallory that either the map (1) was a modern fraud by someone with a sense of humour or no knowledge of cartographic history, or (2) *had been copied* by Piri Re'is from some much older source-map originally drawn by a cartographer who had known of azimuthal equidistant projection and that had been preserved in the Middle East. Very careful study of the map seemed definitely to rule out fraud. Piri Re'is himself had written that his map was partly based on maps dating from "before the time of Alexander the Great." Judging from surviving examples, the ancient Greeks and Romans were not particularly accomplished map-makers. And what *older* known culture on earth could have developed the projection before we did?

The Hadji Ahmed Map of 1559 may well provide a hint. This map of the world, or "mappamundi" (as academics would term it), was discovered in 1862 in Damascus. It is the work of a mediocre Arab cartographer named Hadji Ahmed who is otherwise undistinguished in the history of cartography. Hadji Ahmed lived and worked during a time of decline in Arabic cartography and maritime commerce, a time when Arab maps were more often artistic creations than geographic depictions. This map shows this tendency in its curious "split-apple" projection, which is based on no mathematics at all.

But this map is utterly priceless and equally remarkable. A careful look at the geographic land masses will reveal that Hadji Ahmed copied *all* of it. He copied Africa from some Portuguese map because the continent is distorted in the way that the Portuguese typically distorted it during the mid-sixteenth century. Europe north to Great Britain is a direct steal from Ptolemy's notion of the Mediterranean, including Ptolemaic distortions of the area that are inexcusable on this map since they had been corrected on earlier maps of the sixteenth century.

It is the New World, the Pacific, and Antarctica that are astounding. The American continents are depicted more accurately than on any map for the next century. Where did Hadji Ahmed get this? Certainly not from existing Spanish maps, or from the latest contemporary maps based on Spanish discoveries. Mercator's best map of South America, drawn ten years later in 1569 and incorporating the latest available Spanish information, is a crudity compared to Hadji Ahmed's South America.

Look at the Bering Strait region, where Asia and North America meet. This, in spite of the "split-apple" gap here, shows no Aleutian Island archipelago. Instead, it shows Asia and North America (Alaska) joined together in a large sub-continental region. This is important. Since about 1850 it has been believed that there must have been a Bering Land Bridge that connected Asia and Alaska during much of the last Wurm-Wisconsin Ice Age. Scientists calculated that water tied up in the massive Ice Age ice caps would have lowered the sea level sufficiently so that, at times, a narrow "bridge" of land was exposed between Asia and North America. This allowed the migration of some species of animals from Asia to America, *including humans*, and this was known to have happened.

But it was not until the 1958 Geophysical Year that an international team of scientists made the discovery that the Bering Land Bridge had not been a narrow "bridge" at all. It had been a great plain, comprising all the land north of the Aleutians — in fact, it had been just as Hadji Ahmed drew it 399 years earlier in 1559.

Look at the bulge on the side of California and Lower California. It does not exist now, and it didn't exist in 1559. But it did exist before the end of the last Ice Age. It was a piece of the Pacific Ocean tectonic plate anomalously held above water by the complexities of the San Andreas Fault when the sea level dropped to reveal the Bering subcontinent. It sank, like Atlantis and the Bering land, in the cataclysm that ended the Ice Age. Hadji Ahmed could not have known about this from sixteenth-century exploration.

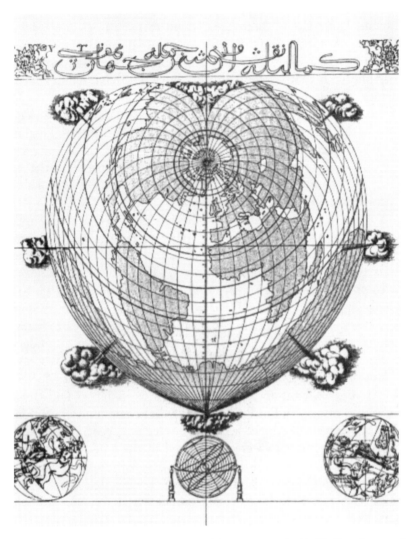

Another Middle Eastern map of inexplicable accuracy, the Hadji Ahmed map of 1559. There is no Bering Strait between North America and Asia, but instead a large land area. This corresponds to the actual size of the "Bering Land Bridge" during the last Ice Age, but modern scholars did not know this until 1958.

Hadji Ahmed also shows the Hawaiian Islands out in mid-Pacific
— but they had not been discovered by Europeans or Arabs in 1559.
Captain James Cook "discovered" them two centuries later. Hadji
Ahmed's Antarctica at the bottom of his pointed earth seems
wholly imaginary. But it is not. Cartographers have compared this
coastline with that of the real Antarctica and have found that it
mimics, in a crude way, the geographical reality.

Insofar as it is possible to measure, the relative distances between
Europe, the Americas, and Asia are about right. Which is to say that
the relative sizes of the Atlantic and Pacific Oceans are more or less
correct — a feat not achieved by any other cartographer for a century.
Also, the absolute latitudes and longitudes of specific, identifiable
places are more accurate than on any map until about 1700.

Except for Hadji Ahmed's slavish copying of Ptolemy's
Mediterranean and Portugal's Africa, this is a fairly accurate general
map of the world. *But it is the geography of the world during the Wurm-
Wisconsin glacial period, not the world of A.D. 1559.*

In the light of the recent Bimini discoveries, plus Plato's
dialogues, plus the Aztec and Mayan memories of Aztlan, so far as we
now know, there was only one maritime civilization on earth before
the end of the last Ice Age that might have been able to produce
such maps. Atlantis. Is it too far-fetched to suppose that this sort of
Atlantean knowledge, these old maps, were preserved until "before
the time of Alexander the Great" and even later? Did these
Atlantean maps give Piri Re'is his azimuthal equidistant projection?
Did they give Hadji Ahmed accurate, but Ice Age, geography?

Both of these maps were discovered in the Middle East. Was
there one place in the Middle East where surviving Atlantean
knowledge might have been preserved? Knowledge, such as old
maps from a lost world, that many subsequent conquerors could
have looted and taken back to their own Middle Eastern cities?

Yes. That place is Ancient Egypt.

There are over sixty pyramids in Egypt and hundreds of huge
statues, but the Giza monuments of three huge pyramids and the
massive statue of the enigmatic Sphinx are so impressive that
they have become the very symbols of Ancient Egypt. This is
highly ironic because there is increasing and converging evidence
that the Giza monuments are not Egyptian at all in any
meaningful sense. True, they are *in* Egypt, but they do not appear
to be *of* Egypt in any important way but one — that what we
know as Ancient Egypt was a degenerated and pallid

continuation of the culture and people who left these monuments several thousand years before "Ancient Egypt" began.

Take another look at that Strategic Air Command map of the world drawn according to that troublesome azimuthal equidistant projection. Note that the official United States Air Force title of this map states that it is centred "near Cairo." That is true, but misleading in a sense. The centre of the map is actually 6 minutes of latitude south of the Great Pyramid of Giza. The longitude is *perfectly* centred on the Great Pyramid. The centre of this U.S.A.F. map represents the precise centre of the earth's land masses, according to the most exact surveys of the late 1950s.[14]

It seems quite obvious that the Great Pyramid at Giza was supposed to be at the exact centre of the earth's land masses, but there's an error of 6 minutes (about six nautical miles — 36,480 English feet). In fact, though, an understanding of the local geology reveals that there was no error in the placement of the Great Pyramid of Giza. There's no bedrock sufficient to withstand the weight of the Giza monuments 6 minutes south of their present location. There's only sand. The first solid bedrock *on the correct longitude* happened to be the Giza Plateau of Tura limestone some six nautical miles (i.e., geographic miles, a true and exact fraction of the earth's actual dimensions) north of the precisely right spot.

In short, the builders of the Great Pyramid at Giza chose the closest possible spot to the exact centre of the entire earth's land masses that would support the weight of a monument conceived, designed, and built to withstand time measured in thousands of years. Eventually, they must have figured, human culture would again attain a level capable of understanding what they knew and what they had done.

The mere placement of the Great Pyramid at Giza tells us that they knew the exact size of the earth and all the major continents and islands upon it. It is impossible to make an azimuthal equidistant projection map of a sphere's geography unless the centre of the map is also the centre of the major land masses. If you try to do it from some other centre, you will find that some geography is hidden and obscured behind other lands. Earth's particular distribution of land and water makes it possible to draw an azimuthal equidistant projection of the land masses of the planet because the opposite "centre" happens to be in a land-empty southern ocean. Even as it is, though, some small oceanic islands are overlapped by larger islands and some land masses. But most of these small islands are in the vast southern ocean and have no relevance to air travel or maritime commerce.

Aside from the fact that the Great Pyramid of the Giza complex is located as near as bedrock will allow to the exact centre of the earth's land masses, various researchers (particularly Peter Tompkins) have demonstrated that the dimensions of the monument, and the angle of ascent of its sides, allow this pyramid to incorporate and embody many different units of measure (some ancient, some still in use) and fundamental mathematical relationships such as the ratios of pi and phi.[15]

Conventional academics, and especially Egyptologists, consider all this to be "coincidence." They would have it that the Great Pyramid was simply planned to be a certain size, and to have a certain angle of ascent, and so the embodied mathematical relationships were merely a natural and inevitable consequence of this, of which the Egyptian builders themselves had been totally ignorant. The interwoven relationships were all "coincidental" from some pharaoh's desire to make it a certain size and height. As for the pharaoh's decision to build the pyramid as near as geologically possible to the exact centre of the earth's land masses, well, few Egyptologists know about *that*. Not many Egyptologists have studied Strategic Air Command maps. And, of course, is it mere "coincidence," too, that the pyramidal shape is the best one for surviving, with the monument more or less intact, any great geologic upheaval?

The building of the Great Pyramid at Giza is attributed by Egyptologists to the first IV Dynasty pharaoh "Cheops" or "Khufu." This attribution rests on the evidence of "quarry marks" daubed onto large blocks of stone in the so-called King's Chamber of the monument.[16] In fact, these "quarry marks" appeared very suddenly after the visit of a rather dubious British adventurer and incorporate hieroglyphic mistakes that no Egyptian living in 2600 B.C. and who could write at all is likely to have made. These marks had not been noted by many previous visitors, some of them "scientists," who had made careful surveys and inventories of everything in the King's Chamber.[17]

But Egyptologists eagerly accepted this dubious evidence because it gave them a comfortable date for the most impressive monument in Egypt — and there was otherwise no clue to its age because the Great Pyramid is nowhere mentioned in any of the known Egyptian texts and inscriptions. This date also gave

Egyptologists an answer to popular tradition, which insisted that the Great Pyramid had been built "before the Flood" by a king named Surid for the purpose of ensuring that human knowledge would survive the coming deluge.[18]

In the early 1990s, a Belgian astronomer, Robert Bauval, noticed something about the Giza pyramids that seemed to be a new and original insight. The three pyramids are arranged in a roughly diagonal relationship to each other, but it is not perfectly diagonal. Their corners are not strictly in alignment. Bauval saw that the Giza pyramids bore the exact same orientation to each other as do the three stars in Orion's belt.[19]

With a computer program widely used by observatories and other professional astronomers, Bauval re-created the night sky over Giza. Now the "declination" of all heavenly bodies — their angular height above the horizon — changes constantly during all hours of the night because of the earth's rotation. But there's also another and much slower change in the declination of stars, planets, and constellations like Orion. Any declination of any heavenly body at precisely midnight on any given year will be very slightly different from its declination at midnight the next year. This is because of another motion of the earth, a motion called the precession of the axis.

The earth wobbles, very slowly, like a giant spinning top. Its axis from the North Pole, through the centre to the South Pole, describes a huge circle in the heavens as the earth wobbles. This is a slow wobble, and so the earth's axis takes 25,000 years to complete one precessional circle. The effect on the declination of heavenly bodies is that at any precise time, say midnight, the star, planet, or constellation will be in a slightly higher or lower position above the horizon from year to year. But the precessional motion of the earth places a limit on this kind of change in declination. It is as if each star, planet, or constellation has a slot in the heavens, a slot of a very precise length. The heavenly object moves very slowly up and down this slot as viewed at midnight over 25,000 years. The object will move up the slot for 12,500 years, and then down its slot for the next 12,500 years until it again reaches the point where the precessional circle began. Then, of course, the cycle starts again.

Because the Giza pyramids seemed to mimic in size (brightness) and position the three stars of Orion's belt, Bauval re-created his computer image of the Giza night sky to study the declination slot of the constellation Orion. He found, and not particularly to his surprise, that Orion culminated — reached its highest point in the night sky on any given nightly rising and setting — directly above Giza. In short, the stars of Orion's belt blazed down onto three pyramids, which were their exact mirror image with regard to size-brightness and relationship to each other. As for Orion's precessional slot, Bauval discovered, to his considerable amazement, that the south-facing so-called air shaft in the King's Chamber pointed *exactly* to the place that was Orion's lowest possible precessional declination. Orion is not there now because it is climbing towards its highest precessional declination, a point it will reach in a few years. But Orion had been there — 12,500 years ago, or 10,500 B.C.[20]

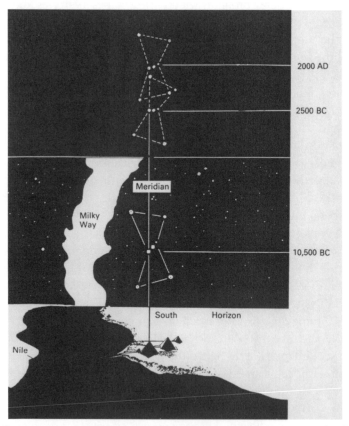

The three major pyramids of the Giza complex exactly represent the "size" (apparent brightness) and relative positions of the three stars in the belt of the constellation Orion. This relationship was discovered by Belgian astronomer Robert Bauval. Supposed "air shafts" in the King's Chamber of the Great Pyramid are oriented precisely to the lowest precessional declination of Orion, which occurred about 10,500 B.C. Further, the Nile River and the Milky Way appear to flow from each other on the southern horizon if viewed from the Great Pyramid.

Beside the three pyramids on the Giza Plateau is one of the largest and most enigmatic sculptures in the world — the Sphinx. It is a feline form, currently with a much-eroded human face, that was carved out of the solid Tura limestone that supports the nearby three pyramids of Giza. The Sphinx has several times been almost covered by drifting sand, and more than one pharaoh of Ancient Egypt has recorded that he had had the sand removed from around the monument. The erosion of the sculpture has always been attributed to blowing sand.

Bauval turned his attention to the Sphinx. Using his computer re-creation of the Giza sky, he found that the Sphinx would be directly facing the brightest star in the constellation Leo as the Zodiacal lion lifted above the Giza horizon in 10,500 B.C. In short, a feline form on the Giza Plateau would be precisely facing its heavenly counterpart during spring dawns of the Ice Age's final years.

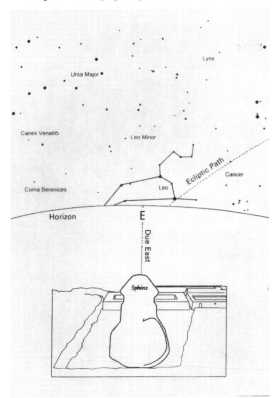

The Sphinx is placed so that it would have faced the constellation Leo at dawn on the spring equinoxes of 12,500 years ago. Originally, did the Sphinx have a lion's head? Since Robert Bauval has discovered new, original, and highly significant relationships between the Giza complex (the three pyramids and the Sphinx) and the sky around the constellation Orion, I've taken the liberty of reproducing his illustrations so as to avoid misrepresenting his ideas.

Between 1990 and 1993, a team of American geologists travelled to Egypt to study the erosion of the Sphinx. By taking photos and doing computer simulations, they concluded that erosion of the Sphinx was a textbook example of *water* erosion, coming from above, due to heavy rainfall. During the 1994 Annual Conference of American Geologists held in Los Angeles, California, after the report and videoed presentations, the conference unanimously agreed with this finding. The question of *when* Egypt had ever experienced such heavy and prolonged rainfall naturally came up. The answer was during the end of the last glacial period — from 15,000 to about 10,500 B.C. when the Wurm-Wisconsin Ice Age reached its maximum and when the snow precipitation elsewhere fell as rain in warmer Egypt.[21]

Therefore, the Sphinx had been made at some time before 10,500 B.C. and the water erosion began shortly thereafter. This evidence was not confused and increased by sand erosion, since the Sphinx, for most of its lifetime, has been covered up to its neck by sand, preventing erosion by blowing sand. The *face* of the Sphinx has, indeed, been eroded by blowing sand, causing its head to be smaller than it should be in relation to the feline body. Bauval and many others believe that originally the Sphinx had a lion's head that was in correct proportion to its body. But the erosion erased the lion's face as well as reducing the entire size of the head. At some point in the distant past, but still long after the Sphinx had first stared into the Giza sunrise, a human face had been rather clumsily carved and grafted onto the head of the statue. Kaphre, a successor of Cheops, may have done this, as Egyptologists rather desperately insist against the available evidence, but he didn't order the original creation of the Sphinx. The Sphinx was staring into the dawn long before the Ancient Egyptians had their first pharaoh.

Egyptologists insist that this human head of the Sphinx is that of Kaphre, who supposedly commissioned the Sphinx to complement the Great Pyramid — and of whom there's supposedly a carved bust in the Cairo Museum. But American professional police forensic artists, who were sent to Egypt to compare the supposed bust of Kaphre with the facial features of the Sphinx, state that there's no significant resemblance between the two. The re-carved human face on the Sphinx is not the supposed Kaphre in the Cairo Museum, but someone else.[22]

In passing, it is interesting to note that Robert Bauval apparently stumbled on another insight. As it happens, the bright, elongated

cloud of the Milky Way (an arm of our spiral galaxy) appears to flow
past Orion, north-south in the sky, as viewed from Giza. The Nile
River flows beside Giza, also in a north-south direction. As you look
south from Giza, the Nile and the Milky Way seem to begin at *the
same place* on the horizon.

In short, the builders of the three pyramids and the Sphinx had
another reason for choosing Giza beside the fact that it was the only
bedrock near the exact centre of the earth's land masses. It was also
the only place where they could construct, on the ground, huge and
enduring monuments that were a mirror image of part of the sky —
the region of the Milky Way and the constellation Orion. In the
earliest known form of Egyptian religion, Orion was the heavenly
abode of Osiris, the first and greatest god. At Giza, someone went to
immense labour to make an earthly abode for Osiris that reflected
his heavenly one. According to the ancient Egyptians, every
pharaoh was a "Horus," a "son" of Osiris, during his life. But, at
death, he transmuted into a sort of Osiris himself and journeyed to
the celestial abode of Osiris, which is to say to the constellation of
Orion. Within this context of the Egyptian Osirian religion, it is
interesting to note that Orion (in Greek mythology) was the son of
Poseidon.[23] Poseidon was the founder and first ruler of Atlantis.
Therefore, one could say, *all* pharaohs were descendants of the ruler
of Atlantis in life and got a bit closer to him in death, merging more
completely into the identity of Poseidon's son.

Egyptian chronology rests basically on the work of an Egyptian
priest who lived very late in Egyptian history, in the third century
before the time of Jesus. Manetho was the High Priest of
Heliopolis and he wrote a history of Egypt in Greek. His account
states that the gods had ruled Egypt directly until 14,000 years
before and then had departed. Semi-divine "guardians" had then
ruled Egypt for many thousands of years before the first pharaoh,
Menes, unified upper and lower Egypt about 3,200 years before
Manetho's time. Thereafter, up until the conquest of Egypt by the
Greeks of Alexander the Great, Manetho listed the successive
dynasties of pharaohs.

"Scientific" Egyptologists of the nineteenth and twentieth
centuries relied on Manetho, who proved to be generally accurate
about the successive dynasties, but they naturally rejected the
fanciful, mythic and legendary parts of Manetho's chronology. The
gods and guardians were eliminated. Egyptian history was deemed to
begin with Menes in 3200 B.C. Therefore, every monument,

inscription and text in Egypt must have been created since then. And most of them have been. It is only the most remarkable irony that the most characteristic monuments of Egypt, the Giza complex of three pyramids and the Sphinx, cannot now be attributed to Pharaonic Egypt at all.

There are now three "locks" on the approximate date of 10,500 B.C. for the Giza pyramids and the Sphinx. First, there's the geological conclusion of water erosion by rain on the Sphinx, and this means the Ice Age "Pluvials" from 15,000 B.C. until about 10,500 B.C. Second, there's the fact that the original lion-like Sphinx would have faced the Zodiacal lion rising in the vernal equinox dawns of 10,500 B.C. Third, there's Robert Bauval's discovery that the "air shafts" of the Great Pyramid are sited at the lowest point of Orion's declination — again 10,500 B.C.

There is a fourth fact that used to stand puzzlingly alone, but that begins to make sense when correlated with these dates. Egyptologists have long known that there was a "Premature Neolithic" period in Egypt. Now, the true Neolithic, the time when humanity began to invent and practise purposeful agriculture, animal domestication, and village life, began about 8000–7000 B.C. in Anatolia (the village of Catal Huyuk) and Palestine (the town of Jericho).

But there was a time in Egypt, about 11,000 B.C., when someone briefly practised agriculture along the Nile. Radiocarbon dating of grain kernels indicates this activity. But the period was brief, the agriculturalists went away, and Egypt had to wait five thousand years for the Neolithic to arrive in predynastic times, in the Nile Delta, about 6500 B.C.

Within the context of the dates for the Giza complex, 10,500 B.C., perhaps this Premature Neolithic in Egypt can best be understood as a temporary agricultural foundation to sustain the construction of the Giza pyramids and the Sphinx. Once the monuments were completed, the agriculture purposefully ceased.

I have placed the Giza monuments under the heading of "Atlantis" because it now seems obvious, with these dates, that the monuments at Giza were not raised by "Egyptians" in any meaningful sense, but by Atlanteans near the end of the last Ice Age. And the reason for the monuments is not hard to guess — Atlanteans may have had the technology to be able to predict the impending end of the Ice Age, and to know about the coming geophysical or celestial cataclysm that would cause it. They left huge, indestructible, and enigmatic monuments on the best bedrock they could find that was near the centre of the earth's land masses.

The very location of these monuments, plus the mathematical relationships embodied in the Great Pyramid, were a legacy for the survivors of the coming cataclysm — if, indeed, humanity survived at all. But if there were survivors, sooner or later they would scrabble upward towards civilization again in that faltering and brutal way of humanity. Sooner or later they would begin to recognize the knowledge left for their benefit and sooner or later they would realize that humanity had reached a pinnacle before them, and had perished. The Giza monuments are also an Atlantean affirmation: "Humanity! Behold, we lived!"

Perhaps they could not have expected that something so fragile as knowledge on their maps would also be preserved. But, as we have seen, it was. One wonders how many other Atlantean artefacts exist that have been denied or misidentified or are yet to be discovered.

Christopher Knight and Robert Lomas, two Freemasons, set themselves the task of trying to discover the identity of "Hiram Abiff," a central character in Masonic lore who was brutally murdered for refusing to reveal the secrets of a Master Mason. Knight and Lomas rather suspected that Hiram Abiff existed only in a "moral" sense — an invented character to dramatize the loyalty expected of Freemasons. Their research is recounted in *The Hiram Key*. Surprisingly, and certainly unexpectedly, Christopher Knight and Robert Lomas discovered that some Masonic rituals dramatized real, historical events dating from Ancient Egypt to medieval Europe. That is, some Masonic rituals and teachings preserved very ancient human history that had been lost in the conventional version.

With respect to Hiram Abiff, they finally not only established his identity (an Egyptian pharaoh) but located the mummies of his murderers. What concerns us here is that the secrets of a Master Mason, which Hiram Abiff heroically refused to yield, were allegedly given to the Egyptian priests and rulers by an earlier and more advanced people. From our very recent knowledge of things, these people can only be Atlanteans. They apparently chose Egypt to be a repository for knowledge that they feared would be lost. They apparently chose Egypt because the centre of the earth's land masses happens to be almost exactly on the Giza Plateau, and some of their knowledge of the world would be demonstrated merely by their choice of this location. Also the Giza Plateau boasted solid bedrock that could support massive monuments, which themselves could be designed to embody in their very dimensions yet more knowledge, and which had some chance of surviving the coming cataclysm intact.

We will recall that even in Plato's story of Atlantis, it was an *Egyptian* priest of Sais who recounted the tale of Atlantis to Solon. We should remember, also, that the Egyptian priest spoke of many earth upheavals, not just the huge one that destroyed Atlantis and that has impeded humanity's attainment of civilization. An Atlantean connection with "Ancient Egypt" cannot reasonably be doubted if we accept the new Bimini and Giza facts, and if we accept the implications of the Piri Re'is and Hadji Ahmed maps (and several others), and if we are now prepared to accept Plato's account as, at least, a generally accurate memory of a former Atlantic civilization.

The point of all this, for our limited purposes here, is that much of this ancient, pre-Christian source of knowledge and tradition making up one part of the Grail religion came from Atlantis. It was preserved in Egypt first. Then it was passed on to other places in the western world, either by foreign conquerors like Greeks, Romans, and Turks who carried off ancient curiosities (like the Piri Re'is map) or more gently by people who preserved ancient knowledge and tradition as religion.

And one aspect of this knowledge was knowledge of America. Plato says that the Atlanteans were great mariners, and the Egyptian priest emphasized that Atlantis held sway over many islands westward to the true continent beyond. Christopher Knight and Robert Lomas discovered that a star called Merika represented these western lands. This name probably came out of Atlantis itself, was preserved in Egypt, and later reached certain religious sects in Turkey and Palestine. Merika or A-merika, was thus known from the earliest times of western civilization.[24] It is a legacy of Atlantean seafaring, and the knowledge was never wholly lost.

Before leaving this section on the Atlantean contribution to the Grail religion and knowledge of land to the west, I would like to suggest a scenario that intrigues me. I admit that it is not, strictly speaking, within the bailiwick of this book.

Some of the Bimini discoveries included glyphs, some in animal form, that resembled nothing so much as Magdalenian Ice Age art from southern France and northern Spain. Since we now know that there was an Atlantis, a glance at a map will show that the shortest route from the Azores Plateau into the Mediterranean is not through the Straits of Gibraltar but to the coast of France at the mouth of the Gironde River, along the Garonne-Aude rivers which are the present course of the Canal du Midi, and out onto the Mediterranean via the inland lakes around Narbonne. We do not know much about the fluctuations in local water levels during the later Ice Age. Land can sink, or rebound upwards. Water levels can rise and fall. It is difficult to know the distribution of land and water in any specific place 12,500 years ago. This route across southern France may have been more watery then than it is now, and so might have encouraged the passage of Atlantean maritime traffic with few portages, or none at all.

If Atlantean travellers passed this way — and maybe they did so many times during the later Ice Age on missions of conquest, commerce, or just hunting expeditions — finally to raise their monuments at Giza, it is possible that contact with them rubbed off on European "cave dwellers" during the Upper Paleolithic. This may account for the astonishing virtuosity of the later Magdalenian cave artists. It may also explain the Magdalenians' acquisition of the atl-atl, or spear-thrower, which may have been originally an Atlantean invention but which is primarily known as a New World innovation — and how Ice Age Europeans got it has always been something of a minor mystery.

There's another point about this hypothetical travel route that may have much relevance to the Holy Grail and Rennes-le-Château. The village of Rennes-le-Château, where the modern Holy Grail research began in the 1950s, has a definite and important association with Jesus. This will become clear when an explanation of the Grail religion and its history is given in Chapter 6. Rennes-le-Château plays a part in the purely Christian component of the Holy Grail.

This small village with its many enigmas is also located on this Atlantic-to-Mediterranean river route. Its undoubted importance and sanctity may be due, in addition to its Christian associations, with the fact that it played an important part in the preservation and rebirth of ancient knowledge — the other component of the Grail religion. Since we don't know the distribution of land and water during Atlantean times, it may well be that Rennes-le-Château was closer to an inlet of the Mediterranean than it is today. The contours of the land (as shown on large-scale topological maps) lead me to suspect this, particularly since at the close of the Ice Age the sea level rose because of rapidly melting glaciers. The Gironde-Garonne-Aude river route across southern France may well have become a temporary drainage spate of the "Deluge," a natural route for surviving Atlantean refugees. If so, Rennes-le-Château may have been an Atlantean refugee community for a while. They may have left some monument to their knowledge there.

Henry Lincoln discovered, and demonstrated without question, that Rennes-le-Château is one point of a huge geographical pentagon. The other points are the castle of Blanchefort on its hill, the Templar castle of Bézu on its hill, and two natural elevations that have no known constructions on them. The resulting pentagon is about four miles across, and it is geometrically perfect within a matter of feet. The hills seem to be natural formations, but Lincoln didn't rule out the possibility that the elevations had been artificially shaped to ensure that the highest points formed a perfect pentagon.

Although Christian churches and medieval castles currently mark most of the geometric figures that radiate with mathematical precision from this central pentagon, some of the points are marked by standing stones dating from long before Christianity. In other words, the Rennes-le-Château pentagon was made many thousands of years ago, but the Grail religion recognized a sanctity about the place. Churches were raised and Templar castles were built at some of the geometric points. Now, of course, since the Albigensian Crusade, the Templar castles are ruins and the churches are all Roman Catholic. But the fact of the pentagon remains...and so does the fact that the pentagon was laid out according to English miles!

I believe it is at least possible that the Rennes-le-Château pentagon was originally an Atlantean monument embodying useful knowledge — a standard of measure based ultimately on the English foot and inch. Livio Catullo Stecchini, along with other modern experts on the history of measures, has concluded that the English foot and inch are very ancient units.[25] Further, they are earth-commensurate, meaning that they are fractions of an actual earth dimension, in this case of the earth's equatorial radius. The English yard is, indeed, more accurately earth-commensurate than the metre because the scientists of the French Academy could not measure the earth accurately enough in the eighteenth century when the metre was established and defined. The metre was supposed to be 1/10,000,000th of the distance from the equator to the pole, but the scientists measured the earth inaccurately.

Now, who would construct a pentagon four miles across, using natural but sufficiently altered elevations to make it perfect, at least 3,000 years ago (if the megaliths within it are any guide) using earth-commensurate units of measure? This assumes, besides sophisticated surveying techniques, that the surveyors of the time knew the exact size of the earth. So far as the evidence indicates (remember those maps!), we know of only one culture capable of making such a pentagon: Atlanteans.

My partner, Joelle Lauriol, was born in France and knows French fluently. In spite of her demanding job at the Ontario Government's Ministry of Education (Francophone Division), she translated parts of the Larousse history of France for me, for I didn't trust my own limited French. I was somewhat surprised to learn that the people of the so-called early neolithic Cardial culture of Provence (and possibly Languedoc) had been building villages with stone houses, cultivating certain agricultural crops, and domesticating goats, sheep, and cattle as early as 6000 B.C., according to the latest radiocarbon dating.[26] Evidence shows that they had boats good enough and large enough to reach some of the larger Mediterranean islands before that. This is getting very close to the earliest dates for the "true Neolithic" at Catal Huyuk and Jericho — and there's been little archaeological work done in Languedoc, which, if this Atlantean route idea has any merit, should have *earlier* dates than Provence.

According to the Larousse history, there's definite indication that the megalithic cultures of northwest Europe actually began with the Cardial people about 6000 B.C. and spread to some Mediterranean islands, such as Mallorca, Corsica, Sicily, and Malta. As the megalithic tradition approached northwest Europe, the stonework became more massive than among the Cardials themselves, particularly in Brittany (Carnac) and Britain (Stonehenge, etc.). The same evolution took place on some of the islands, such as the large Maltese megalithic works, but the idea clearly began with the Cardials. Some people view the megalithic tradition as being an Atlantean style of building that, since Atlantis itself has been lost, can still be seen in various surviving ruins in South America (Tiahuanaco), the Levant (Baalbek), and, of course, Egypt. If this opinion is correct, then it seems there was also Atlantean influence on the Cardial culture of Provence and Languedoc.

To conclude this little detour inspired by my curiosity, now that the Bimini finds prove that there was a real Atlantis with a relatively high culture, I wonder if the Rennes-le-Château area wasn't one of the first places where descendants of Atlantean survivors gave knowledge to the local inhabitants so that western civilization could begin again. I wouldn't go so far as to say that it was *the first* place of such a renaissance. But I will point out that Rennes-le-Château and the Mediterranean coast of France is an obvious place for "civilization" to have broken into the Mediterranean if culture was primarily inspired by the Atlantean tradition. Archaeological research in the Languedoc might well turn up some surprises about the general flow of civilization in the Mediterranean world.

Egypt and "The Curse of the Cocaine Mummies"

Now that we've dealt with the Atlantean contribution to knowledge of "America," knowledge that was never entirely lost although the source of it may have been forgotten, we can turn to the next people known to have had contact with the New World. These people were the *real* "Ancient Egyptians." Whether their voyages were inspired by older Atlantean traditions or were intellectually independent episodes of maritime adventure, it is impossible to say at this time.

The modern, "scientific" aspect of Ancient Eygyptian contact with the American continents, which is to say indisputable, factual evidence of such contact, begins with what we might call "The Curse of the Cocaine Mummies."[27] On September 16, 1976, the mummified body of Rameses II arrived at the Museum of Mankind in Paris. It had been sent there from Cairo so that repairs could be made to the damaged mummy. One of the members of the scientific team that had been assembled to deal with the damage, Dr. Michelle Lescot of the Natural History Museum in Paris, discovered traces of vegetable fibre tangled in the wrappings of the mummy. Under the microscope, this vegetable turned out to be tobacco. According to the best evidence, tobacco was originally a New World plant. It was supposedly unknown in the Old World before Columbus, and a seventeenth-century Frenchman, Pierre Nicotin, is credited with introducing its use into Europe.

Although this discovery deep within the mummy wrappings was witnessed by other members of the scientific team, Dr. Nasri Iskander, chief curator of the Cairo Museum, said that the idea of

Ancient Egyptian contact with the Americas in the time of Rameses II was absurd. Rameses II was the son of Seti I, but not the heir. He usurped the throne and reigned as pharaoh from 1292 B.C. until his death in 1225 B.C. Dr. Iskander stated that the tobacco must have got into the wrappings from the pipe of some Egyptologist or archaeologist.

Dr. Michelle Lescot then took three tissue samples from the mummy's abdomen, which were subjected to standard tests for nicotine addiction. All three samples indicated that Rameses II had used tobacco twenty-seven centuries before Columbus was alive. One would think that this would have caused excitement among Egyptologists, but the Establishment simply ignored the amazing facts. The story died for a while.

Then, in 1992, toxicologist Dr. Svetla Balabanova of the Institute of Forensic Medicine in Ulm, Germany, heard of the 1976 tests by Lescot and decided to test another mummy for narcotic addiction. This mummy was that of Henut-Tawy, Lady of the Two Lands, which had been purchased by King Lugwig I of Bavaria. Dr. Balabanova found traces of nicotine and cocaine in the mummy's tissue. Both of these are American plants. Balabanova was astonished; she sent tissue samples to three other laboratories for independent testing. These other labs reported the same results. In co-operation with two other scientists, Drs. Friederich Parsche and Wilhelm Pirsig, Balabanova published "First Identification of Drugs in Egyptian Mummies" in the prestigious German journal *Naturwissenschaften*.

Balabanova had been surprised at the test results, but was even more surprised at Egyptologists' response to the journal article. They were vehement in their agreement that the results were "absurd." Dr. Balabanova was even accused of perpetrating an outright fraud. Someone suggested that the *mummy* was a fraud, that it had always been a nineteenth-century fake that had been bought by King Ludwig I, who had not been renowned for his mental stability. But hasty and rather desperate "re-research" by Dr. Alfred Grimm, curator of the Egyptian Museum in Munich, which owned the mummy of Henut-Tawy, verified that the mummy was a genuine Ancient Egyptian one.

Dr. Rosalie David, Keeper of Egyptology at Manchester Museum, pontificated that the idea of cocaine mummies was "quite impossible," but she had the courage to take up the challenge. She sent samples of her own mummies out for narcotics testing. The results showed that most of the Manchester Museum's mummies had once used tobacco. Dr. David was at least honest enough to admit that she was "very surprised about this." Most Egyptologists simply ignored the evidence.

Meanwhile, Balabanova obtained tissue samples from no less than 134 separate mummified bodies from Egypt and the Sudan. She made sure that all of them dated from before 1000 A.D. (the time of the Vikings), but some of them were from the Nile Delta and dated back to 5000 B.C. Forty-five of the 134 mummies, including the samples from predynastic times, revealed evidence of both nicotine and cocaine use.[28]

This can only mean that Egyptians of the earliest times had some contact with the American continents. It is written, for example, that one Egyptian pharoah, Necho, sent ships to circumnavigate Africa; the voyage required three years. Ancient Egyptians made numerous voyages to the "Land of Punt" from early dynastic times (3000 B.C. or earlier). Experts have naturally disagreed on the location of Punt. Most have placed it at the southeastern end of the Red Sea near present-day Yemen and Somalia, the Horn of Africa region. Queen Hatsepshut's celebrated and large-scale expedition to Punt, undertaken by this XVIII Dynasty lady usurper, was made about 1500 B.C. in imitation of many earlier ones. To some degree her expedition was a public relations event to associate her rule with great achievements and traditions of the past since she herself was anything but traditional: a woman who had proclaimed herself pharaoh.

But since the mineral antimony was one component of the rouge in an XVIII Dynasty princess's cosmetic case, several authorities think that Punt must have been somewhere in South Africa where the only African deposits of this substance have been located. Egyptian artefacts from the XVIII Dynasty and earlier have been found in southern Africa. The point is that a voyage to Punt was a long-distance voyage, as Hatsepshut's carved reliefs at Dendera plainly show. Even if Punt was located in southern Africa, the return voyage was made on the Atlantic, and through Gibraltar into the Mediterranean to Egypt. Senmut, a vizier of Hatsepshut, not only recorded this route and the commodities of Punt, but boasted that he himself had made eleven round-trip voyages to Punt.

The Egyptians plainly had ships capable of sailing long open-water distances on the Atlantic (again, shown in Hatsepshut's Dendera panels). Even if old Atlantean knowledge of Merika had been forgotten, Atlantic storms would have driven at least some of the Punt-faring ships to the New World. Some of them would have returned to Egypt. "The Curse of the Cocaine Mummies" proves that there was transatlantic contact before 3200 B.C. Hatsepshut's ships of about 1500 B.C. are depicted as wooden ones, but ships made of reed were used long before. As early as about 4500 B.C., according to the evidence of Nagadeh II pottery from "pre-Egypt" in the Sudan, reed boats were used for river navigation on the Upper Nile.

It is a curious circumstance that boats made of reeds represent a cultural trait found in the Americas, and in Ancient Egypt and Sumeria. It is not so odd that reed boats were made on both sides of the Atlantic at a very early date, but it is curious that the design of some are actually identical. Boats made by the Aymara Indians of Lake Titicaca are absolutely identical to reed boats made in Egypt and, further, the Aymara craft carry sails. Sails are most unusual in the New World. Thor Heyerdahl showed that the upturned prows of these reed boats, whether in Egypt or among the Aymara, persisted from a design originally developed from experience sailing on the open ocean. The upturned prows were not necessary for lake navigation (as with the Aymara of Lake Titicaca in Bolivia) or for Nile navigation by the Egyptians.[29]

Heyerdahl was intrigued by this distribution of reed boats of identical design on both sides of the Atlantic. He decided to find out if an Ancient Egyptian reed ship could cross the ocean to the Americas. His book *The Ra Expedition*[30] covers Heyerdahl's successful voyage from Morocco to the Caribbean. Later, with *The Tigris Expedition*,[31] Heyerdahl made another reed ship according to Sumerian specifications and sailed it around the Persian Gulf and the Arabian Sea. These voyages demonstrated that reed ships were cheap and easy to build, were extremely seaworthy, and had incredible carrying capacity. Contrary to expectation, they would last for months before the reeds absorbed too much water; if the reeds were coated with bitumen, which the Sumerians sometimes used, the ships would last for years. They proved to be very slow and clumsy sailers, however, and Heyerdahl agrees with other experts that they must represent a very early answer to the challenge of making an ocean-going cargo sailing ship. How early? Perhaps as early as 4000 B.C.

"The Curse of the Cocaine Mummies" proves, however, that there can be no doubt that the Egyptians crossed the Atlantic in reed ships and in wooden ones. The "Ancient Egyptians" sailed to America.

The Minoan-Mycenaeans

After the Egyptians ceased to be a major Mediterranean power, the Minoans of Crete took over most of the carrying trade. We know that the Minoan fleets must have been vast. Minoan maritime supremacy was so unchallenged that their capital, Knossos, did not even have protective walls. Like Britain many centuries later, the Minoan walls were wooden ones — the hulls of their great naval vessels. But we have no record at all of where their ships may have sailed outside the Mediterranean. Except, curiously enough, in Britain. At Stonehenge there's a carving of a Cretan double axe or *labris,* and also a carving of a dagger of typical Minoan-Mycenaean style.[32]

Mycenaean Greeks inherited maritime dominance from the Minoans but we don't know the extent of their adventuring. The legends of Jason and the Argonauts and the *Odyssey* of Homer are Mycenaean Greek seafaring tales. Most experts believe that these voyages were confined to the Mediterranean and Black Seas (and, for what it is worth, I tend to agree). One reason for thinking this is that British adventurer Tim Severin constructed a replica Mycenaean oared galley and, following details in the Jason legend, was able to locate many landmarks mentioned in the yarn. This modern *Argo* reached Colchis, now known as the Caucasus coast. Severin even discovered the meaning of "the Golden Fleece."[33] However, two scholars of repute, Alexander von Humboldt[34] in the nineteenth century and Henrietta Mertz[35] in the twentieth, have tried to show that most of these adventures took place in the Atlantic beyond the Pillars of Hercules — but this is a matter of interpretation, not explicit statements in the legends themselves.

It is a fact, though, that curious figurines have been discovered in North America (in Mexico) that depict distinctly eastern Mediterranean bearded men, but not Egyptian-looking men. These figures most often wear a close-fitting vest and a conical, floppy cap. These items are similar to the clothing worn by figures in some Minoan frescoes and to the clothing depicted on some Greek ceramics of the pre-Classical era. These little statues may represent sailors from Crete and Mycenaean Greece, but, more probably, depict typical maritime clothing worn in all of the eastern Mediterranean during a thousand years and more. They could equally represent Phoenician or Carthagenian sailors.[36]

Phoenicians-Carthagenians-Celtiberians

The fact of the matter is that almost all the seafaring people around the Atlantic "discovered" America long before Columbus. Most of them left evidence of their presence, and bits of the evidence have occasionally been recovered since North Americans became interested in such things. Of all these discoverers, it seems that "Ancient Celts" were the most important. They not only made apparently frequent voyages of discovery, but actively undertook both colonization and economic activity. We will get to these "Ancient Celts" in due course.

The first certain mention in European literature of continents westward across the Atlantic occurs in two dialogues of Plato (427?- 347? B.C.), *Timaeus* and *Critias*. There is reason to believe that these two dialogues were written in the last years of Plato's life, possibly in 348 B.C. Many amateur historical enthusiasts know *Timaeus* and *Critias* almost by heart because these dialogues contain the first mention of Atlantis. We have already dealt with Atlantis, and Plato's tale of it is important to our purposes now because he wrote (quoting the Egyptian priest of Sais):

> There was, beyond the straits you call the "Pillars of Hercules" an island, larger than Asia and Libya together, from where it was still possible then to sail to the other islands, and thence to the whole continent on the other side, which encloses the sea truly named after it. For everything that is situated on this side of the strait of which we are talking appears like a bay with a narrow entrance; that sea may properly be called an ocean and the land enclosing it as properly a continent.[37]

This seems perfectly straightforward. Beyond the Pillars of Hercules there's an island of large size in the Atlantic ocean (Atlantis). It is possible to sail beyond the large island to, first, some other and presumably smaller islands, and then on to a true continent westward of the islands. This is a good, general description of the islands of the West Indies with the true American continents beyond. Indeed, it is so clear that it is difficult to see how it could have ever been misunderstood, and why so many writers have "found" Atlantis somewhere else.

In a work attributed to Plato's most famous pupil, Aristotle (384–322 B.C), the tutor of Alexander the Great, but in a passage more probably written by a student, part of Section 84 of *On Marvellous Things Heard* says:

> In the sea outside the Pillars of Hercules they say that an island was found by the Carthagenians, a wilderness having woods of all kinds and navigable rivers, remarkable for various kinds of fruits, and many days' sailing distance away. When the Carthagenians, who were masters of the western ocean, observed that many traders and other men, attracted by the fertility of the soil and the pleasant climate, frequented it because of its richness, and some resided there, they feared that knowledge of this land would reach other nations, and that a great concourse to it of men from various lands of the earth would follow. Therefore, lest the Carthagenian Empire itself suffer injury, and the dominion of the sea be wrested from their hands, the Senate of Carthage issued a decree that no one, under penalty of death, should thereafter sail thither, and they massacred all who resided there.

Diodorus Siculus (d. circa 21 B.C.) wrote an account that may well be just a copy and elaboration of "Aristotle's":

> Over against Africa lies a very great island in the vast ocean, many days' sail from Libya westwards. The soil there is very fruitful, a great part whereof is mountainous, but much likewise a plain, which is the most sweet and pleasant part, for it is watered by several navigable rivers....The mountainous part of the country is clothed with very large woods, and all manner of fruit trees and springs of fresh water....There, you may have game enough in hunting all sorts of wild beasts....This island seems rather to be the residence of some of the gods, than of men.
>   Anciently, by reason of its remote location, it was altogether unknown, but afterwards discovered

on this occasion: the Phoenicians in ancient times
undertook frequent voyages by sea, in way of traffic
as merchants, so that they planted colonies in
Africa and in these western parts of Europe. These
merchants, succeeding in their undertaking, and
thereafter growing very rich, passed at length
beyond the Pillars of Hercules into the sea called
the Ocean. At first they built a city called Gades
[that is, Cadiz in modern Spain]. The Phoenicians,
having found out the coast beyond the Pillars, and
sailing along by the shore of Africa, were on a
sudden driven by a furious storm off into the main
ocean, and after they had lain under this violent
tempest for many days, they at length arrived at this
island, and so they were the first that discovered it.

It is very clear that these Greek and Roman writers have some
vague general knowledge about some vast land mass across the
Atlantic, but no detailed information. We may be quite certain
from these accounts that the Carthagenians and Phoenicians knew
a lot more, and kept it to themselves. Phoenicians lived in the
eastern Mediterranean, in the region of present Lebanon, as a loose
confederation of sometimes-allied coastal city-states. The three
major Phoenician cities were Tyre, Sidon, and Byblos.

Phoenicians fell heir to maritime supremacy in the eastern
Mediterranean after the Minoan civilization was destroyed by
Mycenaean Greeks about 1500 B.C., and after the Mycenaeans
were themselves destroyed by invaders from the northeast, possibly
Dorian Greeks, five hundred years later. From about 1000 B.C.,
Phoenician sea power was supreme in the eastern Mediterranean
until Persians conquered the area about 600 B.C.

Carthage was a Phoenician colony established by emigrants from
Tyre about 850 B.C. in present-day Tunisia in North Africa.
Carthage survived as a major power longer than Phoenicia itself,
dominating the western Mediterranean until its wars with Rome
and final defeat in 146 B.C. by Scipio Africanus Minor. In its 600-
year heyday, though, Carthage itself founded colonies all over the
Mediterranean coasts of Spain and North Africa and its mariners
pushed out into the Atlantic. Other colonies were founded outside
the Pillars of Hercules. Cadiz, on the Atlantic coast of Spain, has
already been mentioned. But there was also Lixus on the Atlantic

coast of present-day Morocco, a city that eventually became larger than Carthage itself. Cadiz and Lixus were ports and emporiums of Atlantic trade. They became immensely wealthy and equally exciting. "Wicked Tarshish" of the Bible was Cadiz in Spain.[38]

The Phoenicians and Carthagenians sort of merge into the "Ancient Celts." Some readers of Holy Grail Across the Atlantic wrote letters to chide me, very justifiably, for an error that not one professional historian or newspaper reviewer seemed to notice. I had penned a too-hasty identification of all these peoples: "They [Phoenicians] were the original 'Celts'." At best, this is a gross over-simplification; at worst, some would consider it gross inaccuracy.

Celts are defined as people who spoke a branch of the Indo-European language and who were originally indigenous to the Russian steppes, whereas Phoenicians are regarded as a Semitic people because they spoke a Semitic language. However, language is not necessarily any indication of genetic origin or affiliation since there's nothing easier to adopt than a language. For example, the vast majority of Afro-Americans and remaining Native Americans speak only the American dialect of English today, although not one of their pre-Columbian ancestors did.

It is thought that Phoenicians invaded the eastern Mediterranean coastal region from the northwest, from Anatolia in modern Turkey. Phoenician means "red" or "red haired," a natural characteristic of most Celts (but a characteristic sometimes artificially produced, or enhanced, with an application of pigment and lime by those who either lacked red hair or wanted to exaggerate it). The Greeks first encountered the Keltoi in Anatolia, but they must have come into Anatolia from the Caucasus. Therefore, before either the Keltoi or the Phoenicians got into Turkey, they must have come from the Russian steppe region. This would have been long ago, sometime between 10,000 B.C. and 2000 B.C.

My notion was, and remains, that the Phoenicians and the Celts were originally the same people, Indo-European speakers migrating from north of the Caucasus into Anatolia. This group split and went in two different directions. The "Phoenician" contingent migrated southeast and encountered a Semitic culture and linguistic sphere of influence, and they adapted to it. It is worth noting that linguists maintain that the Semitic languages originated in western Arabia, the exact opposite direction, as far as Lebanon is concerned, from which the Phoenicians supposedly arrived.[39]

The Phoenicians adapted to their Semitic neighbours and languages, but they did not assimilate into either the Canaanite or Hebrew cultures — as we shall see with the "Benjamite tribe" of Hebrews, who appear to have been related to the Phoenicians and fought a war against all the other tribes of Israel. They lost the war, but survivors were carried to Arcadia by coastal Phoenicians. These former Benjamites eventually entered France as Sicambrian Franks, and have much to do with the Holy Grail. The Phoenicians remained culturally distinct in their coastal enclave and expanded westward, by sea, throughout the Mediterranean and North Africa. By planting colonies like Carthage, Phoenicians spread into Morocco on the African side of the Strait of Gibraltar, and into Spain, and even into parts of southern France, on the European side.

The other group of Anatolian Indo-European speakers, called *Keltoi* by the Greeks, went westward by land, crossed the Bosporus into "Europe," and followed the course of the Danube. They seem to have been deflected from pouring down into Greece *en masse*, although some may have done so. Robert Graves, the English poet and linguist, has pointed out the many parallels between early Greek myth and language, and Celtic myth and language.[40] These *Keltoi* created the Hallstadt bronze age culture in Central Europe. They migrated on to western Europe where they evolved into the La Tène iron age Celtic culture in France, Spain, and Britain.

These two streams were, in a way, "reunited" in Spain (and, of course, modern Portugal). They may have retained enough cultural similarity, and even some linguistic affinity, so that they encountered each other as long lost, if by now rather distant, relatives. In any event, the so-called "Celtiberian" culture was the result, a voluntary or enforced fusing of the two peoples.

As Carthagenian associates, the Celtiberians sailed widely on the Atlantic. We will probably never know how widely, although Aristotle and Diodorus assure us that they reached the marvellous "island," that western land that was "rather the residence of some of the gods, than of men." We know that they were primarily traders, that they prospered, and that some of them lived in the western lands.

It is quite obvious, from the accounts of Aristotle and Diodorus, that the best known part of the marvellous western "island," at least the best known to the Greeks and Romans who picked up mere snippets of information, was in latitudes directly westward from the Atlantic coast of Africa. This indicates the Caribbean and the coast of South America. But we know that Phoenician-Carthagenians sailed in more northerly latitudes, too, because in 1753 an earthenware pot full of Carthagenian coins was found on the island of Corvo in the Azores group.[41] The coins dated from the fourth century B.C. The ship, which apparently came to grief on Corvo, would most likely have been bound for North America to have been wrecked at that latitude.

Irish tradition insists that the first Celtic speakers came by ship from Spain and the Mediterranean, not from La Tène culture of mainland Europe. Supporting this tradition, perhaps, is the fact that there are two forms of Celtic language in the British Isles. Goidelic or Gaelic (Irish) seems to be the earlier form, and it did come to Ireland from Celtiberia. It was taken to Scotland in historical times. Dialects of Gaelic are still spoken in Ireland and Scotland and are enjoying a revival today. It is fascinating to note, however, and in passing, that when these Goidelic-Gaelic Celtiberians first reached Ireland from Iberia about 2000 B.C., they encountered a tall, blond, and blue-eyed race they called the Tuatha de Danaan. They spoke the "Elder Tongue" (i.e., Elvish!) and knew the *Oran Mor* (i.e., "The Great Music," an actual form of communication). No one knows for certain who these "Elvish-speaking" people were, but there is said to be a bit of *Oran Mor* in every Irish tune, a few borrowed "Elder" words in Gaelic. They were most likely a people descended from Atlantean survivors who managed to reach Ireland after the catastrophe. There is some slight evidence for this. The so-called *Guanches*, a tall, fair, and blue-eyed people with a very low cultural level, were discovered on isolated Atlantic islands, including the Azores, when European mariners arrived in the fifteenth century. They had been more or less marooned because they could not build boats. They claimed to have descended from people of a great sunken empire that was remembered in their oral traditions.[42]

The other form of Celtic, "Belgic" or Brythonic, apparently came straight to Britain from across the Channel. This branch of Celtic includes the Welsh, Cornish, Manx, and Breton languages. They, too, are enjoying a cultural renaissance. *Brythonic* (with the "th" pronounced as a "d" or "t") was the basic language of the "Ancient Britons" and had many regional dialects. It was overwhelmed, in England, by Latin, Angle-Saxon, Danish (in parts), and Norman-French successively.

Therefore, it seems, the Celtiberians sailed as far north as the latitude of Ireland, about the latitude of the estuary of the St.

Lawrence, with an island-hopping route (Ireland-Iceland-Greenland-Newfoundland) to the Atlantic Coast of continental North America. This route, in the summer sailing season, may have seemed preferable to a longer North Atlantic passage via the Azores, or the even longer tradewind passage to the Bahamas and then north along the Florida, Georgia, Carolina, and mid-Atlantic coasts. But, most probably, all these routes were used depending on the point of departure and the destination.

The Irish and "Iargalon"

One thing is certain. A blessed and almost magical land to the west was ingrained in Irish myth, legend, and folklore. One of the earliest names for it was Tir a nOg (the meaning is disputed). A slightly later name was Iargalon ("The land beyond the sunset"). Still later, about A.D. 400–500, after Irish Christian priests took to sailing out into the Atlantic to find solitude, and as the sailing legends coalesced around the person of St. Brendan, the land was sometimes called Brendan's Isle. This island persisted on maps for a long time, though it was placed with a lot of imagination, and gradually became corrupted into "Brazil."

Phoenicians dominated Mediterranean trade from, perhaps, 1200 B.C. Tyrians founded their colony at Carthage in the ninth century B.C., but must have known the region very well before deciding to build a city in modern Tunisia. There's nothing improbable in the idea that Phoenicians sailed beyond the Pillars of Hercules as early as, perhaps, 1100-1000 B.C. Thus Phoenician/Celtiberian/Celtic voyages to "America" could have been made over the long period of 1,800 years — from the time of Phoenician maritime supremacy until the sailing monks of St. Brendan's time. This is a lot of time, almost as much time as the centuries that separate us from Jesus. Celtiberians could have become very numerous in America during these centuries.

Modern scholars have doubted, though, that Celts from Ireland could have made voyages across the Atlantic once Phoenicia and Carthage declined. For, with their decline, the Classical world's knowledge of making ocean-going ships also supposedly died. The Romans constructed giant merchant ships, primarily to carry grain from Egypt and North Africa to Italy, but it is true that they were built for Mediterranean conditions. Rome never had much of a seafaring tradition. Therefore, once Phoenician and Carthagenian ships were gone, Celts in Ireland were left with their native curraghs. Until recently, scholars felt, with some justification, that a curragh wasn't likely to be able to cross the Atlantic.

A curragh is a boat constructed with a wooden framework that is lashed together. A flexible and waterproof hull material of some sort is fitted over the outside of the framework. The Irish used a matrix of ash lathes for the frame matrix and oiled bull hides sewn together into the appropriate shape for the hull. In short, it was a wood-framed leather boat. Curraghs are often confused with coracles and, for some reason, British writers especially seem prone to this mistake. Curraghs possess a true boat shape; some have been very graceful and surprisingly large, carrying a crew of twenty to thirty. A coracle, on the other hand, is a round watercraft along the same lines. Coracles carried one to three people at most and were used for river and coastal fishing.

Could an Irish curragh cross the Atlantic? Tim Severin decided to find out. He researched everthing he could about curraghs, using various sources of Irish folklore, but particularly the *Navagatio Sancti Bendanis Abbatis* (*The Voyage of St. Brendan, Abbot*), a compilation of, probably, the Atlantic adventures of many Irish monks attributed to, and condensed into the tradition of, the most notable sailing priest, St. Brendan. Many scholars considered this collection of tales to be charming myth. But Severin, who was a sailor, realized that some of the accounts referred to true oceanic experience. He built *Brendan*, a thirty-six-foot curragh, following ancient specifications and in 1976 sailed it from Ireland to Iceland. In 1977 he completed the voyage to Newfoundland.[43]

Tim Severin and his crew quickly discovered that *Brendan* was not only impressively seaworthy, but was a surprisingly swift sailing boat. The flexible concept had both advantages and disadvantages. On the one hand, *Brendan* would bounce away from collisions with solid objects (like ice) that would have cracked a wooden hull. On the other hand, *Brendan's* leather hull could be punctured by sharp objects that might not have penetrated a wooden hull. But, with extra leather, needle, and thread, *Brendan's* hull could be repaired very effectively at sea, whereas a wooden boat would have presented more difficulty.

Severin and his crew proved that a curragh could have crossed the Atlantic, and a lot of them must have done so. The New England Antiquities Research Association (NEARA) and the Early

Sites Research Association (ESRA) have, between them, identified over three hundred Celtic sites in New England. There are some in Canada also. All of these are disputed and denied by conventional academia. A few maverick professors have had the courage to investigate some of these sites and to express the opinion that some are genuine.

Thankfully, for our purposes, most Celtic stonework differs in very obvious ways from medieval construction. Celts raised single "standing stones," *menhirs* in Europe; they built dolmens or cromlechs, a large stone perched on top of three or four other supporting stones. When the Ancient Celts constructed buildings, they didn't use mortar and they didn't make any attempt to square most of their stones. They made walls in the "rubblework" tradition and used the corbelled arch, not the true arch.

The "Vikings"

By the eighth century A.D., Vikings began to raid and then to conquer parts of Ireland. And then they too learned about Tir a nOg, Iargalon, and the ancient traditions of land to the west. The Norse explorations in America are beyond our scope to cover in any detail, but four primary sagas recount the Norse experience in the West.

The *Flateyjarbók* ("Flat Island Book," a record of Icelandic families), *Hauksbòk* (a history commissioned by a descendant of Thorfinn Karlsefni), *Landnámabók* ("Taking of the Land Book," chronicle of Icelandic colonization) and *Eriks Saga Rauda* ("Erik the Red's Saga") tell us that "Vikings" explored the entire Atlantic coast of North America from at least the year A.D. 1000 to about 1030. These sagas, originally transmitted as oral epic poetry by skalds, were written down in the thirteenth and fourteenth centuries and, together with purely mythic and legendary stories like the *Njáll Brennu Saga* ("The Burning of Njáll Saga"), make up the core of Scandinavian literature. The Atlantic sagas tell us that the first known Norseman to sight the coast of North America was Bjarni Herjulfsson.

In the year A.D. 986, Bjarni set sail from Norway to visit his father in Iceland. But, when he arrived there, he learned, somewhat to his surprise, that his father had decided to move to Greenland. Bjarni asked his crew if they would risk voyaging on to Greenland, which, he admitted, "must be considered foolhardy since none of us has ever sailed thither." Nonetheless, his men were willing to follow him. They set sail from Iceland but almost immediately encountered a great storm. It blew them westward for many days.

At last the storm abated and they found themselves off a hilly, wooded coast. This did not look like Greenland to Bjarni — and he'd certainly got all the information he could while in Iceland. The sagas relate that Bjarni knew he was too far south for the land to be Greenland. He therefore sailed north, but was pushed ever eastwards by the trend of the coast. After an open-water passage of undisclosed length, they came to another land northeast of the first. This land was not particularly hilly, but was clothed with a forest of vast trees. It didn't conform with Bjarni's description of Greenland either, and so they sailed on. After another open-water passage, they sighted a third land, which was barren rock with glaciers inland and they coasted it until they left it astern. This third land could not be Greenland, "according to my information," said Bjarni, for he knew that they were still too far south. They left this third land and sailed northeast for four days before sighting Greenland. As luck would have it, Bjarni arrived in Greenland not far from his father's new residence, Herjulfsnes ("Herjulf's Cape").

This passage has been studied and re-studied by amateurs and academics alike because, with very little additional direction given in the original Old Norse versions of the sagas, these are the only sailing directions to Vinland and North America ever offered by the Norse. They were sufficient for Leif Eriksson; Leif's half-sister Fredis and the Icelandic brothers Helgi and Finnbogi who sailed their ship in company with hers; Thorfinn Karlsefni and his three-ship expedition, Thorall the Huntsman and Thorall the Drunkard.[44]

Bjarni Herjulfsson never landed in any of the new lands he sighted, and for this he was much criticized in Greenland and Norway. Finally, Leif, son of Erik the Red, decided to find the lands that Bjarni had seen. He did this by reversing the course of Bjarni's voyage.

Although the location of Vinland has been much debated and is a fascinating puzzle, it is not really sufficiently within our bailiwick to justify detailed discussion. I will give my opinion herewith that the interested reader can best disregard the literary experts in Old Norse who have pontificated on this subject. By changing the directions given in the sagas, which a seafaring audience would not have tolerated, and by making some lubberly translations that would make any seaman roar with laughter, the academics manage to place Vinland any number of unlikely places. The worst, and most pompous, offender of this ilk is, in my opinion, Gwyn Daniels's *The Norse Atlantic Sagas*..[45] But there *is* a legitimate scholarly debate about whether Vinland means wineland or grassland.[46]

Most of this scholarly wrangling is irrelevant to our focus. Readers interested in the Vinland question are referred to the bibliography. We only need to know that Leif Eriksson found Vinland, believing for good reasons that it was the land Bjarni had first seen, and made shelters for himself and his men there. The place was called Vinland the Good thereafter, but also sometimes Leifsbudir ("Leif's Booths" or "Shelters"). Following Leif, all of the above-named Norse were able to find Vinland/Leifsbudir.

Wherever Vinland was, it was not the Norse name for North America as a whole. I think they came to regard Vinland as a sort of Plymouth Rock. It was the first place Leif decided to stay for a while, but as the Norse came to know the land better other places became more important. The name Irland ad Mikla was sometimes applied to North America as a whole in the sagas. This means "Greater Ireland" and the Norse explicitly state that many Irish had been there before them, and some were there when the Vikings explored the coast. Gudrid, the wife of Thorfinn Karlsefni, accompanied him on a three-year expedition to the new lands. Aside from the fact that she gave birth to a son, Snorri (the first known European child born in America), at a place called Straumfjord, she actually met an Irish woman in the New World.

One lengthy section of the coast was called Hvritmannaland ("White Man's Land"), although the inhabitants lived a few miles inland.[47] The characteristic activities of the residents of Hvritmannaland involved marching in processions, chanting and carrying banners. This may call to mind the devotions of Irish priests but, whether or not that is the case, the sagas record that an Icelandic merchant called Ari Marson, a pagan, became a baptized Christian in Hvritmannaland.[48] More often, at least later, the sagas refer to the totality of North America as Markland. This was a name first given by Leif to Bjarni's second land, but was gradually applied to the whole. This means "Forest Land" and it was completely appropriate for the Atlantic seaboard from Florida to Labrador.

The sagas refer directly only to the years A.D. 1001-1030, but Icelandic annals indicate ongoing Norse activity until 1347 when the last recorded "Markland ship" arrived in Reykjavik.[49] We have no certain knowledge of what this Norse activity was. We don't know how many Norse came to America over 350 years. We know that they established a settlement on the northern tip of Newfoundland at L'Anse aux Meadows. We know that Norse artefacts, most of them of disputed authenticity, have been recovered as far west as Minnesota and as far north as Lake Nipigon in Ontario.

When does a Viking become a Norwegian, Danish, Swedish or Icelandic warrior or "knight"? According to Icelandic annals, the last ship to sail from Markland (America) into Reykjavik harbour arrived in A.D. 1347. This is forty years after the Knights Templar were crushed in France, forty years after the Templar fleet disappeared into Atlantic waters. In short, in the year 1347 there could have been both "Vikings" and Grail-related Templars in North America. America is so large that, if representatives of both groups were here, they might not even have suspected each other's existence.

On the other hand, they might well have known of the other's existence. There is reason to believe, for instance, that some Norse chieftains assisted Grail refugees as early as the beginning of the Albigensian Crusade (1209-1244). The Bavarian "troubadour," *or minnesinger* to use the correct German analog, Wolfram von Eschenbach, wrote in his Grail romance *Parzival* that "Greenland knights" played a major role in the medieval chapter of the Holy Grail story. *Parzival* was written in the early 1200s.

Then, the question of who was "Norse" and who wasn't even gets difficult to answer.

All the "Normans" of Brittany, who invaded and conquered England under Duke William in 1066 (and all that), could, by a stretch, be called Norse. The famous Bayeux Tapestry, which chronicles the Norman invasion and conquest of England, is "a purely Norse thing," according to art historian Ian MacLaglan. And, in fact, the Bayeux Tapestry has some later relevance to our theme. "Norman" meant *Northman*, and the Normans were, in theory, descendants of Vikings who had raided Brittany and had settled there. By extension, then, all the Normans in England could also be called Norse. The Saxons, whom they defeated at the Battle of Hastings to win England, were just as Norse as the Normans — they descended from Angle, Saxon, and Jute invaders from Denmark, Germany, Friesland, and Scandinavia.

To make matters more confusing, much of Scotland was held by the "Normans," but some of it was held by the "Norse" in medieval times. Henry Sinclair, Baron of Rosslyn and Earl of Orkney (1345–1400), whom we will meet soon, was a genuine Norman whose ancestors had fought beside Duke William himself, but he was also very much Norse: he held the Orkney Islands for the King of Norway and was a Jarl (Earl) in the Norwegian court.

So, in some instances, it is impossible to determine whether some ruin or artefact should be ascribed to Norse entrepreneurs in America or to Grail-related refugees and their protective knights. They often descended from the same group of ancestors, and both were active in North America at the same times. The Newport Tower in Newport, Rhode Island, is, for example, a building that could have been constructed by either group. But, and this is important to realize, it could have been occupied, or used, by *both* groups at different times — or even simultaneously if the "Grail-people" and the Norse were sometimes allies in the new land. We will discuss the Newport Tower a bit later.

So, even if we find whole or ruined stone structures in improbable places in North America which seem datable to medieval European times, and there are quite a few such ruins that have been discovered (and who knows how many yet to be found?), we cannot with certainty ascribe them to "Grail people" unless an artefact or inscription undoubtedly associated with the stonework suggests some connection with the Holy Grail story. A Templar banking token, for instance, would certainly provide a legitimate connection with known Grail refugees. In fact, several such tokens have been found in excavated sites along the St. Lawrence.

The Welsh

Previously, we asked when a Viking was transformed into a medieval Scandinavian warrior or knight. St. Brendan lived in the sixth century A.D., the so-called Dark Ages after the fall of Rome, and could (I suppose) be considered an Ancient Celt. Prince Madoc of North Wales presents us with a problem similar to the Viking transformation. Madoc, it is written, found a land across the Atlantic and, thinking it a good place for a colony, returned home and then set sail with a small fleet and a number of colonists in the year A.D. 1170. He never came back, and neither did any of his colonists, so we don't know if he made it back to America.

But the important point is that Madoc and his people would

certainly not have made stonework, if they constructed any, in the rubblework-and-corbelled-vault manner of his ancient Celtic ancestors. He would have been much too familiar with Saxon and Norman castles made of squared stones and mortar. Therefore, any given piece of such stonework in America could be attributed, not to medieval Norse or to medieval "Grail people," but possibly to Prince Madoc and his colonists. We just don't know, but the idea is not altogether fanciful.

Captain John Smith (1580–1631) of early American colonial history was not saved by the love of Pocahontas but because Captain Smith could speak Welsh. His Indian tormentors could speak Welsh, too, and one naturally wonders how. Indeed, in very early colonial American accounts, we find reports of Welsh-speaking Indians all along the Great Smokey Mountains (the Appalachians) from North Carolina to Pennsylvania.[50]

In the 1170s or so, the "Welsh princes" were being subjected to Norman conquest from England. Prince Madoc was only one of many clan chieftains of that time who may have considered that colonizing a new land across the Atlantic was much preferable to becoming serfs of Normans. And this land was not really "new" to Celts. It was attested to in many songs and stories. Perhaps it had never really been forgotten since the time of the Phoenician-Carthagenians, Celtiberian-Celts, and its memory had been revived by St. Brendan.

Aside from Atlanteans, Egyptians, Minoans, Mycenaean Greeks, Phoenicians, Carthagenians, Celts, Vikings, and Welsh, we cannot absolutely rule out the occasional voyage by Romans. Roman-looking amphorae have been found off the coast of Venezuela in the Caribbean, indicating a wrecked ship nearby. But what kind of ship? Only the cargo might have been Roman amphorae. The ship could have been Greek or Phoenician.

We cannot absolutely rule out the possibility that Jewish survivors from the Roman conquest of Judea about A.D. 70 not only took refuge in Spain, as they are known to have done, but that some pushed on across the Atlantic. Alleged first-century Jewish inscriptions have been discovered on rocks at Bat Creek in Tennessee. There is, naturally, much dispute as to whether these are genuine, accidental weathering and cracking, or modern forgeries. I have no opinion on this matter and am certainly not competent to judge the linguistic crux of it.

But...some of these hypothetical Jewish voyages may have been

Grail-related. "Terrorists" (from the Roman point of view) were within the entourage of Jesus. At base, both John the Baptist and Jesus were executed because they posed a perceived threat to Rome's authority, and to the authority of local Jewish puppet kings (Herodians) who enjoyed the support of the wealthier Jews. It is at least possible that some refugee Jewish voyages would have included hunted Zealots who knew the Grail version of the lives of John and Jesus. They would have been hunted by both Romans and all right-thinking Jews, whether in Palestine or in Spain. The Atlantic might have seemed preferable to crucifixion. Doubtless, however, the vast majority of hypothetical Jewish refugees would have been from Judea after the fall of Masada in A.D. 70, but this doesn't rule out Grail knowledge and even belief. They were radical in their outlook.

Now that we have mentioned the Jews in Spain, we may as well mention the Moors. When the Berber chieftain, Tarik, invaded Spain in A.D. 711 at Gibraltar (i.e., *Jabal Tarik* — Tarik's Mountain), he brought into Europe the world's most sophisticated maritime culture of the time. The Arabs had developed ships that would sail to windward, as the Europeans failed to do until seven centuries later. The Arabs had developed navigation and mathematical cartography. This is why so many navigational terms, like "azimuth," are Arabic, and why so many stars have Arabic names. British adventurer Tim Severin built a replica Arab ship of about A.D. 800 and sailed it from Oman to Canton. *The Sindbad Voyage* recounts this adventure, and the ship, *Sohar*, was found to be quite adequate. Sindbad's activities took place in the Indian Ocean and the Far East, but the Arabic culture of his time also ruled much of Spain.

Although, to my knowledge, there is no record or evidence of Moorish voyages from Spain to the New World, the Arabs certainly had the ships and navigational techniques to do it. Indeed, they could have done it better than anyone else before Columbus. A French source, the *Encyclopèdie Alphabètique Larousse-Omni*, states that the Moors of Spain used the Azores as a refuge during the Christian "re-conquest."[51] This would have been from about A.D. 1070 and the exploits of "El Cid" to A.D. 1492 and the fall of Granada — a suggestive date! But the *Larousse* also mentions (vaguely) possible Moorish voyages to the Azores as early as the eighth Christian century. My own view is that there must have been Moorish voyages across the Atlantic.[52]

The French national epic, *The Song of Roland*, supposedly written about A.D. 900–1000 but recounting events of the 700s, mentions a great Moorish fleet. Since the action is taking place at Roncesvalles, this fleet must have been based on the Bay of Biscay. On the other hand, *The Song of Roland* is so inaccurate, exaggerated, romanticized, and embellished that it is historically worthless. The historical Roland, prefect of the Breton march and commander of Charlemagne's rear guard when the army was returning from Spain, was ambushed (in A.D. 778) by the Basques, not Moors, and not at the pass of Roncesvalles but at another pass further to the west in the Pyrénées.

I find it much more interesting, for example, that before his third voyage in 1498, Columbus asked for, and received, three Arabic interpreters. Why did he need them in the New World?

Later, we will visit some ruins in North America that have been radiocarbon-dated to the Moorish period. It is also interesting to point out that Moors were amalgamated into the Grail religion. Indeed, Wolfram von Eschenbach in *Parzival* tells us that the first account of the Grail was written in "confused pagan writing" (Arabic) and was from Toledo. Therefore, some Moorish voyages on the Atlantic may not have been entirely unrelated to the Grail.

Canadian archaeologists and historians, while unaccountably hostile to Celtic and Norse visitation in North America even though written documents, ruins, and artefacts support it, are willing to grant the Basques almost any pre-Columbian transatlantic achievement despite the fact there are no known pre-Columbian documents to prove Basque voyages and settlement. I have no doubt at all that the Basques voyaged to North America before Columbus, just as many other mariners did. I have nothing against Basques, but I cannot understand the exclusive "Basque favouritism" among Canadian scholars.

When we think of the Basques, though, we should remember they they also lived in the Pyrénées region. They, too, suffered in the Albigensian Crusade. Basque voyages to the New World may sometimes have been Grail-related. Grail refugees and Basques may have set sail together on Basque ships to find a haven from their tormentors.

We now approach our main theme. Two years before the last "Markland ship" dropped anchor in Reykjavik, Iceland, in the year A.D. 1345, a child was born in Scotland who was destined to become one of the greatest explorers of European history. He was also one of the greatest knights in the long and heroic chronicle of the Holy Grail. Though his name will be unfamiliar to most

Americans, the United States owes a great debt to him. His achievement makes him a worthy companion of Joseph of Arimathaea, Mary of Magdala, King Arthur, Galahad and Parsifal, Godfroi de Bouillon, Jacques de Molay, Joan of Arc, and other great heroes and heroines of the Grail.

His name was Henry Sinclair.

3

Crusades and "The Cross"

My introduction to fieldwork on the Holy Grail came just before Christmas 1981. This was before the explosion of *The Holy Blood and the Holy Grail*, and I had not seen any of the three BBC documentaries produced in co-operation with Henry Lincoln.

Nonetheless, I had long been interested in the troubadour ballads of courtly love that had been written shortly before, during, and after the Albigensian Crusade. This body of literature included the so-called Grail Romances. In the late 1960s, a Toronto high school teacher friend of mine, Lillian Perigoe, had asked me to read over some of this literature. She was planning to introduce it into a classroom full of more or less delinquent girls in a special teaching program. She wanted my opinion as to whether the moral, ethical, and sexual content of these works would be suitable for these young women.

So, as a favour to Lillian, I read a lot of southern French romances of the thirteenth century (in English translation). I never could decide whether this literature was suitable for modern young women — and perhaps I was not the person to ask — but I became fascinated with the romances. The literary style didn't impress me, but what did was the quite self-evident fact (to me) that the troubadours were trying to convey factual information within the guise of harmless romances. Sometimes, obviously, this was accomplished only at the cost of straining the literary structure of a work. *Something* was being said, but it was a code. I was particularly impressed with the amount of geographical information being conveyed and also was puzzled that some of the authors invited rather complex chronological calculations in their stories. I told this to Lillian, but it wasn't her primary focus or interest in the material.

I then began to research the history of the region and naturally learned of the Albigensian "Heresy" and the Albigensian Crusade. The more I read, the more it seemed that some momentous turning point in the history and structure of Christianity had happened. I even managed to get some inkling of what this was.

During the mid and late 1970s, I was writing a book, *The Iceman Inheritance*, on the cultural evolution of western humanity. This was published in late 1978 in Canada, and in 1980 was published by Warner Books in the United States. I thought that the Albigensian Crusade had been so important a turning point in western culture that in the book I attributed crucial influence to it.

I am relating this, quite frankly, because since the international success of *The Holy Blood and the Holy Grail*, many authors have done quick research, usually re-hashes of other work, and have jumped on the Grail bandwagon. I had been doing independent research before the Grail became a popular subject. I planned a book on the Grail to follow *The Iceman Inheritance*,[1] but, as fate would have it, my Grail book wasn't published for ten years — and it was a much different one from the book I'd envisioned in 1978.

As I said, my invitation to do fieldwork on the Holy Grail came from a reader of one of my books in the form of a letter sent to my publisher and forwarded to me. And by then I had the general background to accept the invitation with enthusiasm. As it turned out, this letter was to affect my life profoundly, and it began a chain of events that apparently also changed the lives of many others. At least, many people, all of them unknown to me at the time, claimed so some five and ten years later.

In my case, and in the experience of most others, the change or effect was one of a shift in perspective about the true nature of individual human endeavour, progress, culture, and history. Many people later wrote to me saying that they no longer felt so alone in their values and life commitments, no matter how insignificant these works and feelings had been made to seem by others. This, more or less, was precisely the insight that the letter and its repercussions forced on me.

Therefore, it may not be wholly inappropriate to recount what was going on in my life when the letter arrived. It was one of those times, common to everyone I think, when the fabric of life has been torn, and seemingly beyond any hope of mending. My fourteen-year marriage had broken up in the early summer of 1980, in Halifax, where my wife had been attending social work school. I'd gone to Halifax with her to offer financial and logistical support, and to provide day care for our child, Jason. But once she'd graduated, she decided to end the marriage. She elected to remain in Halifax (she was a native Maritimer); eight-year-old Jason was to live in Halifax with her. How could I maintain a relationship with my son in Halifax and revive and preserve a fledgling writing career?

I was not so well-established as a writer that I could work, and sell, effectively from Halifax. I still needed to be in or near some major market where I could earn bread-and-butter income by being available for whatever writing contracts might come up while I wrote books. Indeed, in return for postponing my own writing career in order to help my wife in Halifax so that her degree could be upgraded at her old familiar school (although other schools in central Canada had accepted her), we had agreed to return to Toronto — or, perhaps, move to Los Angeles — after she had obtained her M.S.W. degree.

But, with the hindsight of eighteen years as of this writing, I can see that a new tapestry of life was already being woven even if I didn't know it. And it had started its career on the loom even before the breakup. If I had not been utterly determined, against difficult odds, to keep a promise to my puzzled and frightened son, the pattern would never have been born. If, further (having nothing to lose), I had not re-vitalized a once-derided and once-ridiculed social commitment based on "childish" experiments with old-style boats, the pattern of the new tapestry would not have emerged.

The bright, golden thread of that AE might never have been noticed. We might never have seen the hint of a great human treasure, the glint of the Grail. A promise to a child, and childish experiments with boats, began a chain of "coincidences" (or synchronicity, as Jung would have it) that led to a glimpse of the Holy Grail and to the discoveries of Henry Sinclair. It was only my interest in ancient boats that gave us the location, income, and leisure to research the Castle at The Cross.

Although I had promised Jason to arrange things so that I could spend two full years in Nova Scotia, during 1980 I had incurred obligations with various publishers that involved media appearances in the United States and Canada; I also had obligations in Los Angeles, where I had agreed to do some screenplays and other writing based on the previous, and now suddenly annulled, domestic agreement. I remember the next few months as hectic ones, jumbled memories mostly of airports because I was determined not to spend too long away from Jason. I would return to Halifax after every business meeting, and even on free days during promotional tours, so that I could see him frequently if not regularly.

Halifax is somewhat remote from other North American cities, so this took its toll financially and in other ways. Finally, in the spring of 1981, I was able to satisfy writing and promotional obligations that might cause long absences from Jason, and I rejected further writing opportunities so that I could spend the promised two years near Jason.

But one May evening in 1981, on a layover in Toronto waiting for what I hoped would be my last early-morning flight into Halifax for a while, I ran into Deanna Theilmann-Bean again. I'd not seen her for a couple of years. Several years before we'd been colleagues at Adcom Research Limited in Toronto. She had just left her job there, wanting to experience an environment other than a large corporate one. She decided then and there to throw in her lot with me, and to help *me* over a difficult time of transition. She had always been fond of Jason and was distressed at his current situation.

Taking an extra day to clear up her affairs and to put most of her possessions in storage, we bought a car, hopped in it, and drove to Halifax. On the long drive to the Atlantic, I told her about my situation. I was going to put my writing career on hold and try to start a boat-building business in Nova Scotia along lines that had interested me for some time. I've always just loved boats of all kinds. But because of my research into ancient and non-western ships and voyages, I had also become interested in the world's fisheries, since wresting food from the sea had no doubt inspired the idea of boats in the dawn of human time. I'd been thinking for the past few years that ancient and non-western ideas of boat-building, if rendered in modern materials, might make seaworthy and inexpensive boats for village fishermen in developing countries. I had long been toying with the idea of putting some money and effort into this, although I well knew it was not a venture likely to make much profit — indeed, my notions of obligation and commitment to humanity had been the source of at least some domestic discord.

During 1979–80 in Halifax, while my wife had attended university, I managed to get a job as a part-time lecturer at Dalhousie University's Centre for African Studies. Not only did this pass the time in an interesting way, but I could refine my research on aspects of ancient navigation, voyaging, and migration. And, as "semi-faculty," I was able to wheedle access to libraries and facilities that I would not have had otherwise. Jason and I had fun spending days and hours (after school and on weekends) tank-testing models of traditional Irish curraghs, Andean log rafts, African reed boats, hull forms derived from Chinese junks, and so on. We did this both at the Dalhousie University Faculty of Mechanical Engineering's ultra-sophisticated test-tank and in our apartment's bathtub. Jason learned a lot.

I learned a lot more — that ancient Irish curraghs were exceptionally seaworthy because of their ultra-lightweight construction; that if a raft is three times as long as it is wide it *cannot* be capsized, assuming equal flotation over its surface, because that key proportion makes it slide over waves rather than flip (as the ancient Andeans and Polynesians discovered long ago, and we have not); that Chinese junks had, for three thousand years, used their deep-immersion rudders as a means of keeping the hull from heeling over in the wind just like the latest "trim tabs" on America's Cup yachts. My respect for traditional knowledge, and traditional boat designs, increased dramatically because of these scientific (and quasi-scientific) tank tests with scale models. I became even more convinced that a combination of traditional boat designs and modern materials could provide inexpensive yet seaworthy craft to help revitalize the world's "artisanal fisheries." The usual western aid agency approach had been to supply western boat designs rendered inadequately in local materials.

Because "westernization" of fisheries had over-fished many Third World waters, just as it was to destroy Canada's own Atlantic cod fishery with the help of "scientific" expertise a decade later, desperate efforts were being made by many nations to stop or roll back "westernization" and to support the rebirth of primitive village fishing traditions. The trouble was, that during the years of mechanized sea-harvesting, most of the village fishermen had been driven out of making even a subsistence living, and wood formerly used for boat building had been diverted into Western European and North American furniture manufacture to the profit of already wealthy countries.

The same old story. Much of western aid, particularly USAID and the World Bank, is but another thinly disguised way of "developing" Third World resources for easier exploitation by *ourselves*. Right-wing American "rednecks" have no reason at all to criticize USAID, the World Bank, or the International Monetary Fund — these aid agencies are right in there pitching with the multinationals.

The tragic result was that developing nations increasingly lacked even the basic materials for making fishing boats that were desperately needed to supply protein to expanding populations. Because I have this penchant for tilting at windmills, I had set my lance firmly on behalf of reconstructing so-called primitive fisheries in the Third World, and knew even then that our own western European and North American fisheries must someday revert to more "primitive" and more "traditional" methods. Otherwise, soon, there would be no more fish to catch — and eat. This is a serious matter since about 70 per cent of the world's protein and vitamins come from fish, in one way or another. Fish meal is the largest component of most agricultural fertilizers (with chemical additives), and it is used for high-nutrition supplement in poultry and cattle feed; it is the main source of A, D, and E vitamins in morning pills.

I knew that we would revert to primitive methods of fishing at some point in the not-so-distant future. The only question was *how*. Would we do it by intelligent policy, or would starving, vitamin-deficient survivors of our cultural rubble stumble down to the nearest water to fish for supper with hand lines?

The fish depletion crisis was self-evident, even back in 1980, to anyone with a modicum of common sense and intellectual integrity. True, so-called primitive and traditional fishing methods were labour-intensive and spawned all sorts of supportive small businesses that employed even more people. But this merely reduced and dissipated the per-unit profits of multinational owners of giant, mechanized and "progressive" factory ships. And these corporations pay the taxes that enable governments to employ fishery scientists, experts, and officials. It is easy to see, therefore, why most fish protein now derives from rat-tailed fish, sharks and squid, and no longer from cod, halibut, and bluefish. But soon even the rat-tails, sharks, and squid will be getting scarce.

This is not an inevitable problem of world over-population. It is the fact that factory ships are wasteful. A high percentage of every trawler haul is crushed to uselessness in the bottom (or "cod end," as it was once called) of the trawling net. Tons of protein are thrown overboard. Then trawling scoops up immature fish and scrapes fish eggs and larvae from the sea bottom, greatly reducing the ability of species to reproduce in naturally viable numbers.

China, the most populous nation on earth, whose people eat more fish per capita than any other nation on earth, has maintained a viable fishery for four thousand years. Why? Because China rejected the 1945 U.S. offer to mechanize its fisheries.[2] The Chinese fishery still employs millions of men and women, still employs traditional methods, and employs other millions in spin-off industries that serve the junk fleets (net-making and mending, sail-making and cordage, wooden ship repair and refitting, transport of fresh or salted product to daily markets without canning, refrigeration, or dehydration). The only concession to "modernization" the Chinese have made is that fishing junk hulls are now being produced in ferro-concrete, in three sizes, to conserve woods and forests that stabilize hills against erosion. The West would be wise to follow the Chinese example before it is too late.

It may not be too much more of a digression to mention that, as early as 1975–76 when we lived in British Columbia on the opposite (Pacific Ocean) side of Canada, and I was alternately writing *The Iceman Inheritance* and working on a salmon boat named the *Florence C*, Canadian Prime Minister Joe Clark requested me to write a long research paper on how both the Atlantic and Pacific fisheries might be saved. I took time out from my own writing, and fishing for a living, to prepare a one hundred-page situation report (unpaid) that opined that the Atlantic cod fishery was doomed anyway because reproductive stocks had fallen below the species' critical level, but that Canada could "hope" to revive it by outlawing mechanized trawling and immediately instituting Chinese-like primitive methods; this would boost badly needed Maritime employment and stimulate labour-intensive small spin-off businesses anyway.

But, I wrote, this was only a faint hope at this late date for the Atlantic fishery. I felt that the Pacific salmon and halibut fisheries might still be salvaged, however, if Chinese-like methods were introduced as a test measure in certain restricted waters. When such tests demonstrated an ongoing, viable catch, with no serious depletion of breeding stock, greater employment among fishermen, with a small reduction in fishermen's income partly offset by lower fuel costs, etc., then the wisdom of the idea could be "sold" to both U.S. and Canadian fishermen.[3]

Readers might wonder why the prime minister of Canada would ask *my* advice. The reason was that I had come to notice as a popular science newspaper and magazine writer, with *some* biological credentials, even if my notions were (even then) thought to be a bit eccentric. Joe Clark's brief days as prime minister were still ones in which wide-spectrum opinion was sometimes sought. Those days are past, and were passing even then. Now, we are at the mercy of conventional, accredited experts stamped with some university's Good Housekeeping Seal of Approval (and the seals, of course, are headed for the endangered species list).

The prime minister duly thanked me for my trouble, but I was informed that fisheries experts considered my perspective naive and that the real solution was further research into the dynamics of fish populations. While these studies were going on...well, in 1989 Atlantic cod became decidedly undynamic. Suddenly, for the first time in five hundred years of European experience, they just didn't appear in numbers worth catching, and most of those caught were immature fish. They remain undynamic, too, and the Atlantic fishery, which has sustained Indians for about eight thousand years, and has sustained European fishermen since the 1470s, is virtually dead.[4]

By 1995–96 American and Canadian west coast salmon fishermen escalated a confrontation, which continues still, about who should get what share of an ever-dwindling salmon catch. Dolphins, seals, and Indian "poaching" were blamed for decreasing fish stocks; but of course dolphins, seals, and Indians had fished gloriously abundant salmon for thousands of years before the Europeans' mechanized trollers arrived on the scene. The truth is hard to face.

Even if our own Atlantic and Pacific fisheries seem doomed, it appeared that Third World nations (at least, forty-four of them) had awakened to the brutal cost of western-style "modernization" of their fisheries. I could do something about that, perhaps, with my boat designs. I could help Third World nations to revitalize village fishing and the supply of inexpensive protein to starving people. Maybe, someday, the designs would become both appreciated and valuable to western Europe and North America — but not until scientific expertise had brought us to the brink of starvation. As Dr. James Bertin Webster wrote in his introduction to *The Black Discovery of America:*[5]

> The West insists upon seeing the world as it wishes
> it was, or thinks it should be. All our claims to
> rationality, objectivity and the scientific approach
> stop at the borders of our own culture. We will pay

heavily for this failure to extend the fairness of objectivity to other peoples and their history. Somewhere in our collective instinct we know it, and we clearly appear to prefer to melt the entire planet (or pollute it past redemption), destroying life totally, rather than become recipients of Third World charity in the form of humanitarian and psychological insights.[6]

So, as I said, with my lance firmly couched and my convictions finally uncompromised and unfettered by those tender, ruthless spider webs of domestic entrapment, I drove towards Halifax and Jason with my new lady's scarf fluttering in the breeze of a fast Fiat X-1-9. I swore to make the two years in Halifax with Jason not only the fulfilment of a promise, but also fulfilling in themselves, to create a platform from which Jason, Deanna, and I could clearly see and experience some basic issues in our complex and conflicting world.

But to return to the book that had inspired a reader's letter, a Christmas gift that changed our lives. This book had been a spin-off from research into ancient boats and navigation. During the course of my study of ancient and non-western voyaging, it occurred to me that a very neglected aspect of history had been the discovery of America by Black Africans from south of the Sahara in present-day West Africa. Actually, and this is no more than the simple truth, it had been five-year-old Jason who, a couple of years earlier, had first pointed out to me that West Africa was the closest part of the Old World to the New and that the oceanic currents flowed in a direction favourable for transoceanic contact. I subsequently discovered that there was no lack of evidence that sub-Saharan, Black Africans had crossed the Atlantic to Central and South America. Their black skins were clearly depicted in paintings in Yucatan, on the Temple of Warriors at Chichen Itza. Huge stone heads, also near Yucatan, had been anciently carved with unmistakable Negroid facial features. Tropical African plants grew wild, or became domesticated, throughout "America," and some of these could not have drifted across the ocean but must have come by the hand of man.

A little research showed that ancient West Africans had had the boats to cross the ocean: rafts of all kinds, giant dugouts as large as an *average* Viking ship (and considerably stronger), and reed boats like those on which Thor Heyerdahl had crossed the Atlantic and had sailed many seas. Early in 1980, I borrowed the typewriter during an academically lethargic February and wrote a book about this. An abridged version of this book was given as a paper to the 10th Annual Conference of the Canadian Association of African Studies, May 1980, by Dalhousie professor and close friend, Dr. James Bertin Webster. The book itself was published in the spring of 1981 by Personal Library of Toronto. It was called *The Black Discovery of America: Daring Voyages by West African Mariners.*[7]

And it was this book that had inspired the letter from the reader. As irony would have it, this reader was a Nova Scotian. She had written to my publisher in Toronto, her letter was faithfully forwarded "back" to us in Halifax, and we opened it just before Christmas 1981.

We debated whether to answer this utterly fascinating letter. Deanna and I had established CanTraid Export Limited in June 1981, with me as chief (and only) designer and her as president and CEO; we had opened a shop and were developing prototype boats using funds primarily derived from the U.S. sale, advance, and royalties of a previous book, *The Iceman Inheritance,* and we were otherwise occupied with trying to be occasional parents to Jason. I also had a personal career worry. I had to keep looking over my shoulder, on this modest corporate ladder we had constructed, to ensure that my ten-year-old son would not usurp my proud position of chief designer. He had ideas aplenty about boats, but thankfully his involvement in CanTraid was limited by school and visiting arrangements. In a word, Deanna and I were busy.

But, of course, the letter was much too fascinating to ignore. The woman had read *The Black Discovery of America,* but she wasn't interested in ancient African voyages. However, knowing that I was interested in obscure transatlantic navigation, she had written in the hope that I might be able to help her.

The problem was the ruined castle on her property.

She lived in a small, mid-peninsular village of Nova Scotia. The village had once been called The Cross, but another and official name had been bequeathed to the village during the 1950s for the benefit of the postal service.[8] It was now called New Ross. Her letter told us about the apparent castle ruins and the artefacts she and her husband had unearthed during a decade of dedicated gardening. She had informed the Royal Nova Scotia Museum years ago. A museum expert from Halifax had travelled down to have a look at her ruins. He pronounced them to be "of either French or Indian origin" dating "to the seventeenth century at the earliest." They were of no interest to the museum. But the lady and her husband knew that there was no historical record of an Acadian French settlement near The Cross (or New Ross) and knew that the Micmac Indians of Nova Scotia had never indulged in stonework of castle proportions. She had then begun a decade-long crusade to have her ruins properly investigated.

She had written to ask if I would come and view her "ruined castle." She wanted to find out what known European expeditions, if any, might be correlated with the apparent ruins. In short, who constructed this castle? When? And why, how, and when did it become a ruin? But her letter contained much more than a request for help. She had also written, at length, to recount the supposed history of the place as she had reconstructed it during the course of a decade's research. I was familiar with some of the history she described, but much was new to me. It was new to me because it was her own family history. The ruined castle was not only partially on her New Ross property, but she had discovered that her own ancestors had had much to do with it.

The "coincidence" of being in Nova Scotia ourselves made it simpler and faster to call the lady in New Ross, rather than to write her, and we arranged to see her "ruined castle" early in January 1982. We drove the seventy-five miles (125 kilometres) to New Ross in our newly leased Nissan diesel truck, a more practical vehicle for a boat-builder than my Fiat sports car, and it was lucky for us that we set out in it. On the way to New Ross, the first blizzard of the winter descended upon us. Aside from the fact that the sunny-climed Fiat heater was a grim joke, the volume of snow would eventually have exceeded the Fiat's minimal ground clearance.

At New Ross we encountered two things. First, we met the woman who'd written us, and her husband, whom I choose to call Jeanne and John McKay, and therefore made the acquaintance of one of the most intelligent, articulate and delightfully eccentric couples imaginable. John, a swarthy Welshman, was a chemist by profession and taught at Acadia University. Jeanne, a small, silver-blond, fragile-looking, and completely indestructible Englishwoman, said she was a witch.

The second thing we encountered was a configuration of rocks that puzzles me, and troubles me, even now. While Deanna went inside the McKays' house to warm up, I mumbled hasty greetings and went immediately to examine the "ruins." My action was curt and impolite, but I wanted to see as much as possible before the blizzard covered everything with snow. The letter had given a most complete description, and even a sketched map, so I knew just where to look (and the property was not all that large anyway). I was lucky, all things considered. Although the storm was dumping lots of snow, and although the low, grey clouds simulated the gloom of falling dusk, a cold wind from the Atlantic whipped the hilltop. It had prevented snow from accumulating on the "ruins" and whisked the descending deluge away from the summit in whirls and swirls.

I've often placed quotation marks around the word "ruins." This is to indicate that I wasn't then, and am not now, completely convinced that what I saw *were* ruins. Six years later I wrote a detailed account of our Nova Scotia investigations called *Holy Grail Across the Atlantic* and stated: "I couldn't swear in a court of law that there was a genuine ruin, but I thought so."[9] I will stick to that. This site has inspired mixed impressions in those who have seen it. Nova Scotia's Special Assistant to the Minister of Culture, Alison Bishop, saw the place several times in 1982–83 and has stated publicly: "I have never been satisfied that the [Royal Nova Scotia] Museum follows investigations as far as both common sense and the dictates of scholarship require. I believe this to be the case not only about the apparent ruins at The Cross, but also in several other and non-related matters that have come to my attention."[10]

Andrew Sinclair, a British writer who has made much of his supposed direct descent from Henry Sinclair, read my book in 1989 and came to Canada in 1990 to write a very similar book about the Sinclair voyage of A.D. 1398. He was not impressed with the New Ross "ruins" and derided my opinion. He found the remains of Henry Sinclair's lost settlement elsewhere in the province. I don't know how reliable or significant Andrew Sinclair's opinion can be considered.

Originally, Andrew Sinclair's book was conceived simply as a sort of biography of Henry Sinclair, including his voyage to the New World. The book was at first meant to be entitled "A Sword on a Stone," referring to the Massachusetts petroglyph that we will discuss later, and he ridiculed my idea of a Holy Grail connection with the voyage in the pages of Canada's *The Globe and Mail* newspaper. Andrew Sinclair has precisely the right sort of British accent and background to evoke a sycophantic, fawning, and purely colonial response in what passes for Canada's media. He was widely quoted, deriding my association of Henry Sinclair with the Holy Grail. Later, however, he was either truly convinced from my research that his ancestor had had genuine Grail connections, or he may simply have thought that reference to the Grail would sell more copies of his book, for he changed the title to *The Sword and the Grail*.[11] But naturally the Canadian media people didn't comment on this.

Thankfully, perhaps, Andrew had sent me a copy of his original book outline in 1990, and I still have it, because he wanted me to participate in a film of the same title to be produced by his kinsman, Niven Sinclair of London.

It required several phone conversations for me to convince Andrew that Henry Sinclair had, in fact, been famous because of his Templar and Grail connections. Indeed, the Sinclair coat of arms depicts a knight with an *engrailed* cross. The Grail had loomed large with his voyage.

Terence P. Punch, who was at that time (1980–90) president of the Royal Nova Scotia Historical Society, tended to think that the configurations at New Ross were the genuine ruins of a large "castle-like" structure that had once been erected on the hilltop. I suggested to the Ministry of Culture of Nova Scotia, and wrote in *Holy Grail Across the Atlantic*, that a search should be made for other ruins within a certain swath of Nova Scotia geography that extended from the Atlantic to the Bay of Fundy across the middle of the province. Although the Ministry of Culture itself did not undertake aerial photography of this region, as it promised to do in 1982, Terence Punch wrote to me much later (1991) saying that a team from the society had searched the area on foot. They discovered another mysterious ruin about twenty-five miles (40 kilometres) northeast of The Cross. I've heard nothing further about this, but the gradual construction of other fortified positions toward the northeast and the isthmus of Nova Scotia is precisely the subject of this book.

What I saw that afternoon in January 1982 on the hilltop looked like the outline of an irregular, five-sided perimeter wall. Numerous later visits during 1982–83 supplied a better idea of the entire complex. A fairly sharp corner happened to be on the McKay property, but the outline extended beyond their property onto neighbouring ones. Within this irregular shape, which I suppose would encompass about two acres, were the patterns of two smaller structures.

The largest of these occupied the center of the area and was composed of a jumble of large stone blocks and boulders; some of these were about eight feet long or tall, perhaps three or four feet wide and two to three feet in thickness (2.5 metre by 1 metre by .9 metre). During the course of time, I fell into Jeanne's habit of calling this jumble "the keep," which is a central citadel typical of Norman castles, but actually I've no idea what this ruin once was. A curious feature of this jumble of blocks and boulders was that it seemed to surround a marshy depression in the ground. During the summer of 1982, I was able to establish that this marshiness was caused by ground seepage from a mini-spring on this mini-mountain. A curious circumstance leads me to venture a guess that, at one time not many centuries ago, this spring had a substantially greater flow. I may as well deal with this now, rather than later, although it is all a bit tenuous — but suggestive.

In 1991, Claudette Leblanc of Barrie, Ontario, got in touch with me because she had read *Holy Grail Across the Atlantic*. Aside from coming from that long-established and seemingly ubiquitous Acadian-French Leblanc clan, Claudette is rather famous in Canada. She's a well-known soprano, winner of the coveted Juno Award, and has recorded several albums. She contacted me because, on a recent trip back home to the Acadian country of New Brunswick and Nova Scotia at the head of the Bay of Fundy, she had acquired an unexpected family heirloom.

While sorting out the possessions of a recently deceased relative, Claudette Leblanc came across a framed Currier & Ives print. She was not particularly interested in the print itself, but in the frame. She recognized it as the woodworking craftsmanship of yet another long-departed relative who had been renowned in the family for his skill. After removing the print, intending to keep the frame, she discovered another picture behind the Currier & Ives. This one was an original pencil sketch by someone with a great deal of native talent and, possibly, some formal training. A later dating of the paper by an expert associated with the University of Toronto revealed that the paper, at least, was made in the early seventeenth century.[12]

This sketch depicts a small and rather rustic-looking stonework "castle." The curious thing about it is that there seems to be a spring-fed pond within the walls, and the water flows out of the castle by a stream that passes through an aperture in the walls. When I saw this sketch in 1991, I was immediately struck by the

This sketch of a rustic castle was discovered in Acadian New Brunswick by Juno Award winning Canadian soprano Claudette Leblanc.

fact that this sketched castle seems just about the size of the apparent ruined construction at The Cross, and also by the fact that the pond might correlate to the marshy ground that is surrounded by the jumble of stones.

No one can say who drew this sketch, or what it is intended to represent. It may have been created in France. Or anywhere else, for that matter. How it originally came into the possession of a Leblanc who lived near Moncton, New Brunswick, is completely unknown. But, when Claudette saw it, she assumed (perhaps incorrectly) that it had been created by some past Leblanc ancestor, had been saved for that reason, and was a local Acadian artefact.

I can only say that whenever I look at the photo I took of it at Claudette's house, I am struck by how closely it conforms to my *previous* imaginary reconstruction of the ruins. For my mind had built an image of a modest, rustic castle with a pond in the middle (although I had not imagined any exit for this water!). Shivers down the spine are worth nothing as scientific evidence; but for what it's worth, this sketch produces them when I look at it.

What I can say with some authority is that there is not, and never has been, any known edifice in New Brunswick or Nova Scotia that looks remotely like this sketch — except, possibly, the ruins at The Cross. Therefore, if this sketch was created locally by an unknown Acadian artist sometime in the early 1600s, it is either a work inspired by imagination or memory — or an attempt to record the castle at New Ross as it very probably looked in the seventeenth century. I think that this sketch is worth investigating more professionally than my time and talent permit. I also think that if a castle actually existed at The Cross, there must be some mention of it in Acadian-French songs, literature, and folklore. Indeed, at one time Claudette Leblanc did some research into this, but nothing absolutely definitive emerged. Claudette would be the first to admit, however, that she's not really an expert on Acadian cultural history although she shares the Acadian heritage.

So much for the larger, central stone jumble and this digression.

As for the smaller apparent ruin of a building within the encircling five-sided perimeter wall, it happened to be just within the acute angle of the wall on the McKay property. It is impossible to say, now, what this may have been without proper excavation of this site. Whatever its purpose, the building was a small one, perhaps fifteen feet square (4.5 to 5 metres), and seemed to me to have had a chimney that had toppled over.

Something needs to be said about the appearance of this "perimeter wall." Not one piece of wall was actually standing when I first viewed it. It was like looking at a ground plan of a structure, a ground plan delineated by a path or a lane of fist-and-football-sized stones that meandered over the hilltop. The visual impression was as if someone with a backhoe had dug a deep trench, from two to six feet (.66 to 1.9 metres) wide, and then had filled the trench with stones. Even that first cold afternoon, I chose three random locations and removed stones until I was certain that they extended at least a few feet into the ground. No one had "made" this ruin by spreading a *thin* layer of rocks. What I've called the perimeter wall would account for several tons of rock. That January I also satisfied myself that this pattern ran beneath existing buildings and houses; later I was able to determine that some of the houses had been built more than a century previously.

Mixed with the rocks within the perimeter wall was a fair amount of sand, but elsewhere on the hilltop the soil was not particularly sandy. Mortar appeared to adhere to some of the stones in the wall and it was crumbly, bad-quality stuff. My opinion in January 1982, and today, is that there was an originally mortared structure at The Cross that predated known European construction in the area. I had only one clue to its age and origin. At crucial points, like corners, the wall had been thickened appreciably.

Someone had used a "rock cottage" technique typical of north Scotland and the Isles in order to make a modest stone palisade with other buildings inside. It reminded me of the photo of a "black house" in the Outer Hebrides that I once saw in *Sea and Islands* by Hammond Innes. He kindly allowed me to reproduce this photo in *Holy Grail Across the Atlantic*.[13]

During the early months of 1982, our investigation of "The Castle at The Cross" (as we came to call it) progressed to the point where we could, with a high degree of probability, identify the Europeans who had originally made it, identify the name and significance of their leader, and even assign a date to their transatlantic voyage and the castle's original construction. But, more important than anything else, we could glimpse some idea of the awesome importance of the voyage and the hilltop fortification. When we had progressed this far, we took our research straight to the Nova Scotia Ministry of Culture. Thereafter, during the remainder of 1982 and throughout 1983 (and sometime later), our investigations were no longer merely the personal part-time hobby of Deanna and me. Our research was partly paid by the ministry, we reported directly to the minister's "special assistant" and we agreed to a ministry request that we would write or publish nothing about the site for a period of time.[14]

It is unnecessary to recap all we found out about the castle at The Cross, because this has been covered in detail in a previous book. However, since the Nova Scotia site is the starting point of the Holy Grail story in North America, the beginning of our trail on the track of the Grail Knights of North America, readers should know at least three things that we discovered. These three facts, more than anything else, convinced the ministry that the hilltop site was worth investigating.

First, it gradually became very apparent that the hilltop site at The Cross had been chosen by someone who had explored Nova Scotia adequately enough to apply consummate strategic skill to the castle's location. The site had been chosen by a military man. New Ross is on the mid-peninsular spine of the province. From the hills around The Cross, once called the Rawdon Hills,[15] rivers flow south and east to the Atlantic and, over the modest watershed, they flow north and west into the Bay of Fundy. The castle also happens to be situated at the narrowest part of the Nova Scotia peninsula. It is only here that a smoke signal from either coast could be seen, only here that rivers gave access to two different coasts if attack or retreat became necessary.

At New Ross itself, the Gold River virtually begins beneath the
castle walls and flows seventeen miles to the Atlantic to enter
Mahone Bay near the town of Chester. The mouth of the Gold
River is just two miles from the greatest Nova Scotia mystery of all,
the famed Money Pit on Oak Island. But just northwest of New
Ross, on the other side of the Rawdon Hills, the Gaspereau River
begins its twenty-five-mile (40 kilometre) journey to the Bay of
Fundy, which it reaches at Horton's Landing. At the mouth of the
Gaspereau River is *another* "Oak Island" (although this Oak Island is
now the tip of a dyked-in peninsula constructed during the 1930s).

In short, there are Oak Islands at the mouths of the only two
major rivers originating near the ruins. And they are the only Oak
Islands in their respective bays. The reason why Oak Islands are
almost non-existent in coastal salt water is simple. As I discovered
by tank-testing, fresh ripe acorns don't float. Acorns are not a
favourite food of any bird native to Nova Scotia that might carry
ripe acorns from the mainland to an offshore island. Squirrels carry
acorns, but they avoid swimming. In northeastern North America,
therefore, Oak Islands are very rare in coastal waters. In Europe the
situation is a bit different, and also in North America south of
Virginia. In both places there is a species of swine that eats and
excretes ripe acorns and that can swim. There's the legendary "wild
boar" in Europe, and the collared peccary of the southeastern
United States.

Acorns will eventually float when they become dried and hollow
enough, but then they can't germinate if and when they reach
suitable soil.

All things considered, therefore, I felt that these two Oak Islands
had been created by man. The oaks had been purposefully planted.
Indeed, I combed the records of Samuel de Champlain and
discovered that in 1608 he had been both puzzled and appreciative
of the Fundy Oak Island whose groves "seemed to have been
planted as if for the pleasure of man." But why? My best guess was
that the oaks served as a unique and self-perpetuating navigational
aid. A mariner seeking the castle, whether he arrived in the New
World on the Atlantic side of Nova Scotia or on the Fundy side,
would only have to sail the coast until he saw an Oak Island. There
would be a river mouth right there. Follow the river and he'd end up
at the castle. But the presence of oaks on an island, particularly with
a mainland full of oaks close at hand, would not likely be noted by
anyone not already in on the secret.

Then there was the consideration of the *meaning* of "oak." In every Celtic tongue, "oak" means *door*.[16] That's because oak wood provides the strongest and best doors. And further, albeit in rather esoteric Celtic lore, the oak is considered a masculine tree and is associated with right-handedness (just as the willow, from which we derive wicker, and *wicca* = "witchcraft ", is considered in old-time male chauvinist Celtic lore to be a feminine, *sinister,* and left-handed tree).[17]

Taking all these poetical Celtic allusions into account, the oaks on the two islands are saying that the river is a door to what is sought. And then can it be mere coincidence that if you stand on either oak island you will see the appropriate river mouth to your right?

This oak business derives mainly from the ancient cultural and bardic lore of the Irish *ollaves* (roughly, *poets-magicians-bards-historians*) and the oak symbolism seems both more ancient and more vital in the Goidelic/Gaelic-speaking Celtic culture than in the slightly later Brythonic Celtic culture. For a while, therefore, I mightily feared that we were dealing with those ubiquitous Ancient Celts! Could they have built the castle at The Cross? Yes, and there's an argument that they may have built some structure on the hilltop many centuries before the ruins acquired the character that distinguishes them today. I've discussed this very possible, and much earlier, phase of "Ancient Celtic" occupation in the previous book. Further coverage in detail is out of place here, but it may be worth mentioning that Jeanne McKay believed in it and claimed to have found a Celtic petromantic "herm" and a pair of what she called "testicle stones" nearby — Celtic fertility tokens.

However..."Ancient Celts" specialized in dry-wall masonry — no mortar. I had found (to my satisfaction, at least) traces and remains of inferior gypsum mortar and found gypsum deposits within a mile of The Cross. These had been worked at some time in the past, but not within the living memory of anyone in New Ross or on record in the Nova Scotia Archives. The sand between the rocks was too coarse to provide a durable conglomerate. This case was a bit different from the same situation in Pennsylvania already recounted. There, it was simply too hard to haul fine river sand up from the West Branch of the Susquehanna. But at The Cross the Gold River was within easy distance of the castle; the problem was that at New Ross the Gold River is very new, a small stream. Coarse sand and grit had been washed out of the Rawdon Hills by the spring that gave birth to the river, but the stream wasn't yet lusty and robust enough to wear this stuff down into fine sand. Five miles downstream, yes. At New Ross, no.

The "Ancient Celtic Theory" sort of crumbled with the mortar, as far as I was concerned. But, and undeniably, there was Celtic symbolism in the oak navigational aids and signposts to the castle. This complex of allusion, symbolism, and tradition, so dear to the convoluted Celtic heart, might have been conceived by some lingering medieval "druid" (i.e., drwydd = "oak seer").[18] The inspiration was most likely to have come from either Ireland, the British Isles "homeland" of Goidelic/Gaelic — or from Scotland, to which Gaelic was taken by invading Irish in the first Christian centuries. All things considered, the mortar and the style of stonework suggested a medieval Scottish origin for the ruins.

The second thing that impressed the Ministry of Culture was that several of the earliest maps of Nova Scotia clearly refer to a "refuge" of some sort at the mouth of the Gold River, or at least in the vicinity of Mahone Bay and the famous (or infamous) Oak Island there. The only trouble was that the cartographic references preceded by more than a century any known settlement in Nova Scotia, preceded by almost a century the piratical heyday that supposedly created the Money Pit. Two such maps, both by Gastaldi, date from 1539–56 and show (marked by an arrow I've added) "port refuge" on the shore of a bay that contains many islands. This is a crude representation of Mahone Bay, which does have 350 islands in it. The supposedly definitive book on the subject of Nova Scotia place names states that Port Refuge was named in 1620 because a storm-tossed ship found it a haven in the tempest — but the book doesn't explain why the name appears on maps nearly a century earlier.

But the real shocker to everyone was the Caspar Vopel Map of 1545. This map shows the coast of Nova Scotia illustrated with a sketch of a Templar knight. In *Holy Grail Across the Atlantic*, I merely argued that this figure was intended to represent a Templar because of details of armour and the insignia on his shield. At the time, and I still cannot imagine why, I did not notice that this figure is actually labelled as a Knight Templar! Right beside the figure is a notation: "Ca d. Temp" — abbreviated Italian for Cavalier of the Temple — Knight Templar!

I have previously made it clear that I'm not entirely pleased with Andrew Sinclair's professional recognition of my research, but this

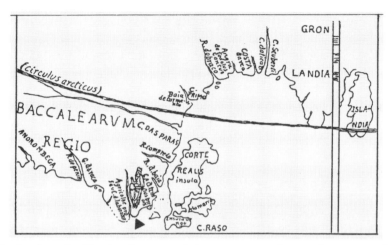

Tracing from the Bjornbo photocopy of the 1570 engraved copy of Caspar Vopel's map of 1545, after Ganong. Note the decorative illustration of the Templar knight on the coast of Nova Scotia. Also, just across the river from the knight is the legend: "Agricolae pro Seu. C. d. laborador."

Reproduced from *Crucial Maps in the Early Cartography and Place Nomenclature of the Atlantic Coast of Canada*, by W.F. Ganong, by permission of University of Toronto Press

is a place where I owe him generous acknowledgement. In 1990, Andrew called me in Toronto. He was phoning from the Nova Scotian Hotel in Halifax, with my own book on his knee, and I was suggesting directions for research. We got onto this Caspar Vopel Map eventually, and Andrew Sinclair wondered why I had not referred to this clear "Knight Templar" label instead of trying to make a case on arguable ground. I replied that I had not noticed any such label. Using my own illustration from Halifax, Andrew guided me to it as I studied another copy of my book in Toronto. I saw it. Talk about egg on the face!

My only excuse for not noticing this important identification by the cartographer himself is that I must have been more intrigued with another inscription that Vopel had made beside the knight: *Agricolae pro Seu C. d. laborador.* This means, more or less, "Farms for the Lord of the Cape of labourers." What farms, what Lord, and what labourers in the Nova Scotia of 1545? And what did Knights Templar have to do with all this?

The Vopel map, above all, had given me some ideas about the castle at The Cross. This was the third major point that impressed the ministry. There exists a record of a voyage to the New World, and the establishment of a settlement in the new land, that took place ninety-four years before the first voyage of Christopher Columbus in 1492, and ninety-nine years before "John Cabot's" alleged voyage in 1497 (more about this later). As of the 1960s, no reputable authority doubted the authenticity of the voyage of Henry Sinclair in 1398. The *Encyclopedia Americana* and *Encyclopaedia Britannica*, for example, both have entries accepting that the voyage took place.[19] Why, then, has this voyage and settlement by Henry Sinclair, Earl of Orkney and Baron of Rosslyn, not become common knowledge?

There are several answers to this question. On the simplest level, people find it difficult and uncomfortable to give up the familiar. Generations of people have been taught that Christopher Columbus and John Cabot first "discovered" America. And that's that. This human tendency, augmented by national pride in some cases, transmutes historical myth into dogma of acceptable truth. The large Italian community in the United States, for example, becomes vehement to the point of violence at any suggestion that Columbus wasn't the first "to cross the ocean blue, in fourteen hundred ninety-two."

But, aside from this natural human tendency to stick to what's familiar, and the tendency to stick up for national pride, there is *one* overwhelming reason why Henry Sinclair's voyage has been studiously ignored by popular media and the vast majority of popular books. Henry Sinclair will lead us into the forbidden and heretical substratum of western history. If attention is focused too closely on Henry Sinclair, then inevitably the story of the Holy Grail begins to unravel. And that would fray the entire fabric of western civilization for the past two thousand years. We have cloaked ourselves in its comfort and security. Most of our social values, most of our cultural beliefs, and even most of our Christian religious dogma, depend for their very existence on the protection of this familiar cloak.

I think there's a concerted effort, by many interested parties, to deflect any effort to bring Henry Sinclair into the realm of common, popular knowledge. Natural human tendencies to stick to the familiar, and to stick up for national pride, are manipulated as emotional allies in this campaign of truth deflection and disinformation.

I will cite just one recent example of this. Most people who will read this book know about the *Matthew* Project of 1997. This was a project to build a replica of the *Matthew*, the ship in which John

Cabot allegedly discovered Newfoundland, so beginning the era of British overseas colonization. The Royal Family supported the celebration. Prince Philip sailed in the *Matthew* for the first few miles down the Bristol Channel on the May 1 departure. Queen Elizabeth flew to Newfoundland for the scheduled June 24 arrival. The Canadian Navy sent warships to protect the tiny *Matthew* en route, and to ensure that it *did* arrive on schedule. Patriotic yachtsmen from English Canada sailed down Lake Ontario and down the St. Lawrence River, in a so-called Unity Flotilla — and naturally had to pass the length of Quebec's St. Lawrence coastline under the disjointed noses in separatist strongholds of Quebec City, Trois-Rivières, Rimouski, and so on.

This was myth-making on a grand scale, a distortion of history that, however, benefited various sociopolitical forces in Canada and Great Britain.

Let's begin with Canada. Since the federal government's biology experts had largely been responsible for destroying the east coast fishery, and with it a substantial portion of Newfoundland's economy, the *Matthew* Project celebration was considered a good way to attract tourist dollars into the stricken province. The federal government therefore spent several hundred thousand dollars to publicize the event and to construct displays and events.

Then someone in Ottawa decided that it would be an "anti-separatist" thrust to support the idea that Canada had first been discovered by someone sailing on behalf of England and who sailed long before the French thought to claim any part of Canada. The notion was that, somehow, the *Matthew* Project proved a Canadian continuity within the Commonwealth by legitimacy of historical discovery. Therefore, the government in Ottawa loudly supported the Unity Flotilla as a way of showing the flag along the entire length of Quebec. I'm not sure exactly what relevance an alleged five hundred-year-old voyage has to Quebec social reality in 1997, but some bright boy in Ottawa obviously thought so.

For "the Royals," the *Matthew* Project in 1997 was crucially important. The public can only absorb so many replica projects and "discoverers." There were some dedicated historians, writers, shipbuilders, and enthusiasts working towards a Henry Sinclair Replica Project scheduled for 1998, the six-hundredth anniversary of Henry Sinclair's discovery of "Estotiland" (Nova Scotia).[20] This project had been beset by financial problems and official obstruction from the start. It kept gamely on, though, and might well have

mounted a "semi-replica" voyage. The *Matthew* Project killed any
hope of this. As luck would have it, Cabot's five-hundredth
anniversary was one year earlier, 1997. This project, therefore, pre-
empted all the funding and interest that most of the public and
corporations could muster for old discoverers and old ships. Cabot's
timing nicely pre-empted Sinclair's. And, unlike the shoestring
Sinclair Project, the *Matthew* replication was lavishly funded by
corporations and individuals that are the "who's who" of British
industry and society, friends of the Establishment and the scandal-
beleaguered Royals.[21] Why?

Well, Henry Sinclair himself was related to the Stuarts. He sailed
under a Stuart king. Any attention spotlighted on this Stuart
discovery of "America" might just dig up the old history of how the
current Hanoverians, alias "Windsors," came to the throne to
replace Stuarts. Any deep look into this sordid history will reveal
that the Hanoverians and their history-rewriting supporters have
lied in maintaining, and publishing in every British school history
book, that Charles Edward Stuart died without a legitimate heir, the
inference being that any legitimate Stuart claim to the throne just
naturally petered out (in addition to the insurance of questionable
legalities). It has always been known by continental historians that
Bonnie Prince Charlie managed to have two legitimate heirs late in
his life. The complete genealogy has just been published in Britain
by Laurence Gardner.[22]

And, as the title of Gardner's book implies, the Stuarts represent a
lineage (as do many other families) that goes all the way back to
Jesus. In our time of almost continuous Royal scandals and churlish
behaviour — well, a resurgence of Stuart credibility might well have
unsuspected appeal. Any public spotlight on the Henry Sinclair
voyage, the Sinclair-Stuart connections, and the saga of the Holy
Grail would not have been in "the Royals'" interests, to put it mildly.

For me, as someone born in the United States, with dual U.S.
and Canadian citizenship, the Hanover vs. Stuart conflict has
always seemed remote, somewhat silly and certainly irrelevant. I
cannot vehemently take sides. But I suppose it is worth noting that
the fledgling United States very seriously offered Charles Edward
Stuart the "Crown of America" in 1776. But Bonnie Prince Charlie
had lost too many battles to the Hanoverians and England to have
much faith that the thirteen rebellious colonies could do any better.
He postponed any acceptance of this offer until he could see how
the American rebels were likely to fare.

By the time the rebels seemed actually to be winning, mostly because of the organizational input by European professional military officers like Baron Friedrich Wilhelm von Steuben (1730–94, infantry commander at Yorktown) and Marie Joseph Paul Yves Roch Gilbert du Motier, marquis de Lafayette (1757–1834, wounded at Brandywine and Valley Forge, cavalry commander at Yorktown), the patriots had decided to offer the "Crown of America" to George Washington instead. History might have been very different if Bonnie Prince Charlie had gambled on the American offer (and left military matters to the likes of von Steuben, Lafayette, and George Washington)...or if Washington had accepted the hypothetical Crown instead of being horrified at the thought of being a king.

But, no matter how my background predisposes me to view the Hanover vs. Stuart claims, it is obvious that these claims are vitally important to the players concerned. *They* take the confrontation seriously, and so do large corporations and prominent people in the current British Establishment. So, too, must the Canadian government for its own political machinations against Quebec separatism. It is easy to see why these interests dovetailed nicely with the *Matthew* Project and why, therefore, this replica project enjoyed so much financial support and Royal-government endorsement on both sides of the Atlantic. It is easy to understand why any focus on Henry Sinclair had to be buried under media hoopla and historical disinformation.

After discussing the voyage of Henry Sinclair, which first established Grail Knights in North America, we will take a brief look at "John Cabot" to compare his claims and credentials with Sinclair's. And further, at the same time, we will present the evidence that a descendant of Henry Sinclair was quite possibly responsible for the magnificent obsession of Christopher Columbus.

4

The Sea Knight

The Henry Sinclair that concerns us (Henry was a popular name in the family), was born in A.D.1345.[1] He was heir to the barony of Rosslyn in Scotland, which was held in fief to the "Stewards" of Scotland — just recently become *Stewarts* (or *Stuart*, as it is usually spelled in genealogies) and kings; but Henry was also a candidate and contender for the title and domain of the Orkney Islands. This island group is north of the Scottish mainland, separated from Scotland by the seven-mile-wide Pentland Firth. It was in Henry's time a possession of Norway, a remnant of former Viking conquests. Orkney (or "Orchadia," "Orchadie," or the "Orchade Isles" as the group was then called) was much richer than the Rosslyn barony because of its great fishing industry based on cod and herring. The Orkney domain also carried with it the title of Jarl ("Earl") and "Lord of the Isles," and so was substantially more prestigious in the feudal scheme of things than the barony of Rosslyn.

When Henry reached his age of majority, Norway was going into a period of decline that was to see it become, before Henry's death, a possession of Denmark. About 1360–70, therefore, the Norwegian king was anxious to appoint an Earl of Orkney who could re-establish control over the islanders, who had become rebellious and semi-independent. There were two major contenders, or claimants, for the title and the king tried both. The first candidate proved unequal to this task. Henry undertook to "subdue" the Orkney Islanders, which he did over a period of almost twenty years, using a policy of mixed firmness (not brutality, strange for the era) and diplomacy, which included assimilating himself in the life of the islanders. By 1390, Henry could call himself Earl of Orkney in fact as well as in title. As a Norman descendant, he'd reverted to being at least partly a genuine Norseman in this process. He learned and partly adopted Norse ways, and it is known that he could speak Norse; it is also known that he was present in Norway on two occasions for important state occasions and was one of the most important Jarls of the Norwegian kingdom.

The stage was set for Henry's remarkable Atlantic adventure. The Orkney domain had provided this sea lord with four crucially important things: first, the Orkney Islands themselves were a superb launching point for a North Atlantic venture, but one sufficiently remote so that much secrecy could be maintained; second, Henry had a modest fleet consisting of thirteen vessels — sturdy, small local ships bred and built for northern seas; third, he had a corps of hardy, competent North Atlantic seamen who were more than just part Viking themselves; fourth, he must have had substantial knowledge of land to the west because he was a Jarl of Norway, and during his lifetime the old Viking sagas were just being transmuted into written literature — they were all the rage at Scandinavian courts.

The contention of my previous book, and this one, is that Henry Sinclair was uniquely placed and purposefully chosen to undertake a desperately needed mission on behalf of the Holy Grail and its beleaguered, battered paladins.

But Henry still lacked two things before he could make Orkney a secure base for the establishment of a transatlantic haven for the Holy Grail. He needed the new-fangled cannons, which, in the semi-barbaric north, would give him a qualitative defensive edge over any regional potential assault on Orkney. He needed not only his tough, practical seamen, he needed the latest navigational and mapmaking skills of the age if the necessary frequent voyages were to be maintained. But both shipboard cannons and navigational expertise were being refined in Italy, and above all in Venice. How could a sea lord in the semi-barbaric north ever gain access to the needed Mediterranean innovations?

By one of the most amazing and improbable "coincidences" in western history — *if it was a coincidence* — Henry Sinclair acquired the expertise he needed from the two people in the entire western world best able to supply it. As soon as the Orkney Islands were at least semi-secure, in 1391, a Venetian ship was wrecked on Fair Island. Fair Island was then part of the Earldom of Orkney and thus belonged to Sinclair, but it is well north of the Orkney group — an eighty-mile voyage north. And, again by "coincidence," Sinclair happened to be on the island just when the Venetian ship came to grief. He was therefore able to stop the time-honoured practice of the islanders which was to massacre the crew and salvage the ship's cargo. Henry Sinclair was able to save the life of a noble Venetian on board, Nicolo Zeno, a navigator and map maker.[2]

The naive story goes that Nicolo was so impressed by Sinclair's knightly bearing and sense of justice that he decided to join Sinclair's service in a life-long bond. Further, Nicolo wrote home to his brother (or son?), Antonio Zeno, and instructed him to come north to serve Henry Sinclair, too. I think this was a carefully planned rendezvous.

Consider how extraordinary all this really was. Cannons had been used first in Europe in 1346 at the Battle of Crécy, fought between the English and French a year after Henry was born. But these early cannon were cumbersome to use, very heavy and hard to move and they could not be said to be user-friendly — whether they were more dangerous to the enemy or to the cannoneers was very much a moot point. Nevertheless, the invention caught on. It was, of course, rapidly refined everywhere, but nowhere better than in Venice where fledgling "scientific" and Renaissance "expertise" (such as it was) was applied to the problem. Eventually, the engineers of Carlo Zeno, "The Lion" of Venice, were able to adapt cannon for shipboard use: they were lighter in weight; a way was found to absorb their recoil (ropes and pulleys and dragged sandbags); their accuracy and range were much improved because the formula for gunpowder was standardized, and calibers and projectile weights were also standardized, so that mathematics could be applied to trajectory to produce more or less accurate range tables for gunners; they were not nearly so likely to blow up. These refined Venetian cannon were called *pietros* ("pious ones," presumably a reference to the gunners, but also "peter" from ancient and obvious male symbolism). With them, Carlo Zeno won the Battle of Chioggia against the Genoese in 1385.[3]

Nicolo Zeno was Carlo's brother. He knew how to "implement state-of-the-art chemically impelled projectile delivery systems" (as we might say nowadays). Although he was also a talented navigator and cartographer, he was not in the same league with Antonio. Both ended up in the service of Sinclair...*and just when they were crucially needed*. Venetian *pietros* gave Sinclair the technological edge to make Orkney secure against any threat by northern neighbours; Antonio Zeno supplied the navigation and map-making skills to ensure frequent transatlantic voyages. Isn't it strange, however, that these two Venetian experts not only turn up in Orkney just when they were needed, but that these two scions of one of Venice's most noble families would stay in the far north with Sinclair until death broke the bonds? Nicolo died in Sinclair's service, probably in 1394, on a voyage to Greenland[4] — and this is thought-provoking in itself, of course; Antonio didn't return to Venice until after Sinclair was killed in a Scottish skirmish in August 1400.

The *pietros* are important to our argument. In my first Grail book, I speculated that Sinclair would probably have brought a few of these cannon to North America with him. They would have helped secure any vitally important Grail haven. If they were not lost or subsequently melted down, their discovery might indicate the location of the transatlantic settlement. I have never found time to track *pietros*, but Andrew Sinclair claims to have located two anachronistic cannons in the armament of the French fortress of Louisbourg on Cape Breton Island, Nova Scotia. In 1995 I was told by an amateur researcher that a British officer's report from the 1750s refers to two bronze cannons of small calibre and ancient make that had been discovered in Guysborough County, Nova Scotia.[5] Again, I have never found the time to verify this. According to the story, the British captured them, but there's no further information in the report. Perhaps they could be traced. Very possibly, because of their "ancient make," they were shipped back to Britain as curiosities, but it seems clear that these two cannot be the same ones that Andrew Sinclair pinned down in Louisbourg. Guysborough County is on the mainland of Nova Scotia south of Cape Breton. But it is interesting that we have four possible *pietros* relating to Nova Scotia.

The document attesting to Henry Sinclair's voyage is called *The Zeno Narrative*. It consists of letters that Nicolo and Antonio wrote home to brother Carlo in Venice while they were in the the north. These letters were kept as Zeno family mementos but a later Nicolo, when a young boy, found them and, as children will, wantonly tore them up. Later, when he grew to manhood, this sixteenth-century Nicolo remembered and regretted this action. He returned to the remote corner of the storeroom in the rambling Zeno residence and discovered the scraps of the letters. As a sort of penance, he pieced them together as well as he could and published the collection in 1558.

This is not the place to cover all the conflict and controversy surrounding *The Zeno Narrative*. This has already been done by the American historian and author Frederick Pohl in his book, *Prince Henry Sinclair* . Although originally dismissed as a "boastful Venetian claim of the discovery of America before Columbus," most authorities now accept that the narrative is genuine. For example, the *Encyclopedia Americana* has, since 1951, accepted that *The Zeno Narrative* is an authentic account of an authentic voyage.[6] Except for scholarly pedantries, it is difficult to see how the account could ever have been doubted. It describes accurately some aspects of Nova Scotia geography that were not known in Europe in 1558. And, aside from the recent references to Venetian *pietros*, there is now proof positive, literally carved in stone, that the Sinclairs of Rosslyn knew of America before Christopher Columbus or "John Cabot."

The Zeno Narrative makes no mention of the Holy Grail, Norse sagas, or ancient tradition when explaining why Sinclair decided to cross the Atlantic. Instead, according to the *Narrative*, an old Orkney fisherman told Sinclair of his experience of being blown by a storm westward across the ocean where he and his companions were marooned *for thirteen years* in some new and vast land. Passing from tribe to tribe of the inhabitants, the European castaways apparently travelled as far south as Mexico, because the old fisherman described Mexican cities accurately. Finally, becoming homesick, and his companions dying one by one, the fisherman made his way back to the northeast coast. There, he married a native woman, but he and his remaining companions secretly built a small boat over the course of several years. When it was finished, they sailed away and managed to return to Orkney.

It is interesting that this Orkney fisherman did not mistake the new land for a part of "Cathay." He told Sinclair that it was a "new world" (*nuovo mundo*) in exactly those words. This is a realization usually, and in error, attributed to Amerigo Vespucci.

Herewith, relevant extracts from *The Zeno Narrative*. The narrator is Antonio Zeno.

> This nobleman, Sinclair, is therefore resolved to
> send forth with a fleet toward those parts, and there
> are so many who desire to join in the expedition on

account of the novelty and strangeness of the thing, that I think we shall be very strongly appointed without any public expense at all....

I set sail with a considerable number of vessels and men, but had not the chief command, as I expected to have, because Sinclair went in his own person.

Our great preparations for the voyage to Estotiland were begun in an unlucky hour; for exactly three days before our departure, the fisherman died who was to have been our guide. Nevertheless, Sinclair would not give up the enterprise, but in lieu of the deceased fisherman, took some of the sailors who had come out with him from the island.

Steering westwards, we sighted on some islands subject to Frislanda, and passing certain shoals, came to Ledovo, where we stayed seven days to refresh ourselves and take on necessaries. Departing thence, we arrived on the first of April at the island of Ilofe; and as the wind was full in our favour, pushed on. But not long thereafter, when on the open ocean, there arose so great a storm that for eight days we were continuously in toil, and driven we knew not where, and a considerable number of vessels were lost to each other. At length, when the storm had abated, we gathered together the scattered vessels, and sailing with a prosperous wind, sighted land on the west.

Steering straight for it, we reached a quiet and safe harbour, in which we saw a very large number of armed people, who came running, prepared to defend the island. Sinclair now caused his men to make signs of peace to them, and they sent ten men to us who could speak ten languages, but we could understand none of them, except one who was from Iceland.

Being brought before our Prince, and asked what was the name of the island, and what people inhabited it, and who was the governor, he answered that the island was called Icaria, and that all the kings were called Icari, after the first king, who was the son of Daedalus, King of Scotland.

Daedalus conquered that island, left his son there for king, and gave them those laws that they retain to the present time. After that, when going to sail further, he was drowned in a great tempest; and in memory of his death that sea is called to this day the Icarian Sea, and the kings of the island were called Icari. They were content with the state God had given them, and would neither alter their laws nor admit any stranger.

They therefore requested our Prince not to attempt to interfere with their laws, which they had received from that king of worthy memory, and observed up to the present time; that the attempt would lead to his own destruction, for they were all prepared to die than relax in any way the use of those laws. Nevertheless, that we might not think that they altogether refused intercourse with other men, they ended by saying that they would willingly receive one of our people, and give him an honourable position among them, if only for the sake of learning our language and gaining information as to our customs, in the same way as they had already received those ten other persons from ten different countries, who had come into their island.

To all this our Prince made no reply, beyond enquiring where there was a good harbour, and making signs that he intended to depart.

Accordingly, sailing round about the island, he put in with all his fleet at full sail, into a harbour which he found on the eastern side. The sailors went ashore to take in wood and water, which they did as quickly as they could, for fear that they might be attacked by the islanders and not without reason, for the inhabitants made signals to their neighbours by fire and smoke, and taking their arms, the others coming to their aid, they all came running down to the seaside upon our men with bows and arrows, so that many were slain and several wounded.

Although we made signs of peace to them, it was of no use, for their rage increased more and more, as though they were fighting for their own very existence.

Being thus compelled to depart, we sailed along in a great circuit about the island, being always followed on the hill tops and along the seacoasts by a great number of armed men. At length, doubling the north cape of the island, we came upon many shoals, amongst which we were for 10 days in continual danger of losing our whole fleet, but fortunately all that time the weather was very fine. All the way till we came to the east cape we saw the inhabitants still on the hill tops and by the sea coast, howling and shooting at us from a distance to show their animosity toward us.

We therefore resolved to put into some safe harbour, and see if we might once again speak with the Icelander; but we failed in our object; for the people more like beasts than men, stood constantly prepared to beat us back if we should attempt to come on land. Wherefore, Sinclair, seeing that he could do nothing, and that if we were to persevere in this attempt, the fleet would fall short of provisions, took his departure with a fair wind and sailed six days to the westwards; but the wind thereafter shifting to the southwest, and the sea becoming rough, we sailed 4 days with the wind aft [i.e., northeast], and finally sighted land.

As the sea ran high and we did not know what country it was, we were afraid at first to approach it, but by God's blessing the wind lulled, and then there came on a great calm. Some of the crew pulled ashore [i.e., rowed ashore] and returned with great joy with news that they found an excellent country and a still better harbour. We brought our barks and our boats to land, and on entering an excellent harbour, we saw in the distance a great hill which poured forth smoke, which gave us hope that we should find some inhabitants in the island. Neither would Sinclair rest, though it was a great way off, without sending 100 soldiers to explore the country, and bring us an account of what sort of people the inhabitants were.

Meanwhile, we took in a store of wood and water, and caught a considerable quantity of fish and sea fowl. We also found such an abundance of birds' eggs that our men, who were half famished, ate of them to repletion.

While we were at anchor there, the month of June came in, and the air in the island was mild and pleasant beyond description; but as we saw nobody, we began to suspect that this pleasant place was uninhabited. To the harbour we gave the name of Trin, and the headland which stretched out into the sea was called Cape Trin.

After eight days the 100 soldiers returned, and brought word that they had been through the island and up to the hill, and that the smoke was a natural thing proceeding from a great fire in the bottom of the hill, and that there was a spring from which issued a certain substance like pitch, which ran into the sea, and that thereabouts there dwelt a great many people half wild, and living in caves. They were of small stature and very timid. They reported also there was a large river, and a very good and safe harbour.

When Sinclair heard this, and noticed the wholesome and pure atmosphere, fertile soil, good rivers, and so many other conveniences, he conceived the idea of founding a settlement. But his people, fatigued, began to murmur, and say they wished to return to their homes for the winter was not far off, and if they allowed it once to set in, they would not be able to get away before the following summer. He therefore retained only boats propelled by oars, and such of his people who were willing to stay, and sent the rest away in ships, appointing me, against my will, to be their captain.

Having no choice, therefore, I departed, and sailed 20 days to the eastward without any sight of land; then turning my course toward the southeast, in 5 days I sighted on land, and found myself on the island of Neome and knowing the country, I perceived I was past Iceland; and as the inhabitants were subject to Sinclair, I took in fresh stores and sailed in 3 days to Frislanda, where the people, who thought they had lost their Prince, in consequence of his long absence on the voyage we had made, received us with a hearty welcome.

...Concerning those things that you [i.e., brother Carlo "The Lion"] desire to know of me, as to the people and their habits, the animals, and the countries adjoining, I have written about it all in a separate book, which please God, I shall bring with me. In it I have described the country, the monstrous fishes [i.e. the basking shark, common in Orkney waters; whales would have been well known to any Mediterranean sailor — Author], the customs and laws of Frisland, of Iceland, of Shetland, the Kingdom of Norway, Estotiland and Drogeo; and lastly, I have written...the life and exploits of Sinclair, a Prince as worthy of immortal memory as any that ever lived, for his great bravery and remarkable goodness.[7]

We know that Henry Sinclair did return to Scotland because it is written in European records:

Henry Sainclaire was advertised of ane army of Southerns that came to invade the Orchade Isles, who resisting them with his forces, through his too great negligence and contempt for their forces, left breathless, by blows battered so fast upon him, that no man was able to resist... was sclane thair crowellie be his innimis.[8]

Most historians are agreed that Henry Sinclair "was slain cruelly by his enemies" in A.D. 1400, a victim of an attempted English invasion of Scotland, but some believe that Sinclair died in 1404. Obviously, the voyage to Estotiland was made earlier. Equally obvious, from Antonio's account, is that Sinclair and his people who had elected to remain over the winter with him also must have built a small ship capable of returning home since they "retained only boats propelled by oars" in the new land. We don't know how many returned, or how many remained in the settlement that Sinclair stayed behind to establish.

There are many points of interest in *The Zeno Narrative*, and I will touch on some of them in notes. Antonio Zeno's "Map of the North," included in the *Narrative*, does, however, deserve later and detailed discussion.

But a few things must be covered here. First, there can be no doubt that "Estotiland" was Nova Scotia. As early as 1951, Dr. William Herbert Hobbs, a geologist at the University of Michigan, pointed out that the *Narrative* contains an excellent description of an open pitch deposit that was burning at the time of Sinclair's arrival. Most likely, the pitch had been ignited by a lightning strike. This is a common occurrence since pitch gives off combustible gases. But the important thing is that, as Hobbs explained, there are only three open pitch deposits in all of the Americas: one is off the north coast of South America on the island of Trinidad; another is the famous La Brea tar pits of Hollywood, California; the third are the flowing pitch springs of Stellarton, Nova Scotia, which are associated with Stellarton's famous coal deposits.[9]

It is clear that only Nova Scotia can be a serious contender in this case.

American historian Frederick Pohl, working backward from this clue, decided that the "great hill" that appeared to be pouring forth smoke in the *Narrative* could only be Mount Adams because it is the only mini-mountain anywhere around Stellarton. With two points plotted, an extended line between them intersected with Guysborough Harbour, which is an excellent harbour. This satisfies the *Narrative* description that they found "an excellent country and a still better harbour." The conspicuous headland that extended out into the Atlantic from the harbour they named Trin, which they called Cape Trin, could only be Cape Canso — the most prominent cape in Nova Scotia. With Hobbs's clue, *The Zeno Narrative* fitted Nova Scotia geography like a glove.

It is obvious that Henry Sinclair would have recounted his later experiences in Estotiland to Antonio Zeno when he returned to Scotland, but before his death. Indeed, we have proof that this happened; Antonio drew a map that shows a country called "Drogeo" (Massachusetts), but Drogeo is not mentioned in the initial voyage to find Estotiland. It was found only after Antonio had already sailed back to Orkney "against his will" as captain of the returnees. Drogeo, or Massachusetts, will be of interest to Americans, but before we can go there, it will be helpful to have a date for this voyage.

The *Narrative* associates "the month of June coming in" with the decision to name the harbour "Trin" and the headland "Cape Trin," so, making a connection, Frederick Pohl consulted Vatican and other almanacs for past dates of Trinity Sunday. He found that the only date that worked was June 2, 1398. And that is the date generally accepted by scholars. If this date is correct — and it dovetails with other events in Sinclair's life — then he certainly spent the winter of 1398–99 in Estotiland. But, at a stretch, since it is thought that he most probably died in August 1400, Sinclair *could* have spent *two* winters across the Atlantic. Antonio's "Map of the North" shows two "towns" in Estotiland, represented in the usual medieval convention by little castles with a flag on top. I take these to be, from their relative locations, the castle at The Cross, which was the settlement that Sinclair himself founded; and the Micmac town of Pictou, near Stellarton, which had "a hundred wigwams" (in addition to some people living in convenient caves nearby).

Antonio's map also shows Drogeo south of Estotiland with a water passage between, and this "Drogeo" is mostly likely the Massachusetts–Rhode Island region, but there are no "towns" indicated in Drogeo.

However, even if no settlements are indicated in Drogeo, there's an existing memento of Sinclair's voyage there. This is the so-called Westford Effigy. For years many residents in and around Westford, Massachusetts, had been aware of the badly weathered "petroglyph" near their town up on Westford Ledge. Everyone just assumed that it must have been scratched by Indians. But in 1940, author and historian William B. Goodwin looked at it very carefully and was shocked to realize that the faded figure was a representation of a knight in armour. Later, Frank Glynn, president of the Connecticut Archeological Society, found out that the armour was of a typical Scottish design dating from the last half of the fourteenth century. Still later, Frederick Pohl and Dr. Donnell B. Young, a local historian, did a painstaking replication of the entire figure and were able to make out the symbols on the shield that the knight is carrying. However, they knew nothing of heraldry and didn't know what the combination of images meant.[10]

It took British experts to discover that the Massachusetts shield carried the coat of arms of the Gunn clan (Sunderland), or the Gunne clan (Caithness), of Scotland. Also, British experts realized that the depiction of the broken sword meant that the effigy had marked the death of a knight. Ian Moncrieffe, author of *The Highland Clans*, states:

> Startling enough, the earliest surviving example of the Gunn chief's coat-of-arms appears to have been punch-marked by a medieval armourer-smith on a rock in Massachusetts. The heater shaped shield there, borne by what appears to be the effigy of a fourteenth century knight, appears to show a distinctively Norse-Scottish character.[11]

Surely, it cannot be *mere* "coincidence" that the arms and armour of this knight effigy not only date from Henry Sinclair's era, but also bear the symbols of a clan which would have been allied to Henry Sinclair. Therefore, we may presume with a fair degree of confidence that Henry Sinclair visited Massachusetts. This must have been after the ship had been made for the trip home, because the open sea distance between Estotiland and Drogeo is too great for "boats propelled with oars" that were just ships' boats of the fleet. Unless further information comes to hand, we cannot say whether Sinclair stayed one or two winters in North America, the first (1398–99) in Estotiland, and the second (1399–1400) in Drogeo. This could have been the case, allowing Sinclair time to return to Scotland in the spring of 1400 to meet his death in August.

Our knowledge of what Sinclair did in Estotiland would seem to end with *The Zeno Narrative* except for the tireless and brilliant historical detective work of Frederick Pohl. It was Pohl who realized that there might be a valuable *Amerindian* account of Sinclair in Estotiland. Although it is quite possibly beyond any absolute proof, Pohl makes a strong and suggestive case for linking Henry Sinclair with the mysterious Micmac culture hero called Glooscap. Glooscap made a great impression on the Indians of Nova Scotia even though he stayed among them for only one winter.

Glooscap explored much of Nova Scotia, crossing the peninsula twice, but he settled for the winter at "Owokun" somewhere on Minas Basin in the Bay of Fundy . In the spring, according to Micmac songs, Glooscap unveiled his marvellous "stone canoe," which was so stable and large that men could walk on it, and it had trees growing on it. Pohl takes this to mean that Glooscap/Sinclair had built a European decked ship near Owokun. And, just before Glooscap left the Micmacs in his stone canoe, he gave a parting feast and then sailed away over the "shining waves of Minas." In memory of his departure, the Micmacs preserved a special song. Pohl discovered that it was a snatch of an old Norse anchor-weighing chantey. Altogether, Frederick Pohl was able to compile a list of seventeen specific similarities between the legendary Glooscap and Henry Sinclair (including the interesting fact that both had three daughters, no sons). All this is covered in Pohl's *Prince Henry Sinclair*.

I may have made a minor contribution to this Glooscap-Sinclair identification. There's a Micmac suffix that was applied to lakes, rivers, and so on, but only where Glooscap was said to have travelled. For instance, there's the Shuben*acadie* River, which flows into Minas Basin. Linguists have not come up with any satisfactory notion of what this suffix means, although some historians believe that it inspired later European names for the Minas Basin region of Nova Scotia: *Arcadia, Acadia.*. Henry Sinclair's major holding was the Earldom of Orkney, and Orkney was called *Orchadia, Orchade Isles*, or Orchadie in medieval times. It was common medieval practice for a nobleman to be referred to by the name of his holding — as any reader of Shakespeare will know. So some of his men would have called Sinclair by the name of *Orchadie* from time to time. If the Micmacs heard this, they might have thought it was one of Glooscap's special names, and so they applied the word to places where Glooscap/ Sinclair was said to have visited.[12]

But we know that Arcadia had another significance, too. There's synchronicity galore in the Holy Grail story.

Before recounting some uncanny synchronicity that affected our study of Sinclair in Nova Scotia, this might be the place to compare "John Cabot's" claims with those of Henry Sinclair. First of all, British propaganda has shamefully anglicized this explorer's name. He was, of course, the Italian Giovanni Caboto of Venice. Second, although the whole idea of "history" is the study of *written* documents, historians have waived that principle in the case of John Cabot. There is no existing log of the so-called first voyage of 1497, and no log of the supposed second voyage, either. The only *written* records pertaining to this voyage are some letters that other people wrote based on what they claimed John Cabot said to them.

These contain descriptions of what Caboto said the new land

was like — and they are not only suspiciously "generic" descriptions of the hazy "spice islands," but are completely inaccurate when applied to any part of northeast North America. The descriptions are simply ridiculous if applied to Newfoundland. Caboto said that the climate was so mild that "brazil" (a tropical dye-wood) and *silk worms* (!) would thrive there. And, although "John Cabot" claimed to have met a "king" across the ocean, and to have exchanged presents with him, he did not bring a single North American artefact back to Europe.[13]

In short, there's no written or hard evidence that John Cabot's voyage ever happened. He supposedly set sail on May 1, reached North America on June 24, and was back in Bristol by August 3, 1497. This is just barely possible in ships of his time. It is not very probable. Then, if John Cabot had sailed directly westward from Land's End at latitude 50 degrees north, he would not have made landfall in Newfoundland or Cape Breton — or any part of Canada. He was using the same sort of primitive magnetic compasses as Christopher Columbus. They were subject to a magnetic phenomenon called westward variation, which was unsuspected by all early mariners. Simply put, the earth's magnetic field is skewed. It makes compasses point west of north as North America is approached. Therefore, a mariner who set a due west course would end up sailing substantially southwest instead. This means he'd end up many miles south of his estimated landfall. This is called "dropping latitude," or "falling south" — and it happened to *all* early trans-atlantic mariners.

Christopher Columbus "fell to the south" some 240 miles on his first voyage of 1492; he "dropped his latitude" by 293 miles on his third voyage. It happens that the phenomenon of westward variation becomes more pronounced the further north you are. Columbus was sailing across the Atlantic much closer to the equator, on much more tropical courses, than John Cabot. Indeed, John Cabot, sailing from Land's End at 50 degrees north latitude, should have "dropped his latitude" much more than Columbus. Cabot should have ended up somewhere between New England and Delaware. And this, by the way, is just where a contemporary navigational expert, Gomera, estimates that Cabot made land.[14]

In contrast to John Cabot's supposed voyage, a written document attests to Henry Sinclair's discovery. Its descriptions are totally accurate. *The Zeno Narrative* even included a map, and it is as accurate as can be expected for the age. The Sinclair expedition brought back an artefact that can only have come from America, and it pre-dates both Columbus and Cabot. This artefact was at least one ear of "American corn" (i.e., *Zea Maize*, agreed to have been unknown in Europe "before Columbus"). This ear of corn was used to design a decoration on a stone column of Rosslyn Chapel. The stone-carved ears of "corn"/maize on this column are so accurately rendered that botanists can distinguish the sub-species depicted. It is a variety native to northeastern North America. Since this chapel was begun in 1441 and completed in 1485, it is absolute proof that the Sinclairs of Rosslyn knew about America before the voyages of Columbus or Caboto. Indeed, including the Westford Effigy, it seems that the Sinclair voyage left artefacts on both sides of the Atlantic.

And it may be worth noting that Sinclair's voyage conforms absolutely to westward variation. Taking his departure from the Orkney Group in the far north of Scotland, he should have "dropped his latitude" by about five hundred miles by the time he reached America. This would land him dead-centre on the island of Newfoundland, or "Icaria" as the *Narrative* calls it. Even the tale of the multi-lingual inhabitants of Icaria lends support to this voyage. In *From Cabot to Cartier*, Bernard G. Hoffman several times states that the Beothuk Indians of Newfoundland had been visited by all manner of European seamen, captured some, and used them as interpreters in barter.[15]

Cabot may not have even crossed the Atlantic at all. But, if he did, he certainly didn't discover the lands that the British later claimed because of him.

So much for the respective claims of Henry Sinclair and John Cabot. We mentioned that Sinclair's voyage may have contributed to the conceptions of Christopher Columbus. It is obvious that Sinclair's life and transatlantic adventure were not isolated events that had no repercussions at all. His exploit was known to everyone in Orkney and Rosslyn at one time; the maize-carved stone column in Rosslyn Chapel was a memento of the 1398 achievement whose existence was only rediscovered within the maze of chapel stonework in 1991. But Henry Sinclair had very powerful friends (the Stuart kings of Scotland), and he had a family. We will recall that he, like the legendary Glooscap of Micmac memory, had three daughters. By the time of the voyage, these daughters were all married to men of suitable rank.

Suspecting that Sinclair descendants might well have

transmitted knowledge of America, the Prince Henry Sinclair Society of North America undertook some genealogical sleuthing between 1992 and 1996. Its members discovered that a great-great-grandson of Henry Sinclair, one John Drummond, resided on the Madeira Islands at the same time that one Christopher Columbus lived there![16] No doubt, this is a meaningless coincidence. Drummond was a sea captain, a writer, and a geographer of minor repute. Columbus moved to the Madeiras in 1479 or 1480 with his new wife, Filipa de Perestrello, whom he'd married in 1479. It was a honeymoon of sorts. Since John Drummond lived there at that time, the two men must have met. There was only one major settlement on the islands then. According to Fernando, the second son of Columbus and first biographer of his famous father, it was on Madeira that Columbus first conceived his obsession: the possibility of reaching the Far East by sailing west. And it was on Madeira that Columbus:

> began to reflect that, as the Portuguese travel so far to the southward, it was no less proper to sail away westward, and land might in reason be found that way. That he might be more certain and confident in this particular, he began to look over all the cosmographers again whom he had read before, and to observe what astronomical reasons would corroborate this project; and he therefore took notice of what any persons whatsoever spoke to that purpose, and of sailors particularly, which might in any way be of help to him. Of all these things he made such good use that he concluded for certain that there were many lands west of the Canary Islands and Cape Verde, and it was possible to sail and discover them.[17]

There is no known proof, at the present time, that John Drummond and Christopher Columbus ever met on the Madeira Islands. Perhaps it is mere *synchronicity* that a Sinclair descendant, who might well have known of land to the west, was on Madeira when Columbus conceived of land to the west....

Synchronicity asserted itself again in March 1982 on our behalf with CanTraid and the Nova Scotia Department of Development. Due to a completely unexpected marketing success with our neo-curragh tropical fishing boat, a success that was to involve several levels of government (for better, and worse), and a success that was to take us to an idyllic Caribbean island on a boat testing project, we suddenly needed expanded design and manufacturing facilities. The province's officials in charge of economic development were willing to help us with low rent and other incentives in an industrial incubator mall for fledgling businesses if we would agree to relocate somewhere other than the capital, Halifax. "The Department" wanted us in Kentville. It became "difficult" to avoid regional government interest in CanTraid because Nova Scotia newspapers had published stories about our boat design and its support by the Canadian International Development Agency. Nova Scotia felt that the province's jobless should have a share of our federal dollars.

Although I had lived in Nova Scotia on several separate occasions, I had always lived in Halifax because my purpose there always had something to do with Dalhousie University. I did explore further afield, but always up and down the "eastern shore" with its famed shipbuilding centres such as Lunenburg and Jeddore and Ship Harbour. I'd *heard* of Kentville, but had never been there. I was not at all sure where it was.

We were primarily busy trying to get CanTraid off the ground, but we were far enough along in our castle-related research to have a suspicion that the ruins at New Ross were Henry Sinclair's settlement in Estotiland. Jeanne McKay was, of course, thrilled with this news. She barraged us with letters urging us to join her decade-long crusade for official recognition and excavation of the site, but I wanted to separate fact from speculation most carefully — and we had battles enough of our own with CanTraid, family courts and counsellors, and seemingly endless spools of red tape unrolled by three levels of government. Bureaucrats didn't share our originally simple goal of helping Third World fishermen, but found other value in CanTraid. In spite of increasing corporate complications, we were far enough along in our research to suspect that Sinclair might well have been Glooscap. I wanted to verify this, if possible, by finding the archaeological evidence that Frederick Pohl had sought in vain. To do this, I had to spend some time around Minas Basin, which seemed to be the core region of Glooscap legends.

Imagine our surprise, then, when we made the more or less "obligatory" visit to Kentville at the "invitation" of the Department of Development for the purpose of looking over the area's industrial incubator mall. We found ourselves on the shore of Minas Basin. In plain sight over the "shining waves of Minas" we could see the peninsula that terminated at Owokun. Checking our road map, we saw that we were only sixty-five miles (100 kilometres) from Halifax, a distance reasonable enough that I could keep visiting Jason regularly. Kentville was just twenty-five miles (40 kilometres) from the castle at The Cross, and one of Nova Scotia's tourist highways, the Glooscap Trail, actually began in Kentville.

Deanna and I grinned at each other because we were getting used to uncanny coincidences. Fate, and the Department of Development, had sent us to the only place where we could do everything we had to accomplish in Nova Scotia. We had had increasingly little to do with the chain of events that was destined to allow us to follow in Glooscap/Sinclair's footsteps. We need not retrace the detective trail in this book, because it was the subject of a previous one.

But, I think, two discoveries need to be mentioned because they have not been recounted before and because, in small ways, they led me to suspect an extensive population with varied activities in the Nova Scotia settlement.

"Owokun," Glooscap's winter camp according to Micmac legends, means "where the deep sea dashes." By following clues in many collections of traditional songs and stories, Frederick Pohl was led to the virtual certainty that Owokun had been located on Cape d'Or. This cape is one of the most spectacular headlands in the Bay of Fundy, and its high elevation affords a strategic view of the Bay of Fundy southwestward. Further, Advocate Harbour, a completely protected little inlet perfect for ship construction, lies under the cape. A winter camp on top of Cape d'Or would have allowed Sinclair/Glooscap to have ample warning of any seaborne intrusion up the long Bay of Fundy. During 1959–62, with funding from the Kermit Fischer Foundation, Frederick Pohl looked for archaeological evidence of previously unknown and unrecorded European construction on top of Cape d'Or in co-operation with archaeologists from the University of Maine. The team found some odd evidence of ancient house sites with "very early Acadian" artefacts in them. But unfortunately, the most promising site had been mostly obliterated by a road serving the copper mine on Cape d'Or.

It is copper, by the way, that gives Cape d'Or its name — the golden-hued cliffs are rich with the mineral. Besides keeping an eye on the Bay of Fundy approaches and his growing ship, Sinclair may also have extracted some of the metal from the cape. The deposits were so rich that, two centuries after Sinclair, Samuel de Champlain called Advocate Harbour the "Port of Mines" — Minas Basin is thought to be a corruption of Champlain's "Bay of Mines."

But, in addition to its view down Fundy, its view over ship construction going on in Advocate Harbour below, and its copper, Cape D'Or may have had a fourth attraction for a man in Sinclair's situation. The cape projects into Minas Channel like a spearhead. This channel, just six miles wide, handles the entire tidal flow of in and out of Minas Basin twice a day. And, since the Bay of Fundy has the highest tides in the world, this is quite a flow. Cape D'Or projects into one of the most boisterous tidal races in the world — it is, indeed, "where the deep sea dashes."

In the summer of 1982, synchronicity struck again because only CanTraid and the neo-curragh boat design permitted our discovery of the crucial significance of this tidal race for someone with Sinclair's concerns.

Perhaps I should explain that my neo-curragh fishing boat design owed both very little, and also a great deal, to Tim Severin's *Brendan*. Long before Severin's *Brendan Voyage* project came to public notice, I had already decided that the Irish curragh concept could provide the cheapest possible kind of boat for offshore fishing: curraghs could be relatively large and extremely seaworthy. They had yet another advantage. They could be made as "kits" to be

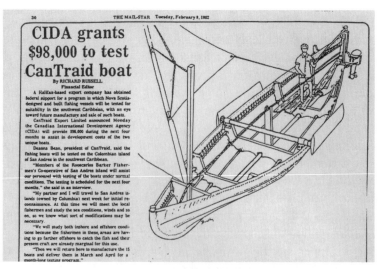

Newspaper article about CanTraid's neo-curragh fishing boat design.

assembled by the buyer and, in this case, I'd calculated that twenty curraghs, each thirty-two feet in length and eight feet in beam, could be shipped in one twenty-foot container! Further, the skin of the curragh could be contrived to be a tough carrying case for all the bits and pieces inside, and this could be made pilfer-proof — a consideration in Third World ports.

What was to become the CanTraid thirty-two-foot (9.2 metre) neo-curragh had been worked out on paper by 1972, and sailed in quarter- scale form off Toronto in Lake Ontario in 1973. I wanted to use modern materials, not traditional ones, for most of the parts because they were manufactured in quantity and were therefore cheaper. For example, Tim Severin had great difficulties in even finding ash suitable for *Brendan* in modern Ireland. The traditional Irish bulls' hide hull also presented formidable supply problems for Severin. The skills of sewing the thick hides together into a hull had virtually been lost. Severin had to recruit leather-working students, and especially apprentice saddle-makers, from British technical colleges in order to make *Brendan's* hull.

Even back in 1972, working the design out on paper, I knew that these traditional materials and skills would never work and would prove inordinately expensive, for mass-produced Third World fishing boats. I had decided to use transverse wooden frames, joined together with short pieces of wood that could be duplicated locally for repairs. For longitudinal frames ("stringers") I'd decided to use epoxy electrical conduit three inches in diameter that had been developed for protecting telephone wires in Arabia. This conduit came in basic twenty-foot lengths, but there were also joining attachments and very sweetly curved segments so that the conduit could be laid around corners. This conduit system, developed by Bell Labs, was stabilized against the ultraviolet rays of tropical Arabia in case the sand in which it was intended to be buried was blown away temporarily and the conduit became exposed to the desert sun. It was light, very strong, abrasion-resistant, and UV-protected. The joints could be sealed watertight with epoxy resin in a simple process designed for Arabian workers in remote places. Just the stuff I needed, and cheap, considering that it defined the shape of the boat when fitted into deep semicircular notches in the wooden cross-ways frames and secured in place with many lashings of plastic cord. A smear of epoxy resin over these lashings made them "permanent" and difficult to loosen. Those sweetly curved corner sections of conduit supplied the boat's bow and stern profile.

For the matrix that would give a boat shape to the basic frame, and that would support the hull against the press of water, I didn't use the traditional Irish ash lathes. It was obvious to me that ash of the required quality was a scarce commodity in today's world, and that the lathes (even if they could be obtained in quantity) must be lashed together in a close diagonal arrangement requiring thousands of individual knots. My purpose, unlike Severin, who must have been working on *Brendan* at the same time, was not to build a replica curragh in order to do historical research, but to build hundreds of inexpensive, practical curraghs for Third World fishermen.

So, instead of clear Irish ash for the matrix, I used mass-produced plastic Canadian snow fencing. This had square apertures of about the right traditional size, but was otherwise moulded of tough, smooth, and rather thick plastic straps. It was also bright orange. Since this material would be visible inside the boat's hull, I thought it might make aerial searching for lost boats easier. The snow fencing was intended to be laid over the basic frame, pressed closely to it, and then secured by lashing it to the frames wherever possible with plastic cord daubed with epoxy resin.

I've mentioned that the epoxy conduit could be joined to be absolutely water-tight. This, indeed, was one of its primary functions to protect electrical wiring. In 1973, more as a joke than anything else, the curragh was sailed in Lake Ontario minus its hull! The frame itself would support three people, the mast, sail, outboard support (and outboard), leeboards and rudder — everything needed for sailing — but it was a cold and wet demonstration.

The hull was a pre-sewn affair of the thickest canvas normally manufactured. The fabric was impregnated with flexible plastic to make it waterproof and was treated with anti-bacterial and anti-fungus compounds for the tropics. The plastic impregnation, by the way, was bright yellow. I thought that this might also enhance the boat's visibility in an emergency situation, but I didn't much like it. We started calling this prototype "the banana boat" because of its shape and colour.

During 1973–74, I had no success whatsoever in convincing aid agencies that a flexible, cloth-covered boat could be a safe and practical proposition. So I put the hull in storage, and just broke up the epoxy-welded frame since I couldn't salvage enough of it to be worthwhile. As I previously mentioned, I went to British Columbia in 1975–76 to work for a weekly newspaper that had advertised for an editor. This was in Powell River, and there I wrote *The Iceman Inheritance*, worked on a salmon boat to learn the practicalities of at least one kind of commercial fishing, studied fisheries in general throughout the world — and wrote my opinions for the prime minister, Joe Clark.

After we returned to Toronto in 1978, Tim Severin's *The Brendan Voyage* was published and caused something of a stir in the media. Even people in aid agencies learned of this voyage. Officials who had rejected the neo-curragh previously were now having second thoughts. I received letters from the World Bank, the Overseas Development Agency of Britain, and Bell Laboratories.

Since my contract with Adcom Research of Toronto left me with some free time, and since I'd completed *The Iceman Inheritance*, I decided to answer these letters and explore opportunities that had not existed before. I retrieved the curragh hull from storage and made some design refinements — one being the addition of a Polynesian sailing rig. Although I was primarily occupied with writing and market research in Toronto, I did start contacting aid agencies again with the vague idea of producing the neo-curragh in Ontario. But we moved to Halifax before anything could jell.

When my marriage broke up and my promise to Jason seemed to signal the end of my writing career for a while, I fell back on this neo-curragh as a way of getting my private sort of aid program off the ground. Most surprisingly, in late 1981 the Canadian International Development Agency decided to support the further development of the neo-curragh (and a smaller inshore design). By this time, Deanna and I had launched CanTraid privately, but more or less immediate encouragement and financial assistance were forthcoming from several levels of the Canadian government involved in aid and development, both foreign and domestic. The neo-curragh designed a decade before, but boosted by Severin's successful voyage, really established CanTraid and got us relocated to Kentville.

We were preparing to supply production models of this boat to Caribbean fishermen, and one of our tests involved anchoring this boat in the Cape d'Or tidal race to see how it would handle short, choppy waves. This was an "exciting" test, to say the least, and we were more than pleased with the result (and quite relieved that we were not drowned). But what made it even more exciting was that we were suddenly surrounded, as the tide surged, with scores, if not hundreds, of small whales — dolphins and pilot whales — from six to thirty feet (2 to 8 metres) in length. The local fishermen, aboard as sailors, had never seen anything like it. Some of them had fished Minas Basin, Minas Channel, and the Bay of Fundy for thirty years. Deanna and Jason, watching with binoculars from the safety of the Cape d'Or lighthouse, were thrilled. And, as I answered a wide-eyed Jason as soon as I could, no, not one of the whales boiling all around the boat even so much as touched it.

I finally figured out a possible explanation because of Tim Severin's experience with his *Brendan*. Our neo-curragh had a flexible hull stretched over "ribs" of plastic and wood. It therefore returned a sonar echo similar to that of a whale's body. It also happened to be about the right size, twenty-eight feet (8 metres) on the water, to be an average pilot whale. Our neo-curragh didn't frighten whales the way a conventional solid hull would have. We were treated to an extraordinary sight, and to a relevant insight about the Sinclair expedition. The whales were not, perhaps, even now as scarce as experts thought — but they had learned to stay away from solid hull boats that would return a "non-whale" sonar echo. What was happening seemed to be that small fry, like herring, were being carried by the tidal stream in their millions; predators like mackerel followed them; and small toothed whales fed on the mackerel. We saw all three — herring, mackerel, and whales — in the tidal race.

This would have been a very convenient situation for Orkney fishermen, and most of Sinclair's "sailors" must have been professional fishermen, particularly in a situation where many castle-builders and ship-builders also had to be fed by only a part of the entire personnel. In addition, of course, provisions had to be laid in for the winter, and also to supply the ship for the return voyage to Europe.

The tidal race provided a most convenient larder. Inshore, in the shallows, fishermen with nets could take herring by the hundredweight. Slightly further out in the water, hook-and-line fishermen could take hundreds of mackerel using herring as bait. In mid-channel, boats with harpooners could take a few small whales at each run of the tide. In Sinclair's time, Fundy whales would have been ignorant of the danger of planked boats. Only at Owokun was all this possible. Can it be just coincidence that Abenaki Indians learned to fish with nets, and very suddenly too, about A.D. 1400? That's when stone-carved net weights first appear in the Abenaki tool kit — although, to my knowledge, no archaeologist has compared the design of these net weights with Orkney net sinkers.

I think it is interesting enough to mention that the neo-curragh experienced much the same thing in the Caribbean. In 1982 we spent some time on the San Andres Islands in the southwest Caribbean assessing our boats in tropical conditions. The fishermen of the Rooscarlos Barker Fishermen's Co-operative helped us. The San Andres group belongs to Colombia (although Nicaragua disputes this claim — the islands are closer to Nicaragua), and are about two hundred miles north of the Colombian coast. The fish there reacted similarly to fish in Nova Scotia. The more natural sonar echo of the flexible hull did not scare them away and the yellow hull seemed actually to attract them.

I had been worried about this, thinking that a green or blue hull would have been better. But the bright yellow seemed to appeal to even some of the smaller fish — and it certainly attracted barracudas and sharks. This might seem unfortunate (particularly, maybe, with a cloth-hulled boat!), but the San Andres fishermen were happy. Their favourite victim is the "kingfish," an Atlantic version of a tuna, but they happily take barracuda and shark too. Very few fish dishes can beat grilled barracuda for taste. Shark meat, and there's plenty of it on every fish, is also very good (and boneless, of course) if the meat is soaked in salt water to remove the ammonia, squeezed, and then sun-dried.

The experience in the tidal race gave us the chance to make a tentative identification of a curious object, the second discovery, that was found in Windsor, Nova Scotia, during the summer of 1982. A glance at the map will show that Windsor is on the shore of Minas Basin less than a day's sail from Owokun; it is also at the

Deanna Theilmann-Bean holding an iron trident discovered near Windsor, Nova Scotia.

mouth of a river that is mightily tidal. The object, found three feet (1 metre) beneath the surface when someone was excavating a basement for a new house, was a very heavy iron trident. It was about four feet (1.25 metres) in length, about nine inches (.23 metres) across the tines and from one to two inches (3 to 6 centimetres) thick.

The Windsor newspaper published a photo of this thing, along with an account of its discovery. The local historical society put it on display for some time with a sign above it, reading "What is it?" Many suggestions were made, including one that it was an old Acadian implement for breaking ice, but nothing definitive was learned. It may still be unidentified.

My own investigation of it indicated that it had been puddle-cast in its present form, but had not been completed. That is, molten iron had been poured into a simple sand mould that was nothing but a carefully levelled depression in sand. The pattern had been defined by a wooden template that had been surrounded with hard-packed sand. One could clearly see, on the "upper" side of the object, a sharp edged fringe all around the implement where the molten iron had adhered to the edge of the sand mould during the cooling process. This object was much too heavy to have been used as a tool for any sort of continuous work, and no one could suggest what sort of job it had been designed for. It is no more than a guess, like others, but it might have been intended as a harpoon "blank" for small whales.

The tines were thick enough that they could have been hammered into barbs at the ends; its weight would ensure penetration of a pilot whale's blubber if cast by a strong man. The shaft would have been forced into a hollow wooden haft, or handle-shaft, designed to break free when the whale dived. The hollow handle would float and be recovered for further use. A rope could have been tied securely around the central tine and the shaft. Leather or (back then) seal skin bags filled with air could be tied onto this rope as floats in order to tire the whale and ensure its capture.

Whether or not this object had been intended as a harpoon, it would certainly make a good one with the tines heated and hammered into barbs of the desired shape. It would be sufficient for whales from ten to thirty feet (3-9 meters) in length.

CanTraid and our neo-curragh had demonstrated that small whales still abounded in the Bay of Fundy and went in and out of

Minas Basin with every tide (even if they were not often seen from conventional boats). We could form a possible answer to the problem of how a small portion of Sinclair's men could have fed a large number delegated to other tasks.

It was only after CanTraid had been wrapped up, after Deanna and I had decided to return to our separate life paths, and only after *Holy Grail Across The Atlantic* had been published in 1988 that, one lazy day in 1990, I happened to be re-reading *The Zeno Narrative*. Something elusive kept teasing my brain. In certain ways, the *Narrative* is quite unsatisfying. There's a lot that Antonio neglects to say. But, presumably, a more detailed account had been contained in his book that he had promised to bring to brother Carlo. As I read it over again, a phrase dropped like a bombshell: *"Neither would Sinclair rest, though it* [i.e., the "smoking hill"] *was a great way off, without sending 100 soldiers to explore the country…"*

A hundred soldiers? On a routine reconnaissance expedition? Sinclair would certainly not have sent *all* his soldiers on such a mission. He was in unknown country with a fleet to protect, and his experience with the islanders of Icaria had been unpleasant. What percentage of his armed strength would a seasoned and successful military man like Sinclair assign to a mission towards the smoking hill? I read the *Narrative* yet again. Antonio is clearly describing a rather massive expedition: *"I set sail with a considerable number of ships and men"*.

By consulting with military people, I learned that Sinclair would not have sent more than 20 per cent of his force on such a reconnaissance — Possibly not even as many as that. Was I seriously to believe that Sinclair arrived in Estotiland with *over five hundred soldiers?* And, I noted, Antonio always differentiated between soldiers and sailors. Were these soldiers *additional* to the fleet's sailors and support personnel? It seemed so.

Then Sinclair decided to establish a settlement, and presumably he left some people in it when he returned to Europe in his "stone canoe." How many people chose to remain over the winter with him? How many men would it take to build a ship *and* to build a castle like The Cross? Under the feudal system, it would have been impossible for Sinclair to have demanded that some of his vassals remain away from their own homes, families, and holdings in a distant new settlement across the ocean. Terms of service were strictly codified in the feudal bond. Those who stayed in Estotiland did so voluntarily, and they must have had a strong reason for pioneering in a new land rather than staying in familiar Europe. How many "soldiers," how many *people*, remained in Estotiland? Who were they?

Also, one Micmac legend mentions a "sorceress" in connection with the Glooscap tradition. The feminine gender is stressed. Were we to believe that a number of women voyaged to Estotiland? If so, it would seem more likely that Sinclair had planned to establish a settlement across the Atlantic even before the expedition set sail. The more I studied the *Narrative*, the more curious it seemed. One thing kept gnawing at my mind. *Only one ship, with Sinclair himself aboard, returned to Europe*. Micmac legends spoke of only one "stone canoe" and, besides, it would be unrealistic to build a fleet of ships over the time of just one winter.

The way the *Narrative* is worded, it is impossible to come to any firm conclusions about the number of ships and personnel in the departing expedition, the number that returned with Antonio, the number that stayed over the winter with Sinclair. But it began to seem as though the whole purpose of the expedition was to found a settlement and to leave a number of "soldiers" there. And, perhaps, to leave their wives there, too.

Who were these "soldiers"? Why would they emigrate from Europe to a remote, new land? Why (if there were women in the expedition) would they subject their wives to such a primitive relocation? I had already suggested that these "soldiers" had been the Templars of Rosslyn and that Sinclair's voyage had been a purposeful one to relocate hunted and excommunicated Templars and, perhaps, the thing they guarded: the Holy Grail. If I have made any truly original contribution to unravelling the tale of the Grail, it was simply to point out that this Henry Sinclair not only made a transatlantic voyage when his own holdings could not be considered truly secure, but that his barony of Rosslyn had been a known Templar haven. And that the Templars, in turn, had been created for just one task: guarding the Holy Grail. My own idea was that the 1398 voyage had been a mission to find a haven for the Grail and its guardians.

But what struck me so suddenly and so strongly while re-reading *The Zeno Narrative* was the sheer *size* of this expedition. How on earth had I missed these clues before? I began to suspect that a surprisingly large number of people had been left behind in Estotiland. A community of that size would not remain restricted to the initial Nova Scotia settlement. The community would explore and expand.

By 1991, I was on the track of the Grail Knights of North America. It proved a surprisingly easy trail to follow. It led from the Atlantic inland into the United States and Canada.

But...why were so many Templars at Rosslyn that a transatlantic relocation became urgently necessary?

The answer to that question will require a brief look at what has been called "The Greatest Story Ever Told." It is the story of Jesus, true enough, but told from a perspective that differs markedly from anything we have absorbed in any church. It is the tragic, heroic, and supremely evocative tale of the Holy Grail.

5

Le Trésor Maudit

The modern understanding of the Holy Grail began, at least for the English-speaking world, with Henry Lincoln's 1969 vacation in southern France. There, in order to pass the time, he bought a paperback edition of Gérard de Sède's *Le Trésor Maudit de Rennes-le-Château ("The Accursed Treasure of Rennes-le-Château")*.[1]

Lincoln expected a frothy summertime reading diversion about a local mystery, but what he got was an introduction to an enigma that seemed to affect the roots of western culture as well as the very character of Christianity. Following the clues so coyly dropped by Gérard de Sède shaped the next thirty years of Lincoln's life, produced several bestselling books and half a dozen television documentaries — and left many more unanswered questions of great import.

The Gold of Rennes

Gérard de Sède's book was about the strange life of François-Bérenger Saunière, a former village priest of Rennes-le-Château. Abbé Saunière was assigned to the village in 1885, and it was such a poor posting that the priest, according to his account books, which still exist, lived on the verge of starvation for five years and more. He had to depend on gifts of food from his parishioners in order to survive. Some elderly residents of Rennes-le-Château remembered Abbé Saunière when Lincoln interviewed them between 1969 and 1971 as a cultured, educated, and athletic man who took long walks in the rugged terrain of this rather remote region of Languedoc in the Pyrénées foothills.

Sometime in 1891, Abbé Saunière found *something* of immense value. Clues leading him to his discovery were associated with the church's location, its construction, and its cemetery.

His church at Rennes-le-Château had been consecrated to Mary Magdalene in A.D. 1059, but may have been rebuilt on the ruins of a church dedicated to the Magdalene as early as the sixth century.[2] Medieval Rennes-le-Château was called Reddis or Rhedae and was situated in a region then called Razès. It was one of the two capitals of the Visigoths — the other being Toledo, farther south in Spain. In A.D. 600, Rennes-le-Château was a much bigger and more important place than it is today. It was said to have rivalled Carcassonne in size and was called "Royal Reddis" (of the Visigoths). Rennes-le-Château was sacked and almost totally destroyed by the Spanish in A.D. 1361. From then on it was just the cluster of houses, a ruined castle, and the old church that exist today. Indeed, it was so small and obscure that it wasn't (until recently, for reasons that follow) even noted on some French road maps.

What we see of Rennes-le-Château today may actually be only the hilltop citadel of what was once a much larger and sprawling city that extended over several square miles. In the 1970s, Henry Lincoln and a BBC producer discovered hundreds, if not thousands, of curious stone houses (locally called *capitelles*) which are supposedly "shepherds' huts" (!) according to conventional archaeologists. Lincoln doubted this explanation because of the sheer number of these habitations, plus his discovery of massive, ruined walls in the vicinity of these *capitelles*. The *capitelles* and ruined walls are scattered to the southeast, beginning near the foot of Rennes-le-Château's hill. Perhaps these walls and structures are all that remain of the once-great city of Rhedae; perhaps today's Renne-le-Chateau is all that survives of the higher citadel.[3]

Before continuing with the story of Bérenger Saunière's treasure, it seems justifiable to mention that Rennes-le-Château may have existed long before the Visigoths arrived in the area. My partner, Joelle Lauriol, one of many enthusiastic amateurs who volunteered research contributions to this book, discovered a reference to an Ionian Greek colony called "Rhodae" in this very region. She found the settlement marked on a large-scale map of Greek colonies around the Mediterranean in the sixth century B.C. She came across this map in a standard university-level historical atlas. This

Ionian colony city appears to be precisely at the location of Rennes-le-Château. According to the atlas (and other references), this colony was established in 584 B.C. and its name "Rhodae" may have been corrupted into the later Rhedae.[4]

At this time, the inhabitants of this area were a Celtic tribe called the Tectosages ("wise builders") and there is the tradition that Ionian Greek mathematicians from the Pythagorean School sought refuge among the Tectosages when their mystical Pythagorean mathematico-religious beliefs caused them to be expelled from Greek colonies in Italy. It is intriguing to speculate on what these Greek mathematicians may have taught the local Celts — or may have learned from them — if, indeed, people in this Garonne-Aude waterway corridor had actually preserved scraps of much older Atlantean knowledge (as previously suggested in Chapter 2).[5]

The arrival of these Ionian Greek refugee mathematicians may have stimulated the conception, surveying, and earth movements required to produce the perfect (with errors of mere feet) "Rennes-le-Château pentagon." A pentagon is a regular geometric shape consisting of five sides of equal length. It was first noticed by Henry Lincoln when he was carefully studying large-scale topographical maps of the area. This pentagon was laid out over rugged terrain. It is marked by the following points which are exactly (within a matter of feet) two and a half miles apart: the highest spot on the hill where Rennes-le-Château now clusters, the hill on which Blanchefort castle was built centuries after the Tectosages, the hill of Bézu where the Templars built a castle in the twelfth century, and the two elevations of Serre de Lauzet and La Soulane which have no known ruins or constructions on them. Lincoln also discovered later that the pentagon had another, central, hill providing a center that was not exactly on the highest point, but was only yards in error — and, of course, the hill may have slipped or eroded since the pentagon was laid out. There used to be a stone marking this centre.

It happens that a pentagon was, for the Pythagoreans, the geometric figure that was used as a sign to summon members of the secret sect to meetings.[6] The "Rennes-le-Château pentagon" may have been a gigantic advertisement, so large that it would not be noticed except by the initiated, that refugee Pythagoreans had a haven among the Tectosages. Certainly, these Ionian Greeks had the mathematical and geometric knowledge to lay out the huge geographical pentagon, while the Celts customarily built earthworks

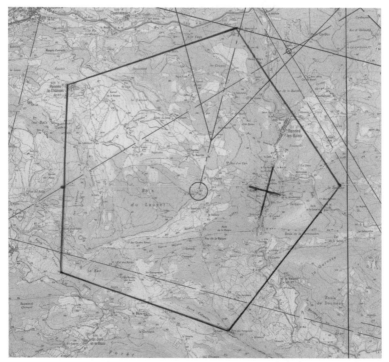

Incorporating as one point the church spire in the present village of Rennes-le-Château, this huge geographic and geometrical pentagon is accurate to a matter of feet. Henry Lincoln first discovered this geometrical figure when he was studying maps of southern France. The pentagon was apparently laid out using measurement of distance in English miles. The author has superimposed this pentagon over the latest French government topographical map of the area.

and could have altered the hills, if necessary, to ensure that the *highest elevations* would mark the pentagon — as they still do today, except for the slight inaccuracy on the cental hill.

But perhaps the pentagon has more significance yet.

As seen from earth, which has its own orbit around the sun, the other planets appear to have conjunctions ("joinings together") with the sun that form geometrical patterns. Mercury, the planet closest to the sun with a relatively small, frequent (eighty-eight days), and highly eccentric orbit around it, appears to merge with the sun three times in every earth year. It forms an irregular triangular pattern if the three conjunctions were to be laid out on a large expanse of earth geography. Mars, with its eccentric orbit, seems to mark out its conjunctions with the sun in an irregular four-sided geometric figure.

Venus, however, currently has the least eccentric and most truly circular orbit of all the known planets in our solar system. As seen from earth, its conjunctions with the sun appear to mark out points of a perfect pentagon. It marks out a perfect pentagon every eight earth years — precisely. Venus was considered the goddess of love, reproduction, and regeneration among the Romans. For the Greeks, she was Aphrodite — goddess of love, beauty, and fertility. It is not surprising, then, that when Christianity superseded paganism (if it has), the planet Venus and the pentagon symbol were associated with Mary Magdalene — by tradition a reformed prostitute, although the New Testament nowhere states this explicitly. Given that Rennes-le-Château is one point of a giant geographic pentagon, it is not surprising that its church has always been dedicated to St. Mary Magdalene.[7]

As explained, the planet Venus appears from earth to have five solar conjunctions every eight years. This ratio, five to eight, happens also to be the so-called Golden Section that was venerated by Renaissance artists as a proportion resonating with something that human psychology, unaccountably but undeniably, finds pleasing, or "beautiful." The pentagon is the geometric figure that incorporates this Golden Section in several ways, and so artists could produce lines of the appropriate length if they underlaid their paintings with sketches based on pentagonal geometry. Both Poussin and the Teniers (and many other Renaissance artists) were known to have done this. The "Golden Section" has been venerated by people other than artists, such as scientists trying to arrive at accurate measurements. A kilometre, for example, divides an English mile into the Golden Section almost precisely.[8] This is no mere accident or coincidence.

But we may wonder whether the Ionian Greek mathematician-astronomer-mystics of the Pythagorean School originated the "Rennes-le-Château pentagon" with the assistance of their earth-moving Celtic hosts, or whether these people came upon some earlier geometric earthwork, were able to notice it because of their knowledge, and undertook any repairs that might have been necessary to restore its symmetry. It is at least possible that Rennes-le-Château is a "Holy Place" because it is part of a gigantic geometric earth-figure left by an earlier, and lost, culture.

From about 1000 B.C., this Pyrénées region of modern France had been in contact with the Phoenician and then Carthagenian colonies in Spain before the Ionian Greeks arrived to plant their isolated settlement. The Rennes-le-Château area can claim to be one of the oldest "civilized" places in western Europe — if we regard civilization as coming from the eastern Mediterranean and not, maybe, radiating at least partly the other way.

After being in a Celtic-Greco-Carthagenian sphere of cultural influence for a thousand years, Rome annexed this part of Gaul around 121 B.C. The Romans eventually called the entire region Septimania because it was allocated as a place of settlement for veterans of the Seventh Legion. The name Septimania lingered long after Imperial Rome lost control of the area.[9]

In A.D. 410, Rome itself was sacked by the Visigoths under Alaric I. They carried off almost all of the treasure that the Romans had amassed over centuries. This included the treasure from the Temple of Jerusalem sacked by Titus 340 years earlier (i.e., in A.D. 70, at the time of the fall of Masada and Judea). Some objects from the Jerusalem Temple are depicted on the famous Triumphal Arch in Rome that was erected in honour of Titus. The Jerusalem treasure alone was a fabulous hoard, but Rome had also ransacked all of the Mediterranean world. In short, the Visigoths made off with the most extensive treasure from one place that the world has ever known. It is possible that the accumulated wealth of the New World, extracted by Spain over three centuries of ruthless exploitation, exceeded the value of Rome's treasure — but it is an arguable point even on the basis of the intrinsic value of gold, silver, gems, etc. It is much more arguable on the basis of art, literature, and religious objects of literally priceless cultural value to the western world.

The Visigoths buried treasure with their kings and nobles. It is known that their habit was to deflect the course of a river temporarily, bury a dead chieftain and his treasure in the exposed river bed, and then allow the river to return to its former course. Alaric I himself died before the Visigoths could leave Italy, and he and his treasure are known to rest somewhere beneath the River Busento.[10]

Aside from Alaric, though, who was just the agreed-upon Visigothic high king of the time, there were many powerful clan chieftains and petty kings who had shares of Rome's wealth. Leaving Italy, the Visigothic horde travelled north and then west around the Ligurian Sea, south around the present Gulf of Lion, and came to rest in Languedoc. Rennes-le-Château was their first and major "capital city" for a century until some clans later travelled into Spain and settled around Toledo. Many Visigothic chieftains must have been buried near Rennes-le-Château during the centuries of occupation, and there are certainly enough tributaries of the Aude River to hide any number of royal corpses under river beds. The treasures that must be buried around Rennes-le-Château have never been (officially) discovered, much less publicized. However, a Visigothic treasure was found near Toledo in the early nineteenth century, at a time when the French Empire under Napoleon occupied that part of Iberia. This treasure was kept and displayed at the Musée de Cluny in Paris until, in 1943, Marshal Pétain gave it to Generalissimo Francisco Franco of Spain.[11]

A Visigothic crown discovered in a nineteenth-century treasure trove near Toledo, Spain.

Although no treasure trove around Rennes-le-Château has ever been officially or publicly acknowledged, it seems clear that Abbé Bérenger Saunière discovered something while taking his long walks. Indeed, as modern researchers have inevitably delved into the slim documentation that exists about this priest, much of his life still remains obscure — but not so totally obscure as it had been. The still scanty evidence has suggested that Saunière actually sought a posting to Rennes-le-Château. Since Bérenger Saunière is known to have been an enthusiast of local history, and was always described as a remarkably learned and cultured man to be a mere priest in a remote village, it is at least permissible to assume that he may have known something about Rennes-le-Château that others did not. Since genealogical research into his background links him with the powerful and Templar-related Blancheforts of the region, this possibility shades off into a probability, if not a certainty.

Researchers do not know, or are not agreed on, what Bérenger Saunière discovered. It is known only that he spent an estimated 1,500,000,000 *old francs* between 1891 and his death on January 22, 1917. This is roughly $300,000,000 in turn-of-the-century American currency.[12]

He built several villas for himself. He bought "vast estates" all over Europe. He brought running water, electric lighting, and a road to his village of Rennes-le-Château. He built a modest medieval castle and tower, called the Tour Magdala, to house his rapidly expanding library of rare books. He built extensive botanical and zoological gardens. He entertained lavishly, hosting royalty and famed opera singers of the day. Some say that he acquired a mistress, Marie Denarnaud, although others maintain that this woman, Saunière's housekeeper since 1885, was never more than a confidante and friend. Abbé Saunière's sudden and immense wealth naturally attracted the attention of Church authorities.

When he was asked to explain his money, Saunière's answer was that it had been given to him by penitents among his village flock! He was eventually removed from the position of village priest, but he continued to live in Rennes-le-Château until his death. At several points during his life after 1891, his wealth seemed to fluctuate down to near poverty, but was always replenished. This suggests that his source of wealth was near Rennes-le-Château. This might be the reason he continued to reside there despite the fact he had various estates all over Europe and powerful (Archduke Johannn von Habsburg in Vienna) and charming (Emma Calvé, diva opera singer, Paris) friends in major cities. He had to keep an eye on his treasure trove.

Bérenger Saunière supposedly confided the source of his wealth to Marie Denarnaud, and he left her an immense fortune. She died in 1953 of a stroke, but she lay in a coma for ten days, unable to speak, and Saunière's secret died with her. However, years before she died, she is reputed to have remarked to a reporter that "people around here are walking on gold and don't know it."

Gérard de Sède called Saunière's treasure "accursed" because the priest of a neighbouring village was brutally murdered, and several bodies were actually discovered buried on the grounds of Saunière's

house in Rennes-le-Château. There is some evidence that
Saunière's Tour Magdala ("Tower of the Magdalene") library-cum-
castle was actually constructed as a fortress to protect him from
those who sought to extract the secret of his wealth. And, although
there is no hard evidence, there is plausible speculation that the
murdered priest, who knew Saunière, was a victim of those seeking
the secret — or that Saunière killed him to ensure his silence. The
murderer of the priest was never brought to justice, and the bodies
on Saunière's grounds have never been identified.

Marie Denarnaud was not being quite fair to the local
inhabitants when she allegedly said that "people around here are
walking on gold and don't know it." In point of fact, stories of huge
buried treasures near Rennes-le-Château had been a part of local
folklore long before Saunière arrived there in 1885. Local tradition
included tales (unsubstantiated) of local shepherds occasionally
finding a pot of gold in remote mountain caves or fissures.

The most obvious answer to the mystery of Bérenger Saunière's
sudden and immense wealth is simply that he found a cache of
Visigothic booty, perhaps because he had more accurate information
about it due to his research and his ancestors. This is the usual
explanation among most of the "Rennes-le-Château enthusiasts"
today. It is equally obvious, though, that in spite of his truly
staggering wealth, Saunière could not have found all of the
Visigothic loot from Rome. Even Saunière's money would account
for but a tiny fraction of it. Since the 1970s, several books of
"Rennes-le-Château Treasure Maps" have been published. The sales
and rental of metal detectors, picks, and shovels has become a
growth industry in Rennes-le-Château and nearby towns.

For people who daydream of buried treasure (and who doesn't?),
Bérenger Saunière's apparent success in finding some has catapulted
Rennes-le-Château from a backwater to a tourist mecca. Many
adventurous young men and women, who might formerly have
offered their services to Mel Fisher in a search for another sunken
Spanish treasure galleon like the rich *Atocha* wreck, are now
freelancing with pick and shovel in Languedoc.

If only things were so simple...

Around Rennes-le-Château one encounters physiological
symptoms atypical of treasure hunters. To be sure, many of them
exhibit the usual frantic, bright glittering eyes of sheer gold lust.
But, surprisingly, one also encounters that benign and ethereal
myopia of spiritual rapture. This is because some of the treasure

taken from Rome consisted of religious artefacts stolen from the Temple in Jerusalem by Titus. This may have included the Ark of the Covenant, although there are problems. One problem is that the Ark of the Covenant impinges upon, and may have contributed a great deal to, the confusion of what the Holy Grail really is. This is a problem we will discuss shortly.

But there are other difficulties with the Ark of the Covenant that have to do with the possibility or probability that it could have been part of the Roman treasure brought by Visigoths to Rennes-le-Château. According to the Old Testament, Exodus, the Ark of the Covenant was constructed soon after the Israelites had escaped across the Red Sea from bondage in Egypt.

Modern engineers have been intrigued by the specifications of the Ark because, if the directions are followed precisely, one ends up making a fairly powerful electrical condenser. It was a box of very specific dimensions made of acacia wood (an insulator). It was covered, inside and out, with gold (an excellent conductor). If the two surfaces of the gold were separated from each other, then a very powerful condenser of electricity is the result. In the dry air of the Middle East, it would accumulate a very powerful charge.[13]

But the Ark was more than just a condenser, it was a "spark transmitter" roughly tuned to a specific frequency by the very precise dimensions given to Moses for the basic acacia-wood box. In this matter, the Ark was similar to early "cavity tubes" in 1930s radar research where the desired radar frequency was obtained by actually machining cavities of various volumes into metal blocks. The Ark was a "cavity" of precise dimensions, and one in a gold-sheathed box.

The Ark also had a top, of the same general construction as the basic box. This lid of the box had golden "cherubim" at each end and a "Mercy Seat." The Bible doesn't tell us exactly how these components were arranged, or how they were attached to the Ark's top. It is well to remember that although Moses is supposed to be the author of Exodus, according to Hebrew tradition, the earliest known written account dates from almost one thousand years later. Moses might not have described everything about the Ark in the first place, but even if he had, it seems probable that some details would have become fuzzy in the one thousand years of oral transmission before the story was written down.

Without assuming any "secret" or "unknown" components at all, but working only with the Ark as described, only two assumptions are necessary in order to construct a fairly powerful spark transmitter. One assumption is that an ancient, pliable insulating material was available so that the parts of the Ark could be attached in ways that both insulated them from, and conducted them to, the basic box condenser-cavity-frequency-modulator in order to produce a "circuit." Such an insulating material was widely available to the ancient Isaelites and Egyptians — bitumen, tar. And we don't need to assume that artisans and priests in the ancient Middle East used bitumen to insulate and to seal simple electrical devices.

Wet-cell electric batteries, using acidic citrus juice as an electrolyte, were discovered in a Baghdad museum.[14] They were sealed with bitumen, and the internal electrodes were insulated from each other with bitumen. These primitive batteries have been dated to about A.D. 700. But fundamental electric devices were used much earlier than that. Tiny golden beads from XVIII Dynasty Egypt (c. 1550 B.C.) were found to have only a thin coating of gold over some base metal. The beads are so small, and also without any sort of seam or hammered edge to the gold layer, that the gold could have been applied only by electroplating.[15] Given a citrus-juice battery like those of Baghdad, electroplating of gold would not have been difficult. So we don't have to assume an electrical insulating material, and we don't have to assume basic knowledge of electricity in Middle Eastern antiquity. We know it.

The second assumption is that there were instructions, or a model, indicating what was to be insulated with bitumen, and what was to be solidly attached with the ubiquitous gold.

Let us consider one "cherub" at one end of the Ark. These "cherubim" seem to have been the Egyptian idea of a "griffon" — an animal with claws and long pointed wings, a sort of cross between a lion and a hawk. Let us suppose that our cherub at one end of the box had one gold claw connected to the inner sheet of gold on the acacia-wood box, and the other claw attached to the gold sheath on the exterior of the acacia box. Further, suppose that this separation was maintained up to the long wings, which were of gold. Suppose that the wings were hinged or pivoted to be able to "flap" like a proper cherub. Maybe they were just mounted in a glob of bitumen with bars, wires, or much more flexible leather-sheathed chain-links of gold maintaining the required connections.

Assembled like this, there would be a very formidable spark between the cherub's pointed gold wings each time they were pushed close together. The Ark would arc — because of the electric charge that had accumulated in the condenser. And it would arc according to a rough frequency dictated by the dimensions of the Ark's basic cavity. Touching both wings at once with bare hands would have resulted in instant death or burn depending on the strength of the charge that had been accumulated. Operating the Ark, or even touching it, would have been a potentially fatal business for anyone not thoroughly initiated into necessary procedures. The Bible mentions at least one instance in which a non-priest fell dead trying to save the Ark —the man grabbed it when it was in danger of falling off its wagon. This was in the early days of Israelite struggles in Canaan.

A priest could move the wings with sticks of wood as insulation, or perhaps some fancier arrangement of moving the cherub's wings was contrived. Maybe there was a simple lever system insulated appropriately with wood, leather and bitumen — pull the cherub's tail (or head) and the wings would approach each other to make an arc, for example. Simple *wooden* linkages.

Making such an electric arc in a dark place like a tent or a central Temple crypt without windows (i.e., the "Holy of Holies") would have been hard on the priest's eyes. If the "stones" in the Urim and Thummim were sheets of mica, common in the Middle East, then The Bible's "silver bows" in which they were mounted would have resulted in granny-style welder's glasses. These would have saved the High Priest's eyesight when communicating with the "Lord."

This sort of "arc-spark" transmitter would have sent bursts of what we call static out into the atmosphere.

What about the "receiver"? Let's consider the other cherub at the other end of the arc. It would need to be completely separated from the structure of the Ark by a layer of bitumen. Its wings were supposedly golden, too, and if they were balanced and supported well, an *electroscope* results. When this cherub was engulfed in a burst of electromagnetic radiation, its wings would repel each other and flap apart. This would naturally happen whenever the cherub at the other end of the Ark was manipulated to produce a spark-arc. If the receiving cherub's wings were delicately counterbalanced, they would close again as the charge on the open wings dissipated.

There would be a charming and satisfying symmetry to the antics of these cherubim wings — a spark made by moving the transmitting cherub's wings closer together would cause the receiving cherub's wings to open.

But the receiving cherub's wings would sometimes open when the spark-cherub was not being operated. This electroscope would also respond to natural bursts of electromagnetic energy — lightning. A nearby storm would cause very definite wing movements indeed, while a lightning strike hundreds of miles away might cause barely a twitch of the wings.

But if at one time there were a number of Arks, all made the same way, the receiving cherub would also respond to electromagnetic energy purposefully caused by a High Priest operating some distant Ark. If the transmitting Ark was many miles distant, the repelling movement of the receiving cherub's wings might be very small — too minute to be detected, with certainty, by a priestly observer. But this problem could be easily solved. With a small light source, like a candle or an oil lamp, "religiously" positioned at specific places near the receiving cherub, even tiny wing movements could be greatly amplified by jewels on the wings. The jewels would reflect the light onto some surface — a wall of a Temple sanctum or the dark cloth of a mobile bedouin canopy — so that, in a dark chamber, the reception could be clearly perceived.

The technology described above was well within the resources and capabilities of the Ancient Egyptian and Israelite artisans. The idea for it is the problem.

More than one modern radio engineer has noted that the Ark of the Covenant was a primitive sort of "spark transmitter" that could send, and receive, strong electromagnetic impulses — in fact, the Ark seems quite similar to the transmitter with which Heinrich Rudolf Hertz (1857–94) was able to demonstrate the existence of "Hertzian" (radio) waves in 1888. With his slightly more evolved spark transmitter, Guglielmo Marchese Marconi (1874–1937) first sent long-distance electromagnetic waves in 1895, and then sent them across the Atlantic in 1901.

The Ark of the Covenant could have been used, and at one time must have been used, to send and receive messages over long distances. If the spark-arc could be generated in a sequence by manipulating the wings effectively, then the bursts of static would radiate into the atmosphere in the same purposeful sequence. In the Marconi "wireless" system, Morse code was mostly used. In the Morse system, for example, three short bursts "dot-dot-dot" represent the letter "S," three longer arcs "dash-dash-dash" represent the letter "O." Therefore S-O-S could be sparked into the air. This is the international code for "Help!"

But every letter and every number can be represented by some combination of dots and dashes. That's Morse code. If you have enough electricity to generate a lot of sparks, and if you have a lot of patience, messages of any desired length and complexity can be sent. And much patience would have been required because, with a transmitter-receiver as primitive as the Ark, purposeful messages would frequently have been confused or completely drowned out by static from distant electrical storms. Our own early "wireless" had the same problem, frustration, and inefficiency.

So much for what might be called the technical aspects of the Ark. What about its provenance? Where did it come from? The Old Testament tells us that it was constructed shortly after the Exodus by an Israelite craftsman according to instructions given to Moses by God. But the Old Testament is, of course, a Hebrew document. It may well be biased. We will recall that Moses had been adopted into the pharaonic family of Egypt and was, in fact, an Egyptian priest. Could Moses have *stolen* this artefact? Or, at least, could he have stolen the plans and specifications of some highly venerated Egyptian religious object? Is this why the Egyptians called the escaping horde under Moses "evil-doers"? Or were the Egyptians just angered at losing slaves?

Considering the dates that have recently been strongly associated with the Giza complex by geologists and astronomers, and the radiocarbon date for the Bimini organic remains — all about 10,500 B.C. — we must consider the real possibility that the Ark had originally been some sort of Atlantean device for long-distance communication. It was a "wireless" and a less sophisticated and refined example of the basic principles than Marconi's 1901 apparatus. It would have worked — sometimes, with optimum atmospheric conditions — and was both dangerous and cumbersome to operate.

But even with marginal or sporadic operational efficiency, it would have permitted a seafaring culture to establish the accurate longitudes of distant places all around the earth. A signal transmitted at noon, "Giza Pyramid time" (just for example), could be compared with the local noon anywhere the signal was received. The difference in hours and fractions (measured by sand glass or water-clock) between "Pyramid noon" and local noon (the sun's highest point in the sky — the "meridian passage"), multiplied by 15, will give the longitude *west* of the "Pyramid Meridian" (Giza), in degrees — and we know that a circle was divided into 360 degrees from very early times, for no very obvious reason. This would have provided better accuracy than was available to Columbus — or to any other European mariner — until John Harrison (1693-1776), a Yorkshire blacksmith, invented a practical marine chronometer in 1749.

Time signals by "Ark broadcast," even if only marginally receivable over long distances (on good days), would eventually result in the mysteriously accurate maps that have actually been discovered. The Ark, since it obviously seems to be a primitive spark generator, naturally becomes linked with the creation of inexplicably accurate maps that apparently date from the last Ice Age (Wurm-Wisconsin) according to the geography depicted. I want to assure readers that the Hadji Ahmed mappamundi is not the only "impossible" map to depict Ice Age geography. The Oronteus Finaeus and Buache maps also show it.

My notion is that most large Atlantean trading ships or warships would have carried an "Ark" on board, and it is possible that large vessels became known as arks (i.e., "Noah's ark") because at one time they carried arc-transmitters aboard. And certainly, every major Atlantean town, colony, or outpost would have had one too. Even if the device never became more refined than the Ark of the Covenant, the technology was still sufficient, over a few centuries of worldwide seafaring, to have resulted in maps of the globe with accurate longitudes. Such maps were actually made, because their inexplicable accuracy and Ice Age geography were preserved through generations of copies on maps that exist today. It is possible that longer and more detailed communications of all kinds could have been sent and received by Atlanteans, but it is not necessary to assume so in order to explain the cartographic evidence that exists.

Modern readers might object that if this sort of spark transmitter had ever been discovered by the Atlanteans, it must have been progressively refined and improved. But this is not necessarily the case, and human history proves it. The Chinese invented all sorts of things that they never developed very much. Gunpowder in China was used for firecrackers and some erratic military rockets at least five hundred years before the invention trickled into Europe. But only European "practicality" conceived the idea of using it in firearms so that thousands of people could be killed in more efficient warfare. It seems that the Chinese had the magnetic compass before Europeans — but they never developed a navigational system to make it truly useful for maritime commerce. The Chinese also invented the vertical axis windmill, from highly efficient junk sails, but they never refined either the windmills or the junks into the ultimate wind-powered mechanisms.

Junk sails revealed the working principles of aircraft wings, yet the Chinese never developed winged gliders (made of bamboo and their silk) which they could have done about the time of Christ. They invented all the items necessary for a steam engine, and even made primitive working ones, but didn't develop practical engines that could supply "artificial power" — which they could have done about A.D. 700 and then applied to their junks and gliders.

The Chinese developed pressure bottles (of bamboo nodes) to hold natural gas for portable stoves intended for travellers, but they never refined the idea to the point of metal containers that would have made steam engines more practical and portable. They invented balloons — paper lanterns sent aloft with heated air from candles — but never thought of sewing balloons from their fine silk and then adding a traveller's natural gas stove to approximate our modern sporting balloons. In short, with that marvellous material called bamboo, and with their silk, the Chinese were technically capable of inventing a more or less practical hot-air ship, kept aloft by natural gas stoves and powered by natural gas steam engines, by A.D. 1000 — but this contraption had to wait 850 more years until a European put it all together and clanked through the sky of Paris in 1863.

As for heavier-than-air flight, "airplanes", the Chinese knew the principles of it before the Christian era. And, they had the principles of an efficient steam engine. An aircraft could have been built, and flown under (cumbersome) power, as early as about A.D.1000.

Human intelligence does not necessarily lead to western humanity's drive towards "progress." The Chinese are supposed to have the highest average intelligence of any major human group, and their numerous inventions (let's not forget paper money, printing, movable type, and even the fishing reel) would seem to confirm this. But technological progress is not solely dependent upon what we call intelligence. Another psychological characteristic is even more necessary for "progress." This leads to interesting ideas about the psychology of progress, which I tried to explore in The Iceman Inheritance twenty years ago.

Therefore, there's no reason at all to doubt that Atlanteans might have stumbled on the principles of a spark transmitter, and no compelling reason to assume that they would have refined it further than an Ark-like mechanism. Was the Ark of the Covenant the last surviving example of an old Atlantean transmitter-receiver? Had it been preserved in Egypt out of veneration for an object made by Manetho's gods of 15,000 years before? Did it still work, or had the insulating acacia wood rotted away? Could a stolen, broken-down Ark have been restored to working order by some of Moses' logic, some of his knowledge and a master craftsman working under his instructions? Probably — but what would the Israelite high priests have received as "messages"?

By 1350 B.C. or so, when the Israelites got the Ark (by whatever means), they could have sent spark-arc supplications into the air — but who was there to answer? Manetho's gods were long gone, Atlantis had perished. But it is certain that the electroscope of the receiving cherub's wings would have moved from time to time for no apparent cause in the wind-proof Holy of Holies. It would have responded to lightning strikes all over the world, just as our AM radios sizzle with static "between stations" (frequencies) for exactly the same reason. Indeed, by responding to distant lightning strikes, the Ark would have predicted the eventual approach of some electrical storms — or the nearby presence, and possible closer approach, of "Jehovah."

This was something mostly to be feared, for Jehovah was an angry and unpredictable God. Was the Ark the reason why ancient Israelites finally determined that Jehovah struck with lightning bolts and earned the epithet "cloud-rider"? Was that why Jehovah was called the Lord of heavenly hosts when the thunderheads piled up? Did Moses impress some tribes of ignorant *Hebiru* ("Hebrew" in Egyptian) nomads with his Egyptian knowledge and "reconstruct" an old Atlantean "wireless" apparatus to establish his leadership, his status, his security, and "The Law"?

"The Exodus" of Moses and the Israelites from Egypt is dated to about 1350 B.C. by some experts and closer to 1250 B.C. by others.[16] The subsequent Hebrew conquest of Canaan was not all smooth sailing, and during this period of two or three centuries the Israelites did not have enough territorial security to keep the cherished Ark in any one place. It moved with them on a special wagon that was covered by a tent canopy. In what seems to have been the "final" struggle for Canaan, against the Philistines, who were also powerful in the region, the Ark was even captured by the Philistines. Its electromagnetic properties are demonstrated by this episode because the Ark caused all sorts of illness among the Philistines who were ignorant of the necessary procedures for handling it. Skin tumours (called "emerods" in The Bible) were produced by proximity to the Ark, and also many other symptoms. Some Philistines died, just as some untrained Israelites who touched the Ark also died. Soviet and U.S. studies have recently shown that skin tumours (among other symptoms) can result from exposure to powerful electromagnetic emissions, an occupational hazard of workers on high-tension power transmission lines. After seven months, the Philistines sent the Ark back to the Hebrews.

After the final struggle with the Philistines, the second king of the Hebrews, David (traditionally considered to have been anointed in 1063 B.C.), kept the Ark in Jerusalem, the old Canaanite capital of Jebusi, which the Hebrews had conquered and occupied. David's son, Solomon, consolidated the occupation and apparently considered Jerusalem secure enough to build a Temple to contain and protect the Ark.

Strangely enough, although the Ark of the Covenant was the prized possession of the Israelites, it is last mentioned in the Old Testament by Jeremiah in 628 B.C.

> And it shall come to pass, when ye be multiplied and increased in the land, in those days, saith the Lord, they shall say no more, The Ark of the Covenant of the Lord: neither shall it come to mind: neither shall they remember it; neither shall they visit it; neither shall that be done any more.
> Jeremiah 3:16

Which is to say (in the style of Jeremiah) that, by 628 B.C., the Ark was no longer among the Hebrews in the Temple. Graham Hancock in The Sign and the Seal gives plausible evidence that the Ark disappeared from the Temple during the reign of Manasseh, King of Judah (687–642 B.C.).[17] Hancock then speculates that the Ark was taken to Ethiopia where it was, as of 1992, in the Church of St. Mary of Zion in Axum under the guardianship of one Gebra Mikail, an old priest. Unfortunately for Hancock's controversial speculations, he could not obtain even one photograph of this most awesome artefact of the Judeo-Christian tradition.

Hancock does note, however, Templar-style chapels around Axum. He speculates reasonably that Knights Templar, searching for the Ark, could have journeyed from Jerusalem to Axum during the reign of Ethiopian King Lalibela (A.D. 1185–1211). This was certainly the time of Templar supremacy and the apex of their power. But this leads to another speculation. If they were so powerful (and they were), why didn't the Knights Templar take the Ark back to Jerusalem with them? This, as we shall see, leads to the distinct possibility that the Ark might well have ended up in Rennes-le-Château anyway!

If the Ark of the Covenant had truly disappeared from the Temple at Jerusalem in the time of King Manasseh, then it could not have been looted by Nebuchadnezzar when he sacked the Temple in 587 B.C., nor could it have been looted by Titus when he sacked the rebuilt Temple in A.D. 70. And, indeed, the Ark does not appear to be represented on the Triumphal Arch in Rome.

But it could have come to Rennes-le-Château with retreating Knights Templar who came to Languedoc between A.D. 1187 and 1244 to regroup from their defeat by Saladin in the Holy Land and to gird themselves for the bloody Albigensian Crusade. Therefore, the Ark of the Covenant could be among the buried treasures awaiting discovery around Rennes-le-Château — or, it could have been discovered by Abbé Bérenger Saunière.

A bit later, I'll suggest yet another place where the Ark of the Covenant could still be hidden — along with a lot of other Visigothic and non-Visigothic gold — a tidbit for North American treasure hunters.

This discussion of the Ark of the Covenant shows that although there must be a lot of precious metal buried around Rennes-le-Château, there may also be religious artefacts of priceless value to the more spiritually inclined. Both sets of treasure hunters have gravitated to Rennes-le-Château after the publication of Henry Lincoln's various books and after the television airings of his various documentaries. This is where the Ark of the Covenant begins to blur with the Holy Grail, and also where the story of the Holy Grail begins at Rennes-le-Château.

The Biblical Israelites regarded the Ark of the Covenant as the actual abode of Jehovah. The Ark *was* God's home, one might put it, when Jehovah was in direct contact with earthly affairs and not in his heavenly and more remote domain. Therefore, one might say, the Ark was a vessel that contained divinity. As we shall see, the Holy Grail was also imaged as a sort of vessel that held the Holy Blood. Sometimes, the Holy Grail was conceived as the Cup of the

Last Supper — it, too, had "held" the Holy Blood in two ways, at two separate times.

First (it *could* be said), it had contained the blood of Jesus when Jesus conducted the first communion ("transubstantiation"), instructing the assembled disciples to think of wine as his blood whenever they should drink it, and to regard bread as his flesh whenever they ate it, as a token of a new covenant. This was at the Last Supper.

Later, during the crucifixion, Joseph of Arimathaea held the *same cup* aloft to catch the blood of Christ when a Roman soldier (traditionally the Centurion Gaius Longinius) pierced the side of Jesus with a spear. Therefore, the Cup of the Last Supper was a vessel that "held" the Holy Blood. The Ark of the Covenant was a container that "held" divinity — and, moreover, they were both tokens of covenants between humanity and divinity — so it is not surprising that these two containers were to become associated and confused with each other, and associated and confused with the Holy Grail.

Before leaving the Ark of the Covenant, and the possibility that it may be hidden somewhere around Rennes-le-Château, it is fascinating to consider that an object called Solomon's Jewel Case was actually captured at the Battle of Juan de la Frontera in A.D. 711.[18] This was the battle in which Roderick II, the last Visigothic king in Spain, was defeated by the Berber chieftain, Tarik. Therefore, the Visigoths under Roderick had possessed this object until their defeat and its acquisition by the Moors. Various traditions attach to this object. It is known that the House of "ibn Da'ud" (i.e., the House of David) came into Spain as allies of Tarik. Some traditions say that this object was turned over to its rightful owners by Tarik. But, whether the Moors or the House of David had it, it was carried to the Pyrénées region when the Moors and their allies began to retreat before the Christian so-called "re-conquest" of Spain. This began, more or less, in A.D.1070 with the exploits of Rodrigo (or Ruy) Diaz, Count of Bivar, much better known as El Cid (from the Arabic *Zayyid* = Lord).

The re-conquest went on, technically, until 1492 and the surrender of Grenada, but the outcome was clear two centuries earlier. So, from A.D. 1070 or so until about 1240 (the time of the Albigensian Crusade), this Solomon's Jewel Case was taken to successive havens progressively deeper into the Pyrénées. Some traditions say that, in the end, it was handed over to the Knights

Templar. Some say it was taken out of the Pyrénées to safety. Some say that it was hidden in mountain caves.

Adolf Hitler thought that Solomon's Jewel Case must have been the Ark of the Covenant, and thought also that the Ark was the Holy Grail. He shared this belief with most of the higher Nazis, and their consensus was that "it" had been hidden in a Pyrénées cavern. For Hitler and some of the other high Nazis, the Ark/Grail/Solomon's Jewel Case had been given to the ancestors of the Aryan race, the Hyperboreans, in the distant past as a way of maintaining contact and communication with divinity. The Jews had somehow stolen this treasure, or otherwise came into possession of it, and falsely claimed it as their own.

Hitler had already acquired the so-called "Spear of Destiny" when Germany annexed Austria in 1938 — this was the alleged spear of Gaius Longinius that had reposed in the Hapsburg Museum in Vienna (it was returned to Austria by the U.S. Army in 1946). For what it is worth, from studying the photos of this spearhead it appears to me that it is not a Roman or Hebrew spearhead of the first century. To me, it is rather obviously a spear intended to be thrown from horseback and looks like existing examples of Bulgarian and Turkish weapons more than anything else.

Immediately after getting this spear, Hitler was determined to possess (or, in his view, "re-possess") the Ark of the Covenant. In 1938, Hitler sent Dr. Otto Rahn, a noted medieval scholar, to the Pyrénées in order to search for Solomon's Jewel Case. Otto Rahn was able to survey and target several likely caves, and later, between 1942 and 1944 when the Germans occupied France, Hitler ordered searches of Pyrénées mountains and caves with the latest metal detectors. No one has said whether these searches were successful in finding anything, but Otto Rahn was promoted to the rank of colonel in the S.S. Otto Rahn also wrote a book, *Kreuzzug Gegen den Graal* (*Crusade Against the Grail*) which was required reading for all S.S. recruits.[19]

We may begin to suspect that perspectives like that evident in William L. Shirer's *The Rise and Fall of the Third Reich* are really fairly superficial views of what Nazism and the great struggle of World War II were all about.

There's much to contemplate in the neighbourhood of Rennes-le-Château.

The Joy of Lex

When Henry Lincoln was reading Gérard de Sède's book, it wasn't the tale of Saunière's treasure that intrigued him, but the mysteries associated with the parchments that Saunière also supposedly found about the same time — that is, 1891. Again, unfortunately, there are several versions of the story. Some researchers claim that Bérenger Saunière was actually searching for these parchments, while others (including de Sède) say that the priest came upon them by chance.

A few researchers even claim that Saunière found no parchments at all, that they are forgeries of the 1950s cooked up by Gérard de Sède himself in order to make his story more enigmatic and appealing. Still others agree that the parchments are modern forgeries, but ones presented to an innocent Gérard de Sède, who included them in his mysteries of Rennes-le-Château because he sincerely believed them to be genuine. New evidence, resulting from research associated with this book, indicates with a probability so high it borders on certainty that the parchments *must* date from before 1800.

In any event, these parchments have been included in almost every book about Rennes-le-Château since Gérard de Sède's *Le Trésor Maudit,* and they have stimulated the curiosity and ingenuity of many agile minds, including Henry Lincoln's. They are certainly intriguing. I think it is worth mentioning that a researcher friend of mine, writer Winnie Czulinski of Toronto, was able to locate an English-language account of the Rennes-le-Château mystery that includes a reproduction of infamous "Parchment No. 2" actually predating Henry Lincoln's BBC documentaries and any published work by Michael Baigent, Richard Leigh, and Henry Lincoln. This account is contained in *Hidden Treasures* by Vezio Melegari.

Four parchments were allegedly found by Bérenger Saunière in the old Visigothic pillars, which proved to be hollow, that had supported the altar of his church dedicated to Mary Magdalene in Rennes-le-Château. Two parchments were genealogies. One genealogy traces a family bloodline up to A.D. 1244, the other traces the bloodline up to 1644 — the most probable date when these genealogies were prepared. These genealogies are certainly relevant to the Holy Grail story, but more recent and more scientific genealogical research has partly verified, absorbed, and superseded the importance of these two pages of genealogies. Therefore, these documents do not concern us further.

The other two parchments were inscribed with coded messages. The story goes that Bérenger Saunière recognized the importance of these encoded documents and took them to his immediate church superior, the Bishop of Carcassonne. The bishop saw their importance, too (or Saunière explained it to him), and Saunière was instructed to take them to the Seminary of St. Sulpice in Paris.

Bérenger Saunière spent some time in Paris after presumably handing the parchments over to the seminary. Gérard de Sède wrote that before he returned to Rennes-le-Château, Saunière bought prints of three paintings from the Louvre Museum: a print of Nicolas Poussin's *The Shepherds of Arcadia*, a print of *St. Anthony Hermit* by David Teniers, and a portrait of Pope Celestine V by an unknown artist. Saunière apparently made these purchases because of an enciphered clue in one of the coded parchments (Parchment No. 2). There's a problem here. To my knowledge, almost nothing is known about what Saunière did in Paris in 1891 except that he went there to take the parchments to the Seminary of St. Sulpice.

What evidence or documents prompted de Sède to assert that Bérenger Saunière bought prints from the Louvre? If any evidence or document exists, I'm not aware of it, and I've read a lot about Rennes-le-Château. Maybe I just missed the evidence, but I rather think that Gérard de Sède was just dropping one more coy clue that he acquired from his secret source. By referring to these paintings, a completely new mystery of Rennes-le-Château was brought to light. I think this was done purposefully in order to intrigue a whole new set of researchers, those interested in art, and thus expand the circle of intrigue beyond treasure hunting and spirituality. As we shall see, this was Gérard de Sède's job.

If we take Gérard de Sède's bait, we immediately run into a perplexing difficulty. There were *two* David Teniers, father and son, both famous painters. David Teniers "the Elder" (1582–1649) and "the Younger" (1610–90) *both* painted pictures of St. Anthony (251?–356), an Egyptian hermit who is credited with starting the monastic tradition. Indeed, the Teniers seemed obsessed with St. Anthony, a man who fled into the desert to escape worldly temptations and thus caused the devil the inconvenience of following him there in order to personally provide some. They painted many "St. Anthonys" and, to make matters worse, the early work of "the Younger" was so similar to his father's style that even art experts have difficulty in distinguishing what was painted by whom. Which "St. Anthony" painting by which Teniers offers a hint of the treasure's nature and location?

An encoded clue in Parchment No. 2 is the phrase "no temptation." The only "Teniers" (the Younger) painting of St. Anthony that does *not* depict the devil tempting the saint is *St. Anthony and St. Paul.*

St. Anthony and St. Paul painted by David Teniers the Younger.

But this painting has never been in the Louvre Museum. This work had once been in the collection of the second Lord Palmerston at his family seat of Broadlands. It is listed in the Broadlands inventory of 1791. It was bought by Edwina Ashley, Countess Mountbatten, in 1942, and is now in the Ashmolean Museum at Oxford. Therefore, according to the "no temptation" clue in Parchment No. 2, which Saunière himself had allegedly found, Bérenger Saunière got a copy of the wrong painting from the Louvre in Paris — and yet he very soon started spending millions of dollars.[20]

This leads to interesting speculations, the most obvious one being that *all* "St. Anthony" paintings by the two Teniers contain some information, and that "no temptation" refers to something else. We will see that this seems to be the truth. As the authors of *The Tomb of God* put it: "There seems to have been a surprising demand for paintings depicting *The Temptation of St. Anthony,* for Teniers was to produce a large number of them. Five major art galleries have examples, while the number in private collection is not known. The Louvre has two."[21]

Perhaps it didn't matter *which* Teniers painting Saunière got a copy of. But this leads to the astounding corollary speculation that, before the days of mass media, some organization had the power and resources to commission *code paintings* by artists as famous as the Teniers and Nicolas Poussin. This would make a mockery of much so-called art history and interpretation by so-called experts of it. The name of this organization was, and is, the Priory of Sion.

The fact of the matter (so far as facts are known) is that Saunière did not start to spend any inordinate sums of money until he returned from this Paris trip. And, since there is no proof that Saunière found any treasure, Visigothic or otherwise, some researchers have speculated that these parchments were of immense importance to someone. This theory suggests that Berenger Saunière stumbled onto a momentous secret that had previously been known only to a chosen few. It was the secret of the Holy Grail. Both the Vatican, which the secret threatened above all, and "Grail supporters" wanted the secret suppressed. The Vatican wanted it suppressed forever, and had tried hard to do so. But even "Grail supporters" wanted it suppressed for the moment, until the time was ripe for revelation. There is, naturally, no proof for this theory...but there *is* some evidence to lend it support.

In this scenario, then, Bérenger Saunière was paid great amounts of money to keep the secret to himself. Either the Vatican paid him, or he was paid off by the "Priory of Sion" — that wealthy and super-secret underground of Grail-related royalty, nobility, business interests, Rosicrucians, Illuminati, and Freemasons. Or he contrived some way to get paid by both and remain alive.

Dozens of serious books about Rennes-le-Château and the Holy Grail have dealt with these parchments, particularly Parchment No. 2, in excruciating detail and also with mind-numbing displays of cleverness. There is no need to do the same, even if I were capable of it. But some idea of the hidden parchment ciphers must be given for three reasons.

First, coded messages contained in the parchments started researchers on the trail of the Grail. And so, if the following tale of the Grail is to become credible to readers who are encountering the story for the first time in this book, some idea of the amazing ingenuity devoted to the preservation and communication of the secret must be demonstrated. The care with which the secret was preserved and communicated shows that some people believed the Grail to be of immense importance to western humanity. They may have been misguided in their beliefs, perhaps, but their commitment cannot be in doubt once the ciphers are confronted.

Second, I think it can be shown that many researchers have been "too clever" — enchanted with their own and the ciphers' ingenuity — and have therefore been led down some irrelevant (but charming) garden paths of ego-gratifying self-delusion. Personally, I feel that this is yet another kind of safeguard for the Grail secret. It screens out people who can't see the woods for the trees, and whose appreciation of their own cleverness reflects an imbalance of ego development. This over-valuation of "self" makes such people dangerous to the Grail, ultimately dismissive and destructive of Grail principles and Grail ethics.

Third, for those who like "The Joy of Lex" — word games — the parchments are more challenging than any crossword puzzle.

My problem in recounting some of the intrigue attached to the parchments is that, although I profess to be a writer, I've never been good at word games and am bored by them. For me, words should convey meaning. They should not be a medium for demonstrating a certain kind of intelligence that is often (in my view) mere vacuous cleverness. I don't bother with crosswords and have seldom even played Scrabble (and have never won). I can smile at simple lexual joys on the level of palindromes (a word, phrase or sentence that reads the same backwards as forwards) like, for example, the way Adam might have introduced himself to Eve: "Madam, I'm Adam."

I can appreciate the cleverness of a more complex palindrome, like this one spuriously attributed to Napoleon: "Able was I ere I saw Elba." But truly masterly palindromes, like this one by writer Leigh Mercer — "A man, a plan, a canal - Panama!" — fill me with helpless admiration for a type of intellect I never want to share.[22]

The Rennes-le-Château parchments are infinitely more complex than the creation of amusing palindromes. Some readers will no doubt enjoy the sheer lexographic virtuosity of these ciphers, but other readers are invited to skip directly to the next chapter.

Both Rennes-le-Château parchments are reproduced here, but we will concern ourselves primarily with Parchment No. 2. Readers who are interested in all the coded messages in these two documents are referred to any of the many books dealing with them.

The easiest encoded message, and the one that led researchers on the first stumbling steps towards the meaning of the Holy Grail, can be found by placing a straight edge under the lines of this inscription. Some letters are raised above the others.

ᵐ
V ÉTFACTVMESTEVMIN
SABBATOSECVNdøPRIMO À
bIREPERSCCETESdIBGIPVLIAVTEMILLTRISCOE
PERVNTVELLERESPICASETFRICANTESMANTbVS + MANdV
CAbANTqVIdAMAVTEMdEFARISAEISAT
CEbANTEIECCEqVIAFACIVNTdISCIPVLITVISAb
bATIS + qVOdNONLICETRESPONdENSAVTEMINS
SETXTTAdEOSNVMqVAMbOC
LECISTISqVOdFECITdAVTdqVANdO
ESVRVTIPSEETqVICVMEOERAI + INTROIbITINdÚMVM
dEIETPANESPROPOSITIONIS   REdIS
MANdVCAVITETdEdITETqVI   bLES
CVMERANTVXÙ̃ qVIbVSNO
NLICEbATMANdVCARESINON   SOLIS SACERdOTIbVS

℗ 𝒮

Parchment One

Parchment I, allegedly discovered in the church of Rennes-le-Château.

⚜

JESVSCVRGOANTCESCXdTPESPASCShAEVENJTThEThqANTAMVRAT
JVERAOTIAZA▪VVSMORTYVVSqVCMMSVSCTYTAVITIYÉSVSFÉdCCRVNT
LAVIEM▪TTCAENAPMTbTCTOMARThAhMINISTRRAbATChASARVSO
VCROVNXVSERATTE▪dTSCOVMLENTdTLVSCVJMMARTALERGOAChCEP
TILKTbRAMYNNGENTTJNARATPFTJTICIqPRETTOVSTETVNEXTTPE
dPCSTERVAETEXTEJRSTTCAYPTIRTJNJVIJPCPdCSCRTPTETdOMbESTM
PLFTIAESTEEXVNGETNTTOdAEREdIXALTERGOVRNVMEXdGTSCTPVhL
TJETVTXTVddXⱱ₅CARJORTISqVIYERATCVhMTRAdTTTVRVSqTVARЕhOᶜCVN
hENVIVMNONXVENV̈TTGRECENPdTSdENAARV̈SETAdATVMESGTE
GENTÉS? dIXTNVFCMhOÉᶜNONqVSTAdEEGAENTSPERRTINEbÉAT
AdᶜVTMSEdqVhInFVRЕLRTÇTLOVᶜVIOShᶜAhENSECAqVAᶜMVTITEbA
NMTVRPOTRAbETEdTXTTCJRGOTᶜShV̷SSTNᶜPTLLAMVNTTXdltεᵐS
ᶜPVLGTVRAЕMSЕᶜASᶜERVNЕTILLqVdPAVPJERESENhTMSЕMPGERhA
hᶜMTTSNObLTTSᶜVMFMᶜAVTᶜTMNONSESMPERhAⱱhЕTⁱSᶜJOGNO
VILIEROTZVRhAMVqLTAᶜXTMVdAᶜTSTqVTATIOLTCЕSTXETⱱᶜNE
ARVNTNONNPROTEPRTESVᵐETANTⱱMMSEdVTLVZARⱱMPVTdER
Éh▪TqVCMKSVSCTAOVITAMORRTVTSᶜPOGTTAVKERVNTAhVTᶜMP
RVTNᶜTPEJSSAᶜЕRᶜdOTVMVMTETLAZᶜARVMTNATᶜRFTᶜTⁱRENTq
LVTAMYLVTTPROPqTᶜRILhXVMAhTbGNTᶜXVGTAₐᶜTSNᶜTᶜRᶜd
dᶜbANTⁱⁱⁿTᶜSVM

                         Ñ
                    NO ₽ IS
                         V

JÉSV. MᶜdÉLA . V̈VLNÉRVM ✟ SPᶜS.VNA. PŒNITENTIVM.
PᶜR. MAGdALÄNA . LAᶜRYMAS ✟ PᶜᶜᶜATA. NOSTRA . dILVAS.

⚜

Parchment II, allegedly discovered in the church of Rennes-le-Château.

Line one: no raised letters
Line two: a,d,a
Line three: g,o
Line four: b,
Line five: e,r,t
Line six:l,l
Line seven:r,o,i
Line eight:e,t,a
Line nine: s,i,o,n
Line ten:e,s,t,c,e,t,r
Line eleven:e,s,o,r
Line twelve:e,t,l,l,e,s
Line thirteen:t
Line fourteen:l,a,m,o,r,t

This reads in French: *"a Dagobert II, roi, et a Sion est ce Trésor et il est la mort."* In English: "To Dagobert II, king, and to Zion (or 'Sion') is this treasure and he is there dead."

This text could not incorporate the accents of French, and so there is a possible alternative rendering which is very slightly different. The second-last word — *la* — seems intended to have a missing *accent grave* to mean "there." But it could be intended as the definite article of the feminine word *la mort* — "death." In this case the inscription would read:

To Dagobert II, king, and to Zion is this treasure and it is death.

This, to me, seems altogether more dramatic and satisfying, but it is probably wrong — at least, according to Henry Lincoln. He notes that the preferred way of saying "it is death" in French, would be *"c'est la mort."* That is true, but I think, in this case, the encipherer has left a clue to tell us that "it is death" is meant. Notice that only one letter (*t*) is indicated on line 13, and that "la mort" is spelled out in line 14. There was no obvious reason to do this, however. Line 13 contains plenty of *l*s, *a*s and *m*s. Part of *la mort* could have been indicated on line 13 very easily. But the word *mort* with its feminine article *la* were all placed on line 14. Since the text is Latin, without opportunity for accents, the code-maker may have chosen this way of showing that the *la* goes with the *mort*. But most probably ambiguity was purposefully conveyed by putting *la mort* on one line, while not absolutely differentiating the *la*s — meaning that the message is to be read either way, and *both* ways. There are good historical reasons for thinking so, as we shall see.

But this is just a quibble with Lincoln's rendering. It doesn't matter much. The general meaning is pretty clear.

Here Lies the Noble M

And now we come to the notorious, infamous monuments to Marie de Blanchefort in the cemetery of Rennes-le-Château's church. There's a vertical headstone with a pointed top, and a horizontal, rectangular slab at ground level over the grave itself. Here's the inscription on the vertical headstone:

The vertical headstone on the grave of Marie de Blanchefort at Rennes-le-Château.

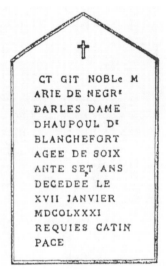

CT GIT NOBLe M
ARIE DE NEGRᵉ
DARLES DAME
DHAUPOUL Dᵉ
BLANCHEFORT
AGEE DE SOIX
ANTE SEPT ANS
DECEDEE LE
XVII JANVIER
MDCOLXXXI
REQUIES CATIN
PACE

The horizontal slab above the grave of Marie de Blanchefort at Rennes-le-Château.

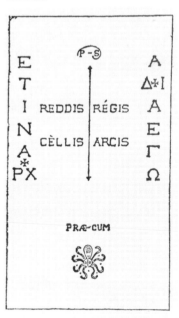

And here is the inscription on the horizontal grave slab.

These churchyard inscriptions have a great deal to do with the parchments, and particularly with Parchment No. 2. The encoded message we have just extracted with a ruler is of Boy Scout simplicity (as Henry Lincoln put it) compared to what follows. There is a *second* enciphered message in the text of Parchment No. 2, *and the key to it is hidden within the inscriptions on the* cemetery monuments of Marie de Blanchefort's grave. Gérard de Sède first published the text of the parchments and the grave monuments in Le Trésor Maudit, and how he was able to do so is a mystery in itself.

Remember, the parchments had allegedly been turned over to the Seminary of Saint Sulpice, in Paris, in the year 1891. Further, by the 1950s when Gérard de Sède was writing, the all-important inscription on the vertical headstone had been effaced. So how did Gérard de Sède know about the parchments and the cemetery inscriptions?

Gérard de Sède claimed that he had got the grave inscriptions from a book called Pierres Gravées de Languedoc (Inscribed Stones of Languedoc) by Eugene Stublein. Unfortunately for Gérard de Sède's claims, this book never existed — at least, no copy of it has ever been found. Researchers have discovered, however, that the cemetery inscriptions were recorded in an exceedingly obscure paper — "Excursion du 25 Juin 1905, à Rennes-le-Château" (Visit to Rennes-le-Château of June 25th, 1905") — by E. Tisseyre and published by the Society for Scientific Studies of the Aude Region (Société d'Étude Scientifique de l'Aude) in 1906. This article, from a regional historical society's sporadic newsletter, is so obscure that it took researchers years to come upon it. It is exceedingly doubtful that Gérard de Sède ever saw it.[23]

As for the two encoded parchments, de Sède neglects to tell readers of Le Trésor Maudit how he learned about them. He reproduced them in his book, and he even gave the solution to the encoded message, but he didn't explain how. As Henry Lincoln and subsequent researchers gradually delved into the mysteries of Rennes-le-Château, Bérenger Saunière, and Gérard de Sède, they were naturally led to the Bibliothèque Nationale in Paris, France's official archives. There, they came upon recently deposited snippets of information about Rennes-le-Château, Saunière, de Sède, and other topics that led them on and on — bit by tantalizing bit — to the meaning of the Holy Grail.

These clues in the Bibliothèque Nationale had obviously been deposited recently, for the most part, because of internal references dating after World War II, but some of the snippets came (neatly typeset) from publications that never existed. Most of them were on microfiche, all right, but lacked the standard, required catalogue data. This could only mean that the enigmatic clues had been placed in the national library by some organization with infiltrators

in the Bibliothèque and the French Ministry of Culture. The reason
why an organization seemed probable, and not just one or two
persons, was that there were hundreds of curious items that were
relevant, many typeset, and it seemed unreasonable that just one or
two people could account for it all. There may still be many
undiscovered documents relating to the various mysteries.

Researchers gradually came to call these tantalizing snippets the
"dossiers secrets" (secret files). And, inevitably, these *dossiers*
introduced researchers to a secret organization called the Priory of
Sion. Apparently, this secret society has been in existence for at
least a thousand years. It quickly became obvious, too, that Gérard
de Sède had close contacts with the Priory of Sion. It began to seem
clear that Gérard de Sède had been chosen by this organization as a
mouthpiece. His job was to start leaking information, in a slow,
regulated, and deliciously teasing way, for the very purpose of
whetting curiosity to the point of frantic obsession among writers,
researchers, and media people.

His books *Le Trésor Maudit* and *La Race Fabuleuse* first initiated
the long and tortuous process of introducing the public to the Holy
Grail. There cannot be much doubt that the Priory of Sion had
given Gérard de Sède access to the Rennes-le-Château parchments
and had given him the solution to some of the ciphers in order to
get the ball rolling. Through his contact with Gérard de Sède,
Henry Lincoln (and his later collaborators) managed to have several
meetings with a man who claimed to be, and seemed to be, the
then-current head of the Priory of Sion. His name was Pierre
Plantard de Saint-Clair (i.e., "Sinclair").

Going back to Parchment No. 2, and before getting into its
second encoded message, it is interesting to note that "Sion" is
written upside down just below the main body of text. The word is
incorporated into a curious "arrow" that points down to the two
lines at the bottom. The word "Sion" appears, *in a geometric code*, on
Parchment No. 1 (the reader is referred to almost any book about
Rennes-le-Château — *The Holy Place*, by Henry Lincoln, for
instance). This word "Sion" appears in the parchments (No. 1)
along with a curious symbol that looks like "P S" with a line curving
over the two letters. It also appears at the top of the grave slab of
Marie de Blanchefort.

The fact that this "P S" symbol turns up on both the grave slab
and Parchment No. 1 is one indication that Gérard de Sède did not
concoct the parchments, nor could the mysterious people who

claimed to represent the Priory of Sion in the 1970s have *wholly* concocted them. Remember, the grave slab was copied on June 25, 1905. The "P S" symbol (with the curved line) was in existence then, and was described by E. Tisseyre as being noticeably weathered at that time. This symbol is on Parchment No. 1, and the word "Sion" appears on Parchment No. 1 in code; "Sion" appears on Parchment No. 2. This does not absolutely date Parchment No. 2 before 1905, but at least suggests (because of the "Sion" on both parchments) that it is legitimately associated with the grave slab and Parchment No. 1.

While we're focused on this grave slab is the time to glance at the two vertical lines of the inscription. The left-hand side of the inscription reads, from top to bottom: "ET IN ARC." The right-hand side reads, from top to bottom: "ADIA EGO." If some readers finds this impossible to make out, it is because some of the letters are Latin and some are Greek. Some letters are the same in Latin and Greek, but some are not. A is common to both alphabets, for instance. A cross symbol (a *Templar* cross) marks out where the Greek letters begin at the bottom of the left-hand inscription. Another cross signifies the end of the word "Arcadi" — which is the French pronunciation of "Arcadie" ("Acadie," etc.) — Arcadia of ancient Greek myth, as Marie de Blanchefort would have pronounced it, but also the French name for Nova Scotia during most of her lifetime.

This second cross on the right-hand side also sets off the last four letters. This is the letter A in Greek or Latin, and the three letters spelling EGO in Greek letters, but it has the effect of having the last four letters start with A (*Alpha* in Greek) and end with *Omega*, the last letter of the Greek alphabet. Jesus said, "I am the alpha and the omega," meaning "I am the beginning and the end" — all that anyone needs to believe in, or understand. The letters *Alpha* and *Omega* also occur significantly in the complex cipher of Parchment No. 2 and therefore reinforce the legitimate association of that parchment with this grave slab and with Parchment No. 1.

In this inscription, we encounter the same phrase we met in Chapter 1. *Et In Arcadia Ego*. It is entirely appropriate that all of the word "Arcadia" is in Greek (remember, *A* is common to both alphabets) because Arcadia was, literally, *in Greece*! But this also draws attention to "Arcadi", and to Jesus with the *Alpha and Omega*.

This inscription on Marie de Blanchefort's grave slab is headed (left) by E and (right) by A. EA, reversed from the AE on Iotigolo's tombstone we discovered in Pennsylvania. In Marie de Blanchefort's case, this EA very obviously heads the phrase "Et in Arcadia Ego." Iotigolo's case is more ambiguous if, as I think, AE also stands for this longer phrase. AE would stand for "Arcadia Ego," and Marie's EA would stand for "Ego Arcadia."

But both mean precisely the same thing: "I am Arcadia." *And in both cases, this is literally true.* In being dead, both Marie and Iotigolo have become the substance of Arcadia. They have become "dust" or "earth" and are now part of humanity's first and enduring home, Arcadia (according to Greek tradition and myth). That's why I think that Iotigolo's AE, and other enigmatic AEs, stand for *Et in Arcadia Ego*.

But there is another indication that Iotigolo's tombstone in Pennsylvania is linked to Marie de Blanchefort's grave in southern France, and that both are linked to the Priory of Sion. At the top of Marie's slab is that P S with the curved line over the letters. Look at Iotigolo's tombstone from Pennsylvania. On it, a curved line connects the *g* (written like a 9 or a backwards *P* with a reversed *S*. What we see is a reversed P S connected with a curved line — very similar to the symbol on top of Marie de Blanchefort's grave slab.

Bearing in mind that Iotigolo's companions may not have had the right tools for cutting an inscription, and bearing in mind that they may have been rushed for time, they had to use the briefest possible inscription. They had to make letters do double-duty. They had a backwards *P* in the form of Iotigolo's runic G, but there was no *S* in his name or in the AE. So, they supplied that one letter, *S*, *backwards* and joined it to their backwards *P* as best they could with a curved line. They interfered as little as possible with Iotigolo's name while yet showing that the backwards *P* went with the backwards *S*. In short, they indicated P S, with the curved line joining these letters, as best they could under the circumstances.

This P S is, of course, the Priory of Sion. I think that the curved line is "over" those in the service of the Priory of Sion, like an umbrella protects those under it.

Soon, we will learn when the Priory of Sion was founded, who founded it...and why. And if the inscription on Iotigolo's stone seems a bit "iffy" and problematical to some readers at this point, the meaning of the AE and the reversed PS will, I think, become increasingly understandable within a few more pages.

If we shift our focus from the grave slab to Marie de Blanchefort's headstone, we will see that the inscription is very odd indeed. There are a number of mistakes in spelling and unlikely mistakes in the general layout. Some people have attributed these to the fact that the stonemason who inscribed the monument must have been illiterate and careless. Plenty of stonemasons *were* illiterate, but few were careless. Their skill consisted of copying out an inscription, written by some educated person (usually a priest), and in spacing the words and letters accurately. That, indeed, was the monument maker's most important job, and it did not matter that he might well not be able to read what he had carved. Marie de Blanchefort was a very noble lady, mistress of Chateau de Blanchefort just a couple of miles from Rennes-le-Château, with a proud lineage that went back to Bertrand de Blanchefort, a Master of the Knights Templar. Clumsy mistakes on *her* headstone would not have been tolerated.

There are eight glaring mistakes:

1. CI GIT ("here lies") has been written CT GIT — an anomalous *T*.
2. The last letter of NOBLE is a small, round *e* — an anomalous *e*.
3. The M of MARIE has been separated — an anomalous M
4. The *E* of NEGRE is smaller than the other letters — an anomalous *e*
5. DARLES should be DABLES — an anomalous *R*
6. The last letter of line four is another small *e* — an anomalous *e*
7. Line seven, the *P* of SEPT has been dropped below, is small — an anomalous *p*
8. In the Roman-style date, an O replaces the proper second C — an anomalous O

It is also of interest, although it is not part of the cipher, that the Latin phrase REQUIESCAT IN PACE ("Rest in Peace") is insultingly broken, and incorrectly broken. It leaves the eleventh line reading: REQUIES CATIN. *Catin* is the French word for whore. And, as Henry Lincoln points out, this is surely an intolerable mistake for the headstone of a noble lady's grave. The stone carver would have been fired (or worse, in 1781) and a new stone would have been made. Lincoln notes the fact that this word *catin*/whore does draw attention to Mary Magdalene who, by tradition but not Scripture, was supposed to have been a prostitute.

But Lincoln *doesn't* point out that this inscription *does* make sense — after a fashion. REQUIES CATIN PACE reads (more or less) in Latin: "Be requieted, Whore! Peace." — as if the headstone were that of Mary Magdalene herself, whose long slander had been avenged. But this is the headstone of Marie de Blanchefort. Was Marie de Blanchefort, who died in 1781, a descendant of Mary Magdalene? As we shall see, the answer appears to be yes. In a very real sense, then, this headstone in the churchyard of Rennes-le-Château is a monument for both women.

Eight glaring anomalies have been identified in the inscription of this headstone.

Four of these oddities involve capital letters, and these letters spell out one word, *and one word only*, in French: MORT — DEAD. There's no ambiguity. Likewise, the other four curious mistakes involve small letters. And they, too, spell out one word, *and one word only*, in French: *épée* — sword. Again, there's no possible ambiguity. *Someone* chose two words, in French, that have no anagrams (i.e., "a word that can be formed by transposing the letters of another word.")

The block of text above the two separated lines in Parchment No. 2 is the Latin "Vulgate" rendering of the Gospel of John, Chapter XII, verses 1–11. This is about the visit of Jesus to the house of Lazarus, in Bethany, where Mary Magdalene anointed his feet with oil and wiped them with her hair. However, there are 140 extra letters scattered throughout this text that don't belong in the passage. These "extra" letters indicate the encoded message.

Gérard de Sède supplied a solution to this cipher. It is:

> BERGERE PAS DE TENTATION QUE
> POUSSIN TENIERS GARDENT LA CLEF
> PAX DCLXXXI PAR LA CROIX ET CE
> CHEVAL DE DIEU J'ACHEVE CE
> DAEMON DE GARDIEN A MIDI POMMES
> BLEUES.

> SHEPHERDESS NO TEMPTATION THAT
> POUSSIN TENIERS HOLD THE KEY
> PEACE 681 BY THE CROSS AND THIS
> HORSE OF GOD I COMPLETE (or "destroy")
> THIS DAEMON GUARDIAN AT NOON
> BLUE APPLES.

This deciphered message turns out to be a perfect anagram of the inscription on Marie de Blanchefort's headstone, plus PS PRAECUM on her grave slab, thus apparently confirming beyond reasonable doubt that her cemetery monuments supply the correct key for the extra- letter code in Parchment No. 2.

Gérard de Sède later revealed to Henry Lincoln (and Lincoln's later collaborators) exactly *how* the cipher had been broken. Gérard de Sède claimed that it had been done with the assistance of French military cryptanalysts with the aid of code-breaking computers. The steps of this decipherment involve mind-boggling complexity and are detailed in Henry Lincoln's *The Holy Place* . Readers who thrill to the joys of lex are invited to try it. The "extra" 140 letters in Parchment No. 2 are (in the order they occur in the text):

V C P S J Q R O
V Y M Y Y D L T
P o h R B O X T
O D J L B K N J
F Q U E P A J Y
N P P B F E I E
L R G H I I R Y
B T T C V x G D
A D G E N E S A R E T H
L U C C V M T E
J H P N P G S V
Q J H G M L F T
S V J L Z Q M T
O X A N P E M U
P H K O R P K H
V J C M C A T L
V Q X G G N D T

Opposite from the "Dagobert" message of *raised* letters, some of these extra letters are *lowered* beneath the general lines of the text. A lowered *Alpha* and *Omega* ("the begining and the end") indicate, in a complex way, that the middle twelve letters ADGENESARETH are to be dropped. In Latin, these letters spell out "AD GENESARETH" — "to Genesareth." (Lake Genesareth, "Lake Tiberias"— or the Sea of Galilee). This is another way of saying "Dump these 12 letters into the sea." There's another meaning in this. The Sea of Galilee is very salty and therefore bitter. So the instructions may mean "Add these letters to the reservoir of bitterness," or something of that sort. When ADGENESARETH is removed, the remaining 128 letters resolve themselves into two groups of 64 letters that are separated by the rejected AD GENESARETH. These 128 letters are the ones of the code in the Parchment.

Step 1. Shift each letter according to a Vigenère Table using the "MORTépée" key word extracted from Marie de Blanchefort's headstone. A Vigenère Table was a standard way of making encoded messages between 1550 and 1850. It is just the letters of the alphabet re-arranged 26 times by successive 1-letter shifts.

The idea is to write out the "key word" above the code letters, and then to shift each code letter to the appropriate Vigenère alphabet indicated by the key word. We'll do this for the first 16 code letters, to give the idea. First, we write out the key word above the code letters.

m o r t é p é e m o r t é p é e

V C P S J Q R O V Y M Y Y D L T

The first code letter, V, is to be changed according to Vigenère's "M alphabet" — this V therefore becomes an I. The second code letter, C, is to be changed according to the Vigenère Table's "O alphabet" and so becomes a Q. And so on. And on.

Encoded messages from the period A.D. 1550–1850 were usually unravelled by just one application of the Vigenère Table according to a key word. This key word protected the secret of the message. Conspirators knew the key word — although this word itself might change according to some pre-arranged schedule. It might be "MORTÉPÉE" in the month of May, for example, but might be different for every other month. Or the key word might be MORTÉPÉE in 1791 and years ending in an odd number, but be another word for even-numbered years.

But, with *this* cipher, one application of the Vigenère Table produces a garbled mess.

Step 2. Take the garbled mess and substitute each letter for the one that *follows* it in the normal alphabet. This also produces a mess.

Step 3. Take these scrambled letters and apply the Vigenère Table again — but use the entire text of Marie de Blanchefort's headstone, add PS PRAECUM on the grave slab (to make up 128 letters for this long, long "key word") to the headstone inscription. Now reverse the order of these 128 letters! This is the new key word. This produces nothing readable.

Step 4. Another one-letter shift down the alphabet. This produces yet another mess.

Step 5. The first 64 letters are laid out in a chessboard pattern from left to right, starting at the top. The second set of 64 letters is laid out in a chessboard pattern the same way.

Step 6. A chess knight's tour around the first square, starting on f6, touching each square only once. A knight's tour around the second square, inverted from the tour on the first square! This produces:

BERGERE PAS DE TENTATION QUE POUSSIN TENIERS GARDENT LA CLEF... and so on. The message deciphered! At last.

Gérard de Sède revealed these steps to Lincoln, including the all-important rejection of the ADGENESARETH before even starting. There is no doubt that "SHEPHERDESS NO TEMPTATION THAT POUSSIN TENIERS HOLD THE KEY, etc.", is the correct solution. It was presented on BBC television in graphically animated steps. Many people who like crossword puzzles and other word games have also extracted it from the text of Parchment No. 2 by following Gérard de Sède's, and the BBC's, process.

The message says that "Poussin Teniers hold the key." This immediately sent researchers to Poussin's *The Shepherds of Arcadia* painting, created between 1640 and 1642, in which the phrase "Et in Arcadia Ego" is depicted as being inscribed on the tomb. Researchers then discovered that Poussin had earlier painted a very similar work actually titled *Et in Arcadia Ego*. It didn't take long for researchers to find out that an Italian painter, known as Il Guercino, had also created a work involving shepherds around a tomb, a skull resting on the tomb (with a bee on the skull), and the familiar phrase "Et in Arcadia Ego" depicted as being inscribed on the tomb.

Paintings by the Teniers were examined, too, and curious things were found in them. In *St. Anthony and St. Paul*, for example, the rock that does service as the hermit's table is five-sided. Joelle Lauriol brought this to my attention and, of course, this must call to mind the Rennes-le-Château pentagon. There's a *skull* unaccountably resting on this rock table in front of a crucifix (which might be expected of Christian saints), and it connects this Teniers painting with the "Et In Arcadia Ego" series by Poussin and Guercino.

If all these convoluted clues are pointing towards a treasure of some sort, *St. Anthony and St. Paul* may give us a hint of what it is. At the base of the rock table, which is to say *below the surface* of the table, some open books are leaning (Joelle Lauriol, again). Does this mean that the treasure consists of *records*, and not necessarily of Visigothic gold? Is the treasure that belongs to "Dagobert II, king, and to Zion" a record of some sort? The parchments were allegedly discovered along with two pages of genealogies. Were these genealogies the record that is the treasure?

By now, hundreds of books have been written and published about Rennes-le-Château and the numerous aspects of the mystery associated with Bérenger Saunière's sudden and immense wealth. The Rennes-le-Château pentagon and the past history of the region have fascinated people who are primarily interested in archaeology, history, and prehisory. The parchments and Marie de Blanchefort's cemetery monuments have fascinated people who are primarily interested in the Joy of Lex. The various paintings that are somehow involved in the mystery have fascinated people who are primarily interested in art and art history. Treasure fascinates almost everybody. The reason why the enigmas of Rennes-le-Château have become a growth industry for publishers and film producers is simply that one aspect or another hooks almost everyone.

But people primarily obsessed with one or two specific components of the mystery are apt to forget that *everything* associated with it leads, eventually, to the story of the Holy Grail. You can approach it by word games, and it leads to the Grail. You can approach it through art, and it leads to the Grail. You can approach it with gold lust, and it leads to the Grail. You can approach it because of an interest in the history of Rennes-le-Château and the surrounding area — and it leads to the Grail.

Before telling the story of the Holy Grail as briefly as possible, I would like to make an observation about Parchment No. 2 and that too-complex cipher that supposedly led Bérenger Saunière to his money.

The oh-so-clever code is irrelevant.

Yes, it does exist in Parchment No. 2, all right. And there's good reason for thinking that most of Parchment No. 2 is genuinely "old" and may (or may not) have been found by Bérenger Saunière. We have only Gérard de Sède's word for this. But there are excellent reasons for supposing that this highly complex cipher was *inserted* into the original "genuine" text by some clever lexophile during the early 1960s, someone who was familiar with the text of Marie de Blanchefort's cemetery monuments from E. Tisseyre's obscure paper. *This cipher did not exist in Bérenger Saunière's time.* And, furthermore, he didn't need to "solve" it in order to find his valuable *something*.

The value, and purpose, of this cipher during the 1960s was simply to captivate minds like Henry Lincoln's, a man whose "mindset" ensured close contacts with similar "intellectualism" within the BBC of that time, in order to keep them enamoured of the mystery. That way, the mystery of Bérenger Saunière and Rennes-le-Château would reach a much wider audience, since English is the dominant language of today's western world. Also, of course, the references to Poussin and the Teniers would immediately widen the net of intrigue and interest to ensnare people who were primarily interested in art and art history, a small but moneyed and influential segment of modern society.

The effort required to decode *that* ridiculous and ambiguous message is, simply, a tidbit for clever lexophiles in order to keep them hooked. Such people's evaluation of their own intelligence would protect them from the suspicion that the oh-so-complex code was mere bait to lead them on to discoveries and revelations that might mean something to other people who didn't revel in cleverness.

Pierre Plantard de Saint-Clair, the supposed and apparent head of the Priory of Sion when Henry Lincoln met him (through Gérard de Sède), implied much of this when he said that the cipher of Parchment No. 2 was merely a "confection" prepared in the 1950s by Philippe de Chérisey, "who was present when this statement was made," according to Henry Lincoln. And then Henry Lincoln wrote: "Later, M. Plantard qualified this statement. 'Dr Chérisey's confections,' he said, 'were based on very good originals'." What does this mean? It seems clear enough. Philippe de Chérisey (who must have been a dedicated lexophile) concocted a delicious cipher confection within the text of a genuinely old parchment. Gérard de Sède only got "copies" of the parchments found by Bérenger Saunière, and he had no way of knowing whether they had been "doctored."

In the 1950s and early 1960s, the task of creating the irrelevant "confection" cipher like that embedded in Parchment No. 2, related to Marie de Blanchefort's headstone inscription (and the PS PRAECUM of her grave slab), would have been a challenging and formidable problem, even for an obsessive lexophile — but it would not have been an impossible one.

One dreary November day in Toronto, after I'd been wrestling with the tortuous steps of this parchment's complex cipher, and accepting Henry Lincoln's admiring acceptance of it, my mind kept niggling at me that something was very wrong. Henry Lincoln wrote:

> The most surprising — and convincing — proof of the validity of this decipherment and the bizarre message it contains is the fact that after having changed the letters again and again throughout the process, the sequence has yet reverted exactly to a group of letters visible from the outset. The final message is a perfect anagram of PS PRAECUM plus the entire text of Marie de Blanchefort's headstone.[24]

On a short walk to the store to replenish my cigarets, and knowing that I was a dunce at word games, my mind yet niggled. Then it came to me. If you start out with a certain collection of letters, however much you scramble them, the final outcome will be the same old original letters. So, the final message *must* be a perfect anagram of the first set of letters (Marie de Blanchefort's headstone plus the PS PRAECUM of the grave slab). There's nothing "clever" about this, it is simply inevitable. It only *seems* clever to people so involved in the exercise of their own ingenuity that they lose sight of the logical hoops they're being goaded (by their tunnel-vision intelligence) to jump through, like trained dogs. The really "clever" part consists in making the final, unscrambled message read as *something* , however meaningless, much like SHEPHERDESS NO TEMPTATION POUSSIN TENIERS HOLD THE KEY...etc.

Even though I am an admitted washout at word games, I didn't think that this sort of cipher would be impossibly difficult for someone "working backwards," and who knew what he (or she) wanted to convey at the end of the "decipherment" — and who could control all the steps of scrambling-unscrambling. But I wasn't about to try it myself, because I was involved in more important things (to me). Besides, lexophilia isn't my particular hang-up.

I was considerably heartened, therefore, to discover that this had already been demonstrated by a computer expert who is also, quite obviously, a dangerous lexophile. In *Rennes-le-Château* by Lionel and Patricia Fanthorpe, Paul Townsend spoofs the notorious Rennes-le-Château cipher of Parchment No. 2 with a cipher of his own *that is more complex*. Townsend uses 162 letters, not the 128 letters of the parchment code, embedded in the text of *Pilgrim's Progress*. He ends up with a much better message, in my opinion, and one that *also* manages to incorporate the alleged encoded stone of Nova Scotia's famed "Money Pit" — a favourite mystery of Reverend Lionel Fanthorpe. (For Paul Townsend's spoof please see *Rennes-le-Château* by Lionel and Patricia Fanthorpe, pages 198-203).

An Enquiry Into the Affairs of Joe Bloggs (Deceased)

The text of Parchment No. 2 (without the extra code letters) can most probably be regarded as genuine. It may, or may not, have been discovered by Bérenger Saunière. It may, or may not, have relevance to his wealth between 1891 and 1917. But the cipher within this probably genuine parchment was *concocted and inserted into* it by a chronic and obsessive lexophile no earlier than the late 1950s, or early 1960s, when primitive computers were available.

Gérard de Sède, to be charitable, was given only a copy of the *doctored* old parchment. He was also given the solution to the cipher because no computer, then or now, could have logically arrived at the *arbitrary* processes of the decipherment. These steps could only have been derived from the code maker and communicated to Gérard de Sède. Gérard de Sède may, or may not, have known (or suspected) a deception. The purpose of this spurious and inserted cipher was to whet the interest of researchers and to widen the circle by introducing the Poussin and Teniers paintings into the corpus of the mystery.

Every clue needed to find the "treasure" is in plain sight on Parchment No. 2. The lexophiles have been so obsessed with the supposed ciphers (they *do* exist) that they haven't seen the woods for the trees. In all the books dealing with this parchment, and that means almost every book about Rennes-le-Château since *Le Trésor Maudit*, everyone has focused on the text *but not on the two lines below the text and separated from it*.

You don't even have to know Latin. These two lines are separated into four segments by small cross symbols. Without knowing Latin, anyone can see that one segment starts with "Jesus." One segment mentions the Magdalene ("by the tears of the

Magdalene"). One segment deals with penance —at least the word looks related to, say, "penitentiary." We don't even need to know that the fourth segment deals with sin and temptation. The crosses separating these phrases invite us to "cross" them in various combinations. Since we're looking for something that must be fairly close to Rennes-le-Château, we look at a large-scale map of the surrounding area. The one we need is "2347 ouest Quillan" of the Institut Géographique National's *Série Bleue* topographical maps in 1:25,000 scale.

We pore over the geographic features in the vicinity of Rennes-le-Château. About two miles southeast of Rennes we find an interesting configuration along the Blanque River. If we mentally place ourselves by the river, to the north along its course is a feature called *le Fauteuil du Diable* (the Devil's armchair). In the other direction, to the south of us about the same distance away is a feature called *l'Hermitage* (the Hermitage). If we face north, to our right will be a statue of Mary Magdalene on a hill. To our left will be a ridge called *l'homme mort* (the dead man).

Since we were, very graphically, invited to "cross" the four phrases at the bottom of Parchment No. 2, let's make a cross with these geographical features. Jesus would be with Mary, so we will connect "the dead man" and the statue of Mary Magdalene with a line. It goes east-west. The devil supplies temptation while hermits flee from it, so we will draw a line from the Devil's armchair to the Hermitage, and this line goes north-south beside the River Blanque. There happens to be a bend in the river at this point. Perhaps it would be a good place to divert a river temporarily — if you regarded it with Visigothic eyes. These two lines form a perfect cross at 90 degrees, depending on which elevation of "the dead man" ridge we select.

As treasure maps say, "X marks the spot." My friend and companion, Joelle Lauriol, quickly discovered this geographic configuration one day in Toronto. After I had roughly translated the Latin of the four phrases at the bottom of Parchment No. 2, and while I was still pontificating to writer Winnie Czulinski about the possible meaning of some of the abbreviations used (not seeing the woods for the trees), Joelle took the information and consulted the map. Within ten minutes of looking at it, Joelle had drawn her cross as described. Gold lust quickly flickered in three pairs of eyes, and we began to glance at each other suspiciously. And edge towards the front door. Who would be the first to buy an airline ticket to France,

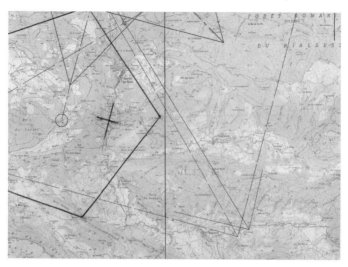

The cross formed by joining four geographic features near Rennes-le-Château, features that are alluded to at the bottom of Parchment II. This association of features was discovered by Joelle Lauriol and are here superimposed over the latest French government topographical map of the area.

buy a metal detector, pick and shovel and start digging? And what would he or she do with the other two of us?

As my hand was turning the door knob, while I was mumbling (*sub voce*) "Sixteen men on a dead man's chest, yo-ho-ho and a bottle of rum...drink and the devil have done for the rest, etc., etc.", Joelle called out that there was bad news. Rejoining her (suspiciously) where she sat at the table looking at the map with a magnifying glass, I looked too. Just where her lines crossed was a small dot labelled "ancient mine." The words "ancient" and "mine" do not have precisely the same meaning in French as they do in English. In French, "ancient" doesn't have to be all that old, and you can "mine" for treasure as well as for iron ore. In English, of course, "ancient" means very, very old; and one "mines" for a natural mineral, but one "digs for" or "excavates" treasure. In short, since this ancient mine on the French map is almost exactly where Joelle had marked her cross, it seemed obvious that someone had beaten us to the "X marks the spot."

On a scale of 1 to 25,000, one millimetre on the map is 25,000 millimetres on the ground — a little more than twenty-five English yards. This "ancient mine" is less than fifty yards from where Joelle's lines, derived from clues at the bottom of Parchment No. 2, crossed each other. This is too close to be coincidence. The difference between our "X" and the dot marking this ancient mine becomes even less depending upon the spot one chooses to fix on *l'Homme mort*. This is a long and gradually ascending ridge with higher elevations at its southern end. But these are not well defined from down near the bank of the Blanque River. Joelle chose the highest map elevation to construct this east-west arm of her cross. It is evident though, even from the map, that from the level of the river, one or two lesser hills would *seem* higher. Choosing one of these hills would make Joelle's "X" and the ancient map actually coincide within a matter of feet. At one time there must have been something marking the exact spot — and nothing would have been more fitting than one of those stone wayside crosses that are so common in France. The fire in our eyes gradually died down.

If it is granted that our "X," derived from Parchment No. 2 and this "ancient mine" refer to the same point of interest, then the age of this mine has much to do with the age of the parchment and its authenticity. For reasons that are discussed more fully in the notes, I'm inclined to think that this mine existed as of A.D. 1800 at the very latest.[25] Therefore, Parchment No. 2, minus the insertion of the modern cipher (the extra-letter code), must have existed before the mine was excavated, say A.D. 1800 or so. For who would leave clues for a "treasure" that was known to have already been recovered?

However, there are several assumptions here, and they sometimes keep me awake at night musing about airline tickets to France, metal detectors, picks, shovels, and so on. First, just because someone mined for treasure in A.D. 1800 or before, especially with the technology of that time, doesn't mean they found all, most, some, or even any of it. Some considerable portion of a Visigothic hoard might remain there today.

Second, the topographical mapping of France by aerial photography did not proceed smoothly because of two world wars and enemy occupation of considerable parts of France. This could be considered a remote region of the country, and we don't know when this "ancient mine" appeared on the earliest modern series of topographical maps. Given the level of accuracy of earlier pre-airplane maps, the mines shown on them may have nothing whatever to do with this one. "Our" mine may have appeared after 1891, in which case Bérenger Saunière seems a good candidate to be the miner.

Third, it is a safe assumption (I hope) that the obvious clues in Parchment No. 2 would not have been leaked to Gérard de Sède for inclusion in a popular book — until and unless the Priory of Sion had excellent reasons for knowing that the treasure was gone. Still, even with mid-twentieth-century technology, a few Visigothic gems or golden beads might have been overlooked.

6

The Greatest Story Ever Told:
The Tale of the Grail

"To Dagobert II, king, and to Zion is this treasure and it is death."
Even some French researchers were a bit hazy about who Dagobert
had been and, of course, the name meant little or nothing to
Britons, Americans, and others interested in the mystery of Rennes-
le-Château. After consulting encyclopedias, everyone scurried to
the Bibliothèque Nationale where genealogies are preserved in the
archives. En route to the archives, researchers came across
fascinating little goads, like this one, from the *dossiers secrets*:

> One day the descendants of Benjamin left their
> country; certain remained, two thousand years later
> Godfroi IV (de Bouillon) became king of Jerusalem
> and founded the Order of Zion.

Godfroi de Bouillon? Another consultation with encyclopedias.
Another trip back to the archives in the Bibliothèque Nationale.
Gradually, the whole thing unravelled.

As of 1998, there have been so many books about the lineage of
the Holy Grail that I do not consider it necessary to "argue" the
basic belief, or to present the lineage itself. The fundamental belief
of the Holy Grail religion has been "argued" by Michael Baigent,
Richard Leigh and Henry Lincoln in *The Holy Blood and the Holy
Grail* . It has been amplified and supported by many historians and
theologians since then, including Margaret Starbird (*The Woman
with the Alabaster Jar*) and Dr. Barbara Thiering, an Australian
theologian and author of several books.

More recently, Britain's Sir Laurence Gardner has traced the Grail lineage through the major European noble and royal families in mind-numbing detail. Gardner is no lightweight. He's a respected British genealogist and is the genealogical consultant to the European Council of Princes and the Celtic Church. You can read about him in *Who's Who in Britain*.

What follows has been known for a long time in certain quarters, but the general public has been insulated from it by the concerted (if not co-operative) efforts of the Roman Catholic Church and all major Protestant denominations.

For several decades, experts in the Jewish and early Christian history of Palestine had quietly suspected that Jesus had been married. Marriage was absolutely expected of all Jewish men of the time; it was mandatory for rabbis. Although the New Testament nowhere mentions the marital status of Jesus, the consensus of Christian historians and theologians was slowly coming around to accept the high probability that he was married. This high probability became a virtual certainty in December 1945 with the discovery of early Christian scrolls at a village called Nag Hammadi in Egypt.

An international team was assembled to study these scrolls in 1961. By the early 1970s it was clear that the scrolls themselves dated to about A.D. 300–400, but were copies of much earlier texts. At least two new Gospels were found: the Gospel of Thomas, and the Gospel of Philip. In some respects, these texts were more trustworthy than the four canonical Gospels because the Nag Hammadi scrolls had been buried in Egyptian sand for 1,600 years. They had not been subjected to any "editing" in the intervening centuries. The four canonical Gospels (Matthew, Mark, Luke, and John, plus the Epistles, etc.) were known to have suffered extensive editing to make them conform more closely to the dogma of "Christianity" as developed by Paul, then adopted by the Council of Nicea (A.D. 324–25) and then by the Church of Rome.

Aside from the fact that historical scholarship was already tending toward the idea of a married Jesus, the Gospel of Philip in the Nag Hammadi collection seemed to identify his wife — Mary Magdalene. Even in the four canonical Gospels, Mary Magdalene plays an important part in the life of Jesus. She, and she alone, was present at every crucial event of Jesus' ministry, and it was to her that his resurrection was first revealed.

The religion of the Holy Grail is the tradition that Jesus and

Mary Magdalene were married and had children and that the descendants of Jesus continued to exist on earth through many centuries. The Holy Grail is the lineage of Jesus. It is the living vessel in which the Holy Blood is held. It is a "cup" or "container" in this allegorical sense. It incorporated, and mostly preserved, the idea that living descendants of Jesus imposed an obligation to try to practise "living love" in day-to-day life, even in warfare if violence became utterly necessary. Since they believed that Jesus and Mary Magdalene had been married, Grail believers generally also gave women a much higher social status than in other parts of Europe during the two thousand years separating Jesus from ourselves. In the realm of warfare and strife, Grail believers invented the idea of "chivalry" — the novel notion that a true knight had obligations transcending the behaviour of a loutish warrior, that mercy should be offered to a defeated foe and that those who could not protect themselves should be defended.

Why was this covered up? Why did official Church dogma become the idea of a *celibate* Jesus whose grace was passed on through a lineage of *male* priests by the symbolic "laying on of hands" — so-called apostolic succession? Why was Mary Magdalene presented, in Church tradition, as a reformed prostitute when even the four canonical Gospels cannot help but show her as an important part of Jesus' life? Why did women have such a low status in the Church and in medieval Europe?

Episcopalian bishop John Spong of Newark, New Jersey, believes that he has the answer. In a painstaking analysis of the writings of St. Paul (in the original Greek), Dr. Spong finds overwhelming evidence that Paul had been a frantic, but frustrated, homosexual. Paul wrote obsessively about the torments and temptations that his "member" (i.e., Greek for "penis") continually caused him. Had Paul been born a Hellenistic Greek, we might never have heard of him because the "decadent" Greeks had long since come out of their closets. But Paul had not only been born Jewish, he was a dedicated Jewish nationalist who abhorred Hellenistic Greek influence in once-Jewish Palestine. He hated the gradual Greek subversion of The Law, hated the all-powerful Roman successors of the Greeks even more — and above all hated Christians, a sect *within* Judaism that undermined The Law.[1]

Paul was a familiar stereotype. A rather prim soul because of his limited sexual experience, he was basically a conservative. Yet his specific sexual orientation prevented his full participation in his traditional native culture. The more his "member's" antics goaded him, the more fanatically Jewish he became — although his homosexual yearnings barred him from full orthodox Jewishness.

In short, Paul was locked into his own private hell, which had both moral and "career" aspects to it. A fanatic, conservative Jew, and aspiring to be a rabbi, Paul knew that his own sexual orientation would prevent him from being a successful husband and father (rabbis were expected to have children). He feared that if he married, and attempted heterosexual sex in order to fulfil the rabbinical expectation of children, his homosexual inadequacies would inevitably come to light. And this would be bad news, not only for his rabbinical career, but for his life — the Jewish penalty for homosexuality was the same as that for adultery: death by stoning. Paul was simply, and hopelessly (as we would say today), dysfunctional within the Jewish society of his time.

Paul "saw the light" on the road to Damascus. Fledgling "Christianity" could offer him a way out of his dilemma. Christ's love was all-embracing. Jesus Christ could love and accept into his group of followers *even a homosexual* — something that the Jewish Sanhedrin was not about to do. But the light shone further yet. In becoming a leading and articulate Christian, Paul could achieve a status in the new sect, "a rabbi," that was denied to him within Judaism itself. And, being a prolific, polemic, and talented writer, Paul set out to do just that.

In promoting the spread of Christianity, however, he also had the opportunity to inject into it some of his own homosexual prejudices (and needs). He denigrated women and their proper place in the Church. He naturally downgraded Mary Magdalene's special relationship with Jesus. He advocated a male and celibate priesthood in which "grace" was transmitted by an abstract, spiritual mechanism and not by messy reproduction requiring women.

In addition to Paul's career ambitions, and apart from the sexual politics he inflicted on new Christianity, there was also a strong and sincere belief among early Christians that Christ's "second coming" was an imminent event. It could be expected any day or, at the most, within a few weeks or months.

Under such circumstances, further human reproduction was unnecessary and, in a very real sense, irresponsible. A certain number of all souls born would be consigned to damnation because they would not believe in Jesus when he came soon to judge "the quick and the dead." Paul may also, with great sincerity, have believed in an impending second coming. In Paul's view, reproductive sex within marriage was certainly a distasteful thought (for him, as a homosexual) and it was also unnecessary (in view of the looming second coming) — but it could not actually be called a mortal sin. Marriage and reproduction were venerated in Jewish tradition (which Paul still secretly respected), and even Paul was not prepared to contradict God's injunction to "be fruitful and multiply." But the best that Paul could say of marriage and reproduction was "It is better to marry than to burn." Paul's personality, according to Bishop Spong, was one beset by so many conflicts and fears that it was certainly neurotic, possibly psychotic. Paul bequeathed this burden to the early Christian Church.

The Roman Catholic Church rests heavily upon a conceptual tripod. The strongest leg of it (for Church structure) is what is called Paulist Doctrine. This is a compendium of what Paul interpreted and extrapolated from the story of Jesus. It has little to do with what Jesus is known, or alleged, to have actually said. And this Paulist Doctrine is so embarrassingly laced with anti-female vitriole that it can only have emanated from a prim, fanatical, and homosexual male mind.

The second leg of the Roman Church's tripod is the so-called Petrine Claim. The idea is that because the Apostle Peter was the leader of the fledgling Church in Rome, the Bishops of Rome had a Jesus-given right to be leaders of the Christian Church. This claim, at base, stems from a pun that Jesus made. When translated into Latin, the name Peter means "rock." Jesus was alleged to have remarked, "Thou art Peter, and upon this rock I found my church." Jesus may have actually said this, but we don't know how. Remember, Peter was the only Disciple/Apostle to have denied that he'd been associated with Jesus in any way. Even the hated Judas did not do this. Peter denied his association with Jesus three times when in danger of being apprehended by Roman/Jewish informants. Jesus reputedly foretold this "thrice-denial" and so may have read Peter's character well. Could the statement attributed to Jesus have meant: "Thou art Peter, and upon *this* rock I found my church?" A wry and bitter piece of Jewish humour — or an injunction?

But, naturally, the Bishops of Rome chose to regard it as an injunction, implying that the bishops descended from Peter were the Jesus-approved leaders of the entire Christian Church. These bishops slowly evolved into popes.

The third leg of the Roman Church's survival is, of course, sheer money. Tithes and donations of land, money, and bequests poured in from the faithful, mostly in the form of donations made in the name of local saints who often had been, in a previous guise, local gods and goddesses of paganism. The votive offerings didn't change, only the ultimate recipient — "Rome," the Vatican.

While what we have come to know as "Christianity" was coalescing around the doctrines of Paul, the idea of apostolic succession from Peter, and political structure borrowed from the once-hated Roman Empire, various sects tried to preserve what "early Christianity" had once been all about. For the most part, these sects were gradually pushed into Anatolia, modern Turkey, by the pressure of jostling empires and emerging "orthodoxies." It would be wrong to say that all of these sects believed in the "Grail" tradition of a married Jesus with descendants, but they sought to preserve the original tradition, and message, of "the Christ" as they saw it. Some of these Christian sects were not "Christian" at all, as we would understand the term, because they believed that John the Baptist, not Jesus, had been the "true Messiah." This belief was based as much upon Gospel as orthodox belief, and perhaps upon earlier versions of the Gospels that were not subjected to subsequent editing and doctoring.

As mentioned before, when Paul went to Ephesus to preach the new Christianity there, he discovered that "Christian" churches already existed in the city — but they held that John, not Jesus, had been the Saviour. This is the so-called Ionnite Heresy, much feared and hated by the Vatican in the early days of struggle for Christian supremacy and orthodoxy. According to Walter Birks and R.A. Gilbert, many Christian sects still exist around Lake Van in eastern Turkey.[2] Some are "Johnites," some believe in the Grail tradition, some are *both* — but all practise a simple, communal, and non-violent life based on the teachings of John and Jesus.

This is where we run into a problem, from the outset, with the Grail tradition. Mary Magdalene *may* have been married to John before she was married to Jesus. She may have had children by both husbands. This would have been entirely in accord with Jewish law of the time. A widowed wife was immediately incorporated into the household of her deceased husband's closest male relative. This was a social measure to ensure the survival of widows and orphans. She became a wife in her new household, too, and might well bear children to her new husband.

A wife? It is not generally known by the North American public, and not advertised by the Jewish community, but a Jewish man can have more than one wife under religious law, just like a Moslem — indeed, the Moslem custom of polygamy derives from Jewish religious law. Under The Law, a Jewish man can still have more than one wife, but rabbis discouraged the custom in the thirteenth century in order to make less apparent difference between Jews and their Christian neighbours. Christians in Spain, France, and Germany were all too prone to use any difference as an excuse for massacre. In Islamic countries, of course, civil law coincides with religious law. In western Europe and North America, it does not. Polygamy is illegal under western civil law, but not under Jewish and early Christian religious law.

In short, Jesus could have had more than one wife. And, in fact, Mormon belief asserts this. The Mormon doctrine of "multiple marriage" is based solidly and squarely upon ancient Judaic scripture and law. The Mormons have sometimes encountered difficulty and hostility in attempting to place religious law above civil law. Joseph Smith, the founder of Mormonism, was lynched because he advocated this (and other things). The Jews have been smart enough not to make the same mistake in North America. According to genealogies that one can obtain from the Mormon Church's giant computerized Family History Center in Salt Lake City, Jesus was married to Mary Magdalene, Martha (of Bethany?), woman named Anna, and a few others.

Before leaving the Mormons temporarily, because we must return to the story of Joseph Smith later in connection with North American "Grail-related" artefacts and traditions, I would note that it is odd and ironic that the Mormons are associated with "family values" in the minds of many Americans. Mormon television commercials have much to do with this. But if one examines the doctrines of the Church of Latter-Day Saints closely, the "family values" are there, all right — in spades — because the idea is multiple families deriving from multiple wives. Also, although the Mormons accept that Jesus was married to both Mary Magdalene and Anna and had children by both women, the rather blood-chilling doctrine is that his descendants by Mary are "Canaanite" (damned by blood taint) while his descendants by Anna are "Israelite" (blessed by pure blood). There's nothing that can be done to purify a Canaanite except what Mormons call a blood atonement (in the words of Brigham Young) — death, voluntary or otherwise.

Unfortunately for the vast majority of humanity, most of us are Canaanites — most "whites" (even including Jesus' own descendants by Mary Magdalene), all blacks, and all Asians. So who is Israelite and blessed in the Mormon view? Well, Mormons, of course, and some American Indians.

Luckily for Mormons, they can discover whether they are Canaanite or Israelite by sincerely praying to God to grant them the death of "blood atonement" if they are impure. Most often, God doesn't instantly kill these supplicants and so Mormons who survive this sincere prayer know that they are "Israelite". The whole idea behind the Church's Family History Center in Salt Lake City is to determine who is Canaanite and who is Israelite. Therefore, if there's ever a breakdown of civil law, or if Mormons come to control civil law, those people destined for the blood atonement can be identified, for, as Brigham Young said in one of his speeches as governor to the Utah Legislature, "there is no higher service these people can render to God."[3]

So much for family values — don't believe everything you see on television.

As we've seen, according to the Jewish laws and customs of his time, Jesus could have had more than one wife — and also would have been expected to marry Mary Magdalene if she had been married to John the Baptist. *If* Mary had first been married to John, and *if* she had borne children to him, the matter of children becomes complicated. These children would have become Jesus' own (under Jewish law) when and *if* Mary, as John's widow, came into his household according to Jewish custom. Therefore, the "bloodline of the Holy Grail" (as Laurence Gardner put it) is complicated right from the start.

Three children of Jesus and Mary Magdalene have been tentatively identified. Sarah, according to Barbara Thiering, was possibly the youngest child "of Jesus," born when Mary Magdalene first fled from Palestine almost immediately after the crucifixion. Another daughter named Tamar has been identified by Laurence Gardner. There were also (possibly) two older boys: Jesus Justus and James. Jesus Justus is even mentioned in the New Testament. If someone knows the real father of these children, because of some priceless early genealogy still hidden away, it has not yet been revealed to the general public. Laurence Gardner, who apparently has access to very old and jealously guarded noble and royal genealogies because of his official position as genealogical consultant to the European Council of Princes, focuses on two boys as the children of Jesus.[4]

The whole idea of the "Holy Grail" is a bloodline deriving from Jesus. I cannot state, from my own knowledge, whether this belief is a "true" one. That is, I don't know if this belief is founded on actual fact. What can be said with absolute certainty is that many men and women have believed in the Holy Grail during the past two thousand years. They may have been misguided. Or they may have had very good reasons for their belief. Our belief in the "orthodox" celibate Jesus may be misguided. Bishop John Spong has observed, "Orthodoxy is orthodoxy because it won, not because it is true." And Pope Leo X is said to have quipped: "It has served us well, this myth of the Christ."

For our purposes, it does not matter at all whether belief in the Holy Grail is misguided. Grail belief motivated the actions and activities of hundreds of influential people in western history. Their belief, motivations and actions shaped much of the western world, including the discovery and settlement of the Americas. Tracking their explorations is what *Grail Knights of North America* is about — not the validity or delusion of their beliefs.

The story goes that after arriving in Alexandria, Egypt, from Palestine shortly after the crucifixion of Jesus, Mary Magdalene and other members of Jesus' immediate family then took a ship from Alexandria to Marseilles. All accounts agree that Mary was accompanied by Joseph of Arimathaea, but the stories differ concerning who else was in this group.

Gypsy legends say that the Queen of the Gypsies of the Marseilles area, "Black Sarah," swam out to meet the arriving ship and guided it to safety in the maze of the Rhone River delta. And, in fact, there's the famous shrine of Les Saintes Maries (the Holy Marys) near Marseilles to this day. No one knows for sure when this shrine was founded, but it was very early in the history of Christianity. The idea is that Mary of Bethany and Mary the Virgin accompanied Mary Magdalene to Marseilles. The bones of *someone* are venerated at the shrine of Les Saintes Maries currently — it is the foremost Gypsy shrine in Europe.[5] Who is this Mary?

Theologians generally consider that "Mary of Bethany" and Mary Magdalene were the same person. The medieval Church accepted this.[6] The proliferation of Marys in Jesus' life was just one way in which early Paulist editors tried to confuse and denigrate Mary Magdalene's role. The Virgin Mary is thought to have died in Ephesus (in modern Turkey). Could Mary Magdalene have died in southern France? Are her bones the ones still venerated at the shrine?

Possibly. In this case, Joseph of Arimathaea is supposed to have taken her surviving child, or children, on to Britain.

In any event, after staying briefly in the area around Marseilles, Mary Magdalene(?) and Joseph of Arimathaea travelled on to Glastonbury, in Britain. This is quite plausible. If these people were fleeing from both Roman authorities and Jewish ones, neither Alexandria nor Marseilles would have been very safe. Rome was solidly in control of both cities. Both cities had large and thriving Jewish communities. Glastonbury makes sense. It was still within "civilization," the Roman Empire, but was on the extreme western fringe of it. It was about as far from Palestine and Rome as it was possible to get without venturing into barbarian territory.

On arrival in Glastonbury, Joseph of Arimathaea is said to have stuck his thornwood staff into the ground in order to mark the site of a church he planned to build in honour of Jesus. The church, a modest affair of mud and wattle on the shore of the interconnected lakes and bogs which then almost encircled Glastonbury, was duly and quickly built. It was the first church in all of Christendom. Joseph's thornwood staff supposedly took root and grew into the famous Glastonbury Thorn tree. This tree still exists (or, rather, a tree still grows from a cutting, planted in 1690, of the original tree), and it is a Palestinian variety of thorn, not the species common to western Europe.[7]

Rome, under pressure from encroaching barbarians, evacuated its troops from Britain between A.D. 418 and 425. Thereafter, Romano-Celtic kings and chieftains defended Britain as best they could against invading Angles, Saxons, and Jutes — Teutonic tribes from Scandinavia, Germany, and Friesland (Holland).

The most famous defender was, of course, King Arthur (A.D. 490?–542?). According to legend, as *dux bellorum* (war leader), he revived an old Roman plan for defending Britain with a mobile strike force of heavy cavalry that would reinforce local defence against Saxon landings. He may, or may not, have been the official and recognized High King of the Britons — but he was certainly the most powerful and respected chieftain in Britain during his life. Arthur's only title appears to have been *Comes Britannarium*, Count of the Britons. A *comes* was just an old Roman word for a cavalry commander. It is asserted in folk tales and later troubadour poetry that Arthur had *something* to do with the Holy Grail. If one or more children of Jesus had arrived in Glastonbury with (or without) Mary Magdalene, these descendants of Jesus would have had more than four centuries to marry into Romano-Celtic families by the time of King Arthur.

In the beginning, perhaps, being the child or descendant of Jesus might not have been too much of a recommendation for prospective parents-in-law. But the Emperor Constantine ("the Great," A.D.288?–337) actually became a Christian on his deathbed and had previously (313) proclaimed Christianity to be an official religion of the Roman world. Constantine had always been attracted to Christianity, and this was known throughout the Empire. He convened the famous (or, infamous) Council of Nicea in 324–325 even if he knew pitifully little about competing Christian scriptures and doctrines. But his conversion to Christianity would have had special impact in Britain because Constantine had served with the British legions and had been proclaimed Emperor at York (306).

It is intriguing to speculate that Constantine's exposure to Christianity may have come from his contact with the Glastonbury community, intriguing because his attraction to Christianity had immense repercussions. Christianity was suddenly catapulted from the status of a persecuted sect to the status of the official religion (337) of the Roman Empire. Is it possible that Christianity's first step into prominent respectability was made possible because of this Emperor's early exposure to the Holy Grail community in Glastonbury? If so, it is one of the supreme ironies in the history of religion because Constantine's "Council of Nicea" helped, eventually, to damn the Grail tradition as heresy.

But all that lay in the future. From Constantine's death in 337, then, the powerful and noble Romano-Celtic families of Britain would have sought out marriageable descendants of Jesus and Mary. This is almost two centuries before King Arthur's time and doubtless, by then, most of Britain's royal and noble houses (of which there were many) could boast mixture with the "Holy Bloodline."

But, unfortunately for Arthur, the "Holy Grail," and Romano-Celtic remnants of civilization, the barbarians were too many and too strong. It is said that Arthur's son, Mordred (or Medraut), allied himself with the Saxons in a bid to take over Arthur's Britain and "Camelot." The resulting battle, Camlann (542), was a bloody draw in which Mordred was killed by Arthur, but in which Arthur was mortally wounded. This was the end of the cohesive defence of Britain, although kingdoms in the far west (Somerset and Cornwall) held out against the Saxons for another century or so. These legends are misted by time, but it *seems* that this last-ditch defence of Cornwall by "King Mark" gave us the "Romance of Tristram and Isolde" and other stories that are vaguely (and confusingly) linked with King Arthur.

However, the history of the Grail insists that before the last Battle of Camlann, when the writing was clearly on the wall, members of the Holy Bloodline were evacuated across the Channel to France. In point of fact, though, there's not much doubt that descendants of Jesus from Britain would have begun marrying into powerful "French" families just as soon as Christianity had gained the status of Imperial favour — from A.D. 313 on.

These Franks, contemporaries of "Arthurians," were fighting against incursions on their own northern and eastern borders by the same Teutonic barbarians that Arthur opposed. They were called Sicambrian Franks and had long been civilized by Rome. Some were Christian, some were pagan. They boasted a most curious history. According to their tribal traditions, they had once been the Israelite Tribe of Benjamin!

The Benjamites had fought a losing war against the other eleven Israelite tribes because the Benjamites refused to participate in an attack on the "Sons of Baal" — which must mean the coastal Phoenician cities of Tyre, Sidon, and Biblos. The Benjamites lost this war, but the survivors were taken to safety *in Arcadia, in Greece*. Some of the defeated Benjamites remained in Palestine, and the tribe apparently remained powerful. Jerusalem was itself allotted to the Benjamites along with many of the larger Canaanite cities. Israel's first king, Saul, was a Benjamite. This war between the Benjamites and the rest of Israel is mentioned in Judges. It therefore took place about 1100–1200 B.C., about the time of the Trojan War — which gives an idea of how ancient, and possibly garbled, this tribal tradition was.

In any event, those Benjamites who took refuge in Arcadia (and they must have been taken there in Phoenician ships since the Israelites were landlubbers), eventually joined the long Celtic migration westward along the Danube. By the time of Jesus, they had reached the Rhine and crossed into France where they became influential in Roman Gaul. Many became Roman citizens, and there were even Sicambrian consuls in Rome's history. By the second or third century of the Christian era, these Sicambrians had reached the Channel.[8]

Although it is something of a digression here, I would like to mention briefly the hazy matter of "Lyonesse."[9] It may be of unsuspected importance to the story of the Holy Grail, Christianity, and Rome. Lyonesse is something of a void in conventional history — and literally, because it supposedly sank into the sea. It is an accepted geological fact that much coastal land off the shore of the present French *département* of Morbihan did sink beneath the sea during the third to sixth centuries A.D. This land had supposedly been Lyonesse, a powerful country composed of large and small islands that stretched across to Cornwall. Ruins can be seen under the water from glass-bottomed tour boats, just off Land's End in Britain. There are megalithic sites under the sea off today's Morbihan coast of France. According to legend, all this was once part of Lyonesse.

The country of Lyonesse seems to have begun sinking as the land around Glastonbury started to rise, in some sort of compensating and reciprocal local crustal shift.

The point of all this is that Lyonesse must have been important in early French and Holy Grail history. It is not mentioned in Roman sources — which can only mean that Rome didn't conquer it! Rome (Julius Caesar) conquered the rest of Gaul, however, and in no uncertain terms. But Lyonesse, which was known to be at least partly above water for four or five more centuries, was not listed among Caesar's conquests. It must have remained Celtic and independent. Lyonesse, because of its geographical position, would have been much less vulnerable than Britain to Irish and Saxon raids.

And because of its geographical position, squeezed between Roman Britain and Roman Gaul, it could not have escaped the influence of Roman civilization even if it remained independent. Lyonesse might have been an important and unsuspected link between Arthurian Britain and Merovingian France that has eluded researchers' attentions. Lyonesse figures in the Arthurian legends as an important place. The enchanted forest of Brocéliande, now reduced to the Forest of Paimpont southwest of the city of Rennes in Brittany (not to be confused with Rennes-le-Château, or *was* it?), was Merlin's summer home in the romances. Merlin, of course, was King Arthur's primary advisor. The Holy Grail was often sought in Brocéliande.

Forested Lyonesse must have been an important route between Britain and Gaul in early Christian times, an important route of retreat from Saxon invasion for the Holy Blood and Arthurian protectors — and yet almost nothing is known of it. We know only that Merlin was in partial residence there, that one of its rulers (perhaps an Arthurian contemporary) was the fairy, Mélusine, and that knights seeking the Holy Grail had to pass through its enchanted forest. Julius Caesar conquered Gaul just before the time of Christ, 58–51 B.C. He doesn't mention Lyonesse.

If it remained independent of Rome, and substantially above water, it might have been a better haven for Joseph of Arimathaea and the "Holy Grail" than Glastonbury. This is not to suggest that Joseph of Arimathaea did not come to Glastonbury, did not plant his staff there, and did not build a church there — but Glastonbury might not have been his only, or primary, residence. An independent but civilized Lyoness might have been the centre from which the Grail influenced both Arthurian Britain and Merovingian France. It might be worth some research.

Sicambrian Franks established the so-called Merovingian kingdoms of early post-Roman Gaul, named after a Sicambrian high king, Mérovée. From about A.D. 490, the Merovingian royal houses began to claim a mysterious, or magical, infusion of lineage from a sea creature. No one knows precisely what they meant by this, but the name Mary means "of the sea." It is also fascinating to note, however, that the traditional ruler of Lyonesse, Mélusine, was a "fairy," and an aquatic one. She became, on occasion, a "mermaid" with a fish tail — highly appropriate for the queen of a recently sunken kingdom. Did Mélusine have Holy Blood in her veins? Was she the Holy Grail link, or one of them, between Britain and France?

It is at this time, the time of Mérovée and the known geological disappearance of Lyonesse, when the central story of the Holy Grail shifts to France. There had been, of course, many descendants of Jesus who had remained in Britain and who still lived in regions not overrun by Saxons — Wales, Ireland, Scotland, etc. But with Mérovée, the story of the most direct descendants of Jesus moves across the Channel.

In another coy book, our old friend Gérard de Sède claims that the Sicambrians-Merovingians were not wholly human and possessed a special claim to divinity. Strangely enough, the Bible makes the same claim about the Tribe of Benjamin. Merovingian royalty indulged in polygamy, which they justified by ancient Jewish law, and therefore there were numerous royal offspring who married into almost all the other royal, noble, and powerful families of

Europe. This has prompted one historian to assert that the foundation of European nobility is Jewish!

In any event, from the time of Mérovée, the Merovingian kings adopted rather curious symbols for their flags and battle banners. Clovis, a very powerful Merovingian king, adopted a battle flag adorned (if that's the right word) with a toad or a frog. This must surely be a strange symbol for a famous warrior like Clovis, and some researchers think that this frog or toad is intended to represent the aquatic sea creature that supposedly enhanced the Merovingian line about the time of Clovis. Perhaps this makes some logic (of a sort) — if the sea creature was fully aquatic, and mixed with terrestrial Franks, the resulting Merovingians could be regarded as amphibious, like a frog. It is just a thought.

Another Merovingian symbol was a bee, and no one knows why. Three hundred golden bee figurines were found in the tomb of Childeric (another Merovingian king), which was excavated in 1649. Napoleon appropriated Childeric's golden bees for his own coronation robe in 1804 — no one knows why — and then turned them over to the Louvre, where they are still on display. These odd Merovingian symbols have exercised a lot of imagination among historians and writers.

It is alleged that an important event in the history of the Holy Grail took place at this time, the era of the first Merovingians (about A.D. 450–500?). With the collapse of Imperial Rome, the Christian church desperately sought some temporal and military power with which it could ally itself. All of Europe seemed in danger of being overrun by pagan barbarians. Christianity seemed in danger of being inundated beneath the old pagan gods of the Teutons. Sicambrian Franks in Rome's most civilized province, Gaul, seemed the logical power to save the Church.

True, some of their royalty were pagans (most were not), but they were not barbarians. They were highly civilized and, like the Arthurians in Britain, they preserved what was left of Roman culture. But, unlike Britain's Arthurians, the Sicambrians did not inhabit an island that could be cut off from remnants of Roman culture. Also, the Sicambrian Franks were much more powerful and numerous than Arthur's Romano-Celts. Being civilized, these Franks could be converted. The Church of Rome set out to do just that.

Some of the Frankish kings were astute enough to realize that military power alone was insufficient to hold a society together. A deal was made: the Sicambrian Merovingian Franks would become the Church's chosen temporal power, while the Church would become the sole spiritual power of post-Roman Europe and supply the cultural infrastructure to hold what was left of civilization together. At this point (it is asserted), some higher officials in the Church knew full well that descendants of Jesus had married into the Merovingian royalty and knew that this was a source of pride to them.

But the deal was that the dogma of Rome would be tacitly accepted as orthodoxy by the Franks, while the Church would turn a blind eye to the lineage of Jesus (which threatened the validity of the so-called Petrine Claim). The secret of the Holy Blood would be kept by both parties for the benefit of society as a whole — and themselves, of course.

The problem with this arrangement was that after Clovis (c. 466–511), Clotaire (d.561), and Dagobert I (d. 639?), the Merovingian kings became progressively weaker and less able in war. French history calls them "enfeebled kings." This was not what the Church needed at all. Rome looked around for a replacement and found it in a secondary level of Merovingian nobility — the "Carolingians," "Mayors of the Palace" within the Merovingian scheme of things, and ancestors of the great Charlemagne.

One of the last Merovingian kings was our Dagobert II (d. 679?). The ancestors of Charlemagne were in the process of usurping Merovingian thrones with Rome's tacit approval, and Dagobert II was one of the victims. He was shot with an arrow while out hunting near the town of Stenay. Dagobert's skull was made into a drinking cup by his Carolingian murderers, an attractive vessel decorated with silver trim, which became famous as a token of the passage of the Merovingians and the arrival of the Carolingians. After Dagobert II, the "Mayors of the Palace" assumed the overt style, if not the title, of actual kings. Dagobert's skull is now in a convent near Mons, and the relic had considerable importance for the Grail tradition.

The series of "Et in Arcadia Ego" paintings seem to depict *this* skull, and not just any old cranium that could represent Death (as M. Owen Lee would have it — see Chapter 1) because two of these paintings, one by Guercino in 1618 and one by Poussin in 1639(?) *clearly show a bee resting on the skull*. This is an unambiguous reference to the Merovingians, and specifically to Dagobert II, whose drinking-cup skull had a certain morbid fame. This reference was necessary since Dagobert II had simply been erased from all

French histories printed before 1649. These histories just skip from Dagobert I to Dagobert III, omitting our Dagobert II altogether!

It was confidently thought that Dagobert's son and heir, Prince Sigisbert III (or IV?) had been hit and killed as well, but a loyal retainer took the boy to safety in the southern French dukedom of Razès, to live among his mother's people. This brings us to Rennes-le-Château again — it was then the capital of Razès, a Visigothic region.

If it is true that a pact between the Merovingians and the Roman Church had been made, and also true that the Church broke this pact because the Merovingian kings had become useless, then it is obvious that some attempt to exterminate the "Holy Blood" would have been made. The broken pact made the Roman Church, and the usurping Carolingians, aggressors against the descendants of Jesus. The only way in which this betrayal could be covered up would be to wipe out the known descendants of Jesus, destroy genealogical evidence of them, and deny that Jesus had ever had any lineage. The Vatican has worked hard at this for more than thirteen hundred years.

The story goes that the Holy Bloodline found a haven around Rennes-le-Château for several centuries. They were able to survive in southern France only because the region was *not* securely controlled by Christians. Remember, in A.D. 711, the Berber chieftain Tarik had invaded Spain and had defeated Roderick II of the Visigoths. By 730 the Saracens had invaded France. Islamic armies were stopped by Charles Martel ("Charles the Hammer"), a "Mayor of the Palace," at the great Battle of Tours in 732. Tours is less than two hundred miles from Paris.

The Holy Bloodline found a sanctuary in the Pyrénées foothills only because the region was a confusing patchwork of shifting Christian and Moorish kingdoms, princedoms, dukedoms and alliances. No single major and cohesive power had sole and secure control of the area. Given the timing of the Moorish invasion of Spain, and considering that the House of ibn Da'ud came into Spain as allies of Tarik, it is intriguing to consider the possibility that the Moorish invasion of Spain might have been encouraged by the Holy Blood. That would have been one way of avenging and limiting the usurping Carolingians' power.

Rome did crown Charlemagne as Holy Roman Emperor in the year A.D. 800, thus officially and overtly repudiating the earlier agreement allegedly made with the Merovingians. But, although Charlemagne controlled a vast amount of European land, he never could control the Pyrénées. The Moors not only offered effective opposition in these mountains but were a serious threat to the security of France itself for three centuries. The French national epic, "The Song of Roland," is specifically about an episode of Charlemagne's attempted and unsuccessful occupation of the Pyrénées — but more generally about the long French struggle to secure a border against the Moors.

Genealogies of this period exist in the Bibliothèque Nationale. They lead cohesively from Sigisbert to the next major historical figure to emerge from the Holy Blood. This was Godfroi IV de Bouillon, leader of the First Crusade (1096–99) and conqueror of Jerusalem in A.D.1099.

Apparently, Godfroi could produce plausible and convincing proof that he descended from Jesus because he was acclaimed king of Jerusalem for no very obvious reason. True, he'd been one of the three main leaders of the Crusade, but there were his co-leaders (and others) who could claim greater nobility. Godfroi, however, declined the kingship. He claimed only the title Protector of the Holy Sepulchre, and it is said that he founded the Order of Zion. Godfroi may have declined the kingship because he knew that he was dying. En route to the Holy Land, he had been mauled by a bear. An infection set in that never truly healed. No one would accept the kingship until Godfroi died in January 1100. The next month, his younger brother, Baudoin ("Baldwin") became the first Frankish King of Jerusalem.

The Vatican and the Roman Church could not do much about this. By "freeing the Holy Land" Godfroi became, in the eyes of millions of ordinary Christians, the greatest religious hero since Jesus himself. Although Godfroi's name is completely unknown to most North Americans today, he was the most famous man in Europe for a century or two. He was ranked with David and Moses in the Judeo-Christian tradition. Rome could not oppose this popular adulation. The best that the Vatican could do was to negotiate the survival of, and practice of, "outward and visible orthodoxy" by de Bouillon's dynasty — but only at the high cost of making certain concessions in Europe.

One of these concessions concerned the two new orders of knighthood formed by Baudoin I of Jerusalem, Godfroi's brother. It was agreed that these new knights were to be absolutely independent of all secular authority. They were to have a free hand throughout Christendom, answerable only to the King of Jerusalem and the pope. The most prestigious new order was called Knights of the Temple of Solomon, much better known as the Knights Templar. Their primary task was guarding the "Holy Grail" — that is, they were the elite guards of de Bouillon's line. Templars also engaged in banking, revitalized European commerce so that trade again approached the volume and value that had once flourished under Rome, and financed the construction of the famous European cathedrals in the new "Gothic" style.

Being independent of local princes, dukes, and counts, Templar fiscal activities absolutely undermined the very foundation of European feudalism. Their activities brought a new class into being, a middle class of merchants, traders, and skilled artisans. Although some astute minds in the Vatican knew that this would eventually undermine the Church of Rome itself, nothing much could be done about it. A glance at any modern map will show that Vatican pessimism was realistic and justified. With few exceptions, the north and west coastal areas of Europe, the richest regions that developed trade, commerce, and manufacturing, were to turn away from the Church of Rome as "Protest-ants." The central, agricultural regions of Europe remained predominantly Roman Catholic, but these regions were also the poorest, least educated, and least cultured. Rome's income suffered.

The Order of the Knights of St. John of Jerusalem, Hospitaliers was also an elite force, but their main task besides fighting was to establish hospitals and medical knowledge in the Holy Land and back home in Europe.

In Chapter 1, we hinted that "Grail values and knowledge" might have prevented our modern plague of new viruses and bacteria like Lyme disease, Ebola, Lassa, and HIV. This is because, as early as the twelfth century, the Knights of St. John began translating Arabic and Jewish medical books into Latin. Aside from basic principles of public and medical hygiene, which they introduced into Europe, they also began the "scientific" study of epidemic diseases. It was primitive and it was rudimentary, but they early realized that "new" afflictions seemed to appear with travellers who had been to remote and unexplored places. If this observation had been developed over centuries of uninterrupted study, we might have grasped the nature of epidemics much sooner than we did. But the knowledge was interrupted by a period of Church-dictated medical and scientific ignorance that lasted until the 1700s. Then, the work began again...but from scratch. In the 1850s, European doctors still believed that malaria, for example, was caused by "bad air" (mal-aria). The Knights of St. John grasped its association with mosquitoes in the thirteenth century. They used primitive antibiotics in the thirteenth century, too.[10] Who knows what medical knowledge we might have built on this foundation if it had been allowed to flourish? Who knows what new epidemics we *might* have been able to contain?

The hospitals established by the Knights of St. John undermined the Church monopoly in healing and "infirmaries". New medical knowledge undermined the idea that disease was a manifestation of God's displeasure in which priests might be able to intercede — for a price. The Knights of St. John struck at another area of Church authority but, again, not much could be done about it. For readers with interest in such matters, today's St. John's Ambulance organization is a direct descendant of these knights.

In short, with the Templars and the Knights of St. John, a social, economic and health revolution was loosed upon Europe. Within these cultural departures from feudalism and the Church, the seeds of the modern world were planted. But they were fated to lay dormant for several more centuries.

The Saracens under Saladin launched a massive counter-offensive in A.D. 1187. The Frankish kingdoms in the Holy Land crumbled under this onslaught. The Knights Templar retreated back to the centre of "Grail Belief" — southern France primarily, taking treasures discovered in the Holy Land with them. As we saw in Chapter 2, some of these treasures must have been ancient maps filed away in the archives of Middle Eastern cities that fell to the Templars. These maps, the final generation of numerous copies, preserved Ice Age geography that showed, however, another continent westward from Europe and Africa. They depicted accurate longitude, which the Templars and later "discoverers" could not know, *but which were distances that could be roughly measured, using European distances as a guide.*

As for the Knights of St. John, they conducted some of the most masterly retreats in military history. They fell back on successive island fortresses in the Mediterranean. The last one was Malta, and so they are better known as the Knights of Malta today. As island-bound knights they began to specialize in aspects of seaborne commerce: navigation, map making, naval architecture, and the "scientific" improvement of ships. Their activities had immense influence on Europe's so-called Age of Discovery. Knights of Malta were leaders of, or consultants to, almost every major European voyage of discovery up until the 1680s. Maps copied and prepared by the Knights of Malta guided voyages of exploration.

Although the redoubtable Templars "dug in" throughout southern France and the Pyrénées foothills, the Vatican saw its chance to exterminate the Holy Grail once and for all. In 1209, Pope Innocent III (1198–1216) called for a "crusade" against the "heretics" of southern France (in Provence and Languedoc, primarily). Northern French barons, attracted by the wealth of the progressive Provençal culture, participated in the crusade under the initial leadership of Simon de Montfort.

The heretics of southern France and the Provençal culture had a significantly higher level of civilization than the rest of Europe. Meg Bowen in *The Women Troubadours* has shown that the legal status of women was much higher among these heretics than elsewhere in contemporary Europe. Women could own their own property and were not themselves chattel.[11] Women could be priests (*parfaits*) among the heretics, and they could also be military commanders. Art, literature, medicine, and commerce flourished. Religious toleration was also practised among the heretics. Not much of this progressiveness endeared the heretics to the Vatican, needless to say, while the wealth of this society inflamed the greed of neighbours.

One of the most savage religious wars ever fought raged in the Pyrénées foothills until the last great heretic fortress, Montségur, fell on March 16, 1244. But it is said that the Holy Grail was taken to safety while doomed Montségur fought hopelessly on.

Even though the heretics were defeated, they were not quite exterminated. Although having to profess careful orthodoxy in public, they found ways to communicate their beliefs. One way, as Margaret Starbird has shown through her study of thirteenth-century French watermarks of paper makers, was with symbols. Grails labelled "MM" (Mary Magdalene) became a popular watermark.[12] Unicorns (the married Jesus) suddenly became popular too. Secret "Grail Believers" used paper marked with these symbols in order to write notes to other known heretics.

It may be of interest that even our modern deck of playing cards reflects this great struggle in the south of France. The first known deck of playing cards dates from 1327.[13] The suit of hearts "Amor" (love) represents the heretics and is "Roma" spelled backwards. The suit of spades looks much more like a mitre (and always has); this

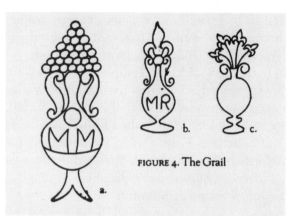

FIGURE 4. The Grail

"MM" water marks of medieval southern French paper makers. The "MM" traditionally stands for Mary Magdalene, the wife of Jesus, according to the Grail tradition.

represents the Vatican. The meaning of clubs and diamonds is disputed but there is no dispute about the Joker, the card that can (in some games) beat any other card. The Joker, or Fool, was a "fool for Christ" because he believed in the Grail truth. The Joker is the heretic. Is it any surprise that one pope denounced card-playing, not as immoral, but as heretical?

Although the details of this culture are well beyond the scope of this book, it is interesting to note that the region's knight-poets, or "troubadours," were famous for inventing the first "Grail Romances" — sometimes called "Arthurian Romances" because they *all* involve King Arthur. How did southern French poets come to learn about an obscure British *dux bellorum*? The Grail Romances seem to be sort of a eulogy for, and epitaph for, the Holy Bloodline of Godfroi de Bouillon — which, as we have seen, stretched back past the Merovingians to Arthur's Britain and further to the arrival of Mary Magdalene(?) and Joseph of Arimathaea in Glastonbury.

Although King Arthur figures in all the known Grail Romances, he is a rather shadowy and obscure (but powerful) personality in the background of the main action of the stories. This obscurity is natural enough, given the centuries that separated Arthur from the troubadours. What is truly astonishing is that the thirteenth-century troubadours of southern France would have heard of Arthur at all.

There's a possible answer to this mystery, although it will find no favour with modern literary experts. There are various odd traditions in English folk memory. One of them, for instance, and it seems to be confined to the immediate neighbourhood of the small

Dorset village of Priddy, is that Jesus (as a boy) came to Priddy with Joseph of Arimathaea. The tradition is so detailed that places where Jesus allegedly walked can be pointed out to visitors. Priddy is about ten miles from Glastonbury. If this Priddy tradition is true, it suggests why Joseph of Arimathaea might have decided to bring descendants of Jesus and Mary Magdalene to Britain after the crucifixion — he had some friendly contacts around Glastonbury from previous trips in the metal business.

Another such stubborn memory attaches to King Arthur. It is believed by some that when Arthur was still a young man, before he became *dux bellorum* but when he knew that he would be a leader against the Saxons, he made a trip to Septimania. His purpose was to buy the larger strain of Septimanian horses to be cross-bred with the small British hill ponies. This would give him horses large enough to mount heavy cavalry, or *clibanarii* (as the Romans termed mailed and heavily armed horsemen). These horses existed in southern France, remnants of Roman cavalry horses that had been mixed with the Goths' own large horses. Rennes-le-Château was the actual capital of Septimania when Arthur could have come — say, A.D. 510–515.

Rosemary Sutcliff, author of a very popular fictional "biography" of King Arthur, makes this stubborn tradition into a prominent episode of the young Arthur's life in *Sword at Sunset*.[14] Since Rosemary Sutcliff is respected for the research behind her historical novels, we may be assured that she gathered as many existing versions of this tradition as she could. It is at least very plausible that a young Briton, planning a corps of heavy cavalry, would have journeyed to the Visigothic horse fair at Narbo Martius (i.e., modern Narbonne) to purchase a string of breeding mares and stallions. If he did, he must have visited Rennes-le-Château early in the sixth century — about the time when Bérenger Saunière's church was originally built. Is it possible that some lost document or Pyrénées tradition preserved the memory of this visit by the young Arthur? Or did Arthur do something more memorable than buy horses? Or was a vague memory of him preserved among the Merovingian refugees in Rennes-le-Château? No one knows — but what is certain is that troubadour romances from this area feature King Arthur.

This is the place to mention that the word "Grail" (or *Graal*, as the troubadours spelled it) begins to appear in western literature in the very late twelfth century and more commonly in the early thirteenth. This was the time when the Jerusalem Franks were retreating back to southern France and when Vatican retaliation could soon be expected. *Graal* is a concocted word, being a composite of the Provençal French word for a vase or container (*grasale*), the Latin word for a prayer book (*graduale*), and the Arabic word for anything inscribed upon (*al gor'al*).[15] It was a coded reference to the Holy Bloodline of the de Bouillon lineage, a living "vessel" that held the blood of Jesus, that could answer humanity's prayers, and that was "inscribed" with a lengthy genealogy plus the names of many heroes and heroines. Stories of the Grail were created between 1187 and 1220, mostly, and sought to tell the story of the Holy Blood because there was an excellent chance that it would be wiped out — if not by the Saracens, then by the Vatican. They were both eulogies and epitaphs "in advance," in case they became necessary due to present and impending conflicts.

The "Cathar" or "Albigensian" heretics were crushed by 1244, but the Holy Grail was supposedly taken from the fortress of Montségur before its fall on March 16 of that year. Is it significant that one of the Rennes-le-Château genealogies recorded a lineage up to the year 1244?

French historian Maurice Magre judged the outcome of the Albigensian Crusade as "the most crucial turning pont in the religious history of Mankind." Magre may not have put it stongly enough. In *The Iceman Inheritance* , I seriously suggested that it might have been the most significant turning point in the *entire* history of mankind. Progressive seeds of a more modern world were planted and they sprouted — but the hopeful crop was ploughed under. A religion or philosophy, the "Grail religion," held the promise of reconciling Christian, Moslem, and Jew, but reactionary forces were victorious and guaranteed more centuries of religious violence. Indeed, the Arab-Israeli conflict in today's Middle East, which may yet become our nuclear Armageddon, stems from the destruction of a composite religion that could *possibly* have defused extreme parochialism. Medicine, science, the social status of women, trade and commerce leading to technological progress — all were retarded, perhaps fatally for humanity's survival, by the outcome of the Albigensian Crusade.

Further, although it is not difficult to show that "Grail refugees" influenced the development of Protestantism, the defeat of the Albigensians meant that Protestantism could not unfold more gently and naturally in sympathetic soil. It was forced to confront a Roman Church made stronger by its victory in southern France. Under this duress, Protestantism betrayed the promise of its early ideal of religious tolerance to rival the intransigence and fanaticism of Rome itself.

This had repercussions all over the world, involving millions of non-European people. It is not difficult to demonstrate that the "Age of Discovery" was initiated by Grail refugees seeking a transatlantic haven from the Inquisition. But because of their defeat and near-extermination in southern France, the "Grail Complex" could not hold, colonize, and administer the lands they originally "discovered" and tried to settle. One by one, these discoveries were appropriated by stronger nations who were either fiercely Catholic or fiercely Protestant, and who shared equal ruthlessness and intolerance. Native populations were conquered, not "met," by Europeans who had no margin of tolerance to accord them respect or even mercy. The Age of Discovery for Europe *might* not have also been the Age of Bondage for non-Europeans if the process had been guided by "Grail Heretics," who had achieved a progressive society in southern France.[16]

There is positive evidence for this. It is the Age of Piracy. Not having vast resources that could rival national navies, the Grail religion struck back at Roman Catholic exploitation of the Americas with the only weapon it had — individual captains of pirate ships flying the so-called Jolly Roger flag. The skull and crossbones on this black flag were a common symbol on Templar and Masonic tombstones. The message was a vow to fight minions of Rome to the death. The first Jolly Roger had flown above the ships of Roger II of Sicily, a Templar. Roger was "jolly" because his court at Palermo was bright with learning and art (and because Roger himself loved Arabic and Hebrew love poetry and had a taste for women to match the beauty of the verses). Roger's ships preyed on Vatican vessels.

Christopher Columbus himself had flown the Jolly Roger, on behalf of René d'Anjou, capturing the Spanish galley *Ferrandina*. And when we also consider that "Columbus" (from the Latin word for "dove") was a popular name among surviving Pyrénées heretics, we may suspect that the matter of "Christopher Columbus" is more complicated than it is presented in text books.

The early pirates, like Drake and Hawkins, were known for their chivalry. Later, of course, psychopaths like L'Ollonaise, Blackbeard, and others got on the bandwagon.

True pirates, however, continued to exist and they tried to find remote places where they could establish a base for ship building (and repair), supplies and so on. One such place was Madagascar and there, between 1500 and 1690, pirates created the most progressive society the world was to know until two centuries later with the birth of the United States. It was the Republic of Libertatia, in Madagascar, based on Freemasonic political philosophy.

In Libertatia, sexual discrimination was illegal. Slavery was illegal. Freedom of religion was guaranteed. An elected goverment of checks and balances was created.

A fundamental activity of Libertatia pirates was to attack slave ships, free the captives, and either repatriate them to Africa or offer them Libertatia. A leading captain of this operation was one Captain Mission, a former Roman Catholic priest. After capturing one slaver off the coast of Africa, Captain Mission's speech to his crew (see notes) reads like something Abraham Lincoln might have said in 1865 — indeed there's evidence that Lincoln copied parts of it for his Emancipation Proclamation.[17] The world might have been much different if the heretics had won the war in the Pyrénées.

However, by discussing Captain Mission, Libertatia, and other anomalously progressive and humanistic pirates, we are running far ahead of our story. But perhaps a last, brief question can be permitted. Why did a pirate named Jean Lafitte arrive just in time to help Andrew Jackson win the Battle of New Orleans in 1812? Lafitte got nothing but damaged ships and casualties for his effort. But the United States was able to preserve its recent Louisiana Purchase against British aggression, so that the American democratic experiment could proceed on a continental scale. It must have been a strange sight, the Jolly Roger and the Stars and Stripes flying together over New Orleans — until one considers that America was just a bigger Libertatia. There's more to history than meets the eye.

Having defeated the heretics, the Vatican turned its attention to the Templars. They were so powerful, however, that it required fifty years to contrive a coalition willing to confront them. The King of France, Philip the Fair, was attracted by Templar wealth. On Friday, October 13, 1307, French forces and Vatican mercenaries simultaneously attacked all Templar priories in France. Surviving Templars were accused of heresy, tortured hideously, and killed. (This is why Friday the thirteenth is considered unlucky.) Special attention was accorded the last Grand Master of the Templars, Jacques de Molay. He endured years of torture in French dungeons until being granted the mercy of being roasted to death, over a slow fire, by order of king and pope. The cruelty of the Vatican and the ruling dynasty of France was never to be forgotten or forgiven.

Templars were attacked by Philip the Fair in 1307 — but it seems that the Templars had some advance warning of the impending simultaneous raids. There is actual evidence that Pope Clement V, although entangled in the French king's machinations, actually got this warning to the Templars. Clement was a Frenchman from southern France, related to the Blanchefort family — Bertrand de Blanchefort had been Master of the Templars in the Rennes-le-Château area and was one of Marie de Blanchefort's most illustrious ancestors.

Because of this warning, the Templars' Atlantic fleet, based at La Rochelle, was able to put to sea in advance of the raids. This fleet has never been heard from since. We do not know what treasures it may have carried. We don't know its planned destination or whether any ships ever arrived there. Pope Clement V performed a second service for the Grail Believers. He could not prevent Philip's raids on Templar priories in France and, in fact, he dared not prevent enthusiastic Vatican forces from joining the operation. He could not prevent the unspeakable torture deaths of thousands of men at the hands of his own Inquisitors and Philip's dungeon masters, nor could he prevent the confiscation of most Templar wealth in France by French and Vatican forces. But, as pope, he could and did officially disband the Templars and award all their surviving wealth (i.e., outside of France) to the Knights of Malta! Thus, the Grail Complex was left with considerable resources even though it had suffered a crushing defeat and near extermination.

Surviving Templars fled to the fringes of Europe, and mainly to two places — Portugal and Scotland. In Portugal they simply changed their name to the Knights of Christ and found favour in high places. The King of Portugal himself became Grand Master of the new Knights of Christ —he needed these seasoned warriors in his struggle against Spain to create a strong and separate Portugal. Later, Henry the Navigator (1394–1460) also became a Grand Master of the Knights of Christ.

Henry the Navigator began Portugal's great Age of Discovery and my notion is that ancient maps from the Middle East assisted Portuguese voyages of discovery. Diaz had a map showing the southern termination of Africa (and thus the route to the East Indies) before he discovered it in 1485. Magellan had a map of

South America, before he set sail in 1519, showing that he was to search for "an obscure strait" that would take him into the Pacific Ocean.[18] Where did these maps come from? The most likely answer is that they came to Portugal with refugee Templars who had got them out of Middle Eastern archives. But eventually, it may be, they go back to Ancient Egypt and to truly ancient Atlantean knowledge.

Did Portugal make a deal with the Templars and with the "Grail Underground"? It seems so, or at least it is possible. In 1492–94, Pope Alexander VI was asked to arbitrate between Spain and Portugal about the new lands being discovered. Alexander solved the danger of confrontation between the two most loyal Catholic powers by dividing the whole world. The pope drew a line down the Atlantic Ocean and on to the other side of the world (no one knew quite *where* on the other side because Magellan's expedition didn't sail around the world for another generation). The idea was that everything east of this Line of Demarcation would be for Portugal to discover, conquer, and colonize, everything west was Spain's — until their holdings met again somewhere in the unknown Pacific. This line was adjusted several times, but it eventually sliced through the easternmost parts of North and South America. Brazil, projecting out into the Atlantic east of the line, belonged to Portugal — which is why Brazil to this day, alone among South American countries, is a Portuguese-speaking country.

But unknown (because nobody could calculate longitude) amounts of New England, Nova Scotia, and Cape Breton were also east of this line and belonged to Portugal. Portugal colonized Brazil and defended this territory vigorously against all comers. But Portugal did not colonize or defend its possessions in North America. Portuguese fished off the Grand Banks, but they planted no colonies east of the Line in the north. Was this a payment to the Grail Complex and Templars in exchange for those priceless maps that the Templars had brought to Portugal? Maps that gave Portugal a world empire...

Perhaps this deal was cut. It was only because Portugal neglected to colonize and defend this territory that it became an objective for Scottish, French, English, Swedish, and Dutch explorations. And can it be mere coincidence that most of these explorers and settlers happened to be religious refugees from the countries named? America's Pilgrims are well known. But what about the other refugees — French Huguenots (Protestants), Dutch Protestants,

Swedish Protestants? A haven was available only because the Portuguese didn't assert its possession — and call in Roman Catholic aid. Do we owe this vital negotiation to the Grail? It seems so.

In Scotland, Templars arrived just in time to play a role very similar to the one they filled for the King of Portugal. Fleeing from France in 1307, there were enough Templars in Scotland by June 14, 1314, to win the Battle of Bannockburn for Robert the Bruce. This preserved Scottish independence from Britain for four centuries.

Scotland was the home of the Sinclairs. The family of Sinclair, or "Saint Clair" (and ninety-odd other spellings) had always been special defenders of the Holy Blood. Early Sinclairs had intermarried with the Holy Blood when it was hiding in the Pyrénées. It is written that Henri de Saint-Clair actually fought shoulder-to-shoulder with Godfroi de Bouillon, as Godfroi's picked battle companion, to take Jerusalem in 1099. No less than six Sinclairs had fought beside Duke William and Eustache (Godfroi's father) to "retake" Britain at the Battle of Hastings in 1066.

It was natural, therefore, that refugee Templars would have gravitated to the Sinclair domain in Scotland — the Barony of Rosslyn. Rosslyn Chapel, which remains a tourist attraction today, is nothing more or less than a monument to the Sinclairs and the refugee Knights Templar that fled to Scotland. And, just like in Portugal, the Knights Templar brought the treasure of ancient maps with them, maps showing land across the Atlantic. We know this because the so-called Zeno Map of the North, supposedly drawn by Henry Sinclair's captain, Antonio Zeno, around A.D. 1400 is inexplicable. It is in the same class with other maps we have seen. According to the Strategic Air Command cartographic experts who have studied it, the map is drawn on a polar, conic projection that was not conceived until three centuries after Antonio's time. It shows accurate longitudes for Greenland and Estotiland, but no one could compute longitude in A.D. 1400. It shows places on a *partly unglaciated* Greenland that no known human being had visited as of 1400.[19]

There can be little doubt that this map led Henry Sinclair across the Atlantic, just as similar maps brought by refugee Templars depicted the discoveries of Diaz and Magellan in advance.

Rosslyn Chapel holds irrefutable proof that the Sinclairs knew about America before either Christopher Columbus in 1492 or John

Cabot in 1497. The Chapel was built between 1441 and 1485 and it is a maze of Templar-Masonic stonework. It was not until 1991 that Philip Bryden noticed that one of the stone arches in Rosslyn Chapel was carved in a motif representing ears of American corn (*Zea maize*) and photographed the archway. This photo is illustrated in Andrew Sinclair's *The Sword and the Grail* (1992) and also in *The Hiram Key* (1996) by Knight and Lomas. American corn (maize) was supposedly unknown in Europe before Columbus — he brought some back to Spain. John Cabot should have brought some back too, since he claimed to have met an Indian king in America, but he did not.

After the completion of Rosslyn Chapel in 1485, we hear no more of the Templars who had taken refuge there. The chapel was

Depictions of American corn (*Zea maize*) carved in stone at Rosslyn Chapel, Scotland. The chapel was completed in 1485, seven years before the first voyage of Christopher Columbus and twelve years before the voyage of John Cabot. This carving could date from any time after 1441 when the chapel was begun, but the actual ears of corn must have been brought to Rosslyn even earlier.

the memorial for those who had fought for Scotland and who had died there. Surviving Templars and their descendants simply disappeared. In Scotland, the Templars did not form a new order of knighthood as they did in Portugal. Instead, it has been shown that they gradually merged into the organization called Freemasonry, *with the Sinclairs as* its *hereditary heads.*

But what about the hundreds of Templars and Templar-descendants who just seem to have disappeared from Rosslyn before 1485? Given the fact of the Sinclair voyage to Estotiland, and evidence of medieval Europeans in North America, it seems that we must search for them across the Atlantic.

Thus we bring the Tale of the Grail full circle to the voyage of Henry Sinclair and the later explorations of Grail Knights like Iotigolo. It is easy to see why Gérard de Sède called the treasure of the Grail accursed. The story is one of great courage, love and sacrifice...but also of terrible tragedy and inhuman cruelty.

7

The Newport Tower

Henry Sinclair could have spent the winter of 1399–1400 in the New World and, after leaving Nova Scotia in the late spring or early summer of 1399, could have spent it in New England.

We will recall that the Westford Effigy of a medieval knight in fourteenth-century arms and armour, apparently of the Gunn or Gunne clan, both of which would have been allied to Sinclair, was marked on a stone ledge in Massachusetts. Therefore, this is an indication that all or part of Sinclair's expedition may have visited New England in 1399–1400, in addition to the depiction of Drogeo on Antonio's map. This must have been after his winter in Nova Scotia because Micmac legends from the Bay of Fundy are both insistent and detailed that Sinclair spent one winter among them and built his "stone canoe" during the winter, for he invited Indians aboard in the spring. Also, we will recall that Sinclair and his companions "retained only boats propelled by oars" when Antonio Zeno sailed back to Orkney in the late summer or fall of 1398.

Sinclair would have needed a ship, and not just rowing boats, to reach Massachusetts in the spring or summer of 1399. The open-water passage across the Gulf of Maine would have been too risky for rowing boats and, according to Sinclair/Glooscap's travels in Nova Scotia (as related by the Micmacs), Sinclair simply had no time to coast along the shore of New England southward to Massachusetts in 1398. There's little mystery about how Sinclair would have known about land to the south of Estotiland. Micmacs would have told him.

The Micmacs of Nova Scotia are part of the larger Abenaki

tribal and linguistic group, which itself is a major subdivision of the Algonquin language group. Abenaki Indians inhabited New Brunswick, Nova Scotia, and Prince Edward Island in Canada, and ranged down the Maine, New Hampshire, and Massachusetts coasts of the United States. American folklorists have confirmed that the Glooscap tradition extends as far south as Boston, although there it is not as detailed as the Nova Scotia legends. According to an Abenaki Indian woman living in Massachusetts in the 1870s, it was "Kuloskabe" who divided the single mountain of Boston into the three hills that are conspicuous today.[1]

Therefore, it seems reasonable to conclude that Sinclair visited Massachusetts and the surrounding region, using his new little ship, in the summer of 1399, perhaps wintered there during 1399–1400, returning home to Scotland in the summer of 1400 in time to fall in battle in August of that year. This seems reasonable but, of course, it is not certain. Very little is certain in the field of history. Some historians maintain, for example, that our Henry Sinclair did not die until 1404, a date that allows much more time for North American explorations.

The Zeno Map of the North, drawn by Antonio Zeno about A.D. 1400, bears evidence that some geographical details were depicted after Sinclair returned to Orkney and after Antonio had had the opportunity of consulting with him. I have covered this in *Holy Grail Across the Atlantic*.[2] Also, of course, we can never forget that Antonio Zeno did not truly create this map entirely from his own knowledge and skill. There is no doubt whatsoever in the minds of Strategic Air Command cartographic experts that Antonio had some inexplicably accurate map of the North Atlantic, with a modern conic projection that Antonio didn't understand, and upon which he changed, added, and "improved" geography according to his own experience, his own cartographic skill, and his consultations with Sinclair.

Antonio's map shows a land, Drogeo, south of Estotiland, separated from it by a fair expanse of open water. Since we know that Estotiland must be Nova Scotia because of the open-pitch deposits that occur nowhere else on the North American continent (except for Hollywood, California), this Drogeo most likely represents the Massachusetts/Connecticut/Rhode Island peninsula south across the Gulf of Maine from Estotiland. Sinclair must have visited Drogeo and then must have told Antonio about it upon his return to Scotland, for it to be shown on Antonio's map. Antonio himself never saw it, according to his own words in *The Zeno Narrative.*

Estotiland is drawn with two settlements on it. These are represented by two little castles with flags on top — a common medieval convention. I have illustrated an enlargement of the Zeno Map of the North here, showing these two castles. I take these to depict first, the Micmac "town of a hundred wigwams," Pictou, which Sinclair encountered (north); and second, Sinclair's own settlement farther to the south — "the castle at The Cross."

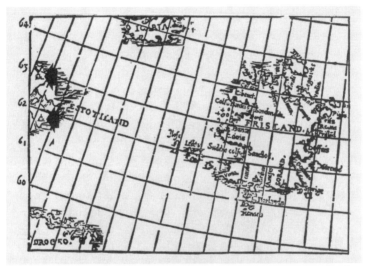

Close-up of Estotiland on the "Zeno Map of the North" (c. A.D. 1400) showing two castles representing settlements. As early as 1954 Estotiland was identified as Nova Scotia because of the open pitch deposits described in *The Zeno Narrative* that are the pitch deposits of Stellarton, Nova Scotia — the only open pitch deposits on the Atlantic coast of North America.

There are no settlements shown in Drogeo. But it is probable that Sinclair's entourage visited it because of the memorial to the dead Gunn(e) chieftain. If Sinclair himself had left a settlement of any kind in Drogeo, he would have recounted this to Antonio upon his return to Scotland and Antonio's resulting map would show it. Therefore, based on the evidence we have, it appears that Sinclair may have visited Drogeo, but left no settlement there during the *initial* 1398–1400 adventure. This may be a disappointment to American enthusiasts. Indeed, Americans tend to assume that any important event of transatlantic discovery must have taken place on what is currently U.S. territory. There have been some recent interpretations of the Sinclair voyage by Americans, suggesting that the entire episode must have taken place in Massachusetts and Rhode Island. This is too typical American chauvinism and parochialism at its most exuberant. It is not supported by the facts we have.

Nonetheless, there's another artefact in Drogeo in addition to the Westford Effigy. It is European, but pre-Columbian, and it is a good deal more substantial than the Westford Effigy — or anything so far discovered in Nova Scotia. That's also a fact, and one that upsets some Canadian enthusiasts. It is unfortunate, but probably human nature, that modern nationalism can sometimes seriously distort any objective understanding of what happened in times long before present national boundaries existed.

Standing on a gentle knoll in the middle of Newport, Rhode Island, currently surrounded by an iron fence to keep tourists at a distance, is the so-called Newport Tower. Aspects of its architecture and construction date it to the middle or late fourteenth century — say, sometime between A.D. 1350 and 1400.[3] There is no colonial reference to its actual construction, although early colonial Americans used it for various purposes, including the foundation of a windmill. There seem to be some vague references to it that predate the founding of Newport by William Coddington in 1639. If this squat tower were standing in Europe instead of in New England, it would automatically be described as "fourteenth century, of Scandinavian origin."

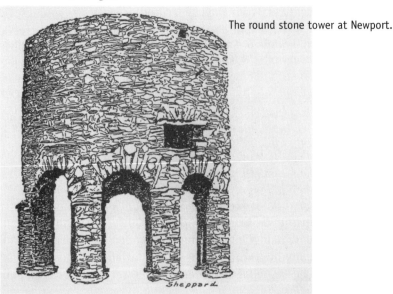

The round stone tower at Newport.

The tower is round, about twenty-five feet in diameter and about thirty feet tall. It stands on eight columns, one of which is oriented to True North based on Polaris; each column is about three feet in diameter. The tower is of rubblework construction, but it incorporated mortar and was obviously built with further construction in mind. The columns, up to the level of the first "floor," are truly vertical. But at that point there's a kind of niche all around the tower, and then the tower widens out several inches in diameter just above this indented niche. Obviously, some other sort of building had once been planned to surround the tower, using it as a sort of central supporting "core." There's no evidence that this further construction ever even began. The Newport Tower very much resembles the core of Great Hedinge Church in Denmark, St. Olaf's Church at Tønsberg, in Norway, and the Church of the Holy Sepulchre at Cambridge, England.

At the base of the columns, the tower may be said to be truly circular because the error is just one to two inches. Higher up, though, the tower is as much as eighteen inches out of round. It stands within a hundred yards of the highest elevation in Newport, and on ground that is only five feet lower than the highest land. Above the columns in the two habitable "floors," windows have been purposefully "sighted" to overlook the water approaches of Narragansett Bay and the Atlantic Ocean. The window openings are therefore placed at irregular intervals around the circumference and also at different heights above the floors. Loopholes have also been let into the sides of the tower, at various points on both floors, and they are not the long, vertical "arrow slits" that bowmen would require. This tower was built for people who had either crossbows or primitive firearms that could be aimed through smaller apertures. This is an observation that, to my knowledge, has not been made before. It may have some bearing on the age and builders of the structure.

The only entrance to the tower, as it now exists, is a square aperture, slightly more than two feet two inches on a side, but the edges of it are angled at 45 degrees on the outside and about 30 degrees on the inside. This doorway enters the lower habitable room about eighteen inches above the floor. This doorway is about fifteen feet above the ground. Entry required a ladder.

Although the structure seems to have done service as a small church, and there is apparently an altar in the lower of the two habitable sections along with a niche in the wall for a religious relic, it was obviously intended to be the core of a larger church that was never built. But, just as obviously, it served as a small and impromptu fortress in the meantime. The provisions for entry show this. A rope ladder could be pulled up and inside by defenders. Anyone else reaching the small entrance, perhaps by a wooden ladder or tree trunk leaned against the tower, would discover that only one man could enter at a time — and the aperture was just the right height off the floor so that anyone entering had to use both arms and hands in order to scrabble through. An enemy doing so would be vulnerable, virtually helpless, and could be conveniently knocked on the head by the waiting defenders inside.

But the doorway could also be effectively closed against attackers. There are no provisions for hinges, hooks, or crossbeams to hold an ordinary door. Nonetheless, the angular splays of the masonry would permit two heavy square wooden panels to be secured together by a central chain that was attached to the middle of the outer panel and that passed through a hole in the middle of the interior one. A spike passed though the chain on the inside of the interior panel would secure this doorway very solidly. Since the walls are about three feet thick, the outside wooden panel could certainly not be pushed inwards — yet the panels could be loosened and moved to permit a fairly wide field of action outward past the angled stonework. Swords, spears, or crossbows could be used against an enemy trying to enter. This is a fourteenth-century type of door used for small strongholds, or where iron for proper door hooks, hinges, and crossbeam straps was unavailable.

A fireplace with two flues was also built into the tower on the first habitable floor. These flues rise vertically inside the stone walls and then turn at right angles to exhaust from the tower's sides — obviously, if the wind happened to be blowing directly at these openings, the smoke would be backed up inside the tower. This, again, is a fourteenth-century style of flue. It was not until a century later that people discovered that if the flue was carried high above the roof, by the addition of an extension flue called a chimney, the hot air draft would be carried up and away no matter which direction the wind blew, and further, that any wind would assist the drawing of the flue.

The Newport Tower betrays a general style, plus architectural details, that date its construction to the fourteenth century. In this date, it agrees with the arms and armour depicted on the Westford Effigy knight of the Gunn(e) clan. The tower was clearly a chapel-fortress and habitation for a few men, but was intended as the core of a larger building.

Local residents tend towards the belief that the "Vikings" must have built the tower because of its obviously Scandinavian looks. Perhaps they are right — and, in any event, this general opinion is likely to be more correct than the opinion of conventional historians and archaeologists who insist that the tower was built by colonial Americans in the mid-to-late 1600s.

I think that the smallish loopholes may tell us something important. Not only are these not the long vertical slits required by bowmen, these loopholes could not have been intended for individual firearms.

The earliest shoulder-held "matchlock" arquebus in European warfare is dated to about 1485, but this primitive precursor of the rifle was rare until 1520. The tower cannot have been built between 1485 and 1520 because it would have incorporated the new-fangled chimney for its fireplace. Then, there's the consideration that the interior of the tower is cramped. Room for wielding bows is scarce — and I (for one) would not like to have been "secured" inside with co-defenders using early arquebuses. Aside from the noise which that have been literally deafening, early gunpowder would have created so much smoke inside the tower that all the defenders would have been asphixiated. Aside from mere discomfort, there's the small matter that early arquebuses commonly blew up. With one or two of these contraptions in use within a small masonry tower, there was an excellent chance (especially with matchlocks) of igniting the whole available powder supply. A matchlock was only a contrivance for snapping the burning end of a long fuse, itself sprinkled with gunpowder, against the gun's powder charge so that the gunner could choose an exact moment to fire without using his hands to push the burning fuse into the explosive. This mechanical trigger left the gunner's hands free to hold the weapon and left his attention free so that his eyes could focus on aiming it. The matchlock fuse burned until the fighting stopped. The glowing, sputtering, and sizzling fuse made life interesting in proximity to gunpowder, and re-loading a matchlock with a new charge of powder was an exercise for those who could boast steady hands.

With matchlocks at work within something like the Newport Tower, my opinion is that the first (and last) defence would doubtless have been successful, because many of the attackers would have been felled by flying rubblework. But little or nothing would have remained of the defenders. An enclosed cylinder made of three-foot-thick masonry makes an excellent bomb. All woodcuts of early fuse-fired hand-cannons and matchlock arquebuses invariably show them being fired in the open. There were good reasons for this.

The loophole size, and these considerations of early firearms, tell us that the defenders of this tower were crossbowmen. There's no particular problem with this — except that "Vikings" and North Europeans generally did not represent a crossbow culture. Almost invariably, during the 1300s, "Vikings" and other North Europeans used the longbow, when bowmen were employed at all. But commonly, in the North European culture, the art of the archer was frowned upon as being cowardly. The proper way of fighting was hand to hand. Probably also, the longbow was frowned upon because it was so lethal, was cheap, and made any good yeoman (i.e., "yew-man", since the bows were made of yew) the fighting equal of several knights in full armour. Longbows thus undermined the feudal scheme of things. English kings and princes turned a blind eye to feudal proprieties when they faced the French knights at Crécy (1346) and Agincourt (1415) who not only outnumbered the English, but were considerably better equipped and much more competent. Longbowmen won both battles for "English chivalry" by decimating the charging French knights at ranges of from 500 to 1,000 yards. The mark of a good yeoman was to put twelve arrows in the air before the first one hit the ground. Most of them found specific targets, too.

The North European longbow was so formidable that even evolved muskets were no match for a master archer. As late as 1815, the Duke of Wellington, victor at Waterloo but a shaken man after the charge of Napoleon's cavalry, advocated the establishment and training of a corps of traditional English longbowmen in case the British should have to face another such charge. They could shoot farther, faster, and more accurately than the ordinary infantry armed with the Brown Bess musket.

The major drawback to the longbow was that, although it was clearly superior to even the evolved muskets of less than two hundred years ago, it took many years to acquire the skill of an archer. Yewmen were scarce; being a longbowman was a lifetime career, not just a skill.

That's why even primitive firearms superseded the longbow. Almost anyone could become reasonably proficient with a gun. And that is also the reason why crossbows became the south European and "Crusader" answer to the longbow and also to the Saracen double-recurve bows of the Holy Land. Almost anyone could become proficient with a crossbow — assuming that he had the strength to draw the short, stiff bow. But all sorts of levers and ratchets (called "goat's feet") were devised for this purpose. Crossbows didn't usually use arrows, and certainly not the three-foot-long ("clothyard") arrows of the English and Scandinavian longbowmen. Crossbows shot a very short bolt or "quarrel" — something like a stubby arrow, about six to eight inches long, carved from wood, complete with carved or inset fins, and both tipped and weighted with metal at the lethal end.

The crossbowman's weapon and ammunition were both more compact and less fragile than the yeoman's. The crossbow could rival a longbow in range and accuracy and striking power. They could not fire nearly so quickly, but many more men could learn to use them with great skill. So, crossbows became the "projection weapon" of choice among the Normans, French, Italians, Swiss, South Germans, and so on. It became the projection weapon of choice among commanders who had seen service in the Crusades against the deadly Saracen horse-archers — and the Templars, for example, had an entire second grade of knights who were primarily mounted crossbowmen.

The preferred types gradually standardized into two basic models: a giant Swiss thing, using cast all-metal bolts, which could knock a horse flat at 1,000 yards, but which was heavy and bulky and required the brawn of a Swiss mountaineer to use (even with levers and rachets); and the Italian or Genoese type, of much less power (it was comparable to a longbow) but light, robust, relatively easy to use, and deadly accurate. This type became "standard Templar issue," one might say, because of all these practical qualities. A characteristic of these Italian and Genoese crossbows was an extremely short, stiff bow, sometimes of tempered steel but more usually of laminated and bound layers of wood and horn. They were therefore convenient to operate in a confined space — like on the crowded battlements of medieval fortresses. Since they could be shot through small splayed (conical) holes in walls and didn't require the larger arrow-slits, the defenders did not have to worry quite so much about enemy missiles whizzing through larger apertures in the parapets.

The loopholes in the Newport Tower, about seven inches in diameter on the inside and about twice as large on the outside surface of the wall, suggest but by no means prove that the builders came from a Scandinavian architectural tradition, obviously, but had designed for weaponry that was more commonly associated with south European, Templar, and Holy Land fighting experience. And, for what it is worth, there was just one Scandinavian place where these two traditions were most likely to merge: Sinclair's Earldom of Orkney and his Barony of Rosslyn.

Having studied the Newport Tower for some years, I'm absolutely convinced that it was designed to be defended primarily by crossbowmen who must have represented most of the garrison initially. The reason for this is that the impromptu fortress is ridiculously vulnerable to a determined enemy. There's no entrance, and no loopholes, on the bottom of the tower between the columns. If one or two warriors could gain this sanctuary beneath the tower, they could not be harmed by the defenders inside. But they could build a fire under the tower if they carried some brushwood with them. This fire could be fed by waves of further attackers willing to sustain some casualties. The defenders would be roasted to death within a stone oven. The defenders must have been well aware of the tower's vulnerability — and they must have felt that they had an answer to it. The tower is sited on the highest land in Newport, with superb fields of view for long distances all around. This is an ideal situation for crossbows — and the tower's garrison must have put their faith in them.

The defenders must have felt, for adequate reasons, that they could kill enough attackers at long range to prevent any large fire from being maintained beneath the tower. In short, they must have been highly skilled crossbowmen using the Italian-Genoese version of the weapon because of the restricted space inside. And, I think, this shows that when the tower was first built in this configuration, the defenders did not plan for defence against potential European adversaries. European armour and shields would have rendered the crossbow defence much more marginal, and a fire beneath the tower would have been more of an eventual certainty. This tower was designed as a temporary fortress against local Indians only. But since the further construction that was clearly planned to surround this structure seems not to have even started, it is possible that European enemies showed up sooner than expected. In this case, the Newport Tower would have been virtually indefensible against determined and numerous attackers. Since there are no signs of scorching or heat-cracked rocks in the rubblework, it is possible that the garrison either just surrendered or took to the surrounding forest. A completed structure around the tower might have offered successful resistance to European adversaries, the tower as it exists could not.

However, with the loophole size and the field of fire as it exists, European crossbowmen could have held off any attack that the Abenaki Indians could mount. These Indians were primarily harvesters of edible roots and berries, and coastal seafood — like clams and oysters. They were not particularly warlike and they were not great hunters. Compared to the inland Iroquois and Plains peoples, their weapons were weak and inaccurate. They customarily went into their skirmishes naked and, of course, had no armour. European crossbowmen would have decimated these people before they could get anywhere near the tower.

What about the possibility of a stealthy night attack in which defending crossbowmen might not have the opportunity to prevent some Indian warriors (and fire fuel) from reaching the tower? It seems that these coastal Indians *never* attacked at night. The four Viking sagas recorded several skirmishes between the Indians and the Norse during the period circa A.D. 1000 –1030. Thorfinn Karlsefni even anticipated a night attack after one of these skirmishes and disposed his men accordingly, but it never came.

The Vikings did not know why the Abenaki would not fight at night (at least, it is not recorded in the sagas), but modern anthropologists do. The night environment of these coastal Indians was inhabited by various demons, ghosts, and goblins that were more terrifying than any human foe. These Indians therefore made human mayhem a purely daylight activity...after the sun was actually above the horizon, but hesitated to fight on dark, gloomy, or overcast days when lingering demons might still be abroad. Their attack, when it came, was preceded always by a prolonged period of yelling, whooping and screaming — in order to inspire their own courage. The sagas call them "skraelings" ("screamers") for this reason. The defenders of the tower knew that they need fear no night attack and would have some minutes of noisy warning of any attack. This, by the way, argues considerable knowledge of the local Abenaki on the part of the tower builders.

The Norse had such knowledge from three centuries of contact with the Abenaki, and this insight could have been passed on to allies. But castaways from Europe would not have had such knowledge, and so probably didn't build this tower as it has been preserved. In one way or another, the tower's defenders were content to leave their structure uncompleted in this particular

240 Grail Knights of North America

way because they felt that their crossbows could deal with the local Indians.

Some readers may be interested that I have tested this empirically. In my misguided youth, I had allowed myself to be trained in the use of a crossbow for clandestine and "delicate" military operations, and an interest in archery lingered from this sordid experience. In 1995, in Ottawa, I reproduced the loopholes of the Newport Tower and shot through them with a Leopard Mark III ex-Vietnam War crossbow and discovered that, even using the standard-issue eleven-inch aluminum arrows with the triangular-section "broadhead" razor-edged points favoured for assassination, one could get a reasonable field of fire through the conical, splayed openings.

This "research" was undertaken when I was employed — believe it or not — to defend the home of a stalker victim (threatened with death, many times and not having adequate protection from local police) in Ottawa. Since guns are frowned upon in Canada and very difficult to possess legally (except by the police, of course) but crossbows were still quite legal, I dusted off the old Leopard for renewed, and perhaps much more moral, usage. I determined to secure firing angles from her house against all comers. This reminded me of the Newport Tower's loopholes, and so I decided to mix the business of 1995 defence with the pleasure of fourteenth-century research.

I asked a master bowman who owned an archery shop in Carleton Place, Ontario (near Ottawa), to try out these loopholes and measure the angles he could cover. He could not attain nearly the same field of aim using his thirty-two-inch arrows, which were shorter than the medieval "clothyard" (thirty-nine inches) shafts of traditional longbowmen. His accuracy, though, within the field of his arrows, was much better than my own. I believe that the preferred 11" modern aluminum arrows, with their owl-quiet semi-foam plastic fins, are no match for the shorter medieval quarrels. The quarrels would have increased the field of crossbow fire, probably had better flight characteristics, had greater striking power, and probably had greater range.

This experiment and its results does not necessarily mean that the Newport Tower was built by Sinclair's expedition during that winter of 1399–1400, which could have been spent in Drogeo. The Sinclairs held the Orkneys for another seventy years, and they must have made at least a few more voyages across the Atlantic after the initial one.

The opportunity for later Sinclair family voyages also means that the Gunn(e) effigy at Westford, Massachusetts, does not, necessarily, date from Sinclair's first visit in A.D. 1398-1400. Some later voyage, under a trusted and allied chieftain, could have accounted for it equally as well. This is a point often overlooked by American enthusiasts.

The settlers would have needed supplies from Europe during their first years in order to maintain, or approximate, their former lifestyle — iron for tools and weapons, cloth, tanned leather, and either dairy products (like cheese) or livestock. Any of these later trips to "Estotiland" could have resulted in the construction of the tower. For that matter, ex-Templar knights exploring the country from Estotiland could have also made it in the first years of the new century. These are not the only candidates, however.

It was a previous voyage across the Atlantic, probably made sometime around 1350–70, that supposedly inspired the Sinclair adventure in 1398. Strangely enough, there are some scanty records of a transatlantic voyage that was made about this time. But it is a long and complicated story. In the year A.D. 986, about a thousand men and women from Iceland packed themselves into thirty-five ships and, under the leadership of Erik the Red, established settlements in Greenland. They landed first at Eriksfjord, which Erik had earmarked for his own homestead, but spread out all up and down the coast on land that Erik had previously surveyed and subdivided. Eventually, there were two major settlements, the Eastern Settlement and the Western Settlement, although both were located on the west coast of Greenland facing Canada across the Davis Strait.

Erik's colonists were able to survive because the climate of that time just barely enabled them to practise mixed farming and dairy farming on the coastal strip of Greenland that was not covered by inland glaciers. Greenland was never "green." It was a name purposefully coined by Erik the Red in the best tradition of a huckster selling swamp acreage in Florida. As the sagas relate, Erik called this icy place "Greenland" because, quoth he, "People will be more readily persuaded to come hither if the land has a good name." Farming was always marginal and fishing must have been a major activity. Greenlanders almost immediately knew about land across the narrow strait to the west because Bjarni Herjulfsson was blown there the same year, 986, that the colonists arrived in Greenland. They must have obtained some commodities in North America, particularly wood for house beams and furniture (there were only dwarf willows in Greenland). It must have been an uncomfortable existence, and a precarious one. Modern excavations have shown that the medieval Norse settlers in Greenland suffered progressively because of malnutrition. Their skeletons became increasingly stunted and malformed. Nonetheless, by the early fourteenth century the tithes, or "Peter's pence," sent from Greenland to Rome indicated a population of 6,912 persons.[4]

Leif, son of Erik the Red, is credited (or blamed, in Erik's view) for introducing Christianity into Greenland. Leif brought three priests with him (called "jugglers" by Erik) when he arrived home from a visit to Norway in A.D. 999. Erik's wife, Thorhild, was converted and, since Erik refused to renounce the old Norse gods, she refused to have sexual intercourse with him — "whereat Erik was sorely vexed," as the saga puts it. Thorhild built a small church not far from their farm, which was named Brattahlid, and this construction must have angered the old pagan even more.

On February 13, 1206, Pope Innocent III appointed the Archbishop of Nidaros (i.e., Trondheim) in Norway to oversee the Orkney Islands, the Faero Islands, Iceland, and Greenland. This, by the way, is the same pope who incited the Albigensian Crusade in 1209. Up to 1206, then, Greenland had not been under much effective supervision from Rome — possibly an important point. The diocese in Greenland was called Gardar, and a modest little "cathedral" was built there that has been excavated. On December 4, 1276, Pope John XXI directed the Archbishop of Nidaros to appoint people to collect the tithes from Greenland. The archbishop of that time obviously wrote to Rome explaining that tax collecting in Greenland was a difficult business (although this letter does not survive), because two years later (January 4, 1279) Pope Nicholas III replied: "From your letters...we gather that the City of Garda is seldom visited by ships because of the dangers of the Ocean surrounding it."

But, by the late 1200s, Greenland's tithes began to trickle into Rome. As mentioned, by this time, the Peter's pence represented almost seven thousand people. On March 4, 1282, Pope Martin IV commented that the tithe sent from Greenland was in the form of cattle skins, skins and tusks of seals (i.e., walruses), and whalebone — commodities that could not be sold at a fair price. But, at some time after 1340, the Peter's pence stopped coming from Greenland. A priest, Ivar Bardarson, was sent to investigate. His report is probably the basis for the following entry in the fourteenth-century annals of Norway: "Inhabitants of Greenland fell voluntarily away from the true faith and the Christian religion, and after having given up all good manners and true virtues, *advertent genestem.*"

These last two words — *advertent genestem* — may hold a wealth of meaning for the story of the Holy Grail and the history of North America. They mean, literally, "turned to the people" — and this has usually been translated as "went native." Conventional historians quite justifiably assume that the Greenlanders, as their climate undeniably grew colder during a well-known phase called "The Little Ice Age" (A.D. 1300–1600, roughly), could not hang on to their already precarious and marginal lifestyle.

The idea goes that these people assimilated into the local Eskimo population. And, this undoubtedly *did* happen in the case of isolated homesteads along the Greenland coast. We know, because of continual Danish excavations from the 1920s to the 1990s, that expanding glaciers did inundate the medieval Viking settlements in Greenland. The people just "disappeared" in about 1340. Greenland wasn't re-colonized by Scandinavians until the Norwegian, Hans Egede, founded the first "modern" colony in 1721.

Early seekers for the Northwest Passage sailed past these ice-buried Norse homesteads and some of them reported "fair and blue-eyed" Eskimos in the Arctic. Such people have been reliably reported, and even photographed, up to truly modern times. So there was Norse genetic admixture with Arctic Eskimos — which cannot surprise us very much — and *some* of the Norse may have "gone native" as the climate deteriorated. But *seven thousand* of them? There have never been that many Eskimos in Greenland at any one time. If seven thousand Norse people had "gone native," many (or most) of the Eskimos in the Arctic would have blue eyes and fair hair, not just a few.

Because of Ivar Bardarson's report that the Greenlanders had disappeared, King Magnus Eriksson, ruler of both Norway and Sweden, fitted out an expedition to go and search for the missing Greenlanders and, if possible, return them to the true faith. In November 1354, the king wrote to his chosen captain of this expedition:

> We desire to make known to you that you are to take the men who shall go in the royal trading ship, whether they be named or not named, from my

bodyguard and also from the retainers of other men whom you shall wish to take on the voyage...Paul Knutson, who shall be captain of the royal ship, shall have full authority to select the men and officers who he thinks are best suited to accompany him...for the honour of God and for the sake of our soul, and for the sake of our predecessors, who in Greenland established Christianity and have maintained it to this time.[5]

There are several points of interest about the king's letter. First and simplest, men from the king's bodyguard would have been Götlanders, southern Swedes called Goths. But second, the last line is somewhat puzzling. If the Greenlanders had not only disappeared, but also had "gone native," assimilated into Eskimo groups — then how could the king have written that Christianity had been "maintained ... to this time"? Obviously, it had *not* been maintained "to this time," its disappearance being the whole reason for the expedition. But perhaps this was merely royal-religious pomposity on King Magnus Erikson's part — unless we are seriously misreading the Greenland situation.

The words "*advertent genestem*" are pregnant with meaning. True, they can be read as "went native." But they can also be read another way.

During its periods underground and in hiding, the Holy Bloodline had often been referred to as a "vine, a struggling plant, or seedling or 'shoot'." The reason for this was that Jesus' blood, from the Last Supper onwards, was regarded as "wine," and grapes grow on vines. Therefore, his embattled, threatened, and fugitive descendants were often called "the vine" or "the plant" that had not *quite* been uprooted or "pruned." The supposed head of the Priory of Sion during the 1970s, that enigmatic Pierre *Plantard* de St-Clair whom Henry Lincoln met, has a name that reflects this tradition. *Plantard* means a plant or a sprout — "of the vine" — one presumes. Is it mere coincidence that Joseph of Arimathaea and Mary Magdalene are patron saints of vineyards?

In addition to this, though, the Holy Bloodline was sometimes called "the people," because of both special lineage and because the meaning and message of Jesus' life had belonged to "the people" — everyone — and not to any favoured ethnic group or caste of "chosen people." I suppose this is as good a place as any to mention that there never was any such person as "Jesus of Nazareth" for the very good reason that, during the lifetime of Jesus, there was no such place or town in Palestine.

The Bible nowhere mentions Nazareth, except in the mistranslated New Testament; excellent, detailed Roman taxation records mention no such town. This manifest lack of any Nazareth in Palestine greatly bothered early Church theologians. Some of them actually lived in the Holy Land, knew its towns and villages well, and had even searched for this non-existent Nazareth. Six hundred years after Jesus, therefore, the town of Nazareth was duly founded in order to make the scriptures read sensibly. Jesus was not *from Nazareth*, he was a *Nazorean* — a member of the *Nazorean* sect, itself possibly a splinter group from the Essenes, which held that the "chosen people" could be anyone who maintained certain values and behaviour. One did not have to be ethnically Jewish in order to be God's "chosen people." This, by the way, along with several other actions and statements of Jesus, truly shows the gulf separating him from the Judaism of his time. Jesus represented a definite and decided departure from "The Law," something that some modern writers have sought to minimize — such as Knight and Lomas in *The Hiram Key*.

Modern Arabic is thought to retain many similarities to Aramaic spoken in the time of Jesus. It is interesting that the Arabic word for both "a school of little fishes" and "Christians" is *al nazrani*.[6] Jesus was a *Nazorean*, a man of the many "little people," not of the few priests and great people. That is another reason why the earliest Christians used the sign of the fish as their symbol— along with the more usual theological explanation that the first letters of "Jesus Christ" — in Greek, "IC" — are also the first two letters of the Greek word for fish (*icthys*). The "orthodox" cross was not adopted as a symbol until two centuries later and was not the first symbol used to designate Christians.

The Holy Grail tradition preserved this idea of Jesus as a man of the people, and so the symbolism of the "vine" and "the people" were merged in designations and code phrases for the Holy Bloodline. One of them, for example, was *planta genesta*, "plant of the people" — now the Latin name of a species of low-growing broom common to Brittany. This undistinguished kind of plant was, it is said, chosen by Geoffrey of Anjou as the symbol of his house. It gave its name to the *Plantagenet* dynasty of English kings — descendants of William the Conqueror, whose family came from Anjou.

Anjou, in Brittany, was one other place where Merovingian descendants of Jesus found a haven. Indeed, according to Wolfram von Eschenbach's *Parzival*, the "Tale of the Grail" began in Anjou, at least as far as France is concerned, with incoming Holy Blood refugees from Arthur's doomed Britain. Between the ninth and eleventh centuries, semi-secret Holy Blood descendants in both Brittany and the Pyrénées began rejoining forces. According to Baigent, Leigh, and Lincoln in *The Holy Blood and the Holy Grail*, this process also began in Brittany, because Brittany was a place of geopolitical activity compared to the backwater Pyrénées, with the arrival of a mysterious "Prince Ursus." This person figures in the Pyrénées genealogies leading from Sigisbert IV onwards to Godfroi de Bouillon, but he "emerged" into geopolitical affairs in Brittany. It is not generally known who this Prince Ursus was, or what he did (although someone must know, most likely the Priory of Sion). It is interesting that his name means "bear" in Latin — a designation that was sometimes, long before, applied to King Arthur (*Arthyr*, as the Celts rendered his name, is not a Brythonic-Celtic word, but is most likely related to the Greek word, and similar, earlier Goidelic-Celtic word for "bear" — *Arctos*). Eventually, because of this Prince Ursus and other leaders, the Brittany and Pyrénées "branches" or "sprouts" of the Holy Bloodline felt strong enough to counter-attack those who had previously defeated them and had driven them underground.

William the Conqueror, with the help of Godfroi de Bouillon's father, Eustache, "re-possessed" England from the Saxons who had inundated Arthur's Britain five hundred years before. The Battle of Camlann (A.D. 542) was avenged by the Battle of Hastings (A.D. 1066). As we have seen, Eustache's son, Godfroi de Bouillon, captured Jerusalem thirty-three years later in 1099 and, as the most direct descendant of Jesus, took the Holy Land. William and Eustache, as another branch of the plant (or vine) "of the people," were "given" (if they could take it) England.

Which brings us back to the errant Greenlanders and that *advertent genestem*. The secret of the Holy Blood was sort of an "open secret." Those who had the blood in their veins knew it as a proud heritage; high officials of the Church knew it also, of course, because it was a threat to the papacy. Does the phrase "turned to the people" mean that the Greenlanders had become, or had been discovered to be, heretics in the style of southern France? Had they turned to the *planta genesta* — the plant of the people, their "vine" of sweet wine that was the Holy Grail? Is that why King Magnus Erikson wanted to send an expedition to those Greenlanders who might still be orthodox, who might be struggling against heretics, and who had "maintained Christianity to this time"?

I think this is more than just possible. We don't know what sort of "Christian" priests Leif picked up in Norway to bring to Greenland. They may well have been Celtic Church priests, or Cathar "Christian" priests, and may not have represented orthodox Roman Church doctrines at all. Leif himself was a young man, just recently a pagan, and could not have been well informed on the finer points of competing Christian doctrines and dogma. All "Christians" would have seemed the same to his father, Erik.

Also, if there were Celtic Christian or Cathar Christian priests as refugees in Scandinavia, they would probably have preached a very "generic" and simple sort of Christianity to their Viking converts. Details of orthodoxy would not have mattered much to these Norse, even if they could appreciate them. And since, as we've seen, there was not much Roman Church interest in, or supervision of, these northern regions and isles until just three years before the Albigensian Crusade and up to the dispersion of the Templars, the north would have been a good place for heretics and disgruntled Celtic Christians.

We know this to be the case. Irish "Celtic Christian" priests who did not accept the victory of Roman Catholic doctrine embodied in the Synod of Whitby (A.D. 664) fled to the northern isles. By about 700 they had reached Iceland. They were there on this otherwise uninhabited island when the Norse first arrived around 750. The Norse called them "papar." Celtic Christian artefacts are occasionally uncovered by modern Icelandic archaeological excavations.

Six centuries later, refugee Templars fled to Scotland from France, starting in 1307, for the same reason that they had run afoul of Rome. They gravitated to Henry Sinclair, Earl of Orkney and a notable figure in the Norwegian court. Others besides Celtic *papar* and the refugee knights of Rosslyn may have also come into the north, and they may have come earlier than A.D. 700 or A.D. 1307. In the Vatican correspondence, we see an interest in Greenland beginning in 1206 and continuing on to Pope Martin IV's mention in 1282 — the time of the Albigensian Crusade and its aftermath.

King Magnus Erikson is thought to have been a zealous orthodox Roman Catholic, known to history as a cruel persecutor of Russian pagans. He was also unpopular among his own subjects because of his brutality and fanaticism. He was deposed in 1364 and was imprisoned until 1371.[7] In 1354, therefore, he might well have sent an expedition to Greenland, both to assist any orthodox Roman Catholics who might have been struggling with heretics, and to destroy the heretics themselves. Was there any hint that the Greenlanders could have been heretics? Perhaps.

I've stated previously that this book would not go into the "Vinland" question in any detail, because it is so complex and convoluted, but we may wonder about the very name of the place (as, it may be, King Magnus Erikson also wondered). It means "Vineland," or "Wineland," according to tradition. It was discovered by Leif Eriksson in the year 1001, who reversed the course of Bjarni Herjulfsson's voyage of 986. The sagas state that Leif named it "Vinland" because of the wild grapes discovered there.[8] In later Norse tradition, the place was called "Vinland the Good," although no Norse visits to it, after about 1030, were recorded in the four existing saga sources. But we know that the Norse remained active in North America until A.D. 1347 because that was the year in which the last "Markland ship" came into Reykjavik harbour, according to Icelandic annals.

Leif's "Vinland the Good" became more famous in Scandinavia during the 1200s and 1300s than it ever was when Leif discovered the place two or three centuries earlier. This later fame is partly explained by the fact that the old sagas were just being written down, forming the basis of Scandinavian literature for those who could read. I've often wondered, though, if this fascination with Vinland the Good during these centuries was also partly because many of the Scandinavian nobles, like Henry Sinclair himself, had been related to the Holy Blood for centuries. Viking conquest of, and intermarriage with, Irish, Scot, and Welsh survivors of "Arthur's Britain" had guaranteed this. Laurence Gardner's *Bloodline of the Holy Grail* gives genealogies of descendants through the most prominent of these northern noble houses.

I wonder if, at some point during the Albigensian Crusade or just after it, Leif's old discovery gained prestige as the Land of the Vine, Land of Wine, the Good place, and so on, because some descendants of Jesus were there.

The "Holy Grail" was supposedly taken out of doomed Montségur before March 16, 1244, by three knights who climbed down the mountain with their burden.[9] The Templar fleet, based on the Atlantic at La Rochelle, escaped the raids of 1307 and put to sea. Did the Grail and some Templar ships reach Vinland the Good?

Survival of the Holy Bloodline through many centuries had relied absolutely upon astute planning (and good luck). As early as A.D. 1200, Templars were in Scandinavia, principally in Denmark, and they must have learned of the old Viking discoveries.[10] Since the Holy Land could not be considered truly secure against the Moslems, and since nowhere in Europe would ever be secure against the Vatican, perhaps Greenland and North America were even then kept in mind as potential retreats.

We know only that the epic poem *Parzival*, written between 1190 and 1220 by Wolfram von Eschenbach, features "Greenland knights" prominently in the early chapters of the work. In *Holy Grail Across the Atlantic*, I drew attention to this, asking how Wolfram von Eschenbach, a Bavarian knight-poet, could have even heard of Greenland. According to his own words, Wolfram got his story of the Holy Grail from Guyot of Provence, a Templar and troubadour. Wolfram apparently got knowledge of Greenland from Guyot as well. When I was writing *Holy Grail Across the Atlantic*, I just didn't see the complex connections between the Norse, Greenland, Vinland, the Holy Grail, the Templars, and *Parzival*.

Nothing certain is known about the fate of King Magnus Erikson's expedition to Greenland under the command of Paul Knutson. However, a runestone discovered near Kensington, Minnesota, in 1898 may provide a hint. Naturally, the authenticity of this artefact has been a matter of heated controversy. Genuine or not, it is now in the Smithsonian. The text on the thirty-one-inch-long and sixteen-inch-wide face of the stone reads, in runic characters:

> 8 Götlanders and 22 Norwegians on
> exploration journey from
> Vinland to the West. We
> had camp beside two skerries one
> day's journey from this stone.
> We were and fished one day. After
> we came home found ten men red
> with blood and dead. Hail Mary.
> Deliver from evil.

On the narrow six-inch-thick side of the stone:

> Have ten men by the sea to look
> after our ships fourteen (forty?) days journey
> from this island. Year 1362.[11]

Kensington, Minnesota, would be about forty days' journey from Hudson Bay via the route of the Ogoki and Albany rivers of Ontario. If we take the alternative reading of "fourteen days' journey," that would be about the distance to Lake Superior. True, this is a lake, not "the sea" (*sia* in Norse). But these Scandinavians may have been stuck for a word to describe a lake so much larger than anything in their experience. Lake Superior is larger than the giant Gulf of Bothnia between Sweden and Finland — a sea, to the Norse. Several centuries later, the French were similarly flummoxed when they encountered the huge expanse of Lake Huron (but smaller than Lake Superior). They called it La Mer Douce — The Freshwater Sea.

A most interesting statement is "(we are) 8 Götlanders and 22 Norwegians." Götlanders were known to have made up the bodyguard of King Magnus Erikson, and we have his letter specifically ordering their inclusion in the Paul Knutson expedition. Therefore, this runestone dated 1362 has a tenuous, but still definite, link with a known voyage.

The Paul Knutson expedition, which most probably set sail in 1355 for political reasons concerning the king, doubtless included Orkney sailors, who had a high reputation as seamen. Orkney was a possession of Norway then, as we know. Paul Knutson's personnel might well have included one sailor who, as an old man, told Henry Sinclair of his youthful journey to a *nuovo mundo*, thus confirming the existence of America.

Several historians, Frederick Pohl among them, have speculated that the Kensington rune stone is an artefact of the Paul Knutson expedition. The idea is that after the expedition reached Greenland and found no one there, the expedition went on to Vinland, which was a logical retreat for Greenlanders. This theory suggests that the expedition pushed on further west because there was good reason to think that many of the Norse from Greenland (and those who may have "always" been in Markland?) had settled around Lake Superior and Hudson Bay. The reason for this would have been access to metal, both iron and copper. There was no metal, at least not within reach of medieval Norse technology, in Greenland itself. Metal was essential to the maintenance of a European lifestyle, and it had been obtained by the Greenlanders from Europe through barter of the same commodities mentioned as Peter's pence. But when the climate began to get colder about 1300–20, the Greenlanders decided to migrate on to Vinland (Markland), North America.

This is a plausible theory. North America was certainly familiar to the Greenlanders. The sagas mention that several hundred Norsemen from Greenland visited the place during the thirty years after Leif landed at Vinland. They must have obtained most of their wood for house-building in North America because there is no useful wood in Greenland, and they probably obtained most of their walrus hide (for hawsers) and ivory from North America. The Davis Strait between Greenland and North America is only about five hundred miles wide near the site of the larger Western Settlement.

But, surely, when life started to become impossible because of the colder climate, *some* of the Greenlanders would have returned to Europe via Iceland? These were highly independent people, and we are talking about several thousand of them. Although many might have perished due to worsening conditions since the Peter's pence representing a population of almost seven thousand was sent to Rome early in the 1300s, some considerable number must have survived. If they had the resources to relocate to Vinland, then they also had the ships and supplies to go back to Iceland. Some of these Norse would have certainly chosen that option under ordinary conditions.

But maybe conditions were complicated. I will suggest that the majority of Greenlanders may well have been heretics — and it is possible that they only gradually discovered this about themselves because of the simplified Christianity of the north and the lack of efficient supervision by the Roman Church. They could not go back to Europe, and especially not to the land of their fanatical king, Magnus Erikson. Those who might have wished to become good Roman Catholics, and who might have wished to return to Scandinavia, may well have been prevented from doing so by the majority — or massacred by the heretical majority. It would have been the only way of preventing the location of the heretics' haven from becoming common knowledge in Europe. And, if North America became commonly known as a religious refuge, some monarch, perhaps at the urging of the Vatican, would have taken stronger action than sending one ship under the command of Paul Knutson.

But this is sheer speculation. The Newport Tower is very tangible. It need not have been built by "Vikings," by Henry Sinclair, or by Templar explorers from Estotiland. It could have been built by the Paul Knutson expedition. Or, it could have been built by the Templars who set sail from La Rochelle in 1307. Any of these potential builders could account for the fourteenth-century characteristics and for the crossbow-friendly loopholes.

All this has been irrelevant to conventional historians. They maintain that the Newport Tower was built by colonial Americans — in spite of its architectural anachronisms. For the conventional "knowledge establishment," the tower was built as a windmill by late seventeenth-century colonials and that's all there is to it. The reason for this definite opinion hinges on the letters first referring to the tower. Windmills are prominent in this documentation, but a careful and chronological reading of this documentation reveals an uncertain situation.

The first reference to windmills occurs on August 28, 1675, when it was recorded that an all-wood windmill built by Governor Easton in 1663 blew down in a storm.[12] This colonial-built mill was apparently the first and only windmill in the Rhode Island colony. Eighteen months later, on February 28, 1677, a deed for a cemetery, a deed involving then Governor Benedict Arnold (not to be confused with the later American traitor of the same name, although the two were distantly related), mentions "the Stone Mill." Eleven months later, Governor Arnold mentions "my Stone Built Wind-Mill," in his will dated December 24, 1677, though he did not say that he had built it.

What seems to have happened is that, when Governor Easton's colonial-built wooden mill blew down in the storm, Benedict Arnold opportunely used the existing round stone tower on his property to become an emergency replacement mill for the colonists. The loss of a mill in August was a serious matter. The colonists were growing English wheat, barley, and rye (all of which the English confusingly term "corn"), and Indian maize (which the colonials also called corn). These crops ripen in August and September and needed to be ground into flour for the coming winter. But the only windmill had just blown down. Arnold may have realized that his round stone tower could be modified and pressed into service as an emergency windmill. It was sited on the highest land in Newport, as we have seen, and could have used the prevailing winds well. The tower seems to have been modified and used, probably as quickly as late August or early September of 1675.

Since, as we shall see, there's a reference from almost a century earlier to a round stone tower in this very area, a scenario much like this must have taken place. For why build a second all-wood windmill if a stone mill already existed? But if a stone windmill had already been built by the colonists, why did they make it so inconvenient to use? Why set it on eight columns, difficult to do and also a weak point of the all-important foundation of a windmill? Why make just one doorway fifteen feet above the ground, requiring a ladder for entry? Why make the doorway so small that only one person at a time could scramble through on hands and knees, making flour hard to carry out?

Also, the tower is "out of round" by eighteen inches at the top, or wind-catching, portion of the tower. To convert this tower into a proper mill, the colonists would have had to construct, on top, a truly circular wooden runway around the tower in order to let the windmill shaft revolve to face into the wind. But if it was necessary to construct a wooden runway atop the tower, and wooden beams to hold the runway as scaffolding — then why construct the out-of-round tower of stone at all if its purpose was to be used as a windmill? Why not make it of wood? The inherent unsuitability of the Newport Tower to be a windmill, in spite of its good location for one, is obviously why the colonials decided it would be easier just to make an all-wooden one from scratch. They did this in 1663, but their mill blew down in the storm twelve years later. It was easier and faster, under these dire circumstances, to modify the existing stone tower, using the salvaged shafts, sails, and gearing from the blown-down one, than to construct a new mill tower from the ground up. The disaster wrought by the storm also came at a time when most of the available labour was required to harvest the ripening crops.

Time being of the essence, to get the grain harvested and ground into flour, and with the reduced labour force, who would build a stone structure on eight columns, with an altar and fireplace and loopholes in it? Aside from the problems of entry in the existing Newport Tower, there is also the inconvenience of the *exit* of finished flour from the two-foot-square "doorway" that was fifteen feet above the ground. The colonists might have bagged the finished flour and just tossed bags down through the two-foot-square opening, but woven cloth was a valuable commodity in the colony. Most of it was imported from England because cotton and flax for "homespun" were not yet being grown in North America. Woollen cloth could have been woven in 1670 Newport, but you can't keep flour in wool bags. More likely, some sort of trough or chute was contrived, of wooden planks, on which the ground flour could have flowed (helped along by brooms) into waiting baskets carried by housewives.

Logic tells us that the Newport Tower was not built as a windmill by the seventeenth-century Rhode Island colonists, but was pressed into service as one in a situation of urgent need.

The first systematic archaeological excavation of the tower was undertaken in 1949 by William S. Godfrey, Jr., then State Archeologist of Rhode Island. Godfrey excavated at points all around the tower, and also under it, but mostly around its perimeter in the assumed and presumed original "construction trench." He found seventeenth-century colonial objects — a piece of clay pipestem, a nail, and a small piece of glass. He states that this "construction trench" around the tower was "completely undisturbed" and that the soil of the trench was "of an olive-yellow color and of a clayey consistency," while the soil of later centuries was a "loam and is dark brown in color." Godfrey insisted that the loam was not mixed with the olive-yellow clay of his construction trench, and therefore the colonial items he discovered dated the building of the tower. Godfrey warns, however, that the results of his excavations did not "resolve the architectural anachronisms or explain the peculiar structural details" of the Newport Tower.[13]

Without calling Godfrey an incompetent, I flatly don't believe that there's *any* undisturbed soil around this tower. It was made into a windmill at one time, so the existing documents state, and this would have required much colonial digging around the perimeter of the structure. Some sort of wooden scaffolding would have been set up to support the outer edge of a truly circular wooden runway around the top of the tower. This runway would have been necessary to permit the salvaged shaft, sails, and gearing from the blown-down mill to be used on the new and emergency stone foundation. It is badly out of round just where the shaft of a windmill would have had to revolve to keep the sails into the wind. This projecting, flat, and circular wooden "collar" around the top would have needed vertical beams to support it. These beams must have been sunk into the ground all around the tower and it would have been best to angle them into the base of each existing stone column. Such beams could then have been lashed around the columns without the need for more time-consuming carpentry.

This means colonial excavations would be undertaken in the presumed "construction trench." And, of course, colonial objects would have been discovered here. Almost equally certainly, any non-colonial objects that the windmill builders found around the tower would have been kept as curiosities. There might not have been any non-colonial objects left for Godfrey to find by 1949. We know, with near certainty, that some odd things were discovered by the colonial windmill builders or later excavators, because the colonial legend grew up that the Newport Tower was the site of some treasure. Many hopeful people dug for it near the stone structure. In the early nineteenth century, the governor himself organized an intensive, if not professionally archaeological, series of digs around the base of the tower. He was after treasure.

Why would colonial and later Americans dig for treasure around a "windmill" that they had made themselves? They would not have bothered, and so logic forces us to conclude that the tower was pressed into service as an emergency mill and, while the necessary excavations and alterations were being carried out, some odd objects were found. These discoveries inspired the idea that some non-colonial treasure might be found under and around the tower. In this case, non-colonial is synonymous with "pre-colonial" since Newport had been founded in 1639. There cannot be much "undisturbed soil" around this structure, and especially not anywhere close to the tower's perimeter or under it.

The latest attempt to date the Newport Tower was a Danish effort of the 1990s. The team had the idea of radiocarbon-dating the air that was trapped in bubbles in the mortar and that must date from the time when the mortar was mixed. The results varied wildly — from A.D. 800 (a date that was rejected as being "anomalous") to A.D. 2015 (also rejected as anomalous, thankfully). Most of the dates, though, clustered around 1500–1600 — but the margin of error was 150 years! The conclusion was that the tower was most likely built about 1645. The basic assumption of this research was quite iffy: that the mortar was sufficiently non-porous to prevent atmospheric carbon from mixing with carbon in the entrapped air bubbles. *All* mortar is porous to some extent. A large block of well-mixed mortar *might* remain non-porous enough, and cohesive enough, to prevent the gradual osmosis of atmospheric air (and moisture) into deeply entrapped bubbles. Maybe.

But there's no large block of mortar in the Newport Tower. In this building, mortar was used to bind irregular pieces of rock together — rubblework. From the beginning, there would have been fissures and cracks in these layers of mortar. The stress of the tower's weight, plus gradual shifting of the soil (even without mild earth tremors over the centuries, which did happen), would have created hairline fractures all through the mortar — and especially with rubblework because the stresses are applied to irregular shapes. Although highly touted by the press (and the researchers themselves) as being a high-tech solution to the age of the Newport Tower, common sense (and some of the C14 dates themselves) reveal this Danish research to be useless.

It is the sort of "research" that represents the apotheosis of our infatuation with technology and that befuddles the average person. If something with diodes and a dial can be applied to a problem, and applied however erroneously with regard to basic assumptions and sheer common sense, the results must be right because the "high-tech" dials and computers say so. We've forgotten about that warning phrase much used in the early days of data analysis: "GIGO — garbage in, garbage out" in our increasing and, increasingly unexamined, faith in high-tech methods of data collection and analysis.

A very low-tech approach has given better results — good, old-fashioned library research. Frederick Pohl discovered a reference to a "rownd stone towre" at Newport, and the reference dates from seven years before the founding of Newport in 1639.

In the 1620s, Sir Edmund Plowden was granted letters patent to establish the colony of "New Albion" on present-day Long Island and parts of the adjacent mainland. The grant reads (in part):

> all of that entire island, near the Continent or Terra
> Firma of North-Virginia, called the Isle of Plowden,
> or Long Island...and forty Leagues square of the
> adjoining Continent with all and singular islands,
> floating or to float, and being in the sea, within ten
> leagues of the shore of said region.

In short, this grant included not only Long Island, but also 120 miles square of the adjoining mainland together with all existing and future islands within 30 miles of the mainland or Long Island. It included today's Rhode Island and the site of present Newport near the mouth of Narragansett Bay.

The Plowden Company must have sent some people to explore this region and to assess its various resources, but we don't know when this preliminary survey took place. At any rate, the Plowden Company published, in 1632, a document entitled *The Commodities of the Island called Manati or Long Isle within the Continent of Virginia.* This was just like a modern corporate prospectus; it listed the good things that existed in the land — assets. It was intended to tempt potential English emigrants to join the colony of New Albion. Among the good things that already existed in the land were vines, deer, turkeys, chestnuts, valuable trees, good places to build and launch ships, good places to set up windmills and sawmills, various kinds of fish, fowl, vegetables, and animals for food and by-products, animals valuable for fur and the possibility of fur trading with the Indians, "spring water as good as small beere," a good place to dry codfish on a bank "60 miles to the northwards," and so on.

The delicate matter of protection against Indian attack makes up almost one-third of *The Commodities.* Potential colonists were assured that the Indians on Long Island itself, squeezed between the Dutch in New Amsterdam (New York) and the New Albion colony, could not be a serious menace. But security required that a watch be kept on the continent to the north, because it was only from there that a large and serious attack could be organized. *The Commodities* (Section 27) therefore states that this watch would be kept by "30 idle men as souldiers or gent be resident in a rownd stone towre and by tornes to trade with the savages and to keep their ordinance and armes neate."

The next section of *The Commodities* (Section 28) again deals with the matter of protection against, and trade with, the Indians. In part it reads:

> The Partners are willing to mentaine the governor
> & 2 men to wayte on him & a Seward and a factor
> & his man theise to be att the chardge of the
> Adventurors and 25 soldiers and 25 marriners to
> truck and trafficke by torne with the Savages, and
> never above tenn of them abroad att once in a
> pinnace planqued against arrowes.

The Commodities, as the word implies, is an inventory of those useful things that *already* existed in the land granted to the proposed colony of New Albion. The "rownd stone towre" must also have been in existence when Plowden's people surveyed the land grant. If it wasn't already there, why specify that it be stone — when a small pinnace planked against arrows was deemed adequate protection for other armed men trading with the Indians? And for that matter, why specify that it be "rownd" when a square tower would have been easier to construct? But, even if this was some structure planned for the future of the New Albion colony, why go to the difficulty of perching it on eight columns — not to mention all the other inconveniences (the chimney flues) and anachronisms it incorporates?

I think we may regard this "rownd stone towre" that was to the north on the mainland to be the Newport Tower, surveyed sometime after 1620 by Plowden's men but not written up in *The Commodities* in 1632 — but still almost a decade before Newport was founded. By the way, it is worthwhile to note that the New Albion scheme was superseded by another grant to Sir William Alexander, Earl of Stirling, who was awarded all the land and islands between the Hudson River and Cape Cod. Therefore, the New Albion proposal never got off the ground. No structures at all were built in the new land by Plowden's people.

It is also worth noting that the more evolved firearms of 1620 — wheel-locks and even early flintlocks with improved gunpowder — could have been used with less smoke and more safety within the Newport Tower than arquebuses of the fifteenth century. But gunpowder in an enclosed space has never been "safe."

There's another early colonial, but pre-Newport, reference to some anomalous and European-seeming construction at the place Newport was to be founded. William Wood visited the Massachusetts Bay colonies and the Newport area between 1629 and 1634. He made a map that was published, in 1635, under the title "New England's Prospect." On his map, Wood showed the then-existing Plymouth, Massachusetts, settlement as "New Plymouth." At the future site of Newport, Rhode Island, Wood wrote the place-name "Old Plymouth." Had he seen the tower on his travels and had he assumed that it was a remnant of a former and failed colony of the Massachusetts Bay settlers?

It is intriguing that there may be a much earlier reference to the Newport Tower and at a time when it may still have been garrisoned or occupied. Just thirty-two years after the first voyage of Christopher Columbus, in the year 1524, Giovanni da Verrazano, an explorer in the service of France, sailed along the coast of New

England. *Somewhere* in southern New England, da Verrazano came upon a "Normanvilla," as he called it. This term can be translated in a number of ways, none of them very helpful. Da Verrazano could have meant "Norman town," implying a small settlement. In the Italian of his time, "villa" was starting to mean a "house, usually by the sea." For an Italian, "Norman" would have meant "Northman" — anyone north of, say, France. What he saw has been much debated, because he didn't land and didn't comment further.[14] Some doubt that da Verrazano saw anything man-made, believing that he mistook some natural stone formation for a building or village. Could he have sailed past the Newport Tower?

If a building like the Newport Tower cannot be dated satisfactorily, it can be measured. Analysis of the measurements can usually, if not always, suggest the original unit of measure that the builders employed, which can sometimes suggest who built the structure and when. The Newport Tower has been carefully measured several times with this in mind. The idea is that any builders would lay out a large building with whole units and simple fractions of their customary unit of measure. The Newport Tower is not made of whole units and simple fractions of the English yard and foot, such as the seventeenth-century English colonists of Rhode Island would have employed.

But, we might ask, have these English units varied greatly during history? The answer is no. I have prepared a table showing the standard English yard that was enforced, by royal decree, between the time of Columbus and the first reference (1677) to the tower:

Standard Yard of	Year	Modern Inches
Henry VIII	1490	35.924
Elizabeth	1158	836.015
Guildhall	1660	36.032
Clockmakers' Company	1671	35.972[15]

We see that the length of the English yard has remained remarkably constant. By royal decree, the yard consisted of "three feete and no more." And "ye foote shall by twelve ynch and no more." And the inch was to be the length of three *average* barleycorns, "rownd & true" placed end-to-end.

These measures would have been used by early colonials because they were the legal ones, and their measuring tools from England would have been calibrated accordingly. The only surviving house in Newport today that was contemporary with the "windmill correspondence" is the Hazard House, built in 1675 (it's possible its precursor was blown down in the same storm that destroyed the wooden-built windmill). The dimensions of the Hazard House conform absolutely to standard English measure. The Newport Tower does not.

It has been known for almost a century, through the efforts of many experts in the study of measures, that the standard unit used for the tower is *longer* than the standard English foot by almost one-half of an English inch. This makes a "yard" that would be an extra inch to an inch-and-one-half in length. This may not seem like much to readers who are not handypersons, but it would have been an intolerable error for any carpenter or mason of the seventeenth century. Accuracy of measure was a matter of professional pride.

It has long been known that such a unit — that is, one that's half an inch longer than a standard English foot — exists. It is the Icelandic *fet* (foot) of 12.35 English inches. It was called "Norsk" measure and was used all over Scandinavia until as recently as the 1930s. Twentieth-century steel measuring tapes were manufactured to this basic unit and its subdivisions and multiples. Three of these *fet* constitute the Norse *ell*. The Newport Tower was laid out using whole units of *fet* and *ells* and simple fractions of the *fet*. The structure was therefore built by people, *or master craftsmen among them*, who used Norsk measure. This can point to "Vikings," the Paul Knutson expedition, Henry Sinclair's expedition and later voyages from Orkney to Estotiland, or explorers from Estotiland. It argues against construction by members of the Templar fleet who left La Rochelle in 1307 — unless the fleet went into northern waters first and acquired additional personnel from Scotland and the Isles, or Greenland, before venturing across the Atlantic.

At any rate, regarding the Newport Tower, my opinion is that it is an artefact genuinely indicative of the Grail Knights of North America — one way or another. Either it was built by Sinclair's people or people that were allied to them, perhaps some Greenlanders, or it was built by their enemies represented by the Paul Knutson expedition to Greenland, Vinland, and farther west in pursuit of heretics.

8

The Case of the Acadia Coin

By 1989, I began receiving letters from readers of my first "Grail" book. Terence Punch, then president of the Royal Nova Scotia Historical Society, wrote to say that he and other members of the society had discovered another inexplicable collection of ruins about twenty-five miles (40 kilometres) north and west of "The Cross." Dr. Gérard Leduc, a retired professor from Montreal's Concordia University, wrote to tell me about strange ruins he'd been investigating near the Quebec-Vermont border. He also wrote about old maps, which he discovered, that showed apparently European fortifications in Montreal before the place was officially founded in 1642. A Burlington, Ontario, business consultant, William F. Mann, contacted me to say that his relatives back in Nova Scotia had discovered yet another strange site near the town of Noel Shore, further north and west of the ruins that Terence Punch and his team had found. He commissioned aerial photographs of the place, and Bill Mann showed them to me. Although I'm no expert on aerial photo analysis, the picture seemed clearly to show some geometrical pattern of eroded earth contours and crop marks underlying modern agricultural fields. But these seemed to me then, and now, to resemble Ancient Celtic circular fields and oval houses more than medieval remains.

And, of course, last but certainly not least, Don Eckler of New York State wrote to me about his own, and Bob Williams's, strange discoveries in New York and Pennsylvania.

And there were other letters, about other odd ruins. Had I seen the Egyptian ruins near Bedford, Nova Scotia, outside of Halifax?

Well, no — I had seen the remains there of a canal system built in the 1850s. Had I seen the ruins on the New Brunswick-Quebec border, on the east shore of Lake Témiscouata? Well, no again, although I had independently heard about these some years before when writing an article for the *Montreal Gazette* about the various alleged lake monsters of the region! Had I seen the ruins on some of the St. Lawrence River islands not far from Lake Champlain? No. Had I seen the Viking runestone near Lake Champlain, and the underground stone chambers there near Bulwagga Bay? No, but I had heard about them while doing "monster research" for the *Gazette* — North America's first lake monster report, by a European, was made by Samuel Champlain himself, in 1609, describing "a serpent as big as a barrel" in Lake Champlain. So my *Gazette* article relied heavily on research around that lake. Inevitably, I'd heard rumours of mysteries other than "Champ," as the lake's monster was fondly called.

At first, I just shrugged at these letters. I was deep into other projects at the time. But the file of letters got thicker. I remembered many of the details because I had written lengthy responses out of both courtesy and interest. One day I decided to read this file again, and it struck me that the accounts of ruins formed a definite pattern. All of these ruins were located along waterways leading from Nova Scotia towards the heart of the continent. Of course, one *could* say that all eastern North American rivers lead inland from Nova Scotia! I kept this wryly in mind. Still, people had written about puzzling ruins where there should have been none and, I noted, these ruins seemed to be located on the largest and most obvious rivers leading inland. Even the American letters conformed to this pattern, as I realized after looking at a map, because the Susquehanna River flowed into Chesapeake Bay from the north, from the direction of the Great Lakes Basin.

If the ruins described in the letters were both genuine and relevant, then it seemed as though the Estotiland settlers had shown a definite tendency to probe towards the Great Lakes. They went about it in two ways. Either they went immediately north and west from "The Cross," encountered the Bay of Fundy and the mouth of the St. John River and travelled up the river to Lake Témiscouata and across "The Great Portage" to the St. Lawrence. Or they coasted southwest along the Maine and New England shores and went up the biggest rivers they could find. These all flow from the north. The Connecticut River takes you straight to Lake

Memphremagog and the Newport-Magog ruins recounted by Gérard Leduc. The Hudson takes you north to Lake Champlain and the St. Lawrence River and all the various ruins clustered there. The next big river, the Susquehanna, takes you north through Pennsylvania and western New York State to very near Niagara and all the ruins described by Don Eckler.

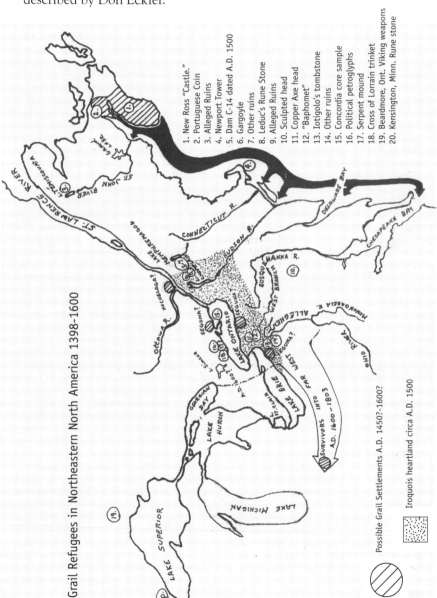

1. New Ross "Castle."
2. Portuguese Coin
3. Alleged Ruins
4. Newport Tower
5. Dam C-14 dated A.D. 1500
6. Gargoyle
7. Other ruins
8. Leduc's Rune Stone
9. Alleged Ruins
10. Sculpted head
11. Copper Axe head
12. "Baphomet"
13. Iotigolo's tombstone
14. Other ruins
15. Concordia core sample
16. Political petroglyphs
17. Serpent mound
18. Cross of Lorrain trinket
19. Beardmore, Ont. Viking weapons
20. Kensington, Minn. Rune stone

Grail Refugees in Northeastern North America 1398-1600

Possible Grail Settlements A.D. 1450?-1600?

Iroquois heartland circa A.D. 1500

After a couple of years, Estotilanders and Micmacs would have
been able to communicate because each would have picked up more
than a smattering of the other's language. Estotilanders would then
have learned about the Great Lakes and the great St. Lawrence
River flowing from them. The Micmacs had a very good knowledge
of Nova Scotia's geography and some of the continent north and
west of it. They traded with Hurons and other Iroquoian speakers
around Lake Ontario. A map on display in the Abenaki Friendship
Lodge in Truro, Nova Scotia, a public motel and hotel owned and
operated by the Micmac reserve there, is a traditional Micmac
creation. After you take into account that the Micmacs reckoned by
time of travel, and not by fixed distances, the map suddenly reveals
itself as being very accurate. This Truro map extends far into New
Brunswick, and the St. John River is conspicuous.

The Estotiland refugees would quickly have learned the general
features of the continent as far west as, say, Niagara. They knew that
metal, in the form of copper nuggets, was available in great quantity
around the giant inland seas because the Micmacs acquired Lake
Huron nuggets by trade. Estotilanders would have known how to
extract and smelt "bog iron" — iron usually found in marshy areas,
where plant metabolism has assimilated and concentrated iron
oxides from the mineral suspended in water, or mineral deposits
under the surface. But extracting bog iron is a laborious process, and
the resulting metal is weak from many mineral impurities. It is
possible that people in Estotiland would have heard of the huge iron
ore deposits at the western end of Lake Superior near today's
Duluth. This is the fabulous Mesabi deposit of iron, the richest in
the world, and very accessible to fourteenth-century technology.
Today, Mesabi iron is still mined in open pits.

Metal must have been a concern for the Estotilanders. They
needed it in order to maintain a European lifestyle and, perhaps
more immediately important, to maintain their military superiority
over the local inhabitants. The Indians knew of copper, and they
used it for implements, but European blacksmiths had almost
forgotten how to make and work bronze from copper. Iron had
supplanted bronze by about 500 B.C. in Europe and bronze had not
been used since for weapons. Iron was stronger and harder. In the
thirteenth century, Europeans were making small quantities of crude
steel, a compound of iron and carbon that was much stronger than
iron. The settlers of Sinclair's haven would have sought out a source
of good-quality iron on the western side of the Atlantic because, if

trade with Europe was ever interrupted for a long period, they could not preserve their way of life or even their lives without it.

We have discussed the possibility that the Paul Knutson expedition of 1355 left the Kensington Runestone dated 1362. Kensington is in the Mesabi region and some of Knutson's people may have recognized the iron deposits. Vikings were always on the lookout for sources of iron in their travels, and it is possible that some unknown Viking explorer had discovered the Mesabi iron long before. In 1937, a complete set of Viking arms was found in Beardmore, Ontario, just north of Lake Superior about five hundred airline miles from Kensington. Stylistically, these Norse weapons date from the early eleventh century, which is when they were made, but weapons were often handed down through several generations until some recipient decided to acquire more modish arms. Therefore, although the Beardmore relics were made about A.D. 1000–50, they could have been buried with a fallen warrior any time over a period of two or even three centuries after that.

It may be that the missing Greenland colony headed into the heart of North America via the Davis Strait and Hudson Bay, and they did so because they had learned, by 1340, that there were vast iron deposits around Lake Superior. If the Paul Knutson expedition trailed the missing Greenlanders from Vinland "toward the west", expedition members may have also noted the iron. If this was the case, Sinclair's colonists might have known the general location of the Mesabi deposits before they left Orkney. Sinclair could have heard such gossip in Norway, to which he travelled on state business, but it was probably common knowledge among the Norse traders throughout the north.

The obvious question is, though, what happened to these hundreds, or thousands, of Greenland colonists who may have moved from Greenland and from Vinland towards the west? Some of them certainly were assimilated with the Eskimo peoples in Greenland and today's Canadian Arctic. But serious scholars, such as Germany's Paul Hermann, have proposed that most of them were assimilated with some native people to form the populous Mandan tribe that inhabited Minnesota, Wisconsin, and northern Illinois. When first encountered by white men in the mid-seventeenth century, the Mandans knew a simple form of Christianity, they worked copper well, but had some iron objects, and many of them had fair skins, sometimes light brown or auburn hair and beards, and blue or hazel eyes. These people were virtually wiped out by the smallpox epidemic of 1816, but some paintings and first-hand reports of them still exist. It may be that the old Viking legacy expressed itself within the Mandans mostly, but neighbouring tribes also show some, but lesser, European admixture.[1]

There is absolutely no proof that the Vikings knew about Mesabi iron, but it is plausible speculation covered in a number of serious and scholarly books about the Norse. One of these, *Westviking*,[2] by the famous Canadian author Farley Mowat, has even given birth to a new Canadian literary genre — historical fiction about Vikings along the shores of Hudson Bay. Aside from Mowat's own *The Curse of the Viking Grave* and *Lost in the Barrens* (adapted for television movies by Atlantis Films), there is also Tom Henighan's *The Well of Time* — all three are about Vikings in Manitoba.

So it seems that the Estotiland settlers must have heard about the copper, and might have heard about the iron, deposits around Lake Huron and Lake Superior respectively, and set out rather quickly to confirm the existence of these metals. They probed purposefully, and by several routes, towards the St. Lawrence and the Great Lakes.

But were there so many settlers in Estotiland that they could undertake so many explorations?

In *Holy Grail Across the Atlantic*, I had already accounted for Sinclair's modest settlement to my own satisfaction.

We may recall that Bérenger Saunière, when he supposedly found the parchments in 1891, was also supposedly instructed by his Church superior, the Bishop of Carcassonne, to take them to the Seminary of St. Sulpice in Paris. Michael Baigent, Richard Leigh, and Henry Lincoln recount correctly that this institution was founded in the late 1630s by a man called Jean-Jacques Olier. But they didn't, apparently, realize the extraordinary implications of this. Jean-Jacques Olier was *also* one of the two primary founders of Montreal in 1642. Not only that, but his Seminary of St. Sulpice was granted the exclusive right to look after the spiritual requirements of the Montreal colony.

The newly founded Sulpicians somehow won this right in competition against long-established orders that were eager to control the spiritual orientation of the new "Ville Marie" ("City of Mary"). Clearly, Jean-Jacques Olier and his Seminary of St. Sulpice had "major leverage." Since Bérenger Saunière had been instructed, allegedly, to take his parchments to the very same seminary, the nature of this leverage wasn't hard to guess.

My notion was that, since it is an accepted fact that Henry Sinclair had close Templar connections and that his Rosslyn had been a Templar haven, the descendants of his Estotiland settlers in Arcadia would be relocated to a safer place inland, Montreal, just as soon as a colony could be set up. Or, at the very least, by mentioning the Seminary of St. Sulpice, the Priory of Sion, through Gérard de Sède, wanted *someone* to make these connections and thus carry the Grail story across the Atlantic via Sinclair's Estotiland and Olier's Montreal. Gérard de Sède even planted *another* clue that this transatlantic connection should be made.

When Bérenger Saunière came into his money, another of his projects was to continue (much more elaborately) with the renovations of his church that had been interrupted by the unexpected discovery of the parchments. Aside from having the words "Locus Iste Terribilis" ("This place is terrible") carved above the door, he decorated the inside in a colourful and bizarre manner. Colour photographs of some of it are in Henry Lincoln's *The Holy Place* — a curious devil inside the door as part of the support for the Holy Water container, full-colour renditions of the traditional Roman Catholic "Stations of the Cross" around the walls (but each with some decidedly untraditional twist). In one of these stations, the Christ child is shown wrapped in Scots tartan!

Now, to me, steeped in the textual and cartographic evidence of Henry Sinclair's transatlantic exploit, and knowing that Rosslyn had been a haven for outlawed Knights Templar, this Child in Scots plaid was a definite pointer to an overlooked episode in Holy Grail history. Baigent, Leigh, and Lincoln noted this Scottish scene in the Rennes-le-Château church, but did not follow the clues even when their research subsequently led to the activities of Jean-Jacques Olier.

Indeed, I suggested that all of the "Et in Arcadia Ego" paintings were also one way of reassuring the Grail Faithful that the Holy Bloodline descendants were being safely "shepherded" to a new haven (in addition to whatever other information these works may contain). *The Shepherds of Arcadia,* the title of one of Poussin's Arcadia-theme paintings, were literally that — people who would oversee the relocation of the Estotiland sheep to the new fold of Montreal. I even suggested that the shepherds in Poussin's paintings, the three men and one woman, were portraits of the four people who were mostly responsible for this — three men (Jean-Jacques Olier and Jérôme de la Dauversière, the founders and backers of Montreal, and de Maisonneuve, Montreal's first governor) and one woman (Jeanne Mance, "the angel of the colony," the spiritual strength of Montreal and the administrator of its hospital).

The reason King Louis XIV acquired this painting and then hid it away was simply that these people were known and identifiable *at the time*. And yet, he had permitted the colony to be established as a "city of the *living* Holy Family" (my italics). This could not have pleased the Vatican very much, which was why the king hid the painting clearly identifying four of his dissident, but powerfully connected, subjects.

It is also quite interesting that some research seemed to confirm my suspicions about this particular Poussin painting. Nicholas Poussin did most of his work in Italy, but *The Shepherds of Arcadia* was done in Paris between 1640 and 1642, according to art historians. Poussin was an acknowledged master, and, as we have seen, he had much to communicate in this painting. He performed "an amazing feat of virtuosity" with it. It seems that he may have done even more — he may have supplied us with the only certain and authentic portraits of four people who were important to the early history of Canada. The bodies of these shepherds would have posed no problems for a master like Poussin. All he would have needed to know was that they were three men and one woman.

But the facial portraits were a different matter. To be faithful and accurate portraits (and why else would they have been hidden?), the subjects would have had to sit for Poussin. I don't pretend to know what he would have required in the way of time. But I do know that all four people — Olier, de la Dauversière, de Maisonneuve, and Jeanne Mance — were in Paris, and therefore available to sit for Poussin, *only* during 1640 and 1641, while this painting was being created. Mere coincidence? Matching the facial portraits in Poussin's painting with sketches or descriptions of Montreal's founders is a research suggestion for a student of art history, and one that might provide not only a new perspective on Nicholas Poussin's life and work, but verification of portraits of four people who were influential in early Canadian history.

Why was relocation inland from Arcadia necessary? Why would the Grail Faithful start worrying about the Sinclair community of Estotiland around 1580-1620? The epic poem *Arcadia* was published in 1590 and the "Il Guercino" (Barbieri) version of the shepherds of Arcadia was thought to have been painted about thirty years later, in 1618.

It seems simple enough. By the time of the Armada crisis in 1588, Elizabeth I had been on the English throne for thirty years. Philip II of Spain, after many unsuccessful efforts to acquire and subdue Protestant England by his marriage overtures to the island's indomitable and "virgin" queen, Elizabeth, decided to take England by force, add it to his possessions, and also return it to the spiritual fold of the Church of Rome. He gathered together an invasion fleet of 130 ships, and an on-board army of 30,000 men, all under the command of the Duke of Medina Sidonia. In addition to this, though, the Armada was to sail from Lisbon to Flanders, pick up the seasoned army of Alessandro Farnese, and convoy it across the Channel to assist in the invasion.

This ambitious undertaking encountered difficulties from the start. Just after leaving Lisbon in May, the huge fleet was delayed by weather at Coruña on the northwest corner of Spain. It did not reach Plymouth until July where it encountered much more severe problems represented by the English fleet. As everyone knows, Elizabethan England was blessed with a remarkable generation of courageous and adventurous mariners. The Armada encountered many of the most famous at once. Under the command of Charles Howard himself (later made Earl of Nottingham) were no less than Sir Francis Drake, Sir John Hawkins, and Sir Martin Frobisher. In a running, roiling battle up the English Channel, this formidable pack of Elizabethan sea-dogs mauled Medina Sidonia's larger and less maneuvrable ships unmercifully. Although most of the Armada escaped being sunk, it was compelled to keep sailing north by the harrying English and was finally beaten by storms north of Scotland and Ireland.

It was, of course, a great victory. But it was also food for thought. It was clear that Elizabeth would not live forever (she was fifty-five years old), and the effort put into the Armada demonstrated the depth of Roman Catholic hatred for Protestant England. Further, it seemed that Elizabeth's successor would be a nominal Roman Catholic, a Stuart from Scotland. Certain political philosophers in England — and most, but not all, were Freemasons — began to think about forging Parliament into an effective instrument for limiting the powers of the monarch. Some steps in this direction had marked the reign of Elizabeth herself.

She lived longer than anyone expected, and died in 1603 at the age of seventy. James I succeeded to the English throne that same year, but his reign was never a happy one. The only positive things about it were the astonishing literary and artistic productions of the English Renaissance and the creation of the King James version of the Bible — but even its worth has been questioned by some modern theologians and historians because of the many mistranslations in it. James, like all Stuarts, was suspected by his increasingly Protestant English subjects of favouring Catholics. Further, like all Stuarts, he was quite extravagant, and this goaded the ever-increasing Puritan population. At this time, and largely because of a Stuart on the throne, there was a highly concerted effort on the part of the English political leaders to make Parliament into a strong institution of government and not just an impotent and irrelevant convocation of Lords and popular representatives that had mostly been ignored by reigning monarchs.

James encountered a renewed effort to assert parliamentary power, and responded by dissolving Parliament (in 1611) and asserting his "Divine Right" to rule. Astute political minds, including those charged with preservation of the Holy Bloodline, could see all too clearly that Parliament and the Crown were heading into a confrontation. Holy Blood Planners (if we can call them that) knew this better than many because they were mostly Freemasons and were themselves developing the democratic thought that would eventually pit Parliament's army against Royalists in the English Civil War.

James I died while in an even deeper confrontation with Parliament. His son, Charles I, came to the throne in 1625. From the first, the new king's contempt for Parliament and the people (and particularly Puritans) was patently obvious. Serious trouble was brewing, but the pot had been heating up since the latter part of Elizabeth's rule, say from 1588, and James I's dissolution of Parliament in 1611 just upped the temperature, but Charles I's arrogance made the pot boil over. In 1628, Charles I married Henrietta Maria, the youngest and most vivacious daughter of Henry IV of France. She brought Arcadia, or "Acadia," with her as a dowry. Which is to say that not only did Acadia pass out of French ownership, but passed to a King of England who was in deep trouble with his own people. Charles I, mostly through his own arrogance, intransigence, and duplicity, forced a civil war against Parliament and the Puritans.

Naturally, Charles thought that his noble cavaliers would sweep the common rabble from the field, but he reckoned without Oliver Cromwell's "New Model Army" — the first armed force since Rome with modern discipline and organization. The "dashing cavaliers" were no match for the "Roundheads" or "Ironsides" (as Cromwell's army was variously called). Charles I not only lost the war, he lost his head when Cromwell had him executed in 1649.

The war between the Royalists and the Roundheads (or Puritans, so-called because of their unadorned helmets) would naturally be played out in mini-wars overseas wherever England had colonies. Acadia had come to Charles I with Henrietta Maria and was Royalist if only because it was marriage property of the House of Stuart, *not England* — at least, that was an arguable perspective (and we must return to this). Acadia would, therefore, be vulnerable to attack by Puritans from the Massachusetts colony. This must have seemed inevitable to Holy Blood political experts. A new haven was needed. Attack by Massachusetts would become an increasingly inevitable matter, and no one in the 1630s could say how long the impending English Civil War would last.

It was a more serious matter then than it would be now. Massachusetts was much larger then than now. The once-humble Puritans of the *Mayflower*, having achieved a certain security and prosperity in their American colony, became intolerant (always a latent fault in their religion), greedy, and ruthless (latent faults in everyone). They became as imperialistic and authoritarian as the Papists and kings they despised. Whereas Charles I clung to his divine right to rule, the Puritans began to say seriously that their expansion was God's will that the new land should be controlled by the "righteous" (themselves). By the 1630s, Massachusetts had expanded to include most of what is now called New Hampshire and some of Maine. By 1677, Massachusetts had purchased all of Maine.

For Henry Sinclair back in 1398, there had been a wide and inconvenient expanse of open water between Estotiland and Drogeo. In the 1650s, just 250 years after Sinclair, there was very little open water between Acadia and bloated Massachusetts. Only the Bay of Fundy separated them — and on a clear day you can see across it.

The problem for the Holy Blood was simply that in the 1620s and 1630s there was little truly unknown and unclaimed geography left in the world. Europe's "Age of Discovery" had seen to that. And the few undiscovered and unclaimed places were in Arctic or Antarctic regions that were uninhabitable, given the technology of the day, or else they were in the fever-ridden tropics of Africa, South America, and southern Asia — which belonged to Spain and

Portugal anyway. There was no longer another "Estotiland" that could sustain colonists in a European lifestyle and that could be kept at least semi-secret. Any new haven for the Holy Blood would have to be a "disguised one," not a truly "unknown one" in the geographic sense. Using their natural cultural orientation (French), and the geopolitics of their era, I argued that they finally decided to plant a well-disguised heretical colony in the very heart of New France. The city of Ville Marie, Montreal, a colony dedicated to the living Holy Family. It would not be vulnerable to attack by Puritans like Sedgwick because of the narrows upstream on the St. Lawrence and the fortress at Quebec City guarding these narrows. It might prove vulnerable to religio-political developments in France itself (but there was a plan afoot to counter this), and it might be vulnerable to the Indians on the seventeenth-century frontier, but these were deemed then to be lesser threats than attack on coastal Acadia by Massachusetts Puritans.

In 1653, Governor Sedgwick and his "righteous" Massachusetts colonists duly attacked the "arrogant" Royalists of Acadia. Sedgwick certainly burned the Acadian stockade-fort at Annapolis Royal, and there are claims that he probed further inland to destroy "the castle at The Cross." Not only the "Holy Grail" had crossed the Atlantic, the English Civil War had also crossed it.

Therefore, it had all seemed fairly simple to me. In the previous book, I had documented the rather hectic activity, starting about 1620, to establish the financial and administrative structure necessary for the founding of Montreal as a secret "heretic" community within the bosom of New France. Also, I had mentioned the "cover" for the relocation of some people from Acadia to Montreal. Holy Blood planners could not simply bring people from Acadia, which was supposedly uninhabited, to Montreal. There had to be some plausible trade and traffic between Acadia and New France in addition to the very few known fur traders operating in both places.

This cover was, I had supposed, the French colonization of Acadia by Isaac de Razilly in 1634–35, when he brought six hundred colonists to Acadia. These industrious people quickly made and launched numerous small ships and shallops for fishing and coastal trade and for travel to New France. Their very existence justified French ships stopping in Acadia before travelling on to Quebec City and other New France settlements on the St. Lawrence. The Acadian colonists made it much more difficult to keep track of who came and went between Nova Scotia and the St. Lawrence. By dint of hard work in France, Montreal managed to become established in 1642, seven years following the colonization of Acadia. After Sedgwick's attack on Acadia in 1653 there was, in fact, an influx of colonists into Montreal.

In *Holy Grail Across the Atlantic*, I assumed that this influx of people in 1654–55 was the core descendants of the Holy Bloodline from Sinclair's old Estotiland. I also assumed that one duty of the Acadian settlers would have been to occupy, or else thoroughly destroy, any former constructions of Estotiland. There would be no obvious evidence to prove that Holy Blood colonists had ever even been there. For me, this explained the curiously tentative nature of the "ruins" at The Cross. I left it at that.

From 1959 to 1961, Frederick Pohl and the archaeological team from the University of Maine had found "very early" Acadian artefacts in the house sites atop Cape d'Or. At that time, of course, the significance of Sinclair's close connection with the refugee French Templars and the Templar connection with the Holy Grail were not realized by anyone (except by the still-secret Priory of Sion). The knight refugees themselves had been originally French, just like the Acadians 230 years later, and the people of Estotiland must have kept up some ongoing contact with France and Scotland (however sporadic) over the intervening years. How could one distinguish between "Late Estotiland" artefacts and "Very Early Acadian" ones? I suggest that someone at the University of Maine should have a closer look at those Cape d'Or artefacts.

I was content to leave the story of Estotiland when the Acadian colonists arrived (1634–35), when Montreal was established (1642), and when new people flooded into Montreal from Sedgwick's attack on Acadia in 1654–1655. But I did point out that the colonization of Acadia by the French could not have been accomplished without Stuart collusion. Remember, Acadia had come to the King of England as dowry with Henrietta Maria. Acadia belonged to the English king, not to France. Indeed, as early as 1628 (as soon as he had it), Charles I began creating "Baronets of Nova Scotia" for cash since Parliament refused to give him any money. So, while Charles I was selling his titles in Nova Scotia to Englishmen, the French were bringing in hundreds of colonists!

Nonetheless, even though the story had its curious aspects, I thought that it was not only straightforward, but also quite limited in time and geography. Estotiland had been a refuge for a very small group of people under the protection of picked guardian "Templars" from Scotland, guardians who might well have been rotated in their duty. The refugees had been relocated to Montreal by "The Shepherds of Arcadia." The faithful had been reassured by all the coded "Arcadia" references in art and literature. The phrase "Et in Arcadia Ego" took on special meaning for those in the know and helped to spread the word that the lineage was safe from the problems of Charles I. (Charles himself read Sir Philip Sidney's long poem *Arcadia*, written in 1590, while awaiting the axe at Whitehall. He was apparently comforted by the thought that the lineage he represented was being protected yet.)

Mind you, even then certain things caused a tiny red flashing warning light to begin pulsating in my Grail-weary brain. Like the first name of Montreal, for example. When Jacques Cartier arrived at the future site of Montreal in 1534, he was told by the inhabitants that the name of the place was Hachelaga (Hochelaga, Chilaga, Hochela, and other variants). But this word does not seem to be an Indian one, as linguists have long remarked. In 1991, I was writing a book on Middle Eastern religions when I stumbled on this passage from Samuel I in the Bible: "Doth not David hide himself with us in strong holds in the wood, in the hill of Hachila…?" (Samuel I 23:19, see also Samuel I 26:1).

David took refuge on this wooded hill, which was in the "wilderness of Ziph," during his guerrilla phase when he was in conflict with the rival king, Saul. With a brief history of the Holy Grail behind us, we can immediately see how very apt it was to name a New World haven "Hachila." Jesus came from the line of David. And, just like David's conflict with Saul, the living descendants of Jesus could be said to be waging their own guerrilla war against a rival, "official" king, the pope.

The name Hachila is also quite apt for the actual site of Montreal. It is a high hill, called a mountain locally even today. Montreal is a contraction of Mount Royal (also the name of a Templar fortress in the Holy Land, and the name of a heretic stronghold near Carcassonne during the Albigensian Crusade). And, in 1534 and until much later, this hill was heavily wooded. Parts of it still are, preserved by the modern city as a park.

Naturally, linguists have been puzzled about the name after discovering that it did not seem to come from any known Indian language in the area. It is good Hebrew. After dismissing the first wild thoughts that came to me, such as all the early colonial ideas that the American Indians were remnants of "the ten Lost Tribes of Israel" and so forth (but we must return to this), I figured it was more probable that some Grail refugees had travelled inland from Estotiland between A.D. 1398 and 1534 (when Cartier arrived), had appreciated the strategic situation of Montreal just as later settlers were to do, and had named their settlement after a Biblical guerrilla stronghold of David's.[3]

Cartier coyly doesn't exactly tell us what sort of people the inhabitants of Hachelaga were, although they had "fortifications." This brought to mind Dr. Gérard Leduc's letter about the old maps showing European-style fortification at Montreal before it was founded.

The Hachelagans told Cartier that there was a larger city of white men towards the southwest on the shore of a great body of water. They pointed, roughly, towards Lake Ontario (or Lake Erie?) and told Cartier that the city was called Seguna. Later, some sources relate that Cartier received a gift of twelve "golden rods" from the people of Seguna. But Cartier's informants at Hachelaga also maintained that some of the people of Seguna had wings and could fly — so I discounted this whole episode as being fanciful Indian myth — until I came across that passage in Samuel I. And then I wondered if the reported "flying men" might have been paintings or carvings of Christian angels. Indians might naturally regard these as portraits of some of the inhabitants of Seguna.

In short, there were some intriguing loose ends about Montreal, Hachelaga, and Seguna. But I found it easier to be satisfied with my scenario and to ignore the stray discrepancies — just like any good conventional historian!

Unfortunately for this tidy scenario, I kept getting letters from credible people who claimed to have discovered ruins. And, unfortunately for the scenario, these ruins formed a pattern that suggested exploration from Estotiland. But the number of ruins, and the size of the explorations, called for a re-think about the size of Estotiland's population. So I found myself re-reading *The Zeno Narrative* after I had re-read all the letters. I had to accept the evidence that Henry Sinclair had arrived with at least four to five hundred "soldiers," that Antonio Zeno may well have sailed back with a largely empty fleet, and that Sinclair himself, with very few companions, returned home in one ship. He apparently left a lot of "soldiers" in Estotiland, perhaps enough to account for the ruins described in the letters and the extensive pattern of geographic exploration.

Something has to be said about these Templars of Rosslyn and the "soldiers" that Sinclair brought to Estotiland in such large numbers. The Knights Templar were attacked, dispersed, and disbanded between 1307 and 1314. The several hundred who managed to flee to Scotland in time to help Robert the Bruce win the Battle of Bannockburn (June 14, 1314) would have been long dead by the time of Sinclair's voyage in 1398. Templars did trickle in after 1314 from various parts of Europe, and they gravitated to Rosslyn, Sinclair's domain. But, by 1398, these Templars would have been greybeards. As we know, the Templars continued on in Portugal as a "new" order, called the Knights of Christ, under the patronage and protection of the king himself. Some of these "neo-Templars" may have travelled to Scotland, and some may even have taken part in the 1398 voyage, and so provided a "genuine" Templar contingent.

The original Knights Templar were sworn to celibacy, but it is hard to say how far this went in practice. Certainly, while the order was official, Templars could not have been married. But many (most?) Templars could have had mistresses — and, indeed, this might have suited them quite well. We know that Roger II of Sicily *was* actually married, even as a Templar, and also kept a court at Palermo noted for its beautiful women. We know that he was termed "jolly," and perhaps this says enough.

However, once the refugee Templars at Rosslyn found their order officially dissolved by Pope Clement V, they were no longer obliged to practise even "outward and visible" celibacy. They were no longer *Templars*, and they were excommunicated, but knighthood itself could not be taken from them. Making knights was not a prerogative of the Roman Church, it was a jealously guarded right of feudal nobility and royalty. But the status of these knights, and that of their descendants, was uncertain. Their children would have been excommunicated, too, from the Vatican's perspective because they were born of an excommunicated father. It is probable, though, that papal excommunication did not overly concern these knights.

Knighthood was not automatically hereditary. Nonetheless, we are speaking of children born of "ex-Templars," once the most exalted and revered knights in Christendom, and now in exile among people who were not only secret allies in the same Grail belief, but who, like Robert the Bruce himself and the later "Stewards" (Stuarts), owed them a great deal. I think we may be certain that the status of knighthood would have been conferred upon male Templar children who showed sufficient aptitude and warrior skills. The "soldiers" of *The Zeno Narrative* must have been knights, although they were were no longer Templars because there was no such order. I think we may be confident that the old Templar values and obligations were passed on to these younger knights by Templar fathers and grandfathers. *They* had had the awesome, evocative, and romantic duty of guarding the Holy Grail, and surely they would have passed this glorious heritage on to their sons.

When these "soldiers" were relocated to North America, they would have remained knights so long as their community preserved European values and lifestyle. While, I think, some of these settlers must have truly "turned native" eventually, the major communities must have tried to preserve their European heritage — even if it grew hazy. The figures argue that four to five hundred knights may have been left in Estotiland. Some of these men would have been married already and would have brought their wives from Scotland. Others would marry any eligible European women who happened to arrive in Estotiland, and there may have been a few. Most, of course, would marry into the native population, and a composite people would have emerged over the years with the European heritage steadily diminishing.

In the immediate neighbourhood of Sinclair's Estotiland, in that part of Nova Scotia that became the heartland of Acadia, the purely European heritage must have lingered in a much more definite form. From the initial voyage in 1398, there must have been at least a few subsequent transatlantic visits bringing supplies, news, and the latest fashions in clothes and arms to the remote refugees. This would have revived the commitment to European values and lifestyle even if such contact became more sporadic. The European lifestyle would have been given new vitality by de Razilly's Acadian settlers and much more frequent contact with France. What happened to those settlers of old Estotiland who did not go with the core descendants to the new haven of Montreal in 1642?

I think that some of them merged into the "Acadian" settlements established by de Razilly in 1634–35. This could have been easy to do, since because there were also French refugees from other nearby French colonies (in Maine and New Brunswick) who merged with the Acadians. In examining Acadian genealogies, I found there were too many generations in some of them to support the idea that certain familes had come with Isaac de Razilly in the official Acadian colonization. I cannot, of course, absolutely prove this, but the case was strong enough to be presented on a National Film Board of Canada 1993 documentary about the huge Leblanc clan called *It's in the Genes*.

In his explorations of the Bay of Fundy in 1604, Champlain reported that he had discovered an old weathered cross standing in the woods on Cape Blomidon. Champlain took this cross as a tomb marker and wrote that the cross "showed without doubt that Europeans had formerly lived here."[4] If they had formerly lived in the Fundy region, these Europeans remain unknown to conventional history, although they conform to Sinclair's Estotiland settlement.

Aside from the ubiquitous Leblancs, though, there's also the common Acadian family name Gallant — this means *knight*. And, strangely, various families called Gallant deny any original connection between them. Several "Gallant lines" started simultaneously in old Acadia. I have the hunch that if anyone dug deeply into the genealogy of the several Gallant lines, a situation similar to that of some Leblancs would emerge — some were in Acadia before the Acadians, so to speak. Scions of the Gallants have achieved fame, too, just as Claudette Leblanc has attained fame as a virtuoso soprano. Mavis Gallant is one of Canada's brightest literary lights, and Patsy Gallant is one of Canada's best-known recording stars. French-Scots were in Acadia before Acadians.

A confirmation of these suspicions may come from the sermons of Monseigneur Bourgeois of Moncton, New Brunswick, who died in 1993 at the age of 101 years. Aside from the fact that this Acadian priest openly kept a mistress for many years, he was nonconformist in other ways. He ended every sermon of his long life with these words to his Acadian flocks: "Never forget that we are descendants of the knights and the Apostles."[5]

But most of the knights of Estotiland could not have been married when the initial settlement was established. There were some women, perhaps, but Antonio Zeno doesn't mention women in the fleet. Micmac legends, however, seem to associate at least one woman with Sinclair and his expedition. She's called the "Sorceress of the Atlantic" in Micmac songs and folklore. We know nothing else about her except that "Glooscap" supposedly met her somewhere on the Atlantic coast during the summer before he set up winter quarters at Cape d'Or. Did this woman "sorceress" lead another exploration party that made a rendezvous with one led by Sinclair? This is possible because we know that in the Grail/Cathar community, women could be both military and religious leaders. Or could Sinclair have met this woman on the Atlantic coast because she was a member of some previous Celtic, Viking, or Templar settlement? We don't know. The Micmacs simply associate a woman with Sinclair, and she was possibly a European woman of such strange appearance as to be called a sorceress. But at least *one* woman has been associated with Estotiland.

There must have been many unmarried knights in Estotiland, and they would have been the ones to go off on various explorations, found many small settlements along the river routes, and inevitably marry local Indian women. As they explored inland, perhaps some married knights from Estotiland among them sent for their wives to join the new settlements, and perhaps some few marriageable women even travelled inland from Europe via Estotiland. But, inevitably, there would have been increasing Indian admixture, and purely European values and lifestyle would have merged with Native American culture and lifestyle.

Hochelaga at the time of Cartier's visit may well have been a somewhat mixed community, but one originally founded by Europeans, and the people knew of another and larger community to the southwest that was "more European" than themselves in 1534.

In short, the more I thought about it, taking into account the letters, *The Zeno Narrative*, and these tantalizing loose ends in my hands and mind, the more it seemed that a fairly large population of Europeans and Métis could well have been settled around lakes Ontario and Erie within a century or so of Sinclair's original transatlantic adventure. They would have left earlier traces all along the river routes to the lower Great Lakes.

It also seemed possible, the more I reviewed English and French colonialism of the sixteenth and seventeenth centuries, that this population had been intended to play a major role in controlling French North America for the Holy Blood...but that is getting slightly ahead of our story.

In trying to get some mental construct about these people radiating inland from Estotiland, I tried to imagine something of their culture and heritage. But this largely defeated me. The original refugee Templars had been mostly French. But by the time of Sinclair's voyage in 1398, they (and their descendants) had been in Scotland for roughly ninety years. If they married, they married local Scottish and Norse women or, perhaps, the very rare woman from France who dared the voyage across the channel and through the North Sea. What language would they speak? Perhaps they would have retained a sort of basic French laced with a little Norse and much more of whatever the Scots of that time spoke. And what was *that*? Scottish Gaelic, seasoned with the lowland English of Chaucer's time? The leaders might have preserved a purer form of French compared to the average knight's family, but the settlers of Estotiland must have spoken a linguistic dialect that was quite distinctive.

As it chanced, because of "lake monster research" I had to read an entry from the *Cronicis Scotiae* that was an account, dating from the year A.D. 1500, about some sort of creature being killed by one Hugh Frissel of Glenconie. This example of written Scottish dates from a century after Sinclair's voyage, but it also comes from a remoter place than Rosslyn. Glenconie is up in the true Highlands. This highland speech, I thought, might well have retained an older style than Rosslyn, which was more exposed to evolving forms of English. Therefore, I guessed that Glenconie speech of 1500 might have been roughly similar to Rosslyn speech of 1400. Without difficulty, one can get the gist of Hugh Frissel's adventure. Some words are out of use, but the Oxford dictionary supplied most of them. In short, with a little work, one could make out the story told in "late medieval" Scottish vernacular spoken in a remote place. Want to try?

> *Anno Domini Mv.* Huchone Frissel in glenconie, the best and maist in estimation of the Lord Louattis kin, he and ane seruand with him beand at the hunting an ane hie land, amang very rank hedder. Tua arro draucht fra him he hard lyk the call of ane ratche and approacheand ner and ner, quhill at the last he saw it, and schot at it ane deid straik with ane arro, quhair it lap and welterit up and doun ane speir length of breid and lenth. The hedder and bent beand mair nor ane fuit of heiht, it beand in the deid thraw brint all to the eird as it had been Muirburn. It was mair nor tua ellis of lenth, as greit as the coist of ane man, without feet , haifend ane meikill fin on ilk syde, with ane tail and ane terribill heid. His greit deir doggis walk not cum ner it. It had geit speid; they callit ane dragon.

This is very possibly the kind of dialect spoken by the Estotiland settlers in ordinary day-to-day conversations. A form of medieval French may have been known, and used, for special occasions. This linguistic investigation and speculation becomes important in a later chapter.

I thought, also, that some memory of arms, armour, and fortifications would have survived, even among well-mixed descendants of the original knights. Is there evidence of this?

In *The Holy Blood and the Holy Grail*, and in even greater detail in *The Temple and the Lodge*, the British duo of Baigent and Leigh showed that the refugee Templars in Scotland (mostly at Rosslyn) did not attempt to organize a "new" cohesive order of knighthood as they did in Portugal with the Knights of Christ. Rather, the Templars merged their secrets and their knowledge and their "religion" into the institution known as Freemasonry. Rosslyn Chapel shows this transition. Purely Templar memorials and symbols are carved in stone beside other symbols that later emerged as Masonic. An important aspect of this emerging Freemasonry was political and philosophical speculation about "building" (hence "Masonry") enduring, compassionate, and productive human societies.

In the light of recent inhuman experience, of course, much of the early fifteenth and sixteenth centuries thought was devoted to ways and means of limiting the Roman Church's power. How could "freedom" from Rome be achieved so that other ideas of human relations with God could find expression? The only immediate answer, in those desperate early days, involved sheer survival and striking back at Rome's power — limited and unremitting warfare. But, in the longer view, the idea evolved into some way of limiting religious control over civil affairs, the seed of the concept of separating Church and State. In a still longer view, was there a way of limiting the State's power over the entire civil organization? Within the context of the feudal system, with nobility and kings, the idea was some institution that represented "the people" balanced against the power of the nobility, and both balanced against the powers of the king — a limited, eventually "constitutional" monarchy, held in check by a parliament. This Freemasonic thought tended towards a system of checks and balances ensuring that no one component of society could come to control all the others.

An English Freemason named Oliver Cromwell reluctantly (at

first) led a civil war against a Scottish, Stuart king (Charles I) to fight for the principle of a limited, constitutional monarchy balanced by Parliament. Cromwell's political philosophy actually owed its impetus to the institution of Freemasonry that developed in Scotland. This shows that the original Freemasonic commitment to the ideals of a "Christian commonwealth" (represented by the life, values, words, and actions of Jesus) superseded their sincere respect for the Stuarts — the Holy lineage flowed more strongly in Stuarts, perhaps, than in any other European royal house. Also, the Stuarts were Scottish, like the early Freemasons themselves and their leaders, the Sinclair family.

Nonetheless, Masonic commitment to a Christian commonwealth such as Jesus had envisioned proved stronger than traditional respect for even Scottish descendants of Jesus. Descendants of Jesus were not Jesus himself; Charles I proved that a descendant of the Holy Blood could be just as arrogant, hypocritical and authoritarian as, say, Caiaphas, Pontius Pilate, or most popes. The letters and speeches of Oliver Cromwell, collected and arranged chronologically by Thomas Carlyle (1845), show that Cromwell bent over backwards to try to deal reasonably with Charles I. It was with genuine regret that the king's antics left Cromwell no choice but armed opposition. And, most unfortunately for Charles, once determined on action, no matter how distasteful, Cromwell proved to be diligent and unbeatable. Oliver Cromwell was not a man to allow his personal regret, or his general respect for kingship and the Holy Bloodline, to stand in the way of what was best for the ideal of a Christian commonwealth. The Stuarts were to learn the hard way that this Masonic social commitment had evolved to outweigh genuine and traditional respect for the Stuarts personally, respect for the Holy Grail heritage, and the fact of mutual Scottish origin.

This gradual evolution was taking place by A.D. 1400. To some extent, it must have influenced the Estotiland community even from its beginning. But, assuming ongoing if sporadic contact with Europe and their Templar-Masonic sponsors, later Freemasonic socio-political thought must have trickled across the Atlantic to the Grail Knights of North America. It would have been a very rudimentary concept of institutional checks and balances. The idea was to ensure as much consensus as possible for any policy undertaken by the society as a whole. Aside from considerations of fairness or equality (not really conceived yet), some semblance of social consensus was likely to make any given policy more effective. A war, for instance, was more likely to become a disaster if it was merely the unpopular whim of a king, but more likely to be successful if it had broader social support. It would have been primitive, but in this trend of thought lay the working political mechanics of modern democracy.

Is there any indication of this sort of political structure in North America between, say, 1400 and 1650? The surprising answer is yes. By the mid-1500s, I think we can see this process at work within North America. In some ways, it flourished more rapidly and more dramatically than in Europe because the ideas fell on virgin soil. In Europe itself, these concepts had to fight a battle against long-entrenched tradition and powerful vested interests. We will encounter this North American political structure shortly.

The letters about ruins, *The Zeno Narrative*, and even the general pattern of historical events, like the colonization and genealogies of Acadia (not to mention curiosities associated with Hochelaga and Montreal), all suggested that the Grail Knights of North America might have been more numerous than I had supposed. There was the possibility, too, that they had played a more important part in the exploration and development of Canada and the United States than I had previously dared to imagine.

It was all plausible and possible — but it was also only hearsay and speculation. I had been on enough wild goose chases after lake monsters and reported ruins to be hesitant about jumping in my van to pursue the evidence described in the letters. The problem with ruins is that there's no certain way to date them just by looking. You have to find some organic evidence, in undoubted association with the structure, that can be carbon-dated. This requires excavation, which consumes time and money. Further, if the excavation is to be taken seriously by experts, it must be under the direction of a trained archaeologist. This costs more time and money, and usually cuts the amateur out of what he (or she) brought to the attention of the archaeologists in the first place. Then, I was primarily interested in Grail Knights— but colonials, Vikings, Ancient Celts, and Lord knows who else could account for any given ruin.

Because of Dr. Gérard Leduc's credentials, I was more tempted by his discoveries on the Vermont-Quebec border than by others. I didn't think that Leduc would have bothered to write if his ruins were plausibly colonial in origin. Nonetheless, Newport, Vermont (not to be confused with Newport, Rhode Island), and Magog,

Quebec, were five hundred miles from Toronto, where I lived. Merely to visit them for a day or so, over a long weekend, would not be enough. Several days would be required. I didn't have the time. I decided to wait for just one piece of indisputable evidence dating from the Grail Period. Further, I stipulated to myself that this additional evidence would have to come from one of the river routes already mentioned in the letters. When and if this evidence came to me, I'd jump in the van and start visiting my correspondents.

Like a taunting challenge, the evidence came within a week of this decision. It came in the form of a letter from Mrs. Marjorie Cove of Amhearst, Nova Scotia. She enclosed a newspaper clipping, "Childhood treasure a rare find," from the *Halifax Chronicle-Herald* newspaper. It included a photograph of the artefact.

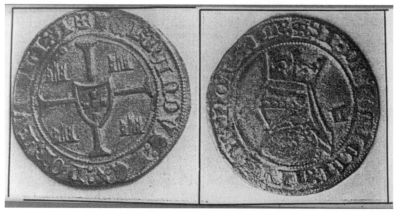

Marjorie Cove's coin. Discovered in Amhearst, Nova Scotia, in the 1950s, the coin is Portuguese and was minted in the late fourteenth century.

I phoned Mrs. Cove at her home in Amhearst in order to get any details not covered in the article. She had nothing much to add. As a young girl of about ten years, she had gone out for an early morning walk along Fox Pen Road on the outskirts of Amhearst. It was a bright morning after a winter storm and Marjorie wanted to enjoy the new fall of snow. She came to a stretch of woods beside Fox Pen Road, which was her destination because she liked to see the branches feathered with new, fluffy snow. She saw that several trees had been blown down in the night's storm and were uprooted. Among the soil and roots of one tree, she saw something glinting in the sunshine. It turned out to be what she later discovered was a gold Portuguese coin struck in 1362. A coin dealer was able to identify it for her, but she didn't want to sell it. When I spoke with her in 1990, Marjorie Cove explained that she kept the coin in a safety deposit box in an Amhearst bank.

I told Mrs. Cove that I was willing to drive to Amhearst if I could see the coin and photograph it. She made a counter-suggestion. She was planning a visit to her sister in London, Ontario, which was closer to Toronto. It would be more convenient for me if she took the coin with her to London and we met there. I agreed to this. Unfortunately, at the time set for our meeting in London, I became seriously ill. So I didn't see or photograph her coin, something I regret intensely to this day. I did not make future arrangements to visit Amhearst because my recovery would take some time, and I didn't want to plan a long trip I might not be able to make. Nonetheless, the coin's existence had been documented in the newspaper article and I had spoken to her about the circumstances of its discovery.

From her own description, and from the newspaper photograph, this coin isn't in mint condition — but it is also not time-worn. Its details and date are still very visible. It could have been dropped at any time since 1362 and dropped by almost anyone who carried around an old Portuguese coin as a curiosity. But, being found in the upturned roots of a large old tree, it seemed reasonable to suppose that the coin was deposited on the ground before the tree started growing. This tree has long since been removed as Amhearst has expanded. In fact, as I understand it, there's no longer any Fox Pen Road (where a local man raised foxes for fur). New houses have covered the area. We will never know how old this tree was by cutting a section and counting the rings.

All that can be assumed, from the circumstances of the coin's discovery and its general condition, is that it was probably dropped not long after it was minted because it is not much worn by handling and was not subsequently found or handled since it was buried. The date 1362 and its Portuguese origin argue the possibility that it was lost during Sinclair's 1398 expedition. It is plausible that Portuguese Templars (Knights of Christ) visited their Templar colleagues in Rosslyn, where the coin may have changed hands. Or it's possible that neo-Templar Portuguese knights actually participated in the transatlantic voyage. Or it could have been dropped by a member of some later Estotiland expedition — but not too much later because the coin is not very worn.

I had the piece of evidence I had demanded. A solid artefact of the "Grail Era," found in circumstances that indicated considerable age, and along a route leading out of Nova Scotia towards the north and west. But since I could not then just jump in my van and go looking at ruins, I began arranging future visits with my correspondents, and I began to think carefully about my own proper role in trailing the Grail in North America.

So far as I know, *Holy Grail Across the Atlantic* was the first presentation of evidence that the story of the Holy Grail had a legitimate and crucial North American chapter. And now I was confronting evidence and indications that there were even more North American chapters to the tale. These were very important ones having to do not only with the settlement of Canada and the United States, but with the evolution of democracy.

It was already becoming clear, to other researchers as well as myself, that the Grail was leading to nothing less than an alternative perspective on at least the past two thousand years of western history. Grail believers had been involved, either overtly or covertly, in most major events of Europe's story since the time of Jesus. Indeed, many episodes of European history are puzzling or more or less inexplicable unless the activities of Holy Grail believers and operatives are factored into the scenarios. It even seemed likely that some Grail-associated evidence, artefacts, and knowledge might well lead back 10,500 years to the end of the last Ice Age — and even further back to Atlantis. To relate the Grail's relevance to this immense span of time will require the work of many lifetimes — just as much work as was required to document the conventional view.

The North American chapters of this story are, perhaps, shorter and less complex. If Atlantean and Ancient Egyptian contact with the Americas proves to have relatively little relevance to the evolution of American history and society, then the American tale of the Grail spans only a thousand years! From, say, Lief Eriksson and the Vikings (circa A.D. 1000) to the present.

But it is obvious that even this more limited span, compared to the European panorama, will require the research of many people over many years. Although I had first associated the Grail with important aspects of North American history, it would be a vanity to presume that the entire story was mine to tell. The emerging torrent of "Grail evidence" made this quite clear, and my own health crisis emphasized it. What, then, was my proper role?

I decided, while writing letters to make arrangements to see ruins, that my obvious job should be as a "scout" or "trail-blazer" for those who decide to follow the fascinating trail of the Grail in North America. Perhaps I had the time, determination, and talent to describe briefly which trails might lead to much more evidence because at least *one* artefact had been discovered along them. Other people, with more time and energy than I could muster, could follow these trails with a certain amount of confidence, and with much greater care and attention to detail, in order to flesh out the entire story eventually.

So, this is what the remaining few chapters of *Grail Knights of North America* will do. We will discover at least one highly suggestive and Grail-era artefact along each of the river routes leading from Estotiland to the heart of the continent. Although at least one artefact will be covered in reasonable detail, hearsay reports of others will be recounted. Future researchers will then have some pointers for the direction of their investigations.

Marjorie Cove's old coin was found outside of Amhearst, Nova Scotia, in the very heart of Acadia around the head of the Bay of Fundy. As I'd decided, I took Marjorie Cove's coin as tangible evidence that the St. John River route to the St. Lawrence had been used by Estotilanders as they probed north and west into the neighbouring continent. Just 100 miles (140 kilometres) south and west of Amhearst is the mouth of the mighty St. John River, by far the largest river flowing into the Bay of Fundy, and the first that would have been encountered by explorers from Estotiland.

Before travelling up this river, though, we should pause to puzzle about the many "St. John" place names in Maritime Canada. There's St. John's, the capital of Newfoundland. There's Saint John, the capital of New Brunswick. The French called Prince Edward Island "Isle St-Jean," and there's the St. John River itself.

We may remember that within the "Grail Religion," and particularly within Templar beliefs (if we can believe Inquisition records), these knights, or at least some of the heretics, also believed in the Ionnite heresy. This was the tradition that John the Baptist, not Jesus, had been the first and real Messiah. Since this area of Maritime Canada seems to have been first explored by "Templar-related" knights of Estotiland, I wonder if the plethora of "St. John" place names reflects their religious beliefs. We will meet with a similar phenomenon in Quebec itself all along the course of the St. Lawrence. In *Holy Grail Across the Atlantic* I mentioned a number of curious place names, most of them given by Jacques Cartier in 1534–35, that recall incidents of the Holy Grail history as we now know it. Cartier named the Magdalene Islands in the Gulf of St. Lawrence at a time when Mary Magdalene had a dubious reputation in the orthodox church. Cape de Raz in Newfoundland (today's Cape Race) seems to recall the dukedom of Razès — Rennes-le-Château — which preserved the Holy Blood by sheltering Prince Sigisbert, Dagobert II's heir. There are, of course many more minor St. John and Mary Magdalene place names as well as others redolent of Holy Blood history — such as the Avalon Peninsula of Newfoundland.

I can tell readers now, and I mentioned it in my first Grail book, that place names on very old maps of Maritime Canada actually seem to spell out sentences with secret significance relating to the Holy Blood. People who like this sort of diversion are invited to get William Francis Ganong's *Crucial Maps* out of the library system and start looking! The early Gastaldi maps are the most fascinating in this respect. To some extent, the basic facts about the Holy Grail were told by the early explorers by the place names they chose for the new geography.

The St. John River is noted for the fact that not far upstream from the Bay of Fundy, the river branches out into a number of large lake-like extensions. Travelling north up the river from the Bay of Fundy, the first one of these is Kennebecasis Bay, the second is Long Reach and the third, some twenty-five miles (40 kilometres) farther is called Grand Lake. I had long suspected that these expansions of the river, because of their good fishing, good hunting, excellent timber, and convenient transport, would have been early sub-settlements of Estotiland. On the north and west shores of Grand Lake, particularly, one comes across towns with names like Camelot and Inland Empire. It is commonly believed by the local people that their region was settled by Europeans long before the Acadians came. In 1992 I saw, and photographed, an old stone cross in the woods near Camelot. It had a very badly weathered inscription on it. I could not make out what I supposed to be the name, but the date appeared to begin MCCCC in a crude Latin style — 1400-and-something — but I could not read the rest. Most unfortunately, I later (1993) lost this photo, and much else, in a boating accident while looking for ruins among the Thousand Islands of the St. Lawrence near Alexandria Bay, New York.

My account, therefore, is no more valuable than Champlain's assertion that he saw an old wooden cross on Cape Blomidon in the Bay of Fundy in 1604. And my account is no more valuable than another statement of Champlain's, dating from 1607, that he'd named some islands The Martyrs because of "some Frenchmen who had once been killed there."[5] "Martyr" is a religious term, and Champlain's use of "had once been" indicates a long time before 1607. Who were these French "martyrs" otherwise unknown to history? I don't know, but I can suggest that the lower reaches of the St. John River, and especially the shores of the lake-like expansions, might turn up some valuable European artefacts and even European sites of archeological interest. The general pattern indicates that these will most likely be outposts of Estotiland dating between A.D. 1400 and 1600.

A recent article from the *Toronto Star*[6] indicates that some very specific artefacts may be hidden on the remoter shores of Grand Lake. The article is about a modern adventurer who wants to investigate a shipwreck in the Jemseg River, which connects Grand Lake with the St. John River. According to the story, a British warship sank in the river. This ship had been ordered into Grand Lake in 1756, during "The French and Indian Wars" (as the Americans call it) in order to mop up French-Acadian resistence there, but it had been damaged so much by cannon fire that it retreated out of Grand Lake into the Jemseg River and tried to make it back to the British base at St. John where the larger river flows into the Bay of Fundy. But the ship was so badly damaged that it did not make it all the way. It sank in the Jemseg, where it was a hazard to navigation for some years until its masts were cut away. Thereafter, the hull settled into the bottom mud.

The curious part of this story is that studies and assessments of known French strength in this fringe of Acadia do not include any cannons whatsoever deployed on Grand Lake. Certainly, the victorious British did not subsequently recover cannons from Grand Lake so, if this story of the crippled British ship is true, the cannons must still be somewhere on the shores of the lake. Perhaps they were buried in the ground, or in shallow water, to prevent the British from capturing them. If they exist, they would probably excite a good metal detector and mildly interest historians.

But there's another possible aspect to this story and these cannons. If the known French strength didn't include artillery, then perhaps these cannons were truly old Venetian ones from Sinclair's Estotiland. Andrew Sinclair illustrated his *The Sword and the Grail* with anachronistic and Venetian-looking cannons on display in the French fortress of Louisbourg (on the east coast of

Cape Breton Island). It may be, however, that not all of Henry Sinclair's Venetian "pietros" have been accounted for. By 1756, they would have been outmoded, but perhaps they seemed better than nothing at the time. A small ship that was not expecting any cannon fire on Grand Lake might have ventured, or have been lured, into a vulnerable position with considerable resultant damage. The cannons of Grand Lake, then, may be more significant to history than anyone might think. Perhaps the possibility of finding these artefacts would appeal to amateur historians in Maine and New Brunswick.

Although I've travelled the entire Canadian length of the St. John River, I've heard no rumours of unknown sites or artefacts until one arrives near the Quebec border with New Brunswick. Here, where Maine meets the two Canadian provinces, geography gets a bit complicated. We are on the watershed between the St. John River system and the St. Lawrence River system. It is here that the mighty St. John River turns west at Fort Kent, and then trends southwest parallel to the Allagash Wilderness Waterway of the State of Maine. The St. John becomes useless as a route north towards the St. Lawrence.

Thankfully for the early fur traders, however, a large tributary of the St. John, the Madawaska River, flows from almost due north out of Lake Témiscouata. This lake is itself some twenty-five miles (40 kilometres) long and so, along with the Madawaska River, covers a substantial part of the distance to the St. Lawrence. Nonetheless, the early French called this "Le Grand Portage" between the St. John River valley and the valley of the St. Lawrence, and it was really two back-breaking portages totalling about twelve miles (20 kilomtres) overland before the rivers on either side became navigable for loaded canoes. In the middle of these two portages, Lake Témiscouata offered twenty-five miles of level water as a respite from the toil just finished and the toil yet to come.

Lake Témiscouata must have seemed like a paradise of relief for the seventeenth-century French fur traders, and for the Indians over thousands of years. It may seem fanciful to modern readers, but it has always seemed to me that a special aura of gaiety, relaxation, and contentment hangs over Lake Témiscouata during the summer. The major town of the area, Cabano, is a village on the west shore of the lake just off the Trans-Canada Highway. And, for me, Cabano is one of the most charming places in Canada. Its long main street is on the lake shore, with water to one side and shops on the other. Cabano's population cannot be more than about four thousand, but it boasted (in 1985) three of the most tasteful lingerie shops outside of Paris, four florists, and several prosperous restaurants and bars — indications of how long, dark, and cold the winters are!

As early as 1967, when I was a history student at Dalhousie University in Halifax and drove past Cabano on my way to and from Toronto several times a year, I thought that Lake Témiscouata would be a good place for a small settlement in the middle of that man-killing "Great Portage." At that time, of course, I was thinking about the known seventeenth century fur traders, and I asked around. Abbé Plant, a local historian from the nearby village of St-Èleuthère, told me that there were ruins at each end of Lake Témiscouata on the eastern shore of the lake, which is accessible only by ferry from the Trans-Canada Highway on the western shore. But Abbé Plant winked, and said that they were older than New France. At the time, I could make no sense of this. I was told the same story by Cyprien St. Pierre of Notre-Dame-du-Lac (south of Cabano on the lake).

In 1992, taking Route 232 northeast out of Cabano, and then taking route 295 towards Lots-Renversés (going around Lac Touladi), I was able to travel parallel to the eastern side of Lake Témiscouata, but a long way from the water except at the extreme ends of the lake. At the northern end of Lake Témiscouata, on Route 232, I photographed a curious jumble of stone that looked, to me, like a ruined rubblework building with several rooms. This was on the same roll of film with the stone cross at Grand Lake, lost in the St. Lawrence in 1993. Someone should investigate this ruin, and there may be other constructions along the eastern shore of this lake. Unfortunately, the roads going around Lac Touladi stay well clear of Lake Témiscouata. To investigate this eastern shore properly will require a largish boat and plenty of time — neither of which I've ever been able to allocate to this area.

From the northern tip of Lake Témiscouata, after a murderous portage, one comes upon streams that reach the St. Lawrence at Rivière-du-Loup and Trois-Pistoles respectively. The larger of these streams is Rivière-du-Loup (Wolf River), and previously unknown artefacts or ruins may be found along it.

It seems evident, because of Marjorie Cove's 1362 coin, that the St. John River to the "Great Portage" and the St. Lawrence was discovered and used by Estotilanders, just as it was discovered and used by traders of Acadia and New France two centuries later. The ruins and artefacts to be found along this long river road may be forgotten trinkets and constructions left by early European travellers of known colonial times...but there may also be articles and ruins left by Grail Knights waiting to be found.

9

The Magog Mill and the Lost Legacy

Following the first of our North American "river roads" from Estotiland, that of the St. John River from the Bay of Fundy to the "Great Portage" and the St. Lawrence, we were lucky enough to find a Grail artefact right at the start. Marjorie Cove's coin, a Portuguese gold piece dating from precisely the right "Grail era," had been left in the soil of old Acadia on the Bay of Fundy. It was a token, a sign, that Grail-related people had been there and that we might follow their obvious route of exploration inland.

With our second river road inland, the Connecticut River, the opposite is the case. To my knowledge, there are no artefacts dating from the Grail refugee era at the mouth of the river on Long Island Sound. Of course, if we wish, we *could* consider the Newport Tower to be such an artefact since it is not so very far from the river.

I prefer, however, to view the collection of ruins and artefacts around Newport-Magog, at the very end of the Connecticut River system, as definitive signs that Grail-related people passed this way. Although the Newport Tower has fourteenth-century architectural characteristics and seems to incorporate a non-colonial unit of measure, the radiocarbon dates must be considered inconclusive. The ruins around Lake Memphremagog, on the other hand, have pre-Columbus C14 dates confirmed by two different laboratories. Two of these dates, relating to a very tangible artefact indeed, are from the fourteenth to sixteenth centuries. Also, for the purposes of this book, the Memphremagog material is more likely to lead interested readers and researchers on to the discovery of more evidence of the Grail Knights of North America.

We are unlikely to come across another Newport Tower. Southern New England has been so built-over from known colonial times to the present that many artefacts have probably been lost forever beneath existing buildings and concrete. There's always the chance, of course, that some bit of evidence remains to be found in southern New England, but the undeveloped region around Lake Memphremagog almost guarantees that more artes and ruins lie waiting to be discovered in Vermont, New Hampshire, and Quebec. Also, as we shall see, the Green Mountains of Vermont play a most curious role in the growth of an American folklore. This folklore may itself have Grail-related origins, but in any case Green Mountain traditions certainly assisted the birth of a home-grown American religion whose scripture may be merely a short history of the Holy Grail in the New World.

I first heard about the Vermont-Quebec ruins in 1990 when Dr. Gérard Leduc, then a professor at Montreal's Concordia University, wrote to me because he'd read *Holy Grail Across the Atlantic*. By the time Gérard contacted me, he had already been inspired to begin research in order to elaborate on my suggestion that Grail-related people had played a significant part in the settlement of the French St. Lawrence. By 1992, Gérard had completed *Templars in New France*, a privately published pamphlet that went far beyond my own research. In May 1991, Michael Twose and I visited Gérard at his home in Mansonville, Quebec, where we saw the various nearby sites in company with Dr. David H. Kelley. Dr. Kelley, New Hampshire-born professor emeritus at Alberta's University of Calgary, is probably Canada's foremost linguist. Kelley and his students have been instrumental in cracking the secret of the Mayan glyphs.

And, indeed, when we first arrived at Gérard's home in Mansonville, it was to find esteemed Drs. Leduc and Kelley on hands and knees in the middle of the living-room floor apparently in mortal combat with what looked like a colourful snake. The tableau was disconcerting, a sort of academic Laocoon. But the serpent proved to be, on closer inspection, a long and unruly roll of painted paper. Mike and I helped subdue this creature and saw that it was a lengthy scroll of curious and bizarre symbols. David Kelley then explained to us that these symbols were Mayan glyphs, and he tried to explain the complicated way in which they had begun to make sense to scholars. The glyphs had posed a fascinating exercise in code-breaking which, even if I understood it, is not within the bailiwick of this book.

Lake Memphremagog straddles the U.S.–Canadian border between the State of Vermont and the Province of Quebec. Newport, Vermont, is at the southern end of the lake. Magog, Quebec, is at the northern end of it. Mansonville is within Potton township on the western shore of the lake on the Canadian side of the border. Most of the currently known artefacts have been found in Potton township, but this is doubtless because Dr. Gérard Leduc has actively looked for evidence in his own neighbourhood.

There cannot be much doubt that, if only researchers looked, evidence would be found on both sides of Lake Memphremagog and down into Vermont. If my tentative construct has any validity, Grail-related explorers from Estotiland coasted New England trying to find a river route inland to the St. Lawrence and Great Lakes. The first large north-flowing river in coastal New England is the Connecticut River. It flows into Long Island Sound near today's Old Saybrook. Going north, it wends its way through southern Connecticut to Hartford and on to the Massachusetts border at Springfield. The river cuts Massachusetts in two from north to south and leaves that state at Bernardston. From the Massachusetts line northward, the Connecticut River forms the border between Vermont and New Hampshire all the way to the Canadian border where Vermont, New Hampshire, Maine, and Quebec meet in jigsaw pieces of geopolitics.

It is true that the Connecticut River does not flow directly to Lake Memphremagog. The river curves east just south of St. Johnsbury, Vermont (note that place name!), but it would have been patently clear to explorers at that point that *some* river route continued north. The valley of the Barton River seems a more obvious continuation of the Connecticut River valley than does the actual Connecticut's valley itself. The Barton River flows some forty-five miles (70 kilometres) from Lake Memphremagog at Newport.

Lake Memphremagog is itself more than twenty miles in length (35 kilometres) and is quite similar to Lake Témiscouata in that it forms a long stretch of level water, a relief from portages, before one crosses over the Green Mountain foothills and comes abruptly into the ancient glacial flood plain of the St. Lawrence. And it is an abrupt transition. Driving on the Autoroute des Cantons de l' Est (The Eastern Townships Expressway — Route 10), you come over the last ridge of retreating mountains at the Waterloo exit, only about ten airline miles from the north end of Lake Memphremagog, and (with binoculars) you can see the skyline of Montreal sixty miles (100 kilometres) away. On a clear day without fog or smog, you can actually see the silver-blue ribbon of the mighty St. Lawrence. For early travellers using Indian canoes, the easiest route from the lake to the St. Lawrence would be the St. François River, although it is not the shortest route.

Therefore, in my view, the ruins around Lake Memphremagog must have a "reason for being" very similar to the reported ruins on Lake Témiscouata. As a respite from portages past and to come, settlements sprang up along the extensive, level, and restful location of the lake.

For me, the most impressive "artefact" of the Memphremagog complex is the ruined mill in Vale Perkins. It is less than half a mile from the western shore of the lake, and it is located on a stream that flows into Lake Memphremagog. Visible now are the remains of a stone-built dam that, at one time, had obviously been built to back up a head of water that could operate a water mill. Any machinery associated with this mill must have been mostly wood, and no longer exists. However, excavations around this mill by accredited archaeologists have uncovered bits and pieces of iron hardware. When we first visited it in 1991, we all made guesses about its age. Both Mike Twose and Gérard Leduc initially guessed that this ruined dam was most probably Ancient Celtic in origin — perhaps as early as 1500 B.C. David Kelley was noncommittal, but observed that it might well be colonial since he'd seen similar ruins in New Hampshire.

Joelle Lauriol standing beside the ruined dam at Vale Perkins in Potton township, Quebec, May 1998, showing the size of the quarried blocks. Surveyors' stakes associated with the dam have been radiocarbon dated to c. A.D. 1400-1500. Photo by author.

I was inclined to think that this dam had never been completed. Just downstream from it, there was a stack of what I immediately called "mattress rocks" because they were the size and shape of double-bed mattresses. They had obviously been cut to their rectangular shape. They leaned against each other like a stack of huge dominoes, but small rocks had been placed between them so that no slab actually touched another. My idea was that this spacing was intended to make it easier to place ropes around these slabs in order to move them into place. And I saw in the ruined dam a place where they might have been intended to fit as the last phase of completion. But the mattress rocks never got there. In the course of examining these slabs carefully, I thought that I could barely make out medieval masons' marks that had been badly eroded by sand and water action. Offering my guess as to the structure's age, I said, "I think it is certainly pre-colonial, probably pre-Columbian, but not all that much pre-Columbian."

Michael Twose sits on a stack of six "mattress rocks" just downstream from the ruined dam at Vale Perkins, Potton township, Quebec. The author's opinion is that the dam is not so much "ruined" as *incompleted*. These large stones, obviously once quarried and purposefully shaped, have now been eroded by five hundred years of weather and spring floods, but were once meant to be placed in existing gaps in the dam. These large slabs do not rest against each other. They are separated by tennis-ball sized rocks, also obviously placed purposefully, to permit ropes and levers to be worked between the slabs so that the slabs could be moved into place on the dam. This work was never completed. Photo by author.

By unceasing and heroic efforts in lobbying the "powers that be" in Quebec, Gérard Leduc finally got the dam investigated, and partly excavated, by "accredited archaeologists." Their report, submitted in 1995, stated categorically that the mill had been built in the early 1800s. Leduc asked for radiocarbon dating of two hemlock surveyors' stakes that had been found in undoubted association with the dam. The accredited archaeologists replied that C14 dating would be a waste of Quebec taxpayers' money because their expertise had already dated the structure with absolute certainty — but they wanted to take possession of the artefacts that had been found, including the precious C14-datable hemlock stakes!

By telephone in September 1997, Gérard told the adventure with a combination of bitterness and amusement, relating to me an informal account of the whole. Gérard Leduc and his associates managed to gain, or regain, possession of these artefacts (but not without difficulties). Finally, Gérard personally paid for two radiocarbon dating tests of the hemlock organic remains. One test was conducted by Isotech Labs at the University of Toronto, the other by a Florida laboratory. The results from both labs agreed on the date A.D. 1450 plus or minus sixty years.

A week after our telephone conversation, on Saturday, September 20, 1997. Gérard and I met in Peterborough, Ontario, at the *Return to the Heart: Earth Mysteries Conference* where Gérard had given the keynote address the previous night, and I was to give a slide presentation that day. One item common to both our presentations was the C14 dates for the "Magog Mill" (actually, the site is closer to Mansonville). Gérard had been kind enough in his keynote address to mention that my medieval date for the mill had turned out to be right, and he emphasized this during discussion following my own presentation. Although the major thrust of this particular conference was Ancient Celtic ruins, my own presentation tried to stress the fact that not all inexplicable North American ruins were Ancient Celtic. We had to contend with other possibilities, too, of which medieval Grail Refugees were one.

Gérard's reported radiocarbon dates for the Potton township mill site — A.D. 1450 plus or minus sixty years — actually indicate a date closer to A.D. 1400, plus or minus sixty years. By convention, radiocarbon dates are calibrated from the year 1950, the year when Willard C. Libby first used the method for field dating of excavated organic objects. Since we're now almost at the year 2000, and fifty years of carbon dating have been done, we should add the past fifty years to the test results. This means that the Magog Mill was surveyed (with the hemlock stakes) between A.D. 1340 and 1460. It is usual to take the middle of the range to arrive at the most probable date, in this case sometime around A.D.1400.

One can see that this date fits well with the establishment of Henry Sinclair's Estotiland settlement of A.D. 1398. Taking this ruined dam by itself, therefore, it most likely represents an early fifteenth-century construction by Grail Refugees rather than by any other known European visitors.

On Friday, May 15, 1998, Gérard opened his Arkeopotton display at the Reilly House in Masonville to show local residents and visiting tourists the archaeological discoveries that had been made in Potton township. Prominent were, of course, photos of the mill and the implements, artefacts, and organic remains associated with it. It was a well-organized display and, in some respects, an astonishing one. But I'm puzzled at the radiocarbon dates attributed to the mill. On the English version of the Arkeopotton brochure, the date of the ruin is given as about 1500 A.D. while in the French version it is given as about 1550 A.D. The information cards beside each item pertaining to the mill agree on "about 1550 A.D." From my understanding of C14 dates from this mill site, recounted personally by Gérard, these dates are roughly a century in error. Still, they make it clear that the mill was constructed before any known "history book" explorers or settlers came to the area.

Arkeopotton gave ample exposure to the aboriginal artefacts that have been discovered at various places in the township, and these include a number of fine specimens of stone club-heads incised around to take a haft handle. The aboriginal artefacts are interesting, but expected. They are not astonishing.

Aside from the mill site, the most astounding item in the Arkeopotton display greets (if that's the right word) visitors first coming through the door. It is a two-foot-high, carved in the round, stone "monster." Its open mouth reveals sharp fangs, and for this reason it is called a lion on the display information card. It was found, in 1985, in a stream bed not far from the mill. Although this creature has fangs, Joelle Lauriol thought that its head looks more like that of a wild-eyed horse or camel. It looks like nothing so much as a European gargoyle of the medieval period — and, in fact, Gérard's information card draws attention to this fact.

Certainly, as Joelle Lauriol pointed out, except for the Eskimo (Inuit) carvings, which are usually of smaller size than the Potton gargoyle, there's no aboriginal tradition of stone statuary (carving in the round) north of Mexico. It is undoubtedly European-looking and could have come off the corner of a cathedral given its appearance. It was found "near" the mill. Perhaps it had been

The "gargoyle" sculpture found in Potton township near the ruined dam. Monica Kuehn, a student in her graduating year at Central Technical College, and her mother Bette Anne, a semi-professional amateur expert in European art history, believe that the style and subject of this Potton "gargoyle" resembles medieval Celtic art more than anything else. The style of the stone carving resembles "The Apprentice Pillar" at Rosslyn, and a gargoyle in the church of St. Léry in Morbihan Departement (France) strikingly. The Kuehns could see no similarity with Quebec's own modern and colonial artistic traditions. The author had refused to give the Kuehns any information (other than the place and date of the gargoyle's discovery "near Lake Memphremagog in southeastern Quebec") before their research. Photo by author.

carved by one of the medieval masons who made the dam. There may be other ruins in this area, yet to be discovered, that this creature once adorned. It cannot, of course, be dated absolutely with present technology.

The problem confronting Gérard Leduc with his Arkeopotton exhibit was simply that there are too many European-seeming artefacts from, apparently, too many ages. It seems as though many European visitors followed the Connecticut River northward to Lake Memphremagog long before our Grail refugees did the same thing. Gérard's Arkeopotton exhibit displayed, and he has personally shown to me in Potton, examples of Ogham writing, a system of writing used by Ancient Celts. Therefore, future researchers who may be guided by this book might find artefacts of medieval European provenance, and these may reveal some definite evidence of a Grail-related origin (or most probable origin), but almost any other sort of European artefact might also be found. Ancient Celts, Vikings, Welsh — almost anyone and everyone, it seems — appears to have found Lake Memphremagog attractive.

Why?

It seems possible that the streams of this area, the foothills of the Green Mountains, washed gold dust and nuggets out of lodes in the mountains. Aside from the ruined Magog Mill, there's another complex of sites near Mansonville. This complex consists of over forty cairns, all about four feet high (1.2 metres) and somewhat less in diameter and all made like a "pine cone" of flat slabs of rock. Each has a large quartz stone nestled on top. We came to call it the Cairn Site. Gérard believes that these are monuments over cremation burials. All or some may be European in origin since an iron chisel was found under the base of one excavated cairn. Radiocarbon dates of A.D. 250 and A.D. 500 have been obtained from organic remains under two cairns.

And yet this site is just ten miles (16 kilometres) from the mill which is totally different in character and which has been reliably C14 dated to a thousand years later! Gérard believes that the place was known as a source of metal by various European cultures and that it was visited by successive waves of European visitors. The first to come were probably those Ancient Celts who left Ogham writing on some Potton rock slabs and who left standing stones and a dolmen in the Potton woods (a photograph of this dolmen was in the Arkeopotton exhibit).

A curious feature of the Cairn Site is a series of settling ponds along the course of a stream that runs down the mountain on which this particular site is located. This series of settling ponds does not seem to make much sense. They are not natural features and yet are too small to collect water for any sort of mill short of an elf-sized one, and are too small to be reservoirs for ditches to irrigate crops. Mike Twose, the technician, came up with the most sensible suggestion, in my opinion, when we all (Gérard Leduc, David Kelley, Mike Twose, and I) viewed this site in May 1991. Mike thought that the ponds were for the progressive extraction of gold. Nuggets would settle in the upper ponds, smaller pieces would settle in the sand of the middle ponds, gold dust would settle in lower ponds, and the finest dust would settle in the bottom ponds at the base of the mountain.

From time to time, the operators would collect the nuggets and dust by panning. It seemed evident that people remained at this site for some considerable period of time. In addition to the cairns (which might be burials, as Gérard Leduc believes) and the curious system of settling ponds, there are stone-built retaining walls down the mountain side that allowed flat, terraced fields to be created. One presumes that these fields were used for agriculture.

Gérard Leduc did much bibliographic research on this site. So far as he could gather from township records and living memories, these mountain terraced fields were not made by known colonial settlers. All sources agree that the stone retaining walls were already there when the known colonists started arriving about 1760.

If these fields were needed by the operators of the gold-settling ponds (as Mike Twose would have it), then it is obvious that a number of operators worked the site over a number of years. A fair amount of gold must have been extracted. It might have been carried out as natural nuggets and dusts, or smelted into ingots and coins on the site so that no dust would be lost in transit. There could have been caches of such gold ingots or coinage that, for some reason, were not carried away by the operators.

Before leaving the Memphremagog area, I'd like to present some of Gérard Leduc's own suggestions and theories. Gérard knows the Potton artefacts better than anyone else, after all. In his Arkeopotton brochure, Gérard notes that during the last century, before they became political and "politically correct," American Indians of the northeast made no bones about the fact that once, long ago, white men had lived among them. The characteristic activity of these white men was mining, smelting metal, and building in stone. We have already seen some stone construction in Potton township that is pre-colonial. According to Gérard, there's a copper mine in Potton township that was worked before colonial times. Sometimes, these white men were also credited with erecting the huge earthworks of the so-called "mound-builders." Finally, the Indians, fearing that these whites were becoming so numerous they would take over the entire country, made a secret plan to massacre them all and did it.

Gérard believes that there may have been a very significant European population in the northeast very long ago. But Gérard is inclined to conclude something else *as well*. In May 1996, the so-called Kennewick Man (9,300 years Before Present) was discovered in Washington State. This individual was apparently Caucasoid. Although other Caucasoid skeletons have been discovered in America, they have been ignored. Gérard thinks it possible that there has "always" been a race of "White Indians" in the New World, people with some Caucasoid characteristics, in addition to the better known "Red Indians" with generally Mongoloid characteristics. These "White Indians" may have done some of the metal-working and mound-building, and they also may have been confused with and also may have mixed with European visitors from across the Atlantic.

In short, Dr. Gérard Leduc is inclined to think that the history of North America is not nearly so simple as "modern science" has presented it in the twentieth century.

Thankfully, for our limited purposes, we can avoid most of this complexity. The radiocarbon dates for the Magog Mill are consistent with the idea that Grail Knights of North America travelled up the Connecticut River to reach the St. Lawrence. The medieval-looking gargoyle is probably an artefact of theirs as well.

We have now reached the St. Lawrence along our two easternmost river roads, the St. John River-Lake Témiscouata route and the Connecticut River–Lake Memphremagog route. The next major route inland, just to the west, is the Hudson River–Lake George–Lake Champlain route, one of the branches of today's New York State Barge Canal. Strangely enough, though, you can reach Lake Champlain directly from the Lake Memphremagog area. I see I've written "strangely enough" when there's no real justification for it except my own continual fascination with the vagaries of watersheds and rivers. It has always captivated me that two streams, just a few miles apart and separated by land that may be mere feet high, can lead in completely separate directions. If you had a light canoe, not so hard to carry around shallows and rapids, you could paddle (for example) to either Nova Scotia or to Virginia — merely by choosing one of two streams in western New York State near Jamestown.

Early explorers of North America travelled the water routes because only rivers and streams cut a clear path through the virgin forests of the northeast. They used the aboriginal Indian birchbark canoe, one of the most ingenious watercraft ever devised — light, much stronger than it looks, and with an exquisite elegance on the water. North America must have seemed much different geographically to these early explorers than it does to us with our land roads, and I think that characteristic distortions on many early maps reflect this.

The Missisquoi River has its source in Vermont's Green Mountains and first flows north to make a gentle loop into Canada. At this point, it is only about ten miles (16 kilometres) from the western shore of Lake Memphremagog and less than a mile from some of the Potton township archaeological sites. The Missisquoi then returns into Vermont and flows westward across the top of the state. Highway 105 follows the river through the mountains to Lake Champlain. By road, which Mike Twose and I travelled in 1991, you pass through Stevens Mills, Richford, Enosburg Falls, East Highgate, Swanton, and on into Lake Champlain in Missisquoi Bay. In 1993, I took the same route in my van with a canoe on top. I paddled from Missisquoi, Vermont (just inside the U.S. border), to Lake Champlain through all of the above-named towns. The canoe trip took three days and was shallow going in places and portages were necessary in others, but it could be done. Even if a canoe is somewhat inconvenient until you reach Enosburg Falls, the Missisquoi would have provided a passage through the virgin forest for early explorers. No need to paddle and portage. They could have walked along the edge of the river.

Early explorers would have known better than modern urbanites that the Missisquoi River, although so close to Lake Memphremagog at one place, flowed into a different watershed altogether. The river didn't flow into Lake Memphremagog, as other streams did nearby; it flowed away from the lake, and so must end up in some greater river or lake farther to the west.

It seems probable that early European explorers, including Grail Refugees from Estotiland, would have ascended the Hudson all the

Dr. Gérard Leduc and the rune stone he discovered near Lake Champlain. Photo courtesy Gérard Leduc.

way to Lake Champlain. But once they reached Lake Memphremagog, and they may have reached it first, they would more usually have cut across to Lake Champlain using the route of the Missisquoi. Therefore, I think, the route of the Missisquoi River would be a good one for researchers to examine. Somewhere along this river, or in the hills flanking it, there's a chance of finding another artefact like the runestone discovered by Dr. Gérard Leduc in 1996.

This inscription has curious features. It includes a depiction of a ship, which looks similar to ships shown on rocks near Boslund, Sweden. The Boslund ship glyphs are dated to the Scandinavian Bronze Age about 1500–200 B.C. On the North American stone, there's a serpent under the ship, a common motif in Scandinavian petroglyphs, and runic (and other) characters are incised along the length of this snake glyph. According to Swedish experts whom Gérard Leduc consulted, the inscription itself makes no sense. But, aside from that, the Scandinavian experts are puzzled because runic characters supposedly date from much later than the Bronze Age. The runes and the ship should not be together. The Scandinavian opinion is that this runestone is a fake. Perhaps it is.

On the other hand, Dr. Gérard Leduc discovered it in a rather isolated place between Lakes Memphremagog and Champlain. It was partly covered with a thick growth of lichen when he found it. If it was faked, it was not faked recently. And who, in the Eastern Townships of Quebec, could have created a runic hoax in the eighteenth or nineteenth century? The lichen growth over part of this petroglyph indicated an age of at least a hundred years. And why create a bogus runestone in a spot where it might never be found? I will say here only that the stone is almost within sight of Lake Champlain.

Readers will have noticed that I have not given the exact location of ruins and artefacts in *Grail Knights of North America*. There are plenty of sincere and responsible researchers out there, but there are also a few vandals, yahoos, and thoughtless souvenir hunters. The material described here is valuable historically, if only because of its controversial nature — and some of it may be the result of hoax. But I think its value goes far beyond mere controversy. Some of these artefacts and ruins, like the Magog Mill, cannot be the products of fakery and therefore compel us to accept another perspective on North American history. There is not much of this "anomalous" material. We cannot afford to lose any of it (possible fakes included) until it has been assessed by truly qualified "experts" (few and far between) and finally assimilated into a historical overview. When I was researching the castle at the Cross, for example, the Nova Scotia Ministry of Culture asked me to disguise the actual location of the ruins in Holy Grail Across the Atlantic. I agreed that it was a wise precaution, and I have followed the same procedure in this book.

Therefore, "fake" or not, the exact location of this runestone remains in the intellectual property of Dr. Gérard Leduc and his associates.

This particular artefact is not genuine, in the opinion of Scandinavian experts. On the other hand, it's hard to see how it could have been faked, or why it might have been faked. I can give no opinion on the matter, but I can say that it would be helpful if additional artefacts were discovered along the route of the Missisquoi. This artefact could then be compared with other inscriptions and motifs.

The Lost Legacy

At Magog we have reached the St. Lawrence River by three of our four river routes because the transverse course of the Missisquoi connects the Connecticut River waterway with the Hudson waterway system. Before going up the St. Lawrence into the Great Lakes, I would like to take a brief poignant look at New France. I think, with regard to the Holy Grail, that the French colony on the St. Lawrence was a lost legacy that affected the future of all North America. This lost legacy was the result of yet another defeat, and a double defeat, suffered by the Holy Grail and its believers and supporters. It may be that this setback (if I have reconstructed the history accurately and responsibly) delayed for a century or so the emergence of constitutional democracy in North America. More certainly, it delayed the maturation of Canada as an independent nation capable of contributing social and cultural gifts to the world.

There is a wry monument to this lost legacy. It is the enigmatic Shepherd's Monument at Shugborough Hall. We have already touched on this curious monument (Chapter 1). It is a relief carved in marble. It is the scene of Nicholas Poussin's "The Shepherds of Arcadia" painting reversed. The Shepherd's Monument was commissioned immediately after the conquest of New France by the powerful Anson family. Why was Poussin's scene reversed? Why is there, beneath the reversed scene, an encoded inscription?

That's the story, and the secret, of the Lost Legacy.

Quebec City was founded in 1607, intended as a fortress to command the abrupt narrowing of the St. Lawrence River west of Ile d'Orléans. The citadel itself was completed by 1617, or so the cornerstone says. This cornerstone was thought to have been destroyed until I located it in May 1991. The citadel had been subjected to several sieges, and the cornerstone had gone missing in the rubble and rebuilding. It is now embedded in the archway over the Canadian National Hotel entrance in Quebec City. I had suspected that it might be there. I took one telephoto slide of the stone at the time, but most unfortunately I subsequently sent this original transparency to *Equinox* magazine as a proposed illustration for a suggested article. The magazine apparently lost it, since it wasn't returned along with the rejected ("too incredible, too controversial") article. But it is no great loss. Anyone who visits the CN Hotel in Quebec City can view it. It reads: "Priory of the Knights of Malta 1617."[1]

We will recall that the Order of the Knights of St. John of Jerusalem, Hospitaliers had been reconstituted by the de Bouillon Dynasty in A.D. 1114, the same year in which Baudouin I, Godfroi's brother, actually created the new order of the Knights Templar. There's evidence that the Knights of St. John existed in the Holy Land before 1114, perhaps as early as the eighth century according to some sources. But the de Bouillon clan took over the order and gave it a new constitution along Templar lines. A new grand master, and new officers were appointed to ensure loyalty to de Bouillon interests and policy. Along with the Templars, these reconstituted Knights of St. John represented the apex and elite of European chivalry. Both orders were deluged with eager young European applicants and could hand-pick their men, so neither order ever had to mount a recruiting drive.

When Saladin led the successful Islamic counter-offensive against the Franks of Jerusalem in A.D. 1187, the Templars mostly retreated to southern France with the remnant of de Bouillons. That was the Templars' job. They were the elite bodyguards, or "sword arm," of the Holy Grail. Templars dug in around Rennes-le-Château, Blanchefort, Carcassonne, and Montségur and awaited the onslaught of the Albigensian Crusade.

The Knights of St. John continued to fight in the Holy Land, conducting a series of masterly military retreats against the victorious Saracens. They retreated to Margat (1187), and then to Acre (1189). They were finally driven from their last mainland foothold in Palestine in 1291 and went to Cyprus. They were there in 1307 when the Knights Templar were dissolved by Clement V. But, as we now know, Pope Clement V was himself related to the Blanchefort family of southern France, Grand Masters of the last Templars. It was Clement V who apparently warned Templars of Philip IV's planned "secret raids" of Friday, October 13, 1307, so that some Templars could escape. We know that the entire Templar fleet at La Rochelle managed to escape, although we don't know what it carried or where it went. It was also Clement V who awarded all Templar property and treasure to — the Knights of St. John!

Therefore, although it was true enough that the Templars and the Grail had suffered a disastrous defeat during the Albigensian Crusade and its aftermath, it is also true that the Grail lineage retained considerable resources. They had the Knights of St. John as a cohesive and formidable military force, and the Knights of St. John were a trustworthy repository for the immense Templar treasure that Philip IV didn't grab. Unfortunately for the Grail survivors in Europe, the Knights of St. John were deployed in the Holy Land far away. And, unfortunately for the Knights of St. John themselves, they were fighting for their very lives against the Saracens.

In 1310, thanks in part to newfound wealth from the Templars, the Knights of St. John were able to finance an expedition to conquer the island of Rhodes. This island had already been well-fortified — one reason they wanted it — and it was a base of convenient size from which to expand their fleet. The "Knights of Rhodes" settled down for 212 years and became immensely powerful and wealthy. They opposed Islamic pirates in the eastern Mediterranean, but were not hesitant to pirate Vatican and Spanish shipping themselves. Rome could do little about this because the knights represented the most formidable European maritime power.

In 1480, Sultan Mohammed II decided to wipe out European power in the Holy Land once and for all, and he made the mistake of trying to attack and conquer Rhodes. Under Grand Master Pierre d'Aubusson, the Knights of St. John successfully defended Rhodes at immense loss to Mohammed II. Finally, in 1522, Sultan Suleiman I succeeded, technically, in capturing most of the island of Rhodes, but not the major strongholds of the Knights of St. John. Suleiman was not anxious, either, to try conclusions with these knights. A kind of stalemate or "Mexican standoff" ensued for seven years. In 1530, Holy Roman Emperor Charles V gave the island of Malta to the Knights of St. John. The knights left Rhodes, and both sides were thankful.

The Knights of Malta, as they now became known, defended Malta against the Turks under Grand Master Jean de la Valette ("Valetta"). They played a major role in the Christian victory at the sea-battle of Lepanto (1571) where Turkish naval strength was finally broken.

We may as well complete their history before turning to the events that concern us. The Knights of Malta played a significant role in the "Age of Discovery." They specialized in map-making, improvement of shipboard cannons, ship design and navigational innovation. They were partners, leaders or consultants in almost every major exploration and settlement undertaken by France, Italy, Spain (where they operated secretly), and Portugal. They were most active in the area of North American exploration and settlement.

The Knights of Malta were "officially" dissolved by Napoleon when he captured Malta in 1798. At that time, their grand master was von Hompsh. Some knights joined Napoleon's army, but most of them left Malta for Serbia, where they came under the grand mastership of Mikal D'Obrenovich.

Because of the immense prestige of the Knights of Malta, Queen Victoria formed a British-based order of pseudo-knights. However, because of Britain's own prestige and power during the nineteenth and twentieth centuries, many people believe these knights to be the original "Knights of Malta."

Even the pope, of all people, got into the act! Once the real knights had gone to Serbia, and because of their historical prestige, the Vatican formed the "Order of Malta" — surely one of the greatest ironies in history. But the pope had decided, just like Queen Victoria, that it was cheaper to reward outstanding citizens with a bogus knighthood than with something more tangible. So, there are now three orders of the Knights of Malta. But, as the *Columbia Desk Encyclopedia* wryly puts it, "as reconstituted, the order bears little relation to the old Knights of Malta."[2] Indeed, when Angelo Roncalli, better known as Pope John XXIII, visited Britain in 1962 (the first pontiff to visit Britain since Henry VIII broke with Rome in 1535), the official excuse for the trip was to sign an agreement with Elizabeth II involving "mutual recognition" of the British and Vatican versions of the Knights of Malta.

What may be termed the "real" Knights of Malta still exist, and they still regard the House of D'Obrenovich as their leader. The last king of this dynasty (in exile), Mikal D'Obrenovich V, died in Los Angeles in 1990. His wife, Dame Thelma Dunlop (of Dunlop Tires), is still alive. Without digressing more than a bit, one can suggest that the current problems in the Balkans are not unrelated to this history. Why do the arms of Bosnia display three fleur-de-lis of France...?

The Knights of Malta played a crucial role in the conflict that Americans call the "French and Indian War." Americans see this war as a long, drawn-out struggle (1689–1763) between Britain and France for the control of North America. This is correct, in a way, but not nearly sufficient. Although only a few iceberg tips of fact now project above the deceptively placid surface of conventional history, I think we may detect that another conflict was raging simultaneously — in fact, two others. The first one was the struggle between the Stuarts and the Hanoverians that took place between 1701 ("The Act of Settlement") and, say, 1746 (the Battle of Culloden Moor). One could say, though, that this struggle continues still.

The second simultaneous conflict within the French and Indian War was an apparent attempt by the Holy Blood to set up a separate state, a constitutional monarchy, in Canada. There are only two really "hard" facts to support this idea, but they are very tangible. The first is the surprising fact that Quebec City (or, at least, the fortress there) was a stronghold of the Knights of Malta as early as 1617. The second fact is that Samuel de Champlain attempted to cede all of New France to the Knights of Malta in 1630. This surprising datum was actually admitted (and not ignored) by McGill University's Dr. E.R. Adair in the ultra-conservative *Canadian Historical Review*.[3] Knowing what we do about the Knights of Malta (which E.R. Adair did not know), it is easy to make several very plausible speculations.

First, because of Henry Sinclair's discovery and settlement of Estotiland with "excess Templars" in A.D. 1398, the Holy Blood justifiably felt that they had some claim on the new territory. It must have seemed rightfully theirs by virtue of discovery and settlement, but the brutal fact of geopolitics was that the Holy Grail lineage did not have the sheer power to compete with emerging nation states. Nonetheless, the Grail Complex had some considerable resources at its disposal. The House of Stuart had much Grail blood in its veins and, in 1603, a Stuart came to the throne of both Scotland and England (James VI of Scotland = James I of England). France had claimed New France, which included Estotiland, with the voyages of Verrazano (1525), Cartier (1534–35), and Roberval (1535–39). Then, in 1628, Estotiland in the guise of Acadia or "Nova Scotia," came into the possession of the House of Stuart as a dowry of Henrietta Maria. And, as we've seen, although most of the Estotiland "Templars" were of French extraction originally, they had no great love for, or trust in, French kings.

The succession of a Scottish Stuart to the throne of England as well as Scotland must have seemed hopeful in 1603. But, as we've discussed, the relations between the throne and Parliament rapidly deteriorated. And, as we've also seen, it was largely the political philosophy of Templars-into-Freemasons that was evolving towards some idea of a potent Parliament and limitation of the monarch's power. This emerging and developing political philosophy was so strong that Freemasons like Oliver Cromwell were even willing to wage war against a Stuart king and behead him (1649) in defence of this political progressiveness.

Nonetheless, the political thought of that era had not apparently progressed beyond the idea of a constitutional monarchy. Europeans were fixated on the idea that "there had to be a king." Even Americans were fixated by the same idea over a century later when they offered the "Crown of America" to Charles Edward Stuart (1776) and then to George Washington (1783). And, I think, the "ideal" king was automatically envisioned as a Stuart because Holy Blood flowed so copiously in Stuart veins. It is an irony of history, and one that no doubt frustrated Templar-Freemason political philosophers as well as Holy Grail believers, that the Stuarts of the seventeenth century had so few of Christ's own virtues. In spite of Stuart arrogance, incompetence, duplicity, and frivolous economic irresponsibility, that almost mystical loyalty still remained — as it does even today in some quarters.

I think that the "Holy Grail–Templar/Freemason–Knights of Malta" master plan had two phases. First, to cede New France to the Knights of Malta and to use the now-dispersed Estotiland people as a core population. It is possible that originally the eventual plan was to offer a constitutional kingship to some cadet branch of the House of Stuart, perhaps the noble Sinclairs.

But then, with the beheading of Charles I, it seemed possible to offer such a constitutional monarchy to the actual House of Stuart.

Charles I's two sons were sent to France when hostilities heated up (1646) and were therefore available as potential kings of a Knights of Malta–controlled New France once their father had been executed. Another advantage of this plan was the legal status of Acadia. It came as a marriage dowry to Charles I. Did it belong to the House of Stuart? Or did it belong to the "Scottish-English throne" which is where Charles sat when he received Acadia? Even if the Stuarts lost the English throne, would the Stuarts and the Scottish throne still have a claim to Acadia? Back then it was (and remains now) a very thorny point of pure legality.

For the Holy Bloodline, this could mean an alliance between a Grail-controlled (through the Knights of Malta) New France and a Stuart-controlled Acadia under closely related kings with (at least) a Freemasonic type of constitutional monarchy in the New France half of the alliance.

For one reason or another, the sons of Charles I did not accept this alternative (if, indeed, it was ever offered). Charles II was restored to the combined thrones of England and Scotland in 1660 and died in 1685. His brother, James II, ruled only from 1685 to 1688 and had to flee to France in the face of the "Glorious Revolution." He tried to establish himself in Ireland in 1689, but was defeated at the Battle of the Boyne (1690). In the meantime, although there were legitimate Stuart heirs, the House of Hanover (which had a bare dollop of Stuart blood) had succeeded in pushing through the Act of Settlement. This stipulated that if the last Stuart ruler, Queen Anne, died without a living heir (all her children died at birth), then a male Hanoverian would become king instead of any Stuart male heir.

Even with English impatience, not to say utter frustration, with Stuarts, the Act of Settlement was not pushed through Parliament without liberal applications of Hanoverian gold. Many English, and perhaps more Scots, considered the Hanoverians to be mere loutish German usurpers. Needless to say, some still do.

This change of dynasty was taking place simultaneously with a geopolitical power struggle between England and France for the control of North America — and we can see how complex and subtle the game was because the Stuarts always fled to France. And even with their dreary history of one political, public relations, economic, or military disaster after another, the Stuarts did not give up. In 1746, Charles Edward Stuart ("Bonnie Prince Charlie") managed to raise an army in Scotland to, once more, make a bid for the Scottish and English thrones. This was the defeat of Culloden Moor. Naturally, the battle was another Stuart disaster. Naturally, he fled to France.

But now the story becomes interesting. In *Holy Grail Across the Atlantic*, I related the family traditions of the Nauss family of Lunenburg, Nova Scotia. They were a family of master carpenters, originally from Germany, who came to the Lunenburg area even before the town itself was founded in 1759. The family claims that their forebears were sent over in order to build a "mansion in the woods" somewhere in Nova Scotia. Sketches of this mansion have been handed down within the Nauss family to this day, and they were sent to me by an unknown and mysterious correspondent. Some sketches bore the signature "Nauss, Lunenburg." I reproduced some of these sketches in my previous book. Members of this family are still living, now in the United States, and I've tried to contact them but without success.[4]

The plans for the mansion called for an inlay of the Royal Lion of Scotland on the floor of the entrance. From the timing of things, this mansion could only have been intended for Bonnie Prince Charlie. After his defeat at Culloden and his flight to France, had he at last decided to accept the Throne of Acadia in a possible alliance with New France?

It is true that Acadia had been attacked and occupied by the British in 1710 (one of George I's first moves), but the British situation was anything but secure, during 1750–60, because of the proximity of New France. Bonnie Prince Charlie in Acadia might well have fomented a successful counter-offensive by Acadians with New France jumping into the fray as allies. That is why, I think, the brutal and unBritish expulsion of the Acadians was implemented. The Acadians were asked to sign a statement of loyalty to Britain in 1755. Those who refused (and some who didn't refuse) were summarily expelled. Behind this still-remembered brutality was concern not only for British security, but even more for Hanoverian security.

The Hanoverian usurpers (as some still regarded them) could not allow the Stuart heir to hold a natural geopolitical power base in North America, especially not one that bordered on French allies. If this construct has any validity at all, then the expulsion of the Acadians may have resulted from an attempted Stuart resurgence in Nova Scotia. And this, of course, leads by definite threads all the way back to Sinclair's discovery of Estotiland under a Stuart king.

Although this departure from conventional history seems more than plausible, all there is to support it is one cornerstone from the Quebec citadel, a known scheme to cede Canada to the Knights of Malta, and some sketches preserved by a family of carpenters named Nauss.

Personally, because of the patterns of history, I cannot help but think that the Stuarts must have been offered the Crown of Canada-Acadia many times while in exile in France — if only because the French must have been growing weary of them. To be sure, the French monarch might not have made such an offer, but Grail Operatives must have done so (just as they were to do later with the Crown of America), and they had the resources and connections to make this sort of intrigue at least possible. And later Stuarts, at least, like James Edward and Charles Edward, had by then absorbed enough political acumen to accept the inevitability of constitutional monarchy and to work within it. This constitutional limitation would have been dictated by the Scottish Freemasons. But either because the Stuart exiles themselves were obsessed with regaining a European throne and nothing else (even Ireland would do) and could not appreciate North American potential, or because the Grail machinations to cede Canada to the Knights of Malta were thwarted at high levels in France itself, this political evolution did not come to pass.

This was certainly a plausible legacy for the House of Stuart, but a lost one. It was equally a lost legacy for Canada. Canada, and not the United States, could have become the first "constitutional monarchy" in North America, and thus the birthplace of evolving constitutional democracy. As it was, the British moved swiftly and brutally to neutralize any potential Stuart foothold in Acadia, and they made every effort to conquer New France. Adroitly, the British guaranteed and supported the orthodox Roman Catholic Church in New France so that the community of the "living Holy Family" was neutralized in Montreal, and the frontier Grail Religion population had to keep a low profile.

As for the rest of Canada, as soon as they could, the British populated it with so-called Loyalist people from the American Revolutionary struggle. While it is true that a very small percentage of these Loyalists had actually fought well and bravely against the American rebels (or, patriots — depending on your point of view), it is common knowledge that the vast majority of so-called Loyalists did not fight for either side. They represented an apathetic segment of the colonial American people, and also usually the least successful segment. But, after the war, merely by professing that they had been loyal, and by accounting what they had lost because of their fidelity (commonly exaggerated), they were given tracts of land in Canada, mostly in Ontario. The British thus guaranteed a docile population in both New France and English Canada. The French were held down by the Church, until recently, and the Loyalists had always been unimaginative, uncommitted, and indecisive people. Innovation, imagination, and determination have never been encouraged in Canada. Canada might have been much different if "Canadians" had been faced with the challenge of establishing, and defending, a constitutional monarchy in the 1750s or even earlier. Canadians would have had to display the imagination, innovation, enterprise, and social courage of Americans.

I think that the Shepherd's Monument at the Anson family's Shugborough Hall in England is a smug and wry cenotaph to Canadian potential. The most famous Anson was Baron George Anson, First Lord of the Admiralty during the final years of the French and Indian War. He was the strategic architect of the defeat of Acadia and New France. The Shepherd's Monument was commissioned immediately after the capture of Quebec City in 1759, and it was in place by 1761. It is a reversal of Poussin's "Shepherds of Arcadia" for obvious reasons. The Holy Blood had not been shepherded from Arcadia, after all. It had been thwarted there, its plans had been "reversed." If this notion has any claim to credibility, then the context of the monument is now clear. With that clue, it may be easier to decipher the enigmatic inscription below the carved scene.

Before passing on, however, it is worthwhile to mention that the French and Indian War also witnessed the emergence of John Cabot and the historical submergence of Henry Sinclair. It is between 1750 and 1760 that Cabot Strait first appeared on British Admiralty charts and that the name Estotiland disappeared from world maps. It seems likely that this was a Hanoverian machination. Giovanni Caboto had been all but forgotten in history soon after 1497, and was remembered (vaguely) only in Richard Hakluyt's (1552?–1616) *Voyages*. Someone in early Hanoverian times came across Hakluyt's account and perceived that it was "politically correct" for the 1750s and 1760s. Maps were changed accordingly to supply a plausible English claim to New France and Acadia. Henry Sinclair's voyage was known to all of Scotland, but what did that matter? Bonnie Prince Charlie had just lost the Battle of Culloden Moor and the Scots were reeling under English atrocities and reprisals. The Scots were concerned with sheer survival, not ancient history.

Thus, John Cabot, virtually unknown and unregarded in his own time (and justly, because his discoveries were dubious), became the justification for the British conquest of New France and Acadia. He also submerged Henry Sinclair, crucial for the House of Hanover at that time, because Sinclair's exploit led directly to the Holy Blood and the Stuarts. It was a connection that the Hanoverians could not allow history to preserve. The charade is still going on with the "Windsor" (alias Hanoverian) support of the "Matthew Project."

Vice Royal

The Holy Bloodline did not give up in its attempts to control Canada. It did change strategy, however. Instead of trying to control Canada overtly, by the establishment of kingdoms and kings, it seems that an attempt was made to control geopolitical events by influencing kings through the pillow-talk of beautiful, beloved consorts.

What are the odds that three girlhood chums, who spent some years together on the French island of Martinique, would grow up to marry, respectively, the de facto King of England, the Emperor of the French, and the Sultan of Turkey?[5]

It happened. Joséphine de Beauharnais married Napoleon. Aimée Dubuc de Riverie married the Sultan of Turkey (and he renounced Islam for her) — and Thérèse de Mongenêt, Baronne de Fortisson married Edward, Duke of Kent, de facto King of England (and the father of Queen Victoria). Although the actual birthplaces of all three women are in some doubt, it is known that they were on Martinique at the same time, at roughly the same ages.

Most unfortunately, the adventures of Joséphine and Aimée do not directly concern us because their exploits and their offspring related more obviously to purely European affairs, although their careers and children molded much of the modern world. As for Joséphine, we know that she descended from the Merovingian lineage, and that's why Napoleon sought so avidly to marry her. We don't know the genealogy of Aimée and Thérèse. Perhaps some of the girls at that special "convent" on Martinique were of the Holy

Blood lineage, while others were simply chosen for fairly obvious reasons and then recruited into the service of the Holy Grail.

Edward, Duke of Kent, was the fourth son of George III and was not considered to be in probable succession to the throne. Therefore, not much attention was paid to him and he was simply allotted that lifestyle of honoured military leadership fated for princelings of British (or any other) royalty. On Gibraltar in command of the regiment there (so the story goes), he began to yearn for a female companion and he commissioned an agent to find a suitable one. This is no sordid tale of finding a mistress, because the woman presented to the Duke was the equal of his own lineage (or better). They formed a life-long bond, had five children (by some accounts), and were apparently married twice. The woman who joined him on Gibraltar was "Julia" de Mongenêt, Baroness de Fortisson. Her name was actually Thérèse-Bernardine Alphonsine de Mongenêt, Baronne de Fortisson, whose husband (she said) had been guillotined in France. When Edward was transferred to Quebec City in 1790 to be de facto governor of New France, he took her with him. In Quebec City, Th_r_se-Bernardine became known as "Julia, Madame de Saint-Laurent," his companion and mistress (according to official British accounts).

I first heard this story from Dr. W.A. Douglas Jackson, Canadian-born professor of geology at the University of Washington in the United States. He'd read *Holy Grail Across the Atlantic*, was passing through Toronto in 1990, and wanted to meet me. Over lunch at a Bloor Street café, he told me this story. He'd got it, in turn, from Alexander Addie, official historian of the Anglican Cathedral in Quebec City. Although I was immediately intrigued enough to read two Canadian-authored books on this story, McKenzie Porter's *Overture to Victoria* and Mollie Gillen's *The Prince and His Lady*, I wanted to go to Quebec City to see if I could find some undiscovered document relating to it. I should mention here that Dr. Douglas Jackson and I formed such an immediate rapport that he wrote the introduction to *The Columbus Conspiracy*, my second more-or-less Grail-related book On a trip to Quebec City in May 1991, I got in touch with Alexander Addie who allowed me to go through the dusty registers of the Anglican Cathedral there; I uncovered the following incredible story and one (hitherto unpublished) document that may support it.

First of all, according to Alexander Addie, Edward and Julia had been married on Malta (!) by the Bishop of Valetta, the capital of the island named after a former grand master of the Knights of Malta (Jean de la Valette). This marriage was a Roman Catholic one and would have cut no ice with the Anglican Church and Parliament. Alexander Addie said that he'd personally confirmed the veracity of this marriage through the Vatican. However, according to Addie, a second marriage was performed under Church of England rites in the Quebec cathedral. Unless there was a morganatic agreement concerning this marriage, and none has ever surfaced, then this marriage must be considered legal by the Anglican Church and Parliament. Offspring born after this marriage would have been, or *should* have been, legitimate heirs of Edward.

According to Addie (and other sources), five children were born to Edward and Julie. The story goes that the boys were all surnamed Wood, the name of the Duke's trusted servant and companion, Robert Wood. The girls were surnamed Green. There were three boys and two girls — or, perhaps, the other way around — the stories differ. The boys remained in Ontario and Quebec, but the girls seem to have been placed within prominent Nova Scotia families when Edward was posted to Halifax as governor. However, there has always been the rumour that their last child was murdered by persons unknown, probably Hanoverian agents, and its little body lies buried beneath the altar of the cathedral. In point of fact, according to Dean Merritt, prelate of the cathedral, there are two coffins beneath the altar, one large, one small. After this attack, so it is said, the rest of the children were dispersed and given code names for their own safety.

Alexander Addie befriended the last male heir of this line, Colonel William Wood, who died in 1947. According to Addie, Colonel Wood had been kept as a virtual prisoner in Windsor Castle during World War II because the King was afraid that the Germans might kidnap him and use him to establish a puppet monarchy, claiming that it would be a truly legitimate one. Col. Wood was forced to sign an agreement with the British Crown that he would never marry, never have legitimate offspring — this, again, according to Alexander Addie. When Colonel Wood died, Addie claims to have witnessed the official burning of all Colonel Wood's effects and papers by the Canadian military and the Royal Canadian Mounted Police.

This story may sound like a wild tale, but Alexander Addie was (in 1991) not only the official historian of the Anglican cathedral in Quebec City, but a well-known local historian with numerous journal publications to his credit. He seemed perfectly calm and straightforward to me. Yet, Alexander Addie refused to tell me all of this story inside the church or inside the office of Dean Merritt. He insisted that we walk through the streets of Quebec City, where our words could not be recorded, because (he explained) there was still danger associated with this story.

A stained-glass window in the old Anglican cathedral in Quebec City. This window and four others supposedly tell the enciphered story of Canada's royal line descended from Edward, Duke of Kent, in the 1790s. Edward was the father of Queen Victoria, matriarch of the present House of Windsor.

However, before leaving the cathedral, Addie did point out the impressive stained-glass windows around the church. He asked me to have a quick look at them. I could see that some were dedicated to the memory of Robert Wood! Addie said that these windows had been paid for by the Crown, and that the entire story was told in the scenes of the windows. (Although some of these scenes are suggestive and unusual for a church, I'm not knowledgeable enough in symbolism to decipher them.

After searching through the dusty church registers for a considerable time, I located two documents. The first is a baptismal record for one of the children of the de Salaberrys, a very prominent and respected French Canadian family. Edward and Julia are listed as godparents. The reason for surprise at this is that back in the 1790s, being a godparent was a serious business. A godparent was, literally, largely responsible for the child's spiritual guidance. The official English story is that Edward and his Julia ("Madame de

Saint-Laurent"), were known to be living together, but not married, in Quebec City. Which is to say, it would have been common knowledge that they were committing adultery.

Baptismal document from the Anglican cathedral in Quebec City. It lists Edward and his supposed mistress, known to have been "cohabiting," as godparents of one of the de Salaberry children. The de Salaberrys were a prominent Quebec family; one de Salaberry son won the famous Battle of Chateauguay, which saved Quebec from American invasion in the War of 1812. Could they have been godparents without being married?

The question is: would the de Salaberrys, and the Catholic Church, allow even royal adulterers to be *godparents*? The answer I got from the Catholic Information Centre's historical expert was a resounding no. Edward and Julia would have had to have been married, and, of course, the Vatican had assured Alexander Addie that they had been married by Roman Catholic rites on Malta. The Roman Church's opinion is that Edward's British royalty would have mattered little to God or the Roman Church — then or now. The quality of the *man* was the criterion of godparenting, and the quality of the woman too. Titles didn't matter. The Catholic Information Office also told me that, back then, the fact that they (possibly) had *also* been married under Anglican rites didn't matter at all. These rites were not recognized anyway by the Church. An Anglican marriage would have been "accepted" and "forgiven" in view of Edward's position — it was a "state ceremony" that didn't involve the Church, not a sacrament.

This baptismal certificate had been discovered, and published, before. It is discussed in both McKenzie Porter's *Overture to Victoria* and in Mollie Gillen's *The Prince and His Lady*. Porter views it more or less as I do, and as the Catholic Information Center does, while Gillen dismisses its importance in a scramble (but a dignified scramble) of literary debunking. Gillen falls back on the crucial issue that there's no proof that Edward and Julie were married under Church of England rites. That is the only thing that matters with regard to succession of their children to the British throne.

There is a page torn out of the cathedral's marriage records, however. I saw it and both Porter and Gillen referred to it. It happens to be missing from the crucial year, 1792. Again, Porter finds this significant (perhaps the work of Hanoverian agents) while Mollie Gillen attaches no importance to it at all.

The second document I discovered is an actual marriage certificate. But notice the date! April 1, 1793. April Fool's Day. But the certificate records a marriage in the Anglican cathedral between "John Wood" and "Mary Magdalen sans Laurent ("without Laurent") Hyot. Before 1800, a way of writing "Christ" was Xyot, with the "X" looking like an "H." Are we reading "Mary Magdalen (no Laurent) Christ"? It would appear that neither the bride nor groom could write, and neither could the male and female witnesses to this marriage — they all sign with the mark of a cross — but there's also a curious "vine-like" symbol just after the "Us" in the printed line "This Marriage was solemnined by Us," and just before the marks of "John Wood" and "Mary Magdelaine."

The marks may be of no significance, and they certainly *prove* nothing — as, one feels, Mollie Gillen would be the first to point out. However, we've come across the symbolism of the vine many times before in the story of the Holy Blood. And everyone signed

A curious marriage certificate discovered by the author in the Anglican cathedral in Quebec City. The bride is identified as "Mary Magdalene *Sans* Laurent Christ" — i.e., "*without* Laurent." Does this enigmatic entry refer to the Baroness de Fortisson, Edward's supposed mistress?

with crosses. Also there's this matter of "John Wood." Was Edward's regiment composed solely of soldiers named Wood? It is starting to seem that way. If this "John Wood" is actually Edward, Duke of Kent, he was prevented from following his usual practice of borrowing Robert Wood's name because Robert had already been married in the same church and was listed in the same registries. "John Wood" may therefore have been used, and it has allegorical significance within Christianity. There are several medieval paintings of St. John's Woods, and it is said (no proof) that the cross of Jesus was cut from this little copse of trees. This document comes from the official registry of the Anglican cathedral in Quebec City. I don't know what to make of it. It seems unlikely that a cathedral would record a sacrament as an April Fool's joke, but who knows? Are these people Edward and Julia (forget the alias "Saint-

Laurent")? Even Alexander Addie had never seen this document. He was quite intrigued with it.

The legal situation is that *people* are married, not the names they choose to use before, after, or during the marriage sacrament. If, as Porter among others suspects, the notorious missing page from the marriage registry was the work of Hanoverian agents covering up the fact of a legal marriage, Edward and Julie might have wanted to record their marriage in some way that might survive. Given the evident danger to their children, a curious marriage certificate like the one I found might have been one way of attempting this. It is not *proof* though, and I feel strongly that if they had been married, absolute proof must have been recorded or deposited somewhere. During this research, two informants advised me to visit the small town of Plantagenet, Ontario. The name of this town derives ultimately from that *planta genesta* we have discussed before — the "plant of the people," an allegorical vine that represented the Holy Blood. At that point, though, the hint seemed too nebulous. I didn't even know what I might be looking for, and I had no time to visit Plantagenet.

The story of Edward and Julie became tragic. Although they were together for twenty-six years, and obviously loved each other, chance brought Edward to the succession for the English throne. By this time, he was deeply in debt from gambling. It seems that he succumbed to pressure from Whitehall and Parliament and may also have succumbed to his idea of duty. He went to Germany and married Victoire of Leiningen, a German princess. Their child was none other than Queen Victoria. Victoria ruled England from 1837 until 1901 and is, of course, the great matriarch of the current House of Windsor.

The Anglican marriage of Edward and Julia (if there was one) was simply ignored, and she was presented as Edward's mistress and no more. Their previous marriage in Valetta was also denied when it could not be ignored. But nothing was mentioned often. Victoria would fly into a rage if Julia was even alluded to, and her father was not a topic of royal conversation.

When I began to suspect sufficient material for a book, which I wanted to call *Vice Royal* because of the triple-entendre, I started trying to locate scions of this union. I found some people who claimed to be descendants of Edward and Julia. I was told of documents in Hamilton, Ontario, in Barton Lodge, the castle-like residence of one the alleged descendants. There were supposedly letters from Queen Victoria herself thanking this lineage for their loyalty during the Crimean War and offering them rich financial concessions in Canada "in return" — a vast interest in the Canadian National railroad, a charter for the Bank of Hamilton (now merged with the old Imperial Bank into today's Canadian Imperial Bank of Commerce). And, indeed, it was because of these fascinating conversations with alleged descendants and their lawyers and representatives that I decided to look for the lost citadel cornerstone in the structure of the CN Hotel in Quebec City. And found it.

Most unfortunately, when I actually signed a contract to research and write *Vice Royal*, my sources had second thoughts and began to clam up. The invitation to Barton Lodge was progressively postponed and finally just dropped altogether. I would not be allowed, after all, to see and reproduce the *alleged* documents — those revealing letters from Queen Victoria. It seemed that there may have been a nightmare in *The National Dream* that Pierre Berton either chose to ignore or never suspected.

So far as I know, these alleged descendants of Edward and Julie are alive and well and living in Canada. Whether or not one of them has more claim on the English throne than the present occupant, the tale of the Holy Bloodline's last attempt to control Canada ended, for me, in closed lips and stubborn silences.

10

The Core of the Matter

We have now arrived at the region of Lake Champlain, and also at the area where the St. Lawrence River flows out of Lake Ontario. The Lake Champlain–Hudson River waterway is our third river route leading from the Atlantic to the Great Lakes. Earlier, I said that I would offer one tangible "Grail-era" artefact for each river route, and then simply pass on reports and rumors of other artefacts and sites.

For the first route (the St. John-Lake Témiscouata Route), I recounted the story of Marjorie Cove's coin. For the second route (the Connecticut River–Lake Memphremagog), we have the "Magog Mill" carbon-dated to "about (or before) A.D. 1500" and also that medieval-looking gargoyle.

For our third river route (the Hudson River–Lakes George and Champlain), I'd intended to use the runestone found in 1996 by Dr. Gérard Leduc near Lake Champlain. Unfortunately, this doesn't seem quite fair since the Scandinavian experts whom Gérard consulted tend to think that this runestone isn't a genuine Norse artefact. This unwelcome news came in late 1997 and early 1998, after I had planned the "geographical artefact" structure of the book. I'd counted on using this runestone because I knew the circumstances of its discovery, and neither Gérard nor I expected the negative verdict of the experts. Because of the lichen growth above the inscription, we both feel that this verdict is wrong.

Anyway, there it is. My "Lake Champlain" example of an artefact may not be genuine. So I thought I'd resort to a little intellectual bafflegab to extricate myself from this predicament. If the experts say that the runestone is probably not genuine, what about an artefact that the experts claim is genuinely medieval, but that is patently not? This will prove nothing whatsoever, but it will indicate that the experts are not always correct. If they're so clearly off-base with the "medieval anchor," they may be off-base with the runestone too. I feel rather safe in resorting to this intellectual chicanery because our journey places us not all that far from Lake Ontario. And in Lake Ontario there's a solid piece of scientific evidence that Europeans had settled around the lake by about A.D. 1500. If they were settled around Lake Ontario by 1500, they certainly knew about Lake Champlain!

Don Eckler called me in 1991 with news about something called the Hanseatic anchor. It had been discovered by a casual acquaintance of his, a scuba diver from New York State. The story first was that this anchor had been found in Lake Champlain, but then it changed to having been found in Lake Ontario or Lake Erie. I suspected that the reason for the changes of venue was not motivated by dishonesty, but by legality. In their infinite wisdom, the governments of most states and the federal government have enacted laws that say, in effect, no matter what research, expense, effort, and even danger an amateur undertakes in the recovery of an artefact of historical importance, the thing belongs to the state in which it was found, or if in U.S. federal jurisdiction, to the United States. It will be turned over to "accredited experts" (meaning someone with a degree from a university) for assessment. The amateur finder may or may not be given money representing some percentage of the artefact's value.

If there's more than one artefact — for example, lots of goodies from a wreck like the *Atocha* galleon — all of the treasure legally belongs to the government having legal jurisdiction over the site. The authorities will keep it, make an inventory (often falsified) with the help of those accredited experts and keep the stuff in vaults. Eventually, and this can take years, the authorities will take their pick of the loot and give the discoverer what's left so he can sell it. And just to make things more frustrating, if the treasure is very valuable (like the *Atocha* wreck), and is found in offshore water, the U.S. federal government is not above claiming all or part of it even if it is within the agreed-upon territory of a state, in this case, Florida.[1]

The rationale is the best one possible. The artefacts are the heritage of the entire state, or nation, and belong to "the people." Therefore, artefacts are claimed and confiscated by the authorities and their accredited experts. There are two major problems, or injustices, from a purely human point of view.

First, the accredited experts usually just sit in their university chairs; do not look for this "national heritage" themselves (too dangerous); usually tell amateurs that the site does not exist or is covered beyond reach by sand, mud, and so on; and generally give no assistance whatsoever. However, the instant something is actually found, they are loud in their insistence that it belongs to the people, not the discoverer, and that they, the accredited experts, have the right to study it and write about it and generally all but claim that they found it (and sometimes they do imply they found it or simply fail to give the discoverer any credit at all).

The second problem has to do with the quality of education, which has deteriorated along with the rest of our culture. The accredited experts are graduates with degrees of more-than-dubious value in many cases. Much scientific-sounding jargon has been substituted for solid knowledge (particularly in a discipline like sociology or social anthropology, but also even in archaeology). For example, in the best tradition of euphemism-befuddled Americans (strangely, few other nations share this particular vice), the time-honoured activity of buffalo hunting by American Indians is now termed "implementing bison acquisition strategies" — how can you trust anybody who talks and writes like that? Richard M. Nixon was impeached for using similar jargon to obstruct the truth.

When I wrote to the director of the Debert (Nova Scotia) Early Man Site asking specifically if any *gravigrade* bones had been found in association with the site, after a time a polite letter came back saying that no, no *mammoth* bones had yet been discovered there. For those who are interested, gravigrades were large ground sloths, not mammoths. Many of these accredited experts don't know the basics of their own field of so-called expertise.

In just such a fashion, one so-called expert at the State University of New York told the scuba diver that the anchor he'd found was a very old Hanseatic type of anchor from the medieval period.[2] Where had he found it? The scuba diver knew enough history to know that it shouldn't have been found in Lake Champlain. But this lake, lamentably, has only a small Canadian section (Missisquoi Bay). In short, the diver immediately perceived that he couldn't create too much confusion of international claim in Lake Champlain, so he changed the venue of the discovery to "either Lake Ontario or Lake Erie," and he was not too clear on where, so that any claim to this suddenly valuable anchor would have infinite international complication. I can see his point perfectly.

The only problem is that this anchor is not Hanseatic and not medieval. I think that any yachtsman would recognize at once that it is a folding stock anchor from a pattern popular from 1850 to 1950 and still used on some larger commercial fishing craft. The SUNY expert explained that it had been cast in three pours of bog iron, probably locally, but to a pattern common to medieval North Europe. This is interesting in view of the foundry marks on it, which have suffered corrosion. Although I haven't researched all the foundry marks of the nineteenth-century western world, I *think* it was sand-cast in one pour (shaft and flukes) by the old Columbia Iron Works of Baltimore in 1882. The stock and its knobs were probably forged, at the same works. Its size and weight would suit a canal barge.

This anchor, supposedly of a Hanseatic style according to experts at the State University of New York, was discovered near Oswego by a scuba diver. The author identifies it as a late nineteenth-century anchor probably cast in Baltimore. Photo by Don Eckler.

Unfortunately for the scuba diver, this anchor is not (to me) a historical treasure of the medieval period. It is worth a few hundred dollars, not thousands — except, maybe, to SUNY experts. Nonetheless, once he'd been told it was medieval and Hanseatic, it's easy to understand why he suddenly became vague about the location of his find.

The only real solution to this "artefact claim game" is for governments to be required to pay the market price for artefacts recovered by private enthusiasts. Admittedly, in the case of something like the *Atocha*, this would have strained Florida's economy since the treasure was worth hundreds of millions. There should be at least two evaluations, one by a private expert (paid by the finder), and one by "accredited academic experts" (paid by the government). Among other things, it would be instructive, and perhaps amusing, to discover how incompetent the government's accredited experts usually are. We are not talking only about the intrinsic value of precious metals and gems, but the cultural and artistic value as well. Professional art appraisers are well versed in this, since it is their business, but one wonders if purely academic experts are competent at it.

My beliefs are founded on my experiences, one of which I will use as an example. In 1969, I wrote to Yale University warning that their so-called "Vinland Map" (see *The Vinland Map and the Tatar Relation*)[3] was probably a fake. Yale University acquired this map for a very large sum. Noted academics wrote a typical "scholarly" book about the artefact and its testing. Long technical articles verified the authenticity of the paper and the ink. Other articles verified the geography according to the literary scholars' conceits. *The Vinland Map and the Tatar Relation* was published as a scholarly tour-de-force by Yale University Press. Surprisingly, this monument to careful scholarship had a moderate popular sale. Why did I believe it was fake? I knew that the paper was going to be of the right vintage, and that the ink was going to check out, at least superficially — any self-respecting forger would be sure of that. The creator of the bogus Vinland Map knew well that dubious academic expertise was the hallmark of our time. So he drew a map to conform to the academic misconceptions. But the geography was wrong. Vinland was depicted as a sort of distorted Hamilton Inlet (in Labrador), and this is where modern Norse linguistic scholars had concluded it must be, based on laughable literary misreadings of the available sagas. Uneducated seamen who had been given good translations of the sagas all placed Vinland in New England, probably Massachusetts. Since Norse seamen had been able to find Leif's Booths by these sagas, a seaman's understanding seemed more likely to be right than a literary interpretation.

In 1973, very careful analysis of the ink indicated not only anomalous impurities (which the forger could not have avoided with modern chemicals), but also that the aging process had been helped more by heat than centuries (careless work on the part of the forger). The map was a modern hoax drawn on proper medieval paper with *almost* proper medieval ink. By this time, of course, Yale's money was lost forever. The curious thing is that no one has yet mentioned that the biggest clue was the incorrect geography, and that is because academics like Glynn Daniels, author of *The Norse Atlantic Sagas*, still incorrectly think that Hamilton Inlet was the site of Vinland. I wonder if my youthful letter to Yale is still on file somewhere in New Haven? In 1992, when I was invited to a Yale University symposium as a guest speaker, I did walk over to the Peabody Museum, but the letter wasn't on file there (where the Vinland Map had reposed while being studied).

Here's another example, and one also tenuously related to the theme of this book. As Henry Lincoln related in *The Holy Place*, he discovered that the background skyline in Poussin's "The Shepherds of Arcadia" is an accurate representation of the hills actually visible from the location of the Arques tomb, and this tomb is, of course, exactly like the one in the painting. The elevations shown on Poussin's work are Mount Cardou, the hill of Blanchefort, and the hilltop of Rennes-le-Château. There's not much doubt about this. Lincoln took a panoramic photo of the real skyline and then superimposed it on the skyline in the painting. They match. Aside from this, and the perfect match of the tomb itself, Lincoln noticed that the tree shown in the painting is still growing behind the tomb — or at least, a tree of the same species is still gowing there. It is either the very same tree as the one in the painting, or it represents younger growth seeded from an older tree. It is a kind of oak, or terebinth, native to southern France.

It is known that Poussin lived much of his life in Italy and did most of his work there. But, as we have observed, *The Shepherds of Arcadia* was painted in Paris between 1640 and 1642. Since so much in this painting actually reflects reality near the tomb at Arques in southern France, Lincoln naturally wondered if Poussin had passed through the Rennes-le-Château neighbourhood on his way from Italy to Paris. He didn't know enough about the details of Poussin's life, but the world's foremost expert on Nicholas Poussin lived and worked in London. This was the notorious Sir Anthony Blunt, at that time curator of the Queen's art collection (perhaps the most valuable private collection in the world).

Sir Anthony told Lincoln in no uncertain terms that everything was a "coincidence" — the tomb at Arques, the matching skylines, the tree, everything. Poussin had never been to southern France. Lincoln asked if anyone knew the route that Poussin had taken from Italy to Paris. Of course the route was known, thundered Sir Anthony, it was "the usual one." Which route was "usual," Lincoln wanted to know. At that, Sir Anthony began to bluster and simply to insist that Poussin had never been near Rennes-le-Château, that he — Sir Anthony — was the greatest expert on Poussin and his opinion should be good enough. Lincoln recounts this experience at length in *The Holy Place.* He had to accept Blunt's opinion, and most of the media did too because the media mentality is oriented to "key word" and "expert." Media people couldn't look at the skylines and see they were the same, look at the painting's tomb and the actual tomb at Arques and *see* they were the same, and look at the two terebinth trees and see the obvious. A world-renowned "expert," Sir Anthony Blunt, had said that Poussin had never been there to see all this, and subsequently paint it in *"The Shepherds of Arcadia,* and that was that.

Just how trustworthy Sir Anthony Blunt was, and how far his pronouncements could be credited, was demonstrated when he was unmasked as one of the Soviet moles who, along with Burgess and Maclean (and who knows how many more), had been working for the KGB for years. Saying one thing, thinking another. Sir Anthony's deception does not necessarily mean that his knowledge of painting and Poussin was similarly untrustworthy, of course. But I think we're allowed to suspect that his pronouncements may have secret agendas. It appears that Sir Anthony was genuinely fond of the Queen, and she of him, in spite of his double life. Now that we know something of the complex interrelationship between Poussin, Rennes-le-Château, the Holy Blood, Sinclair's Estotiland, and the House of Stuart, are we permitted to suspect that Sir Anthony was trying to quash any chance that Henry Lincoln would stumble onto these connections?

Aside from the bogus Hanseatic anchor and the runestone which may also be bogus, I've heard of various ruins around Lake Champlain, and also among the Thousand Islands where the St. Lawrence transforms into Lake Ontario. There are supposed to be two corbel-vaulted underground chambers near St. Albans, Vermont. I believe that I finally traced the location of these chambers to the right farm, but on the two occasions I visited the place no one seemed to be at home. I didn't trespass.

There are also supposed to be underground chambers near the south shore of Bulwagga Bay on the New York side of the lake. I heard about these from Joe Zarzynski, a scientific hunter of "Champ" the monster, when I interviewed him for the *Montreal Gazette*. I've never found these chambers myself.

However, from the brief descriptions, these corbel-vaulted chambers seem typical of Ancient Celtic works found further south in New England. Hundreds of amateurs (and some professionals) are already researching these. For those interested in this level of history, contact NEARA (New England Antiquities Research Association), ESRA (Early Sites Research Association) and the Gungywamp Society of Harvard University.

Ancient Celts seem to have come to North America in rather large numbers. I would not be surprised to find ruins of their constructions and communities around the shores of Lake Champlain and the Great Lakes. However, later visitors who may have come long after the Ancient Celts disappeared, and who had more limited manpower, would surely have camped on islands, if they could, during their initial explorations. Open water around them would have given warning of approach by potential enemies, and if they were medieval Europeans with crossbows, open water would have permitted an effective open field of fire for defence. I was therefore inclined to think that the numerous islands in Lake Champlain and also the Thousand Islands in the St. Lawrence might be a place to look for artefacts and the ruins of temporary fortifications.

Indeed, Gilbert Vachon of Massina, New York, told me of ruins he'd seen near Howe Island in the St. Lawrence when he had been fishing. Vachon spent time poring over a map with me and pointed out the exact spot, as he recalled it. In June 1989, and again in 1993, I made several trips to the Thousand Islands with my expedition barges *Nepenthe I* and *II*, but I was able to find nothing I could swear was a genuine "ruin." I did find several suggestive tumbles of stone on Howe Island and also Wolfe Island that might have been collapsed walls. These islands continue to intrigue me because, if my reconstruction of Grail-related exploration is at all accurate, the islands of Lake Champlain and the Thousand Islands almost *must* have Grail-related artefacts and ruins on them. I'd like to return to these islands some day with a more comfortable boat and a lot more time at my disposal.

Author's sailing barge on the St. Lawrence River in 1989. The search for medieval artefacts and ruins along the New York State shore resulted in an accident and the loss of many photos. Photo by Jim Beard.

The Concordia Core Sample

The Ontario Ministry of Natural Resources operates a fisheries research station at Glenora, Ontario. This station is on the mountain sacred to the Iroquois because of the clear lake on top of it, the Lake on the Mountain. Glenora is located at the mouth of the Bay of Quinte across from Adolphus Reach. In 1986, the Fisheries Research Board of Canada wanted to know how some extensive historical human phosphate pollution compared with modern concentrations. Early colonists used lye-based soap, a powerful agent of phosphate contamination, and they didn't treat the waste water before returning it to the lake. Was their pollution more serious than ours on a per-capita basis?

About 1,200 Loyalists were known to have landed and settled at Adolphustown in the 1790s, and it was thought that this known and concentrated population could provide evidence of pre-modern phosphate pollution. Accordingly, Concordia University was commissioned to take several core samples from the bottom of Adolphus Reach.[4] This was done over several years. The layer of lye-based phosphate pollution left by the Loyalists was duly discovered.

But something else — not expected — was discovered as well. At a level in the cores far below the Loyalist level, another level of intense phosphate pollution was discovered. It, too, indicated the use of a lye soap, but the chemical composition of the phosphates was slightly different, indicating a different process or a slightly different mixture of ingredients to begin with. This second, deeper, and completely unexpected band of phosphate pollution indicated (using the Loyalists as a benchmark) a European lye-soap–using population of at least one thousand persons who dumped waste water in the lake for at least a decade. The date? Based on the depth of the Loyalist layer of the 1790s, this earlier layer dated to about A.D. 1480 to 1520.

Since several cores were taken, and the two separate layers appeared in all of them, there can be little doubt or dispute about the evidence. But who were the thousand unknown Europeans who lived around the sacred Lake on the Mountain about three centuries before the Loyalists arrived at Adolphustown? No one knows.

Aside from the fact that the dates 1480–1520 fits well with the expansion of Grail refugees from Sinclair's Estotiland, the evidence of a thousand people may reflect a realistic increase in their population over roughly a century. Given the natural expansion of population, the Estotiland settlement and this settlement at the Bay of Quinte would not account for all of the Templar descendants. There were probably other Grail-related groups, villages, outposts, and towns, but the Bay of Quinte seems to have been a major population concentration. This is, of course, just a personal opinion based on a plausible correlation, but I think there are three other developments that make it even more likely that the inhabitants around the Lake on the Mountain were most probably Grail-related people.

The first, and least tangible, is the supposed City of Seguna, which was southwest of Hochelaga, the future site of Montreal. Jacques Cartier was told in 1534 that it was a city of "white men." The Lake on the Mountain fits the directions from Hochelaga, and the core sample testifies to a town-sized population of Europeans in the right direction at about the right time.

The two other hints that a Grail population lived on Lake Ontario in the early sixteenth century are more tangible in the sense that their apparent influence changed millions of lives, but also much more arguable because of accretion of myth, fact, and belief.

The Iroquois Confederacy

Henry Wadsworth Longfellow may have been a good poet, but he was a terrible historian. His *Hiawatha* tells of an Ojibway brave who lived on the shores of Lake Superior. I suspect that most Americans regard Hiawatha as a fictional character.

In real life, Hiawatha was an Onondaga from the Finger Lakes region of New York State, and he was the architect of the Iroquois Confederacy. He was also a disciple of a person named Deganawidah, supposedly a virgin-born prophet, who lived at the Lake on the Mountain overlooking Adolphus Reach. That's why the Lake on the Mountain was a sacred site for the Iroquois. In short, Deganawidah lived where the Concordia core samples indicated a "European" lye-soap–using population had also been around the year A.D. 1500.

It seems obvious, from reading accounts of Deganawidah's teachings to Hiawatha — and *The People of the Pines*[5] contains a detailed account — that Hiawatha was exposed to a form of Christianity. Hiawatha was told of the "virgin birth," and he was taught a version of the Golden Rule, but it appears that he confused everything. He thought that Deganawidah himself had been born of a virgin, when that might not have been the import of the teaching. Deganawidah also taught Hiawatha that the Onondagas (and other related tribes in the Finger Lakes area) should not fight among themselves and should not eat each other. This novel perspective on things mightily impressed Hiawatha. He paddled back across (or around) the lake and presented this idea to his Onondaga tribal colleagues. Being successful among his own people, he then travelled to neighbouring Oneidas, Mohawks, Cayuga and Seneca tribes and sold them the idea. The so-called Five Nations was born. The capital of this loose confederacy was agreed to be the main Onondaga town where Hiawatha lived.

It has been estimated that the Confederacy was established sometime between A.D. 1480 and 1580, which is to say when the Concordia core samples show that a European population lived around the Lake on the Mountain. Considering that Hiawatha's spiritual insights have definite Christian overtones, I tend to suspect that the Confederacy's birth at this time might not have been mere coincidence. Did a Grail-related community influence Hiawatha? There is, of course, no absolute proof of this, and it is an idea that will enrage both Indians and university anthropologists.

Several recent writers have noted that the political structure of the Iroquois Confederacy seems to have a system of checks and balances resonant of the later U.S. Constitution. Most often, these resemblances have been cited as an unacknowledged debt that "white" culture owes to native American culture. It has been a minor theme of the recent outpouring of political awareness among non-whites in North America. It is now considered politically correct to admit the possibility that the checks and balances written into the U.S. Constitution may have been borrowed from Native culture. Indeed, some aboriginal leaders insist on this "truth."

I wonder.

According to *The Columbia Viking Desk Encyclopedia*, the Iroquois Confederacy was created about A.D. 1570.[6] I have, however, seen other dates that place the formation about a century earlier. It may be that no one really knows. But taking this date of A.D. 1570, cited by at least one authority, we see that it conforms very well with the Freemasonic thought of the time about limiting monarchy by a Parliament. This date is the second half of Elizabeth I's reign in England. It corresponds to the embryonic ideas about Parliamentary structure of that time. The Iroquois Confederacy reflects this basic structure in a vague way, with something else added that reflects (also in a vague way) the later U.S. structure.

Researching a book with the scope of this one is not an easy task. One can only hope that the researcher does responsible justice to these many aspects —and this researcher prays that he has done so. My understanding of the political structure of the Iroquois Confederacy is as follows, and I hope that this précis, culled from many sources, will not lead readers astray.

First, there was a council of hereditary chiefs. This corresponds (more or less) to England's House of Lords in Parliament. In the Constitution, this became the U.S. Senate, an elected body with longer terms than the House of Representatives since America had no hereditary nobility.

Then, the Iroquois had a council of elected chiefs. This corresponds to the English House of Commons in the parliamentary system. The U.S. House of Representatives evolved from the Commons.

The United States has a president who can block, for a certain time, resolutions passed by the Senate (Lords) and the Representatives (Commons) but who must ultimately accede to the will of these two councils if they continue to agree (i.e., pass the resolution three times). In the British system, the monarch had this power, but the veto power was never really spelled out. Now, the monarch simply rubber-stamps whatever Parliament legislates — but, as compensation, British governments are not elected for a given, guaranteed period of time. A British government can fall over any vote in the Commons. This means that representatives must be very sensitive to public opinion when they cast their votes in the Commons. They might well lose their next election because they supported too many unpopular resolutions. So, in the British system, representatives may well vote against their own party and bring down the government for a general election, rather than risk losing the election when it comes.

In addition to the House of Lords or U.S. Senate and the House of Commons or U.S. Representatives, the United States has a Supreme Court. This is really the last and final arbiter of any given piece of legislation because the Supreme Court decides whether it is constitutional. Even if the legislation is passed by Senate and Representatives, and even if ratified by the president, it may be thrown out if it does not conform to the principles and guarantees of the Constitution. The Constitution itself can be changed — amended — but it is difficult to do. It requires a "more than majority" vote of both Houses to ensure that the amendment truly reflects widespread popular consent.

In the Iroquois scheme of things, the Council of Mothers had the powers of both the president or monarch and the Supreme Court. This Council of Mothers ratified, or vetoed, any proposed Iroquois policy (mostly, new wars). The inherently somewhat matriarchal structure of the Iroquoian-speaking Indians was a departure from European custom with which Hiawatha's prophet had to contend, and the Council of Mothers (at least) existed long before any Europeans influenced the tribal political mechanics. It operated within each tribe when the Confederacy was formed.

With the unique and radical political formation of this Iroquois Confederacy, we can see how certain traditional power centres were reformulated into a structure that allowed these five formerly hostile tribes to operate together. Since we know that some Europeans were living around the Lake on the Mountain, and since the timing fits well with natural expansion from Sinclair's Estotiland, and since it is known that Scottish (and then English) Freemasons were wrestling with the actual forms of parliamentary structure at this very time (i.e., 1570), it is hard to escape the suspicion that the Iroquois Confederacy was influenced by this same source.

Of course, it could be argued that the Iroquois structure inspired the Freemasonic notions of parliamentary structure, and not the other way around. Against this perspective, though, is the fact that the Iroquois Confederacy came into being only after Europeans were apparently living around the place of Hiawatha's inspiration — the Lake on the Mountain in Canada. That is, according to some chronologies... If the Confederacy was structured in A.D. 1480, instead of A.D. 1570, then we have the real possibility that the Iroquois bequeathed a political structure that inspired both Britain and the United States.

This would be an interesting question to settle, but it is beyond my interest and expertise. From the dates and artefacts we have amassed so far, I tend to think that the Iroquois were influenced by European Grail-believing Templar-Freemasons and not the other way around. But this may reflect merely my own ignorance of Iroquois political forms.

Without going into details of Iroquois history, it can be said that the wars and alliances of the Confederacy contributed in no small measure to the defeat of the French in North America. Not only did the enmity of the Iroquois prevent the French from breaking out of the St. Lawrence valley in any cohesive and powerful way, but Iroquois alliance with the English during the French and Indian War demonstrably assisted the ultimate British victory. Hiawatha's visions and inspirations affected the lives of millions of people.

Hill Cumorah

Directly across Lake Ontario from the Lake on the Mountain is Hill Cumorah. Two and a half centuries after Hiawatha, another man was destined to influence the lives of millions of people. Here, on September 21, 1827, Joseph Smith acquired the golden tablets that form the scripture of the Mormon religion. Today, the Church of Jesus Christ of the Latter Day Saints has over four million adherents.[7]

For Mormons, it is a matter of faith that Joseph Smith found these golden tablets in a hill in New York State, that he translated them and transmitted the content of a "New Covenant" to the faithful. Most non-Mormons think that the entire story is bunk, that Joseph Smith was a charlatan, and that only the weak-minded could profess Mormonism. We must remember that religion is a matter of belief, not logic. In the cold view of logic, it is no more ridiculous to believe in golden tablets from upstate New York than to believe that the Holy Ghost (alias Gabriel) impregnated Mary with a supernatural child.

In fact, I think that the idea of golden-looking tablets, recounting the tale of pre-Columbus Christian-Jewish people in America, is less ridiculous, logically, than the belief in Mary's virgin impregnation by an angel. My notion is that the people known to have lived around the Lake on the Mountain may have written a record of their adventures and their beliefs. Joseph Smith found it. I doubt that the plates were gold. But they may well have been thin copper sheets — probably sheathing from a ship's hull.

Joseph Smith's story is a complicated one, and I don't intend to go into it in any great detail. He was born on December 23, 1805, in Sharon, Vermont. His family (on both sides) had lived in the Green Mountains, and Joseph Smith grew up with the legends and folklore of "money digging" in these mountains. Money digging was so much a part of colonial activity in these mountains that a stage play on the subject, *Disappointment; or, the Force of Credulity*, was produced in Philadelphia in 1767. A Vermont weekly newspaper wrote: "We could name, if we pleased, at least five hundred respectable men who do in the simplicity and sincerity of their hearts believe that immense treasures lie concealed upon our Green Mountains, many of whom have been for a number of years industriously and perseveringly engaged in digging it up."

We are entitled to ask how an activity like money digging could have sustained itself, with so many people devoted to it, without occasional results? Were there some caches of treasure in the Green Mountains — at least a few to be discovered at intervals that would keep the hopeful digging? The answer appears to be a probable yes. We have seen, on the Canadian side of the Green Mountains, carbon-dated ruins of medieval Europeans. At the Cairn Site in Potton township on the border of Vermont, there is a system of settling ponds that may have been used to extract gold dust and nuggets. If only someone looked, I have no doubt that curious ruins and artefacts would be discovered in northern Vermont and New Hampshire, perhaps including caches of gold dust, nuggets, ingots, or coinage.

Now is the place to mention a curious story told to me and Mike Twose by Gérard Leduc. Gérard himself was inclined to view the Cairn Site as primarily a religious one, but when Mike Twose suggested the "gold settling pond" theory, Gérard remembered a local story. In the late 1950s and early 1960s, a Potton township boy had paid his way through McGill University in Montreal by spending his summers working in the township. This is not, of course, unusual. But in this case, none of the local farmers or businesses employed him, although he disappeared all during the long days. He certainly worked, and worked hard, at something because he came home tired and dirty. Finally, when pressed about his local summer job, he quipped to his mother that he had his "private gold mine." Perhaps he did.

Since there's evidence of both Ancient Celts in the Green Mountains and later medieval Europeans, and since the local Indians (before they became politically correct) agreed that white, metal-working people had lived among them in the past, Gérard's story and the "money-digging" mania of Green Mountain Vermonters start to make a certain sense. The European miners may have cached much of their treasure until they could return for it. But many may not have returned — plenty of early ships must have been lost at sea. In the end, the Indians say, the remaining whites were massacred. Many caches of lost and forgotten metal in the Green Mountains may remain to be found.

So Joseph Smith grew up in a tradition of Vermont money digging. When his family moved to New York State in 1816 (when Joseph was ten years old), they moved into another area in which money digging was a popular pursuit for some. But this New York money digging was a bit different from the Vermont kind. In New York, it acquired a cultural and "archaeological" aspect because treasures were associated with the Indian mounds that dotted the countryside. Eight tumuli were within twelve miles of the Smith farm in Palmyra, and hundreds more were sprinkled throughout New York State.[8] People dug in them, finding mostly bones, but sometimes "metal plates." In 1821, workers digging on the Erie Canal found several "brass breastplates," according to the *Western Farmer* newspaper.[9]

This brings us to the "Moundbuilders," after which we will return to Joseph Smith and the story told in the Book of Mormon.

Moundbuilders

In the 1780s, American settlers began crossing the Allegheny Mountains heading for the "West" — Ohio, Indiana, and Illinois.

Their Indian guides told them that the Allegheny Mountains themselves had been named after a tribe of white people who had long vanished. In the upper reaches of the Allegheny and Ohio rivers, these new settlers began to see hundreds, or thousands of "mounds." Some were just simple, rounded heaps of earth overgrown with grass and trees. But others seemed to be earthworks of careful geometric shapes that might enclose many acres.

Today, although there are moundbuilder museums in almost every state east of the Mississippi (except for the Atlantic coastal states), it is difficult for us to appreciate or grasp the impact of these mounds on an earlier generation. There were hundreds and thousands of mounds, and sometimes they were grouped in concentrations that suggested ancient, abandoned cities. Unfortunately for the mounds, these "cities" were located at strategic places, and we chose the same places for our own cities. The vast majority of the mounds, and particularly the most impressive city-like concentrations of geometrical earthworks, have been obliterated and built over by our own towns and cities, and our wide highways linking these centres have obliterated many more.

This has had a curious effect even on modern archaeology and anthropology professors and students. Since the fantastic nineteenth-century accumulation of the moundbuilders is no longer so obvious to our eyes, modern "experts" tend to think that the number, complexity, and sophistication of the original moundland had been greatly exaggerated by early, mostly uneducated, settlers. "Uneducated" does not mean "stupid," and these settlers could use their eyes (as modern experts are no longer able to do) to see the immense mystery of the mounds. And there were some educated people among those moving west. Some of them left books with careful maps and drawings of the mounds. Since some of the constructions seem so huge, symmetrical, and sophisticated, these first documents are generally viewed as romanticized. I suspect that it is we, not the early and amazed settlers, who have a distorted view of the moundbuilders.

The whites naturally asked the local Woodland Indians who had built these mounds. The Indians of that time answered either that they didn't know and that the mounds had always been there or that a vanished race of white people had built them in the distant past. When? No one knew, but some inquisitive early investigators cut down the largest trees then growing on the mounds and counted the growth rings. Some of the trees were three hundred years old — in 1800. And, of course, there was no way of knowing how many generations of trees had grown atop the mounds since they had been abandoned.

Since the existing Woodland Indians denied knowledge of, or construction of, the mounds in the nineteenth century, many theories sprang up to explain them. First, whatever the Indians said, it seemed obvious that they had truly not made them. The whites refused to believe that the Indians they knew were capable of the geometric precision of the larger mound "cities." Then, there was the matter of labour. The Woodland Indians had never been very populous. They lived by hunting and gathering, mostly, although some had an agriculture imported (it is thought) from Mexico about A.D. 800, based on maize, beans, and squashes of various sorts. But, except among the Iroquois, agriculture was a secondary source of food production among the eastern Woodland Indians. Hunting, gathering, and marginal agriculture cannot support a very large population. The mounds, however, showed that very large numbers of people must have been concentrated in small geographical areas while the mounds were being built. And if, indeed, the larger mound complexes had truly been cities, there must have been extensive agriculture of some kind to support the population — a much more sophisticated agriculture than the Woodland tribes exhibited. The sheer number of mounds required a much larger population than the Indians represented at the coming of the white man.

Gradually, educated whites, and most educated whites were ministers, began to speculate there had been an ancient North American civilization with a population of millions. With their Biblical orientation, their favourite theory was that the moundbuilders had been the Lost Tribes of Israel who, by gradual assimilation into the Indian population, degenerated into tribal and primitive people with their mounds as monuments to their former existence. The most distinguished American clergymen preached this theory — William Penn, Roger Williams, Cotton Mather, Jonathan Edwards, and many others less well known. In 1833, Josiah Priest wrote in his *American Antiquities:* "The opinion that the American Indians are descendants of the Lost Ten Tribes is a popular one and generally believed."[10]

Up until about 1900, a person who professed some education could still believe this sort of thing — and perhaps will again be able to in the not-so-distant future. It may again become possible and justifiable to believe that if they were not specifically the Ten Lost

Tribes of Israel, some ancient American Indians either were "white" and indigenous or came from across the Atlantic or the Pacific. It may again become justifiable to believe that some Woodland Indians, at the time of colonization, descended more strongly from this ancient "civilization" than others did. As I've related, the totality of the evidence, together with the recent (1996) discovery of Kennewick Man, has compelled Dr. Gérard Leduc to conclude that there were both "white Indians" and "red Indians," of differing cultural levels, living contemporaneously in North America during some past time. This is not so different from that supposedly outmoded and "romantic" view of most early nineteenth-century writers. It is based on Leduc's "re-re-appraisal" of the evidence.

For the record, the modern archaeological dogma considers all of the above to be bunk. A good presentation of the truly "modern and scientific" view of the problem is Robert Silverberg's *The Moundbuilders*.[11] In it, we learn that the moundbuilders were just the ancestors of the Indians the colonials met. Well, not precisely. The actual moundbuilders were more closely related to the Sioux who, for some reason, left their eastern river cities to try their hand at buffalo acquisition on the Great Plains. Mind you, they did not yet have the horse (because the Spanish had not yet come), so they just ran the buffalo down. Other Indians moved into the vacuum left by the Sioux and, of course, the mounds were just as mysterious for them as they were to nineteenth-century settlers.

The first group of Moundbuilders were the Hopewells (1000 B.C. to 500 B.C.) who started the tradition along the Illinois River. They were supported by an agriculture based on wild rice, which grew in some of the shallow lakes but was not truly domesticated. These Hopewells had a far-flung economy and traded in such widely separated places as Lake Superior and the Gulf of Mexico. They made beautiful implements and jewellery of copper, using the metal even for points for spears (which happen to look just like Celtic spearpoints from Iberia). Hopewells travelled widely and left cultural outposts around the Great Lakes.

Eventually the Hopewells merged into the Adena culture, producing a culture often called Hopewell-Adena (500 B.C.to A.D. 800?) and expanding from the Illinois River valley to the Ohio River valley, the Mississippi and the Missouri watersheds. Again, moundbuilding, metal-working, and far-flung trade was the keynote of Hopewell-Adena. Most of the mounds, geometrical enclosures, and "cities" were built at this time.

The decline of Hopewell-Adena was caused by the introduction of maize, bean, and squash agriculture from Mexico. No more metal-working, trade and long-distance commerce. This is called (believe it or not) "the breakdown of the inter-activity sphere," and the Sioux-related people left for the Great Plains. However, as it declined, Hopewell-Adena seeded the rise of the Mississippian Culture (I, II and III), which carried on a reduced and diminished moundbuilding tradition until white men came. Mounds were still in ceremonial use in the 1600s, on the lower and middle reaches of the Mississippi when Spanish and French explorers sailed the river.

So much for the modern view of times past. The only thing this interpretation has to recommend it is "political correctness," because ancestors of existing Indians made the mounds without any outside cultural influence. It certainly has no facts or common sense to support it, however. First, was the Illinois-area "wild rice" ever sufficient to support the first Hopewell moundbuilding culture? I've seen no studies on this, but I suspect not. Archaeology professors are fond of taking a few graduate students to the Illinois River, feeding them on wild rice, supplying them with wicker baskets and letting them have the fun of hauling dirt to make a ten-foot-high mound about thirty feet in diameter. This can be done, with candy bars and Cokes as a dietary supplement, but try to raise over 1,200 much larger mounds (the approximate number along the Illinois) with a minimal population supposedly living on wild rice.

What happened to all the metal (copper) implements and spear-points? Did the Indians find them so inferior to chipped flint that they stopped making them? Who mined the three million pounds of missing copper from the Isle Royal deposits (estimate by geologists of 3M)?[12] Where did all this copper go? Why, for the first time in all known human history, would the introduction of agriculture cause a "breakdown of the inter-activity sphere"? All over the world, the introduction of effective agriculture has done precisely the opposite — it has enabled a greater population to exist, and many of these "extra people" became artisans who produced products that stimulated trade and commerce over wide areas. Civilization thrives on agriculture, it doesn't die from it.

As you may gather, I consider the modern "scientific" view of the moundbuilders to be bunk — and it needs to be debunked. What actually happened seems fairly obvious, even if the details are scanty. About 1000 B.C. some immigrants arrived who knew about the extraction, smelting, and use of metal. More and more came, and there naturally was, at the same time, intermarriage with the local Indians. At some point, these immigrants encountered a disaster that wiped them out. This probably happened about A.D. 500–800. Some of their mixed descendants, to a greater or lesser extent, remembered agriculture, metal working, and moundbuilding, but these arts gradually died out in the northeast.

As for the "Late Mississippian" people who were still adding to mounds and using them for ceremonies when the Spanish and French came onto the lower Mississippi River in the 1600s, it is possible that they were originally inspired by moundbuilders from the Ohio Valley and Great Lakes. Moundbuilding lingered among the Natchez tribe (of Mississippi and Louisiana) because of the proximity of Mexican civilizations across the Gulf who were pyramid builders. Or Mississippian may have been inspired by the Mexican civilization to begin with. Or Mississippian was inspired by both the Ohio–Great Lakes moundbuilders and Mexico equally. As a frontier population between the two different cultures, Mississippian must have absorbed from both. Living on a waterway like the Mississippi River, contact north and south was unavoidable.

That's the scenario I prefer. It fits the facts without insulting common sense.

But who were the immigrants into the northeast who did metal working and who built giant earthworks?

The most obvious, almost obligatory, answer is that they were Ancient Celts, a catch-all term embracing Carthagenians and Celtiberians from southern Europe and North Africa, and including Irish Celts and closely related Scandinavian Teutons from northern Europe. In giving this answer, we are not only relying upon traditions, legends, and folklore, but also upon written documents by Aristotle (his pupil, most likely) and Diodorus.

The Book of Mormon

Joseph Smith's time and culture were dominated by the Christian Bible. Celts do not figure in the Bible. During Joseph Smith's time, Celtic studies had not gained much attention, even in Britain. As far as the Bible is concerned, the only large and dramatically lost population was that of Israel (the northern kingdom of the divided Hebrew nation). These Israelites were sufficiently civilized to work metal and build impressive structures of earth and stone. It is not surprising that they were chosen in Joseph Smith's time as the best candidates to have been the moundbuilders. As we have seen, this was a popular opinion of the early 1800s.

The folklore of digging up treasure left by the supposed ancient Israelites, whether in Vermont or in New York State, involved the notion of instruments that enabled the hopeful seeker to find buried treasure. Dowsing is semi-respectable now. In *The Amateur Archeologist's Handbook*,[13] published in 1974, the State Archeologist of Massachusetts advises dowsing when sites can't be located any other way; helpful directions for making hazel-wood dowsing wands are given.

T.C. Lethbridge, for many years director of the prestigious Ethnology Museum at Cambridge University, racked up an impressive record of finding new archaeological sites in Great Britain mainly by using a pendulum. In fact, he could find sites by dangling his pendulum over *maps* — then he'd go to the place indicated and dig. Lethbridge, by observing his pendulum over a number of years, gradually noticed that it moved to a different "beat" or oscillation depending upon the type of buried material it encountered. Wood, glass, pewter, and various kinds of metal all seemed to make the pendulum swing at specific rates. Lethbridge was therefore able to predict what his archaeologists were likely to find, a quite handy ability that contributed to the success of Cambridge University's archaeological excavations.[14]

Dr. Norman Emerson of the University of Toronto had an uncanny knack for finding Indian sites in Ontario; he used dowsing and a psychic.[15] Of the three psychics he used, his favourite was "George." Emerson relates that once, at a party, he was being chided by a colleague who doubted the value of psychics and who attributed Emerson's undoubted success to luck. As it chanced, George was at this party, and the doubting colleague wanted to test him with a troublesome artefact, a rather odd-looking little wooden figure that had been dug up from a Haida site on Vancouver Island. There, at the party, George held this artefact in his hand and without hesitation announced that it was West African, dating from the 1700s. Emerson was appalled, and both he and George had to endure some good-natured (?) laughter. But Emerson had so much faith in George's proven abilities that he set one of his graduate students the task of trying to figure it out. With much persistence (and great luck) this student was able to find a ship's log from early in the eighteenth century. It recorded that a slave on board, an African known to be a carver of wooden objects, jumped overboard and swam to Vancouver Island. This occurred not five miles from the later excavation site where the West African artefact (according to George) was discovered. Of course, the ship's log *proved* nothing absolutely, but the entry is highly suggestive. In later life, Emerson would tell this story to vindicate his use of psychic archaeology. He told me this story many years ago, and I have also seen it in print.

My friend and companion, Joelle Lauriol, has what she calls a "finding knack." She claims to be able to find things that she wants, and for several years has focused on four-leaf clovers. I've seen her casually find sixteen four-leaf clovers in a few hours' walk along Toronto residential sidewalks. She says that she doesn't actually *see* them among the profusion of clover leaves, they "jump out" at her. And they must, for she can perceive one ten feet away in a growth of clover. No one could actually distinguish the pattern of leaves at that distance. Joelle wears contact lenses but her vision is not abnormally acute. Naturally, I'm trying to convince her to broaden her finding knack to include artefacts and treasure. But, like many people with this sort of gift, Joelle is rightly hesitant to employ it to find things of potentially great value.

All the foregoing has been in aid of Joseph Smith, who has been regarded as a charlatan, during his life and now, because he claimed to be able to "see" buried treasure. He sometimes used a pendulum, but mostly relied upon his "seer stone." According to Smith (and the folklore of his time), every person possessed a seer stone that was waiting to be recognized and discovered. Most people do not know this, or believe it, and therefore never find their waiting seer stone. Joseph Smith found his, however, and it was an important event for him. He was digging a well, with some co-workers, for one Mason Chase when he found his stone. Martin Harris, a friend of Joseph's who was present at the time and who later assisted in the translation of the *Book of Mormon*, stated that it came from twenty-four feet underground. One Joseph Capron actually testified in court that Smith could see wondrous sights with it: "ghosts, infernal spirits, mountains of gold and silver."[16]

Joseph Smith's wife, Emma, described the stone as "not exactly black but rather dark in color." Brigham Young, to whom it was given, exhibited it to the regents of the University of Deseret on February 26, 1856, in Utah as "the Seer's stone with which The Prophet Smith discovered the plates of the Book of Mormon."

Hosea Stout, a Mormon elder who knew Smith well, said that it was almost black with light-coloured stripes.[17]

Joseph Smith had already acquired a modest reputation as a seer, or psychic archaeologist (as Dr. Norman Smith or T.C. Lethbridge might have put it), but with his discovery of his seer stone, his powers were greatly enhanced. It was inevitable that Smith would be hired to locate treasure by hopeful money diggers. Martin Harris was quoted in *Tiffany's Monthly* magazine (1859, pages 163–170): "There was a company there in that neighborhood who were digging for money supposed to have been hidden by the ancients....They dug for money in Palmyra, Manchester, also in Pennsylvania, and other places."[18]

Joseph Smith was the prize seer for this company, and it seems an indisputable fact that he was successful in leading these diggers to some buried treasures that included, at least, some "brass breastplates" (and possibly some other, more valuable, things that were not publicized). This is a matter of court record. The laws of that time didn't recognize the potential of psychic archaeology, and being a paid seer was to be considered an impostor and a fraud. In 1826, Joseph Smith was charged, "by an officious person," and convicted of being "a disorderly person and an impostor" by a Bainbridge, N.Y., court. But the interesting part of the court record is that the man who was paying Smith fourteen dollars a month as a seer, one Josiah Stowel, testified that he "positively knew" that Joseph Smith could see buried valuables. A modern court might have dismissed the case since the plaintiff had nothing to do with the money-digging company and Smith's employer obviously had no complaints about his performance.

I have covered this money digging and seeing stones in rather more detail than some readers may feel is warranted. But there are some important aspects to it that deserve consideration. First of all, the Potton township ruins and artefacts suggest that there was actually some justification, and the occasional payoff, to the Vermont mania for money digging in the Green Mountains. Second, I believe that the "truth" about the moundbuilders is still very much in doubt. The modern so-called scientific construct is, to my way of thinking, so full of holes that it is worthless, and much less likely than the nineteenth century "romanticism" about an ancient high culture in North America — especially in view of some ruins (carbon-dated) and artefacts that we have seen. Whereas this high culture may not have been remnants of the Ten Lost

Tribes of Israel, but more likely to have been immigrant Ancient Celts and later medieval-Templar colonization, the nineteenth-century suspicion of some ancient non-Indian presence seems justified. Third, Joseph Smith's claims (and employment) as a seer for buried treasure may not be without foundation. Many objects currently on display at the Royal Ontario Museum were recovered in exactly the same way by Dr. Norman Emerson's psychics; the Ethnology Museum at Cambridge University is crammed with artefacts recovered by Tom Lethbridge's pendulum. Whether we like it or not, some people do have the gift of perceiving buried objects.

Then, there's this matter of "brass plates." They seem to get found, particularly in New York State. Brass is an alloy of copper (90 per cent) and zinc (10 per cent). Bronze is also an alloy of copper (90 per cent) and tin (10 per cent), although some bronze is made with 10 per cent antimony. The very first brass was made with 10 per cent arsenic. In short, brass and bronze are really the same thing — an alloy of copper with about 10 per cent of some other metal, preferably an inexpensive one. During the European Bronze Age, tin was the most common additive because of the huge deposits in Cornwall. The copper came from Spain, mostly, in later times (although the first copper used came from the Balkans, the "Chalcolithic" phase, about 4000 B.C.).

There's a big problem with these alleged "brass plates." According to conventional archaeology, no northeastern aboriginal people used alloyed copper. They beat natural copper nuggets into ornaments and implements, but they did not melt the copper and then pour it into molds so that it could cool and harden into useful shapes. Nor did they melt copper and then add some other metal to make "bronze" (or "brass"). One presumes that nineteenth-century farmers and smiths could distinguish between copper and brass better than the average person today, for they used both on a daily basis. Copper is redder in colour, and softer, than "brass," which is golden-looking. If brass plates were discovered by Joseph Smith (among others) during his money digging employment, and by Erie Canal workmen, they were not made by northeastern Woodland Culture Indians — at least, not according to conventional archaeology.

Are there, or are there not, "brass" objects in the mounds of New York State and elsewhere? For that matter, are there objects from the mounds that were made by melting copper and pouring it into moulds? Conventional archaeology says a thundering no. So what are these "brass plates" reported in 1820s' newspapers? For that matter, what about the brass plate I saw and photographed in the Niagara region in 1992?[19] The owner of this object said that it had been discovered in the 1820s near Palmyra, New York. I cannot vouch for its authenticity, but it *is* brass.

Also in 1992, Don Eckler of New York State showed me both photos and a crystal analysis of a copper axe-head discovered along the Genesee River. It looked to me as if it had been cast — that is, the copper had been melted until liquid, and then poured into a clay mould of an axe shape. Once the copper had cooled to hardness, the two-sided clay mould was taken apart and the new copper axe-head extracted. This technique was supposedly unknown in northeastern North America. Cast metal typically shows a random crystalline structure under a microscope, whereas beaten objects always show indications of crystal alignment where hammer strokes have arranged the crystals in a definite direction. Microphotographs of this axe-head show a random crystalline orientation. There was no doubt: It had been cast. Therefore, SUNY experts called it a hoax. (The "problem" with cast and alloyed artefacts will again concern us soon within the context of "Indian Awareness" and political correctness around Peterborough, Ontario.)

A copper axe head discovered in New York State. According to crystallographic analysis this object had been cast of molten copper poured into a ceramic mould. But experts insist that North American aboriginals did not know the art of casting. Photo by Don Eckler.

At the time of his conviction as an impostor (March 20, 1826), Joseph Smith was employed as a money-digging seer by Josiah Stowel at a salary of fourteen dollars a month — a fair sum in those days. Smith's task was to find an old "Spanish" silver mine that was supposedly located somewhere along the Susquehanna River. Josiah Stowel testified in court that he had reason to know also that ancient "coined money" was to be found along the Susquehanna. While doing this work for Stowel, and also attending school when he could, Smith headquartered himself in the town of Harmony, Pennsylvania. Now, can it be mere coincidence that Iotigolo's AE tombstone was discovered overlooking a branch of the Susquehanna River? True, the AE stone was found roughly one hundred miles west of Harmony, but on a main branch of the same river. In the next chapter, we will again visit the rugged Pennsylvania mountains on the Susquehanna and Allegheny watershed to see the Templar carvings of the Baphomet and the statue of the Murdered Apprentice. These were discovered about the same distance from Harmony.

I find it curious, to say the least, that in following the life of Joseph Smith from Vermont to Pennsylvania, we find ourselves on waterways that have yielded artefacts of the Grail era. The only trouble is that most of these Grail-related artefacts were discovered after Joseph Smith's time. He could not have known about them and would not have credited the Holy Grail if he'd heard of it. Josiah Stowel alluded to a lost "Spanish" mine and to ancient "coined money" in Pennsylvania. It seems obvious that he found something, and wanted to find more, because he travelled all the way to Palmyra, New York, just to recruit Joseph Smith as a seer. And pay him. And it seems obvious that Joseph Smith must have enjoyed considerable local renown as a seer for his reputation to have travelled 150 miles to Harmony.

Of course, it is only Josiah Stowel's opinion that the supposed mine was Spanish. We don't know his opinion on the origin of the coined money. Josiah Stowel was not a well-educated man. He may have attributed the supposed mine to Spaniards only because he knew that Columbus had come in 1492, that Pennsylvania was colonized officially in the 1680s, and that left almost two hundred years for the Spanish to have exploited the continent. The silver mine, if there ever was one, could equally have been the work of Ancient Celts or fourteenth-century Templars. The same applies to Stowel's coined money.

While in Harmony, Joseph Smith became attracted to Emma

Hale. With Josiah Stowel's help, the couple eloped and were secretly married on January 18, 1827. To escape the wrath of Emma's outraged father, they went back to Joseph Smith's parents near Palmyra, New York. Nine months later, Joseph Smith found his golden plates containing the *Book of Mormon*. But he allowed no one actually to see these plates, not even his mother or his new wife, explaining that it was death for anyone else to see them. He did show them the "magic spectacles" that he'd found with the plates. There are several differing descriptions of these by people who actually saw them but all agree that they had silver frames, just like the description of the Urim and Thummim in *The Bible*. Along with the tablets and the spectacles, he found a large copper breastplate "worth at least five hundred dollars" and also, allegedly, a sword. Many others could, and did, see the breastplate.

According to the official Mormon story, Joseph began translating the tablets at his parents' home, dictating from behind a curtain to Emma, his first scribe — Joseph had not learned to write at that time. But it proved impossible for this work to go forward because of the curiosity of his family. Accordingly, sometime in the winter of 1827–28, Joseph and Emma moved back to Harmony, Pennsylvania. This meant braving the wrath of Emma's father and trying to effect a reconciliation. The reconciliation was accomplished, and Father Hale loaned the couple a house. In April 1828, Martin Harris arrived in Harmony to relieve Emma of the task of transcribing Joseph's translation.

The point of relating all this history is that, although Joseph Smith allegedly found the tablets in Hill Cumorah near Manchester and Palmyra, *he could have actually found them months earlier in Pennsylvania while he was employed by Stowel and before he eloped with Emma.* I'm indebted to Joelle Lauriol, a former Mormon, for this suggestion. This is a possibility that, to my knowledge, has never been broached by either Mormon or non-Mormon historians. Why would Joseph Smith have claimed that he found the tablets in New York State after his elopement? It seems simple enough. If he'd found them earlier in Pennsylvania while in the employment of Stowel as a treasure seer, and if he had let it become known, the tablets would legally have belonged to Josiah Stowel. Smith may have justified this by rationalizing that the tablets were not the kind of treasure that Stowel had employed him to find. But, just to make sure, he let no one see them and claimed that he'd found them in Hill Cumorah after he'd left Stowel's employ.

Did Joseph Smith find tablets?

The answer appears to be yes. He certainly found the spectacles, a breastplate, and (perhaps) a sword. Emma Smith, who was no blind devotee of her husband, never looked at the tablets, which were covered by a cloth on the table. This was not so much obedience to her husband as her own determination to remain distant from these tablets. Indeed, eight years after Joseph had published the *Book of Mormon*, Emma was still attending the Presbyterian Church. It was her duty to help her husband in his work (a duty she was happy to hand over to Martin Harris), but she viewed the tablets with religious suspicion. When she dusted the table, these tablets made "a metallic rustling sound," according to Emma. Others also heard this "metallic rustling". Eventually, Joseph went to a Palmyra carpenter named Willard Chase to have a wooden case made for the collection of tablets. Smith kept this case under his pillow at night. A package of this size could have been sneaked out of Pennsylvania. Perhaps the chance discovery of actual artefacts in Hill Cumorah in 1827 gave Joseph Smith the opportunity of revealing the tablets as being part of the same find.

This leads to the conclusion that the tablets could not have been very large, and the collection could not have been very thick. Yet, the *Book of Mormon* is more than four hundred pages long, set in small type. If all this had truly been engraved on smallish tablets, it would have required very good spectacles indeed to have read the print. Even better spectacles would have been required to engrave it. However, none of this is relevant to Mormons who view the *Book of Mormon* as a divine revelation.

The Notorious 116 Pages

After the arrival of Martin Harris in Harmony in April 1828, he and Joseph Smith worked long hours each day for two months in order to get 116 foolscap pages of handwritten translation. Now, originally, these 116 pages appeared to be the completed work. At least, they seem to have been regarded that way. But they could have represented only a small fraction of the *Book of Mormon* as published in 1830. Martin Harris begged to take these 116 pages back to Palmyra with him so that he might show them to his wife. The story goes that either Lucy Harris stole these pages, or that Martin Harris lost them. Either way, their loss was originally regarded as a catastrophe — the loss of the entire work. In extant letters, Martin Harris lamented, "I have lost my soul; I have lost my soul." Joseph Smith is remembered to have cried out, "Oh, my God! All is lost! What shall I do? And how shall I appear before the Lord?"

This anguish was almost unbearably acute because, I think, Joseph Smith had destroyed his copper sheets (or "golden plates") after successfully completing the 116-page translation. There are three likely reasons for this.

First, he may have genuinely regarded them as Holy Writ and, once "revealed" by translation, they should be destroyed since they might result in the death of anyone who saw them other than the chosen prophet, himself.

Second, he had already announced that he was translating the tablets by divine inspiration, and the divinely given Urim and Thummim. Any second version of the 116 pages should, therefore, be word-for-word identical to the first. But if Joseph Smith had been sincerely trying to translate a difficult Scottish dialect that he could barely read and had to guess the gist of much of it, his second version might differ from the original 116 pages, which might yet turn up. Lucy Harris might even have stolen them and might, out of spite, release them for comparison with any second translation. She had no faith in Joseph Smith and resented her husband's loyalty to him — not to mention the fact that her husband seemed willing to mortgage their farm to pay for the publication of Joseph's "divinely inspired" translation. Also, of course, both Emma and Martin had transcribed parts of Joseph's first translation and might remember departures from it in any second translation.

Third, the Smiths were desperately poor, and Emma was then pregnant. Smith may have melted the tablets down and sold the copper for money as the metal was much more valuable then than now. Remember, the copper breastplate supposedly found with the tablets was "worth at least five hundred dollars" in the words of Joseph Smith. His poverty forced him to be acutely conscious of money.

The loss of these 116 pages was even more of a tragedy because no copy was made. This oversight may seem inexcusable, but it is understandable in the 1820s. Copying was a laborious process — there were no Xerox machines. And, given the Smiths' poverty, even the cost of paper was a burden. The original brief text was so valuable to Martin Harris that there was no question but that he would guard it carefully. Yet, it was lost.

This 116-page handwritten translation (in Martin Harris' rather large, scrawling hand), if it was anything like the much longer elaboration finally published as the *Book of Mormon*, told the brief story of Jewish-Christian refugees in North America. They had fled from destruction in the Holy Land to a secret land across the Atlantic. Jesus was somehow "with" them in the new land. Some inter-marriage with the Indians had taken place, but there remained some pure Europeans. There was increasing danger of wars with the Indians they had originally inter-married with and had helped.

I know that it is only one more notion of the *Book of Mormon*, but my opinion is that this notorious 116 pages may have been a real "translation" from a real (and brief) Grail Refugee history. This concise record may have been inscribed on copper leaves, probably copper sheets from a ship's hull. If it was written in a medieval Scottish dialect like the one we have discussed previously, Joseph Smith, who was just learning to read and write between 1827 and 1829, could actually have got the sense of it with a great deal of sincere effort. I think that's why these original 116 pages took so long to produce compared to the later *Book of Mormon* — a 275,000-word dictation that required less than eleven months.

Joseph Smith just took the story of the lost original 116 pages and spun an elaboration around the basic tale. The story told in the original 116 pages must have been fairly similar to the eventual, much longer and greatly elaborated *Book of Mormon*. Martin Harris had written most of these 116 pages himself. If the later enlarged version had differed radically from the theme of the briefer original, he and others would have remarked on it. He didn't and they didn't. The difference in sheer length Joseph explained by this strategem: the original first 116 pages had been translated from an abridged "political" account, whereas the *Book of Mormon* derived from a much fuller historical and spiritual account taken from other tablets altogether. These, too, could not be seen, although Joseph showed *large* heavy boxes in which they were kept. During the translation of the longer *Book of Mormon*, no one reported that earlier metallic rustling sound.

But why replace the lost 116 pages with another and much longer book?

In fairness to Joseph Smith, he may have felt obligated to do it. If he had actually discovered a brief written record in a difficult but barely readable dialect, he may sincerely have thought that it was a priceless record of "Hebrews" (as everyone believed) who had been the moundbuilders. He had translated it, but had lost it. "*All* is lost! What shall I do? How shall I appear before the Lord?"

He was obviously obligated to supply another version of the record and, possibly, as a penance, to make it longer than the lost one! Assuming that he found a brief "Grail History in America," he may have actually believed that he'd discovered a new sort of "Gospel" or "New Covenant" (which is what the Holy Grail version of Christianity is). This would have become clear as he worked on the translation with Emma in Palmyra, and even more clear as the tale unfolded with Martin Harris in Harmony, Pennsylvania.

There's no doubt that Joseph Smith was fascinated with the moundbuilders. In 1825, he'd considered writing a book about them. Even though he couldn't then read or write, he was not without imagination and certainly not lacking in intelligence. As early as 1823, his mother recalled that he'd entertained the entire family at dinner with a long and colourful exposition of moundbuilder customs, costumes, social organization, military organization, and wars with the Indians. When he sat down to make his second effort with what was to become the official *Book of Mormon*, he unleashed his imagination in a four hundred-page "moundbuilder" story that, however, never deviated from the theme of those original 116 pages. By any criterion, it was a literary and intellectual tour-de-force dictated by an illiterate but intelligent and imaginative man.

One can accept the *Book of Mormon* on faith. One can dismiss it as a hoax and a blasphemy, as many did in 1830 and still do.

Or one can wonder why the *Book of Mormon* actually more or less reflects the history of Grail Refugees in North America, which Joseph Smith could not have known.

Or could he...?

As *Grail Knights of North America* was being finalized for publication, more attention than ever before was being focused on a group of people in the Appalachians who seem to be a population of Europeans left over from some early precolumbian contact. *The Toronto Star's* article "Appalachia's genetic mystery: Who are the Melungeons?" reflects similar recent articles in *The New York Times*, *The Washington Post*, *Newsday* and other major North American media.

Black-haired, blue-eyed and generally tall (Abraham Lincoln may have been a Melungeon), these people were reported from the Appalachians by the very first known explorers and colonials to enter the mountains. Until recently they were accounted for, and dismissed, as the descendants of Welsh and Irish deserters from Elizabethan ships that explored Chesapeake Bay as early as the 1570s. Now, however, some words preserved in their traditional vocabulary have demanded a closer look at the origins of these people. Their name for themselves, "Melungeons" (or Melungians), is one of those words. *Malun can* and *malun djinn* are Arabic-Moorish words meaning "accursed soul." It is difficult to see how this derivation can have come from Welsh or Irish sailors in Elizabethan expeditions. The Melungians themselves have a tradition that some of them were North European slaves who escaped from Arab and Moorish voyages to America long before Columbus and who found refuge in the Smokey Mountains. On the other hand, some Melungians introduced themselves as "Portyghees" (Portuguese) to incoming colonial explorers in the early 1600s.

In looks, the Melungians resemble the striking colouring of the "black Irish" and some Welsh. It is a fact, too, that some Melungian words are of ancient or medieval Celtic origin. They apparently had a form of Christianity before colonial influence reached them, but it was a strange form, with much Jewish and Moorish admixture. And, as was always well known, witchcraft, or *wicca*, flourished in the Appalachians until well into the 20th century. It is probable, some experts believe, that Melungians are a composite people of many European types that sought refuge in the Appalachians before Columbus: Moors, Celts, and others. Not much more is known or suspected because no one has studied the Melungeons...until now.

It seems that at least one strong genetic component of the Melungeons must be Moorish (or "Turkish"), judging from words in their vocabulary. This seems in line with two other odd facts. The first is that the North American turkey of Pilgrim and Thanksgiving fame was given a popular name by early European explorers that had obvious *Turkish* associations. Why? The second is the inexplicable circumstance that when Columbus brought the first ears of American maize back from the New World to Spain in 1493, he called it *Turkish corn*. Spaniards still call it that. Why? We will recall that Columbus asked for, and received, three Arabic interpreters for his third voyage. Why?

As I pointed out in Chapter 2, of all the seafaring people before Columbus, the Moors of Spain and the Pyrénées had the most evolved ships and navigational expertise. They, better than anyone until Columbus, could have made voyages across the Atlantic. Perhaps many Melungian genes derive from these voyages.

However, many Moors were pushed into the Pyrénées as refugees and mixed with the Basques, Celts, Jews, and Visigoths who were already there. These people became, en masse, refugees from the Albigensian Crusade because they were associated with the Cathars and the Provençal civilization. Some of them may have set sail across the Atlantic in desperation. Others may have reached the same transatlantic destination via Scotland and Portugal as relatives and dependants of heretics and Templars. It would not be surprising if the Melungians were, at least in part, living descendants of the Grail Knights of North America.

Remnant European populations like the Melungians, survivors of early precolumbian transatlantic voyages, apparently lingered in the mountains and valleys of the Appalachians. It seems as though they influenced the religious orientation of early American settlers who crossed this mountain barrier on their way west.

Jemima Wilkinson, John Noyes, Annie Lee, and Others[20]

One of the truly astonishing facts about the history of the United States is the veritable explosion of new religions that occurred in Upper New York State between 1750 and 1830. Most of these have been forgotten now, except by historians. Mormonism was the only one to survive and flourish into a sizable church.

As soon as New Englanders crossed the mountain barrier of the Appalachians and entered the beautiful Finger Lakes country of New York State, they seem to have been exposed to some influence that compelled religious experimentation.

The Grail Religion of southern France was composed of many elements that were somehow welded into a cohesive body of belief. This was called "Catharism" or "Albigensianism" by the Roman Catholic Church and was considered a major heresy. A primary component of Catharism was the different version of Christianity we've discussed — a married Jesus (and perhaps John the Baptist) with a lineage of descendants from Mary Magdalen, code-named the "Holy Grail." Another component was some body of ancient tradition and knowledge that supposedly went back to Ancient Egypt and beyond, perhaps to Atlantis (now that there's solid evidence of its existence). Yet another part of the amalgam was truly ancient Judaic tradition preserved not only by the Christian aspect, but also by Merovingian tribal memory as being Benjamites — and this included (along with early Judaism and Christianity) the practice of polygamy. Yet another part of this complex matrix was the survival in the Pyrénées of *wicca*, or "witchcraft" — the old, mostly matriarchal, "Fertility Religion" (and body of nature-knowledge) of Europe and the Middle East.

Many of these aspects might seem to be, and probably were, antipathetic to each other as, for example, patriarchal Judaism and *wicca*, but somehow they accommodated each other. This is probably because the Pyrénées Mountains had always been a refuge for defeated people and their ideas. Celts took refuge there when Carthage conquered Spain and when Rome conquered Gaul. Visigoths fled there after sacking Rome. Merovingians took refuge there when Carolingians ursurped their thrones. Jews fled there whenever Christians decided to massacre them (quite often). Yet another refugee population was Moorish; they fled to the Pyrénées when El Cid began the so-called Reconquest of Spain. And, of course, the Basques with their unique language and original Fertility Religion were already there when these others came, but had probably fled there because of the Celtic invasion of France and Spain (2000-1500 B.C.?). All these refugees jostled together in the Pyrénées. They accommodated each other because they had no choice. The result was a rich material and spiritual culture called the Provençal Civilization with a melting-pot language that was about equal parts Celtic, "French," Latin, Arabic and Hebrew.

In some ways, in fact, this Pyrénées refuge resembled the much later United States. Both were composed of outcast and displaced populations from other places. Disparate ideas and beliefs flourished, and they also evolved into new forms. National literature was born in the Pyrénées, first in "French," as troubadour ballads. The idea of chivalry started there, conveyed by the ideals of the troubadours. The idea of courtly love and the liberation of women was also born in these mountains and, as Meg Bowen has shown in *The Women Troubadours*, legal statutes of Languedoc and Provence gave women a much higher status than elsewhere in Europe.

In the Pyrénées, therefore, the strict celibacy, vegetarianism, and poverty of Cathar "Perfects" — religious "priests" or "ministers" who could be male or female — co-existed with "Courts of Love" in mountain castles. And both of these somehow co-existed with Judaic polygamy. Then there was Arabic literature and music thrown in, with a dash of "witchcraft" and much seasoning of fertility rites.

As we have seen, this rich culture was destroyed by the Albigensian Crusade. One might say that the core or heart of it fled to Scotland, from where it was transplanted across the Atlantic by Henry Sinclair's voyage and (probably) some later ones. If my construct has any validity at all, there was a surprisingly large number of original Estotiland settlers. They began to expand inland in the direction of the Great Lakes, using the river routes we've explored and leaving artefacts and ruins dated to their late medieval era.

Finally, they reached the first great lake, Lake Ontario, around 1480. They probably settled on both sides of it, in New York State and Ontario, simultaneously. But the only hard evidence we currently have is the core sample on the Canadian side at Adolphus Reach and the Lake on The Mountain. In settling around Lake Ontario, they encountered the Iroquoian-speaking tribes then living in the Finger Lakes region of New York State.

According to all authorities, these tribes possessed the highest material culture of any Indians north of Mexico. They had a well-developed agriculture based on the cultivation of maize, beans and squash. They had large villages fortified by modest earthworks topped with wooden palisades. In the fourteenth century they used flint and stone for implements and weapons, but "Indians" formerly living in the same area had once known the use of copper for implements and projectile points. They still used bits of beaten copper for making crude adornments, but true metal usage had declined among the Finger Lakes tribes. They had a complex clan organization with matriarchal overtones — much like the pre-Roman Celts of Europe and the British Isles.

My own notion is that the Iroquoian-speakers represented the last remnant of the Hopewell-Adena moundbuilders. They were probably of mixed native and Celtic stock, and by the fourteenth century the native genetic and cultural influence was much the dominant one.

European Grail Refugees then settled around Lake Ontario starting about A.D. 1480. They came into contact with these Iroquoians who, being the most advanced of the northeastern Indians, could and did adopt some European innovations. For one thing, it seems that their earthwork-and-palisade defensive walls suddenly became much more complex around A.D. 1500. They began to adopt geometric shapes permitting enfilade arrow-shooting to cover entrances instead of being mere square or haphazardly oval ramparts. Their walls began to acquire certain characteristics of medieval European castles. Some excavated sites even began to include an elevated walkway behind the walls, supported by vertical wooden scaffolding, so that warriors could shoot over the walls between purposeful gaps in the wooden palisade. At this time, too, in the early sixteenth century, the first wooden and woven-mat Iroquoian body armour appears.

It was around this time, sometime between A.D. 1480 and 1570, that Deganawidah taught Hiawatha a basic form of Christianity and apparently suggested political and ethical forms for the Iroquois Confederacy. Once formed, the Iroquois Confederacy conceived the notion that they were *Haudosonee*, "Superior Men," because of their dispensation from Deganawidah. They began a program of conquest previously unknown among northeastern Woodland Indians. They carved out an empire that stretched from the Mississippi River to Maine, from Lake Huron to the Tennessee River — about half the size of the Roman Empire at the time of Christ. They exterminated many entire tribes, including the Eries, Mohicans, Ottawas, and Neutrals, sending the captured survivors to hideous tortured deaths. In short, they behaved just like white men inspired by Christianity or Islam. I think that, in the end, they may also have turned on the Grail Refugees themselves.

What happened to these Grail Refugees?

Although we're getting slightly ahead of our story, I think that many of them were wiped out by the Iroquois between about 1550–1600. Some of them just moved further west and melded into the frontier population of New France (which stretched from the Atlantic to the Rockies). They may have first given the French names to such midwest and Rocky Mountain American cities as Des Moines ("Of the monks"), Iowa, St. Louis, Missouri, Boise (i.e., *Boisé*, "wooded"), and Coeur d'Alene ("Ellen's heart"), Idaho and so many, many others. It was not until October 21, 1803, that the United States acquired this vast tract of western territory, which more than doubled the size of the country. Setting out in 1803, Meriwether Lewis and William Clark did not return from exploring it until September 23, 1806. They learned that there was a sizable French population living in this new territory, but we do not have the foggiest notion about the origin of most of these people. I think that some of the Grail Refugees went west along with other people from New France.

It is also possible that some Grail Refugees stayed in the northern Appalachians, and also possible that some assimilated into the Iroquois.

Was there a lingering and confused memory of the Grail Religion when white settlers pushed over the Appalachians and entered Upper New York State? I hesitate to answer this important question with a definite yes. I can only say that the forms of those exploding New York State religions seem to espouse beliefs that represent aspects of Pyrénées "Catharism." Jemima Wilkinson formed her "New Jerusalem" colony near the present town of Penn Yan on Lake Keuka; she advocated celibacy and vegetarianism. John Humphrey Noyes formed a community based on free love and early Christian communism on the shore of Lake Oneida. For those with a taste for the more exotic, Annie Lee's Shaker community, at Sodus Bay on Lake Ontario itself, offered the prospects of naked dancing and sexual orgies — a sort of frontier "Court of Love." Joseph Smith's Mormonism wasn't the only new religion to offer polygamy in New York State. Isaac Bullard's "Pilgrims" were polygamous and communistic. All these religions were also associated with vague ideas of "the ancients," their knowledge and money digging for treasure these ancients had left.

Historian Richard L. Bushman, an American student of this era of Upper New York State proliferation of new religions, has written provocatively:

> The lore of buried treasure was tied into a great stock of magical practices that went back many centuries. A play published in Philadelphia in 1767, called *Disappointment; or, the Force of Credulity* turned on the attempt of a fraudulent magician to find a treasure, and depicted the rite of drawing a magic circle on the ground to ward off an evil spirit. The playwright ridiculed the credulity of those who fell prey to Rattletrap the bogus magician, but the comedy of the play derived from the fact that people believed...Not a hundred years earlier, Goodwin Wharton, a Whig member of Parliament, spent twenty-five years searching for treasure with the aid of spirits and angels, while pursuing a career in the House of Commons that culminated in appointment as Lord of the Admiralty. Before 1650

the search for treasure with stones and rod was still more common and, like most magic, blended with orthodox Christian faith in the minds of the common people.[21]

Richard Bushman is writing here of the colonial American experience. What does he mean, therefore, by a tradition "that went back many centuries" from 1767 (the Philadelphia play)? The grant of Pennsylvania to William Penn, of which Philadelphia was a city (laid out by Penn personally in 1682) was less than *one* century old when the play about money digging was published. Bushman then refers to Goodwin Wharton's money digging of 1650 as being even more typical and notes that Wharton became Lord of the Admiralty (i.e., not of Britain, but of Massachussetts). What can "many centuries" before 1767 (or 1650) mean? Is Bushman trying to hint that a religious and money-digging tradition existed from medieval times in North America? The use of "many centuries" from 1767 might be justified by a date of A.D.1398 (almost four centuries) from the time of Sinclair's Estotiland and almost three centuries from Wharton's exploits in 1650. Or is Bushman referring to an Ancient Celtic tradition even further in the past? St. Brendan lived in the sixth century, 1,100 years before the Philadelphia play — but did he represent "orthodox Christianity" or the heretical Celtic Church?

These many blossoming religions in Upper New York State seem to be exaggerations, misunderstandings, and caricatures of just one or two aspects of the Grail Religion, as if a garbled tradition of it lingered in the Finger Lakes area. Would-be prophets adopted whichever part of the whole that caught their fancy, and left the rest. Joseph Smith was exposed to all these religions as he was growing up in Palmyra and and he may also have absorbed some local Iroquoian legends. These may have vaguely recalled a Cathar-like type of Christianity that once existed in this area, the religion of the not-too-well-defined "ancients."

The Children of Light[22]

There was still another new religion in Upper New York State, and it seemed less extreme than the others. The "Children of Light" believed in a mixture of Judaic and Christian doctrine, preferred monogamy (but apparently allowed polygamy), and stressed family and social values in which women had full equality with men. They believed in private enterprise, but also in a close-knit community with generous sharing at times of need. Of all the new religions of the early 1800s, this one most closely approximates what Catharism seems to have been. A common Cathar saying was "All things are lights," meaning that all things had souls — although some souls were so encrusted with ignorance that the light could barely be seen.

Catharism itself was sometimes called the Religion of the Light, and adherents sometimes referred to themselves as the Children of Light six hundred years before David Wilson established his sect in Upstate New York. In Latin, the word "light" is *lux*. However, Latin originally didn't have a letter "U," substituting "V." In Latin capital letters, LVX spelled "light." It is apparent that just one letter, "X," can accommodate the shapes of the other two. So, sometimes, in a code designed to keep the secret from the Inquisition, heretic Cathars would use "X" to signify their hidden "religion of light." It came to mean anything unknown and sought for, a valuable secret, as in "The X-Files" (for example) or the unknown answer to a mathematical equation. When we find the solution, solve the unknown X, we still say that we've "seen the light."

It was Roman Catholic convention to depict the Virgin Mary in green or blue clothing. Indeed, this convention became a papal injunction in the seventeeth century. Mary Magdalen was traditionally depicted in red, the colour of passion and sin, which suited her debased stature within the Roman Church. What do we do with a painting like "Madonna in Red" by Botticelli? If you look at her bodice, you will see a red "X" in the fabric over her heart. The message: "Her heart was light." This is Mary Magdalen. Painters other than Il Guercino and Poussin knew the secret of the Holy Grail.

David Wilson took his Children of Light from New York to Ontario between 1815 and 1820 and settled north of Toronto, where they built Sharon Temple. A painting from the Temple shows a bare-breasted Madonna in red. The dove is the primary Cathar symbol of all, symbolizing the grace of God.

It is perhaps worth mentioning that the Children of Light played an important role in the so-called Rebellion of 1837. The sect members were financially ruined by their support of William Lyon Mackenzie and were imprisoned. The Children of Light were

Derelicta (circa 1495). This drawing by Botticelli shows the female principle locked out of male-dominated Roman Catholic Church. Do the discarded clothes on the steps suggest the Latin letters LVX, *"LIGHT"?*

Madonna in Red (circa A.D. 1483), painted by Botticelli in a risky and almost heretical departure from both tradition and Vatican decree, depicts an X-shaped ribbon above the woman's heart. The Latin word for *light* is LVX — "Lux." Since the letter X alone could incorporate all the letters of LVX, the letter "X" came to represent the secret tradition, the unknown, the *solution.* We still use this "X," representing the unknown, in math today. It is perhaps more familiar within the context of *The X-Files* television series where agents Mulder and Scully most often seek the unknown, the unusual and the truth, which has been purposefully obscured. Botticelli's message: "Her heart was *light.*"

dispersed, but the rebellion led directly to a softening of imperial British arrogance with at least the semblance of democracy for Upper Canada.

Joseph Smith's Mormonism was the only one of these new religions to achieve any major stature. Why did it, and all the others, emerge in New York State across Lake Ontario from a known European population? It was a population that most likely represented Grail-related natural expansion from Henry Sinclair's old Nova Scotia Estotiland. Adolphus Reach and the Lake on the Mountain flank the entrance to the Bay of Quinte, a name that appears on the earliest known maps of the hinterland, such as the Pierre Descelliers map of 1550. The Bay of Quinte is shaped somewhat like a question mark or a shepherd's crook. The word "quinte" actually means a shepherd's crook — *in a medieval dialect of Scottish!* This word was anachronistic, even in Scotland, by 1500 and only rarely used after that. Is it accident or coincidence that this word shows up on a French-made map of 1550? The "coming forth" (as Mormons say) of the *Book of Mormon* from this particular geographic area may not be divine revelation...but can it be mere coincidence?

Before leaving Joseph Smith and the *Book of Mormon*, we might consider the word *deseret*. This word, which appears only twice in the *Book of Mormon*, signifies a honey bee.[23] Yet, as anyone who's visited Salt Lake City knows, this word *deseret* is ubiquitous. There's the official Mormon Church newspaper, *The Deseret News*. There's Deseret University, the precursor of Brigham Young University. There's even a Deseret Gym spa in Salt Lake City and several Deseret Restaurants in Utah. Much Mormon lore has been handed down by word of mouth, and not by actual documentation. It seems that Joseph Smith communicated the importance of the *deseret*, or honey bee, to his closest Church colleagues. Why? Did he see this bee-symbol on the "golden tablets"? Did he take this figure to be the emblem of the pure Nephites? It seems unlikely that Joseph Smith would invent importance attached to a honey bee. Such importance is more likely to have been impressed upon him for some reason and then communicated from him to the chosen companions who were to become Elders of the Church.

We know the importance of the bee symbol. It was a Merovingian symbol. Three hundred golden bee figurines were found in the tomb of Childeric I, father of Clovis, in 1653. Napoleon had them sewn onto his coronation robe in 1804. A bee appears on the skull in both Il Guercino's 1618 "Et in Arcadia Ego" painting and in Poussin's first

The *Madonna of Sharon* in Sharon Temple, north of Toronto, was painted about 1820. Notice her red dress and the two children. Traditionally, red was the colour associated with Mary Magdalene, not the Virgin Mary who, by papal decree, had to be depicted in blue or green. Botticelli's famous painting *Madonna in Red* was therefore a daring departure from orthodoxy. The two children are enigmatic but recur in many medieval paintings of "the Madonna." According to the Grail tradition, Mary Magdalene was the wife of Jesus and they had at least two sons and (some say) two daughters. A German scholar has dealt with the mystery of the many medieval paintings depicting "the Madonna" with *two* male infants. This scholar's book, *Die Zwei Jesusknaben* ("*The Two Jesus Boys*") has not been translated into English. In these medieval paintings of "the Madonna" with two boys, are we seeing the Virgin Mary — or are we seeing Mary Magdalene with her two sons?

work of the same title on the shepherd theme. We know the importance of this bee-symbol very well by now.

But how did Joseph Smith also know it was important?

The logical answer is that he must have seen this symbol on the "golden tablets" he translated. Perhaps a bee-figure was stamped at the beginning and the end of the brief history from which he translated the original 116 pages. Perhaps it was stamped on every page. We don't know. But the *deseret*, the honey bee, became a sub-text within Mormonism, just as it was within the Grail Complex. Is this mere coincidence?

Although it may not seem immediately relevant to our theme, I would like to reproduce a 1990s greeting card by the Roger La Borde company of London, England. The artwork is by "Haydn Cornner" (i.e., "Hide in corner," if you didn't catch it). A story about this card appeared in the *Independent* newspaper in London. This greeting card is indicative of the underground, or almost- above-ground now, "Grail" revival currently taking place in Europe. On the front is a strange horseman, with three gold fleur-de-lis on his royal blue tunic, approaching a rather spacey maiden in her castle tower. We see that vines, some pruned, grow near the tower. Beneath the rider are literal, and ugly, insects. Do we regard this card as merely curious and rather primitive artwork? Or do we regard it as purposefully disguised Grail-related allegory and symbolism? Is the vine that age-old symbol of Mary Magdalen's lineage? Is the horseman that "fool for Christ" like the joker in the deck? Are the insects those who could not believe in the Grail and chose to destroy it — namely the popes and kings of medieval Europe? Is this sort of interpretation fanciful, or is it intended to be made?

The back of this card tells us in no uncertain terms that, as ridiculous as this interpretation may seem, it was very definitely intended to be evoked. Here on the back of the card we see the fleur-de-lis encircled by honey bees. The fleur-de-lis "of France" does not first appear from France. This stylized shape, representing a lily, first appears on Hebrew coinage. It is the Lily of the House of David. The bees we know too well, by now. They gather the nectar of this history and transmute it into a remembrance "as sweet as honey" so

A modern greeting card created in Europe. Notice the Grail-Merovingian symbolism of the bees flying around the Lily of David, the vines (pruned and unpruned) growing beside the tower, the fleur-de-lis on the horseman — and the insects below. Do these insects represent those who fought against the Grail?

that it will never be forgotten. The Merovingians used the bee symbol because they never forgot their lineage. So the message of the fleur-de-lis is "don't forget the sweet lineage from the Holy Land which pollinated all our humane progress." And it has always been safer if someone with this message "hides in a corner" or keeps a low profile. This sort of card, always with a bee illustrated somewhere in the artwork, is fast becoming a cultural fad in Europe. Since this card was bought in a Toronto shop, the fad is already spreading to North America. The Grail is emerging again.

This card illustrates how potent, persistent, and pervasive symbols can be. The Mormon *deseret* is just another example.

The Politically Correct Grind

The town of Peterborough, Ontario, about seventy airline miles northeast of Adolphus Reach and the Lake on the Mountain, is a centre of curious artefacts and ruins.

About twenty miles southeast of Peterborough on the shore of Rice Lake is Serpent Mound Provincial Park. As its name suggests, the main attraction is a long, low mound built in a serpentine shape. It is nothing so grand as the famous serpent mound in Ohio, but the two are associated. Ontario's serpent mound is generally considered the most northerly outpost of New York State's "Point Peninsula People" who were, in turn, a northerly expression of the Hopewell-Adena Culture. In the late 1950s, the Royal Ontario Museum began excavations at Serpent Mound. By 1974 there was a rather impressive display built over the excavations. You could walk along an enclosed and elevated shelter and look down, through glass, onto the exposed skeletons and artefacts. At intervals within this shelter were glass cases displaying other artefacts that had been discovered. Among these were beautiful leaf-shaped spear points made of copper and, I think, bronze. I examined some as carefully as I could through the glass and believed, at that time (1974), that some of the points had not been beaten but revealed mould-marks — I thought that some of the artefacts had been cast.

The Point Peninsula and Serpent Mound people were supposed to have lived about 500 B.C. to 500 A.D., flourishing about the time of Christ. A single Point Peninsula burial was discovered in the middle of the town of Peterborough itself, and a plaque now marks the spot. This shows that the people were not restricted to their serpent mound on the shore of Rice Lake, but may have lived widely around the Peterborough area. The plaque states that this Peterborough burial had also contained metal objects.

At that time, I was taking many photographs of the Serpent Mound display for a book I was preparing called *Lost Legacy: Social and Commercial Life along Canada's Canalized Waterways*. Although I was researching with the assistance of a Canada Council Explorations grant, no publisher would take the book. It probably was fairly tedious, and eventually, I lost the last remaining parts of the manuscript and also all the many slides with which I had hoped to illustrate it. Now, I bitterly regret this.

I regret it because the Serpent Mound displays no longer exist.

Because of complaints by the Bent Lake Aboriginal Band that the displays were terribly "inappropriate" because they desecrated burials, and because they gave an "inaccurate perspective on the totality of aboriginal culture" — meaning that they showed beautiful metallic artefacts that the Indians no longer made at the coming of the known colonials — the Ontario government closed the Royal Ontario Museum's display. There's no more enclosed walkway. No more cases of artefacts. There *are* so-called information panels, which show drawings of artefacts, mostly ceramics. *There are no illustrations of metal implements or weapons.*

The artefacts are still in the Royal Ontario Museum, but they are not on public display. A museum spokesperson told me that it would be inappropriate for the public to see them.

So far as I'm aware, the Bent Lake Aboriginal Band are Indians that moved south into the Peterborough area after Iroquois power declined in the 1750s. They do not, and did not, have anything to do with the Point Peninsula culture outpost at Serpent Mound — except that both groups are (perhaps) "North American Indians."

A little more than twenty miles northeast of Peterborough is Petroglyph Provincial Park. In the late 1950s, a large outcropping of marble was discovered by whites to have a large number of glyphs incised into the rock beneath a thick growth of lichen. The local Indians did not know of it (or had not mentioned it). A husband-and-wife team named Vastokas from Trent University has studied these glyphs, making a meticulous map. The Vastokases themselves observed that some drawings of "spirit canoes" (with apparent masts and side rudders) were similar or identical to ship glyphs on rocks near Boslund, Sweden. The Vastokases attributed this to coincidence, but noted it in their book on the glyphs.[24]

Rock paintings and inscriptions at Petroglyph Provincial Park near Peterborough, Ontario. Notice the glistening and perfectly circular area (centre of photo) where a former and distinctively European-like boat glyph has been erased by grinding. Photo by Monica Kuehn.

The government considered the site important enough that a protective building was erected around the marble outcropping to prevent erosion of the glyphs by rain (and acid rain) since the protective gowth of lichen had been removed. Inside the building, a winding walkway surrounds the marble outcropping. Any visitor can see the glyphs, but most of them are several yards from the walkway and its protective retaining wall. As it happened, though, one of the more "Boslund-looking" ship depictions was easily visible because it was located not far from the promenade.

I write "was located" because this most easily seen "Boslund-looking" ship glyph no longer exists. In October 1996, I went to the petroglyph exhibit with a television film crew. I was to narrate the story of apparent Europeans in the Peterborough area who had left some (not all) of the visible glyphs. The producer-director of this effort was Rob Iveson of Toronto, well-known in the Canadian film industry. An assistant was Monica Kuehn, Fine Arts student and our still photographer.

First, we discovered that one of the most significant glyphs was "missing," and in its place was a circular and glistening impression made by recent grinding. Second, we discovered that this site had been turned over to the local aboriginal band as a "sacred site." Only Indian medicine persons were allowed to go onto the actual marble outcropping itself to conduct "religious rites" on the stone.

I spluttered with outrage and indignation for a few minutes. Then we pulled ourselves together and took high-definition videotape and 35mm photos of the evidence. Meanwhile, aboriginal guides led a group of Japanese tourists around the walkway explaining the sacred significance of the "spirit canoes" with masts and rudders. Our filming was interrupted so that a shaman could perform a necessary religious rite. He didn't deface any of the glyphs, so far as I could see.

What do the aboriginals have against these glyphs?

In the early 1970s, the late famous (or infamous) Dr. Barraclough Fell of Harvard was sent a copy of the Vastokas map of the glyphs. He immediately saw that the "spirit canoes" with masts and rudders were identical to ship depictions from Boslund and other places in Scandinavia. He also realized, as the Vastokases had not, that some of the curious symbols that accompanied some glyphs belonged to a script called Tiffinagh. This script had been used by early Scandinavians called "proto-Celts" and "proto-Teutons" by archaeologists. Barry Fell also claimed to see Ogham script, mostly used by those ubiquitous Ancient Celts.

Fell agreed with the Vastokases that most of the glyphs were aboriginal in origin, but asserted that some were Scandinavian or Celtic. He then proceeded to translate these European inscriptions. Aside from some references to Scandinavian mythology, including "Mjolnir" (the hammer of Thor) and "Fenris" (a legendary wolf), the glyphs told the story of a man named Woden-Lithi ("Servant of Odin") who was engaged in collecting copper nuggets and smelting them into ingots. The marble outcropping itself was, according to Fell, a sort of "law stone" for this European community of Bronze Age Celtic and Teutonic metal entrepreneurs.

Dr. Barry Fell was a professor at Harvard, but not of anthropology, archaeology, or linguistics. In fact, he was a professor of marine biology. For some obscure reason, professors of biology have a weakness for archaeology and epigraphy. (Gérard Leduc was a biology professor at Concordia before devoting his time to archaeology.) So Barry Fell was not an "expert" in the required discipline, and critics were quick to point this out. Also, Fell had made some momentous blunders in the past. He once translated an inscription, found on a rock in the U.S. southwest, as a North African one left by unknown visitors long ago. Then someone observed that the rock had fallen from a ledge and, in falling, had turned upside down. When viewed right way up, the inscription proved to be an easily read colonial Spanish boundary marker for a hacienda.

Similarly, an inscribed stone had allegedly been found in Nova Scotia's famed "Money Pit" sometime around 1850. The stone itself was subsequently lost, but several copies of the inscription were made at the time of discovery. Barry Fell translated this as yet another North African religious inscription, this time a "Libyan" one. As it chanced, in 1982 the Ministry of Culture of Nova Scotia had asked me to try translating this same inscription. It had been done before, but the government wanted another opinion.

The circumstances of this find were that the company with that then held the licence to work the "Money Pit" was facing financial ruin and needed investors to keep its excavation going. The stone was conveniently found just when some evidence of progress was needed. I therefore made the assumption that the thing was a hoax, probably a simple symbol-to-letter transposition code that could be easily broken — indeed, it was *intended* to be easily broken. So I assumed that the language would be the English used in Nova Scotia in 1850.

Every language has its own "letter frequency." That is, certain letters occur more frequently than others. A table of "letter frequency" can be compiled for every language — they *are* compiled and intelligence agencies use them all the time. Cryptoanalysts know dozens by heart. I didn't, but I knew where to find such tables. In modern English, the most frequent letter is "e," followed by "a" and so on. If the inscription is long enough, just count the number of times each symbol appears and substitute the appropriate letter of the appropriate language. If you're right, the inscription will very quickly start to make sense and the rest can be filled in. If you're wrong, nothing will make sense. Back to the drawing board.

The "Money Pit" inscription is not very long. Nonetheless, it breaks easily by applying modern English letter frequencies:

FORTY FEET BENEATH THIS STONE TWO
MILLION POUNDS ARE BURIED, etc.

What are the odds that a given inscription will make sense in both modern English and "Ancient Libyan"? I asked the mathematics department of Dalhousie. The odds against this happening increase with the number of letters in the inscription. In this case, the probability "against" was so high that it couldn't really be expressed, but I was told that "two billion to one" was close enough.

Because I knew and respected Barry Fell, I wrote a humorous letter to him at Harvard gently suggesting that he should drop his Libyan translation from future editions of his book. He didn't answer that letter, although we corresponded later. One thing about Barry Fell, which everyone who knew and liked him will agree with, is that he was never known to admit a mistake!

And he made a few. But he also, and almost single-handedly, has been responsible for a serious and fundamental contemporary reappraisal of American prehistory. He's been right many times. His opinion commanded, and still does, immense (and cautious) respect.

In 1991, Dr. David Kelley, Gérard Leduc, and I found ourselves at Petroglyph Provincial Park. At that time, all the glyphs still existed. It was easy enough to read the Tiffinagh — all you need to know is the phonetic value (sounds) of the Tiffinagh symbols, and all you need is a Norse dictionary, both of which are available. My opinion and Leduc's were worth nothing, but Kelley's was, and is, a different matter. This professor emeritus of the University of Calgary, influential in deciphering Mayan glyphs, published his opinion in the fall 1991 issue of the prestigious *Review of Archeology* in the United States: Some of the glyphs were Tiffinagh.[25] They told of Scandinavian mythological elements. The ships were identical to the Boslund glyphs.

Further than that Kelley would not go. But, of course, it was far enough. Kelley would not confirm the existence of Ogham, nor would he confirm Fell's long account of Woden-Lithi's story.

The Peterborough Examiner ranted that Barry Fell's ideas were "an insult to Canadian archeologists and an insult to Native People." This is a typical example of irrelevant media histrionics. The question was, and is, not whether Fell's opinion is an insult to these groups or whether they deserve to be insulted, but whether it is the truth. The *Examiner* did not stress the fact to its readers that Canada's foremost linguist also shared Barry Fell's opinion.

Why all this controversy over European glyphs among the aboriginal ones?

Well, if there are European glyphs just north of Peterborough, it suggests perhaps that the Serpent Mound people just south of Peterborough who used copper might have been partly European too. This suggests, in turn, that the culture of Native Peoples around Lake Ontario may owe something to European influence. What's wrong with this? The new politically correct myth is that the white man brought nothing but trouble and disease, and before he came the Native Peoples lived in harmony with the land. This is, of course, nonsense. Aboriginals had no more inherent spiritual harmony than Europeans. They did, however, lack the technology to destroy the environment totally and to exterminate species completely. But they did their best with slash-and-burn agriculture and "bison acquisition strategies" that included the stampeding of herds over cliffs where only a few of the injured and dying animals could be reached and used.

It is not so surprising that weak-minded adherents of the New Age would cling to the new political correctness of aboriginal myth, but it is inexcusable that the Ontario government would hand sites over to aboriginal bands so that unwelcome evidence can be detroyed or hidden from the public. At Petroglyph Provincial Park, at least one artefact has suffered the politically correct grind. At Serpent Mounds there's now nothing to see.

A book called *Allegiance: The Ontario Story* was published in 1991 by Heirloom Publishing, a supplier of many official history texts for the schools of Ontario. Indeed, Joelle Lauriol "borrowed" a copy for me from the Ministry of Education. In *Allegiance: The Ontario Story*, the story naturally must begin with the aboriginal history of the province. There is an introduction by a Native spokesperson for this section. After a rather rosy and euphemistic account of the Iroquois Confederacy (with errors about Hiawatha's tribal lobbying), the Native writer deals with Barry Fell (then in the news), and produces this piece of bafflegab worthy of any white politician, sociologist, or social anthropologist:

> The teaching rocks in the Americas are beginning to reveal new information. Elders have begun to notice and are travelling across the continent to interpret these messages. Western scientists have also become interested.
>
> Barry Fell was one of the first western scientists to state that the North American ideographic record of the rocks contains a report of Celt, Libyan and even Egyptian visits, colonies that may date back 2,500 years. From a native viewpoint, Fell's

work is important because it begins to bridge the chasm that has existed between the knowledge systems and relationships of native and non-native Canadians. Fortunately, there is a growing interest on the part of established scientists, such as Mavor and Dix from Harvard, to build on the foundations revealed by Fell. This is crucial because Native knowledge systems hold a key to mankind's and the earth's long-term survival. Cross-cultural scientific communication and collaboration are essential if our children and their children are to continue.[26]

Winston Churchill once said that "words should convey meaning" — although all politicians and spokespeople know it is much better if words do not convey *clear* meaning. What is the meaning of this passage? Whatever it means, it was written before 1991, the year the book was published. All the glyphs were still in existence then. Kelley, Leduc, and I saw them. By 1996, the most European-looking glyph within clear sight of the tourist walkway had been erased by grinding. It was between 1991 and 1996 that the Government of Ontario handed the site over to Natives. They did not even know about the "teaching rock" when it was uncovered from beneath lichen in the late 1950s. So much for the sincerity of sentiments expressed in a semi-official history.

Thankfully, political correctness has not become quite so oppressive in the United States as it has in Canada. At least, in the United States it is not yet supported by the government. Not a great deal of evidence remains about the European prehistory of North America. Our cities and highways cover most of it. The artefacts and ruins that have been found, and those awaiting recovery, are valuable testaments to our heritage. They must be preserved by those of us who care about such things — and this means preserved against vandalism by tyrants of political correctness as well as vandalism by less sophisticated barbarians.

Perhaps it is appropriate to end this chapter with an artefact and a poem. The Cross of Lorraine crucifix is of pewter and supposedly dates from the 1600s. This particular artefact was found in southern Ontario, in an Iroquois encampment near Lake Scugog (fifty miles east of Peterborough). But other similar ones have been discovered all through New York State's Finger Lakes country and even down into Pennsylvania. Most are of pewter, like this one, but wooden,

This "Cross of Lorrain" trade trinket was discovered near Peterborough, Ontario, in 1928. It is supposed to be of Dutch manufacture dating from the early seventeenth century, and (according to experts) was a common trade item supplied by merchants from Albany, New York. But why would seventeenth-century Christians (either Protestant or Roman Catholics), who were trying to convert the Indians, confuse them with unorthodox symbols? The Cross of Lorrain was traditionally a Grail symbol and was associated with the House of Anjou.

copper, and silver ones have also been discovered. In fact, so many have been recovered from Indian (mostly Iroquois sites) that they are now automatically identified as "trade trinkets" manufactured in Albany by the early Dutch.

Maybe.

But there's no actual Dutch record of the manufacture of such trinkets. And it is a strange trinket to offer to Indians. In the early 1600s, all the colonial powers were trying to convert Indians to their particular brand of orthodox Christianity. Symbols were important in this missionary work, and both Protestants and Roman Catholics were careful to imprint Indians on the standard Christian cross. Why confuse them with the Cross of Lorraine disseminated widely in the form of a cheap trade trinket?

What is the Cross of Lorraine, and where did it come from?

Today, of course, it is the symbol of Easter Seals. But originally it was the cross used by the Merovingians and later by the Cathars. Lorraine is the modern name of Dagobert II's old Merovingian kingdom. The Cathars did not really think that the cross was a proper symbol by which to remember Christ. It was the instrument of his torture-death, not his love. Cathars preferred the dove as a symbol of this love and grace. Early Christians had used the "sign of the fish," as we know, because Jesus had been a Nazorean — a champion of the "school of little fishes."

However, because the cross or "crucifix" became the universal Christian symbol, and because they were also Christians (of a sort), Cathars also adopted a cross symbol. But it was the Cross of Lorraine, the ancient cross of the Merovingians who were converted to Christianity. To document this association between the Grail and the Cross of Lorraine, we can start with a quote from the most famous Grail romance, *Parzival* by Wolfram von Eschenbach. In an introductory explanation of discovering the story, he writes:

> Kyot [i.e., Guiot of Provence, troubadour], the wise master, set out to trace this tale in Latin books, to see where there had ever been a people dedicated to purity and worthy of caring for the Grail. He read the chronicles of the lands, in Britain and elsewhere, in France and in Ireland, and in Anjou he found the tale.

As we've noted before, Merovingian royalty also fled to Brittany (Anjou) as well as to the Pyrénées when Carolingian "Mayors of the Palace" began usurping their thrones. In Anjou, "Kyot" found the tale in Latin books, whereas in the Pyrénées he found it "in confused pagan writing" (Arabic). With the help of Flegetanis, a Hebrew scholar, he read the Arabic version. He combined the two accounts into a cohesive whole that he then told to Wolfram von Eschenbach. Anjou, like the Rennes-le-Château area, was a Grail refuge region. Eventually, as we know, the Brittany-Anjou and the Pyrenees lines joined forces to invade England in 1066 and to take Jerusalem in 1099. So Grail descendants lived in Anjou, also, although the most direct descendant came from the Pyrénées lineage.

In A.D. 1308, a scion of the House of Anjou, Charles, was chosen to be the King of Hungary. It was an honour and a throne

Cross of Lorrain and the arms of the House of Anjou on the royal seal of an early king of Hungary.

with much fighting attached. We will remember that the Templars had been dispersed (in France) in 1307. On his way to Hungary, Charles rallied refugee Templars who had fled eastward into the Rhineland, Denmark, Bavaria, etc. There were many of these, though not so many as had gone to Scotland and Portugal. With his Templars, Charles created modern Hungary from a jostling chaos of petty kings. Perhaps this prince of Anjou and Grail descendant felt far enough away from France and Rome to display the Cross of Lorraine conspicuously. In 1323, he had his new Royal Seal designed and made.[27]

On this seal, Charles I proudly and openly displays the symbols of his faith and lineage — the Cross of Lorraine flanked by the arms of the House of Anjou. Once again, the Grail almost emerged into the light of conventional history. Charles I's Hungary was soon to be inundated by the same Turkish expansion that drove the Knights of St. John from the Palestinian mainland in 1279.

Lest there be doubt that Charles's take-over of Hungary was a Grail-related operation, the fact that Pope Clement V backed his Templar-assisted invasion should remove most of it. Clement V, remember, was the pope who was related to the Blancheforts of the Rennes-le-Château area, the pope who gave Templars advance warning of Philippe IV's 1307 raids, and the pope who awarded all Templar assets to the Knights of St. John. Without digressing too much more, a Grail related take-over of Hungary, naturally to be assisted by Templars, was another sort of compensation Pope Clement tried to make on behalf of the Holy Blood. Most of Europe's gold and silver came, at that time, from the Transylvanian

Mountains of Hungary.[28] Charles was most adept at collecting this gold and silver. How much went to assist the Sinclair Estotiland project, I wonder?

The Cross of Lorraine had become a secret symbol of the Grail version of Christianity when the Crucifix of the Roman Christians supplanted the "Sign of the Fish" in Constantine's time. During World War II, it became the symbol of the French Resistance. Charles de Gaulle chose it as the symbol of his Free French forces. It seems that Charles de Gaulle chose this Cross of Lorraine because of the influence of ...Pierre Plantard de Saint-Clair! Plantard was editor of the major Paris-located resistance newspaper *Vaincre* ("Vanquish") and, in some ways, was de Gaulle's mentor. We know also that in the 1970s Plantard was supposedly the leader of the Priory of Sion who met several times with Henry Lincoln (see *The Holy Place*) and also with Lincoln's erstwhile collaborators, Michael Baigent and Richard Leigh (see *The Holy Blood and the Holy Grail*). We've met Pierre Plantard de *Saint-Clair* previously in these pages.

During the Algerian crisis of 1958, Plantard was so esteemed by the war generation of French people that de Gaulle asked him to give radio speeches of assurance that France would survive. It seems that the Priory of Sion organized much of the French Resistance, backed de Gaulle's formation of Free French forces and probably chose the ancient Cross of Lorraine as the symbol of both.

Is it not curious then, not to mention unlikely, that orthodox Christian traders would offer the Cross of Lorraine as a trade trinket?

If we examine this cross carefully, we will see that if the lower cross-bar is mentally discounted, it has the correct proportions of the orthodox Christian crucifix. But the lower bar is longer. I think this means that two men were sacrificed because of "Christianity" (i.e., "messiahship"). One was Jesus (the top bar), but the greater was John (the bottom bar). Thus, the Cross of Lorraine is the symbol of a quite heretical version of Christianity, one incorporating the "Johnite" tradition along with the Jesus tradition. It represents a secret that was damned by the Roman Church, that was considered a belief of Satan.

It is fitting, therefore, to end with a poem by Charles Peguy. He was also a famous Resistance fighter:

> Les armes de Jésus c'est la croix de Lorraine,
> Et le sang dans l'artère et le sang dans la veine,

Et la source de grâce et la claire fontaine;
Les armes de Satan c'est la croix de Lorraine,
Et c'est la même art_re et c'est la même veine
Et c'est le même sang et la même fontaine.

(The shield of Jesus is the cross of Lorraine,
And the blood in the artery, the blood in the vein,
And the source of grace and the clear fountain.
The sword of Satan is the cross of Lorraine,
The same artery...and the same vein
And it's the same blood, the same fountain.)[28]

11

The Niagara Thicket

The Pierre Descelliers Map of 1550 is interesting for several reasons. First of all, it is drawn upside down. South is at the top. I don't know why Descelliers would have done this in 1550. North to the top was, by then, an established convention.

This map is based on the voyages of Cartier in 1534–35 and Roberval (1539) and probably also on many accounts that have been lost to us. It shows the St. Lawrence inland to a badly imaged lake that, as far as I can make out, does triple duty as Lake Champlain, Lake Oneida, and Lake Ontario. From the number of place names and indicated towns along the tidal St. Lawrence, there was a considerable knowledge of the place — also, perhaps, a surprisingly large population of Europeans. Much of this European population would have been seasonal, of course, summer-visiting fur traders. Tadoussac, at the confluence of the Saguenay and St. Lawrence, was a large and well-known emporium at this time.

I've always been intrigued by the Descelliers Map. Aside from the so-called Franciscan Map of A.D. 1360 (an incredibly early date), which may prove to be a hoax (which is why I have not referred to it), this is one of the first European maps of the North American interior. I also like the artwork. In common with many maps of the era, geographical ignorance was disguised with fanciful visions of the country. Descelliers populates his geography with unicorns, fauns and satyrs, pygmies and so forth. These denizens provide a respite from more serious study of place names and mountain ranges, which, by the way, are generally accurate about as far west as Niagara. Descelliers didn't know about the Ohio or Mississippi rivers.

That is, I *thought* that all of these denizens were fanciful until I received Don Eckler's first letter in 1991. He recounted the curious discoveries he and Bob Williams had made in western New York and Pennsylvania. Between 1991 and 1997, I made several trips to this area, which I call "Niagara" for convenience. Sometimes I visited with Don Eckler and Bob Williams, and sometimes not. Sometimes I travelled with Mike Twose, but other times I travelled alone. I was trying to make some sense of it all. Often it just seemed best to ramble with my own thoughts for company.

Don Eckler's letters and many phone calls were not the first time this area had drawn my attention. Thirty years earlier, I'd joined the Society for the Investigation of the Unexplained, called SITU for short, founded by Cambridge zoologist Ivan T. Sanderson. Sanderson was also the author of many scientific and popular books. I wrote some articles for SITU's journal *Pursuit*. Ivan Sanderson had named it that because one dictionary he consulted defined science as "the pursuit of the unexplained." Sanderson and SITU were then operating from Sanderson's farm in New Jersey.

As SITU members began to contribute articles to *Pursuit*, it quickly became evident that the region of the Allegheny-Susquehanna watershed held a number of mysteries. On the tops of Pennsylvania mountains were tumbles of stone walls, but some of these ruins had been subjected to heat so intense that the rocks had melted together in places. These "vitrified" forts are known from Scotland and Ireland, but now they started being discovered in Pennsylvania.

Then, not far from Renovo, a very large chain emerges abruptly from a sheer rock mountain side. The links are about two feet long, and several of them dangle down the rock. This chain would serve the anchor of a fair-sized freighter. How and why it sticks out of rock is a mystery.

For a while, the "ringing rocks" of Pennsylvania dominated the pages of *Pursuit*. They are not common (as rocks go), but they are found always in fields of a few hundred in any one place. This place, too, is almost always on a mountain summit. There's nothing unusual about them except that they ring like a pure-toned bell when struck with a hammer.

Aside from all this, the watershed has the usual quota of monsters. Black cougars (*Felis concolor cougar Kerr*) are frequently reported in this area. Although they are very rare, in the Allegheny-

Susquehanna country they seem merely usual. In addition to the black cougars, which are at least known to exist, there are supposed to be assorted "wild men" like the "Bigfoot" of the U.S. Northwest ("Sasquatch" in British Columbia). The Pennsylvania wild men are not so large as the Washington state variety, but they apparently have the same sort of liquid, gurgling call — at least, according to tape recordings made in both places.

I originally joined SITU because my lake monster research for the *Montreal Gazette* piqued my originally sceptical interest in this sort of thing. Also, I thought, copies of *Pursuit* would come in handy for writing other newspaper and magazine articles of the same ilk. At least I would have the names of witnesses to contact. With one thing and another, I visited the Allegheny-Susquehanna country several times during the late 1960s and early 1970s.

And, with Don's letter in 1991, here it was intruding upon my world some quarter of a century later.

By then, I'd begun to realize that Sinclair's Estotiland had been more populated from the beginning than I had previously considered. I had already earmarked the St. John, Connecticut and Hudson rivers as routes leading inland to the Great Lakes, and as routes that were easy and obvious for coasting explorers to find. But had they truly penetrated as far west as Niagara? It was then that I looked at all the maps again, including the Descelliers Map of 1550. It was evident that he had vague, but undoubted, knowledge of the interior as far west as Niagara. How had he got it?

The Descelliers Map of 1550.

And I noticed the unicorn in the thicket roughly where Niagara would be.

By this time, I knew that art historians tended towards the idea that a unicorn represented Jesus. Not all agreed, of course. Further, the unicorn watermarks of southern France, dating from just after the Albigensian Crusade, indicated that the unicorn originally represented the married Jesus of the Holy Grail perspective. Was I to believe that Descelliers was giving an encoded message that a "Grail" settlement was located somewhere around Niagara? I still don't believe this — why should the unicorn be more significant than the satyr prancing through what passed for Arkansas? Nonetheless, the unicorn was sleeping there, in his thicket near Niagara. A unicorn did symbolize Jesus, and Don Eckler had reported curious finds. According to my own sleuthing, the Grail Refugees had expanded as far as Hochelaga and (supposedly) to Seguna on Lake Ontario. Why not as far as Niagara? Indeed, once on Lake Ontario, and assuming the basics of a ship or two (or even a sailing raft) and Indian canoes, reaching Niagara would have been easy and inevitable.

The more I thought about it, in fact, the more sense it made that there could have been a major, or *the* major, Grail settlement precisely in Niagara. A city or settlement above the Falls would open an entire continent for exploration. La Salle had thought that way when he constructed his little ship, the *Griffon*, beside a stream a few miles above Niagara Falls. The Americans had thought that way when they went to the immense effort of digging the Erie Canal. It connected the East Coast (New York harbor) with Lake Erie and the three other "upper lakes" — Huron, Michigan, and Superior.

The Unicorn

Unicorn water marks of medieval southern French paper makers.

And when I looked at a modern map, I saw that there was one other river, the fourth one, that travelled north towards the Great Lakes. This was the Susquehanna flowing into Chesapeake Bay at Philadelphia. It curves away from the lakes in its upper reaches, but before doing so it flows near to the Allegheny River. The Allegheny loops into western New York, approaching within twenty miles of Lake Chautauqua at Jamestown, and Lake Chautauqua's northern extremity is only ten miles from Lake Erie. Tributary streams shorten the overland portage distances in all cases. This was the route that Etienne Brulé travelled from Lake Ontario to Chesapeake Bay in 1607.

The Susquehanna-Allegheny was where all those Pennsylvania mysteries seemed to cluster, the ones that had intrigued me in my SITU days. This watershed was where Don Eckler and Bob Williams had discovered curious things.

As far as this book is concerned, I made the firm decision to give these SITU-related mysteries only a brief mention, just to document that curious *synchronicity* that seems always associated with the Grail and that previously drew my attention to this fourth river route, and to confine myself to artefacts and ruins that are possibly related to the Grail Knights of North America.

At various times between 1991 and 1996, in company with Mike Twose and Don Eckler (not always Bob Williams), I visited the site of the AE stone, the "Baphomet" carving on the Allegheny, and the astonishing statue of a wounded head on the Susquehanna.

Baphomet

The Knights Templar were accused, among many other things, of worshipping an entity known as "Baphomet" to the Inquisitors. There has been much debate and speculation as to what Baphomet was or represented. Some think that it is just a complicated anagram for "Wisdom" (i.e., *Sophia*, in Greek). Others think that Baphomet was Mahomet — Mohammed, the Prophet of Islam. Some believe that it was a bodiless head, the revered head of John the Baptist. Still others think that Baphomet was a horned idol, a pagan idol, with some resemblance to a goat. It is fairly certain that at least one aspect of Baphomet was goat-like, whatever his (or its) other aspects and attributes may have been.

A possible partial answer to this is that Joseph of "Arimathaea" may be a corruption of Joseph of the *Amalthaeans*. Which is to say that Joseph may have been a devotee of the cult of Amalthaea. She was a goat-like fertility divinity who enjoyed a certain popularity in Palestine during the last centuries B.C. and the first decades of the Christian era. To my knowledge, the English poet Robert Graves first suggested this. I recount this for what it is worth, but I have no strong opinions about it. It is certain, though, that some representations of Baphomet are goatish, but with four horns.[1] It is certain that Baphomet was associated with the Knights Templar, but only they might have known its true significance.

Just south of the New York State line, in northern Pennsylvania along the "Allegheny return" loop of the river, a goat-like head is carved under a rock ledge. So far it has escaped vandalism (we check it periodically) and I will not give the precise location.

Further south and east is the mountaintop ruin and the AE tombstone. It is on the West Branch of the Susquehanna. (We have covered this in Chapter 1.)

This medieval-looking carving of a horned figure ("Baphomet"?) is inscribed on a rock ledge in north central Pennsylvania.

The Murdered Apprentice

A hundred miles downstream from Iotigolo's resting place, in 1958,[2] a deer hunter noticed a smooth, rounded rock out in the woods. He'd stopped to rest on a log, noticed this smooth rock, and the more he looked at it, the more he thought it looked like the top of a head. It flashed through his mind that it might not be rock, after all, but weathered bone of a skull. Getting up and walking over to take a closer look, he was relieved to find that it was real, hard rock and not a skull. But it looked so much like a head that he started to dig around it with his hunting knife. Within twenty minutes, he saw that it was a statue of a human head. It had been made by someone with some skill, but not by any means a master sculptor. There was no doubt that it was an intentionally carved human head, and not any bizarre natural formation, because it had a neck and this neck rested on a rectangular base.

The hunter took it back home and washed it off. To his surprise, the statue appeared to have been made with two intentionally carved defects or "wounds." One defect was a deep hole in the left side of the neck. The other was an indented slash on the top of the head. Not knowing what to make of this curiosity, the hunter used it as a doorstop for many years.

Carved stone head discovered in mid-Pennsylvania compared with the "murdered apprentice" sculpture in Rosslyn Chapel. Although one sculpture is much more crude than the other, the purposeful depiction of wounds are in the same places (the top of the head, and the left side of the neck). Photo by author.

Don Eckler told me of this artefact in 1993. Like the hunter, he didn't know what to make of its reported description. It made immediate sense to me, though, because I'd been studying the carvings of Rosslyn Chapel. One of the most famous of these is the Head of the Murdered Apprentice." The Rosslyn story goes that once long ago, either a Templar or a Master Mason had set his apprentice to do a certain task while the master went away on other business. Upon his return he found that his apprentice had performed the task very well. So well, in fact, that the Templar or Master Mason flew into a jealous rage. He struck the apprentice's head with his sword, and then drove a dagger into his throat.

This grisly monument at Rosslyn is a kind of warning to Templars and Master Masons against overweening pride. Later, I went to see the Pennsylvania head.

It seems obvious, at least to me, that this Pennsylvania head was carved as a local version of the Rosslyn one, a moral warning for a group of Templars or Freemasons. It was not, of course, carved with the skill of the Rosslyn statue — William St. Clair could afford to hire master sculptors for his chapel. But the identical placement of the "wounds" indicate that the carver of the Pennsylvania head knew the story from Scotland, and may have seen the actual Rosslyn sculpture. Can "coincidence" be stretched to explain two disembodied heads, each with two wounds in identical places? If the wilderness carver had once viewed the Rosslyn original, this can date the Pennsylvania head very roughly. Rosslyn Chapel was built from A.D. 1441 to 1485, and the Pennsylvania head must have been made after that.

There is the possibility, I suppose, that this head had been carved for some colonial Masonic lodge and had been lost or hidden for some reason. But it cannot be a "recent artefact" of the current Grail revival. This head was found around 1958; Gérard de Sède's books were not published until the 1960s, and the English-language version of the story dates from the early 1970s and Henry Lincoln's British Broadcasting Corporation documentaries.

Along our fourth river route, we have now seen three Grail-related artefacts: the AE tombstone, the Baphomet of the Allegheny, and the head of the Murdered Apprentice. And objectively, these have the strongest "Grail associations" of any artefacts we've covered. The Nova Scotia trident was found near Sinclair's Owokun, true enough, but could have been made by any visitor — and there were many in the sixteenth and seventeenth centuries. Marjorie

Cove's coin has a suggestive date (1362), but could have been dropped at any time since then. The Magog Mill dates to about A.D. 1400–1550, approximately the right time, but it has no specific Grail connections. It might have been made by Vikings or by Prince Madoc (see Chapter 2). The Potton gargoyle certainly seems medieval but no specific Grail relationship can be claimed for it. "Hochelaga" is suggestive, but not definitive — it may still turn out to be an Indian word. The Concordia core sample, the formation of the Iroquois Confederacy and its structure, plus the explosion of New York State religions are, together, highly suggestive and intriguing — but there's no definite tie to the Grail Knights of North America. The Cross of Lorraine trade trinkets are anomalous, and also suggestive, but their origin and Grail relationship currently stand alone among the artefacts we've covered..

Only with Allegheny-Susquehannah artefacts are there definite and separate Grail-related aspects. Baphomet, a goat head with four horns, was revered by the Templars and we have one along the course of the Allegheny. The AE is sufficiently well linked to the Grail underground, and we have one on Iotigolo's tombstone above the Susquehanna. The head of the Murdered Apprentice is a well-known feature of Rosslyn Chapel, a Templar memorial, and we have a crude copy from the Susquehanna.

The more I thought about it, the more it made sense that the last, perhaps the largest and the most significant Grail community (excepting Estotiland itself) might well have been located somewhere in "Niagara" above the Falls. It is not possible to be certain, only to speculate.

The world was changing for the Grail Knights of North America. It was no longer medieval, it was on the brink of being modern. By 1550-1600, European nation-states were encroaching on the interior of North America. By that time, too, the Iroquois Confederacy was starting its phase of rapid expansion. The Grail Refugees were being pushed ever further west. One of their last population concentrations, before being dispersed altogether, may have been on the south shore of Lake Erie. It is impossible to say where, exactly, but I think a settlement may have been located between today's Buffalo and the western boundary of New York. A likely spot would be due north of Lake Chautauqua, I think.

The reason for this is that they required, above all, rapid news of developments, and the fastest transport was canoe. They had to plant outposts on the Susquehanna to keep in touch with what the

English were doing in Chesapeake Bay (during the 1580s until the founding of Jamestown in 1607). They had to plant outposts along the Allegheny because it flowed into the Ohio and so to the Mississippi — they had to keep track of possible Spanish expansion from that direction and route. They had to keep an eye on the Dutch in Albany, and on the French along the St. Lawrence — and this could be done via Lake Ontario.

So the centre of this web of communications would seem to be on Lake Erie (to serve as a port) at the north end of Lake Chautauqua where the Susquehanna and Allegheny newslines culminated. I have little doubt that if this area were searched, Grail Knight artefacts and ruins would be found. But there's also more to be found along all the river routes we've discussed. The money-digging Vermonters knew this. Josiah Stowel and Joseph Smith knew there was more to be found along the Allegheny and Susquehanna rivers.[3]

We're nearing the end of our story. From Lake Erie, I think the Grail Knights were dispersed into the truly distant west by the pressure of national colonization and also by Iroquois expansion. They merged into, or actually formed, the core population of the Louisiana Purchase.

They were North America's first *known* immigrants who came to the New World as religious refugees. They were precursors of the Pilgrims, the Baptists and Anabaptists, the Huguenots. Even if they lacked the numbers to create a nation along Freemasonic and Christian Commonwealth ideals, they shared these values with those who later amassed the strength to form the United States.

All but two of the signatories to the Declaration of Independence were Freemasons. All of the generals in George Washington's Continental Army were Freemasons. Of officers below the rank of general, some 1,500 were Freemasons. Ben Franklin was a Freemason. George Washington and the next three presidents of the United States were Freemasons. The City of Washington, D.C., was designed by a Freemason. The Washington Monument was designed by a Freemason and was opened with Masonic ceremonies in 1936.

Like it or not, the United States of America was, originally, a largely Freemasonic creation. The Grail Knights of North America came from the same Scottish refugee crucible that forged the Freemasonic conception of democracy and constitutional government.

From the heights of Iotigolo's tomb overlooking the Susquehanna, it is not so difficult for the eye of imagination to follow the river's course down to Philadelphia where the Declaration of Independence was signed. Where the Liberty Bell rang out its defiance and hope. Spectres of grizzled knights hovered behind those signatories. Their armour had been dented, and their swords had been notched, in the clangour of a thousand battles in defence of the Holy Grail. Their battles had been fought from brave ramparts of Albigensian fortresses to crude palisades in the Appalachians. It was this metallic cacophony of many struggles for human freedom that American rebels in Philadelphia heard as the carillon of one cracked bell.

Templar seal of the early thirteenth century discovered in the Bibliotheque Nationale. It depicts an American Indian holding a bow and wearing a feathered headdress.

ɲotes

Chapter 1. Et in Arcadia Ego

1. Garrett, Laurie, *The Coming Plague: Newly Emerging Diseases*, Farrar, Straus and Giroux, New York, 1994, page 212.
2. *The Unicorn Tapestries*, Metropolitan Museum of Art, New York, 1974.
3. Produced by Monique Leblanc of Montreal.
4. "Maafa" is a Swahili word signifying a holocaust or a major catastrophe and has been adopted by modern Afro-Americans as the general term for the transatlantic slave trade between A.D. 1441 and 1865.
5. Spong, John Shelby, *Rescuing the Bible from Fundamentalism*, Harper, San Francisco, 1991, page 12.
6. Lee, M. Owen, *Death and Rebirth in Virgil's Acadia*, State University of New York Press, page 89.
7. Lincoln, Henry, *The Holy Place*, Little, Brown and Company, New York, 1991, page 63.
8. *The Holy Blood and the Holy Grail* (1982) and *The Messianic Legacy* (1986) were published by Jonathan Cape Ltd. of London.
9. *The Temple and the Lodge* (1989) was also first published by Jonathan Cape Ltd. of London.
10. *The Holy Place*, pages 65–70.
11. Andrews, Richard, and Schellenberger, Paul, *The Tomb of God*, Little, Brown andCompany, New York, 1996.
12. Unfortunately, due to a restriction on the number of illustrations allocated for *Grail Knights of North America*, I decided not to include some "AE" and "15" inscriptions associated with the Baphomet (Chapter 11) and some Pennsylvania ruins (Chapters 1 and 11).

Chapter 2. Merika and Iargalon

1. Moses led the Israelites out of Egypt and into the Sinai Peninsula. Moses had been an Egyptian priest and apparently brought Ancient Egyptian and pre-Egyptian knowledge with him. The idea of some Grail researchers is that a community of priests was established in the Sinai Peninsula that preserved this ancient Egyptian and pre-Egyptian body of knowledge and tradition, and that this community evolved into the Essenes. Jesus is now thought to have been an Essene, or leader of a splinter group from the Essenes, and so knew this ancient body of knowledge and tradition brought into Sinai from Egypt by Moses. Thus, among some Grail researchers, Jesus is seen as a link between truly ancient Mosaic-Egyptian-"Atlantean" tradition and the New Covenant of Christianity. See *The Hiram Key*, pages 148-155 for discussion of the links between Egypt, Moses, Sinai and the Essenes.
2. The first census of New France, that of 1666, omitted at least seventeen people

known to have been in Montreal at the time. They were connected with Jeanne Mance and her hospital in Montreal. This is a strange omission since Montreal, not Quebec, was even then the largest single settlement in New France, and Jeanne Mance's hospital was the official reason for the colony's establishment in 1642, just twenty-four years before the census. In addition to the seventeen people known to have been in Montreal but who were not listed in the 1666 census, there may have been many more people in Montreal and New France who are completely unknown to modern scholarship. See *Holy Grail Across the Atlantic*, pages 280-281.

3. Thor Heyerdahl's notion that Polynesia was settled from the Americas, a theory that was first presented in his popular book about the Kon-Tiki raft expedition of 1947 and later (1954) in a massive treatise called *American Indians in the Pacific,* was bitterly opposed (and often misrepresented) by the conventional historical and anthropological scientists who insisted that Polynesia had been settled from the west, from Indonesia. After 1954, when radiocarbon dating was applied to some early Polynesian sites in Samoa and Fiji, the conventional view seemed vindicated: the early migrations had come from Indonesia against the prevailing winds and currents. And in 1976, the replica Polynesian double-canoe "Hokule'a" succeeded in sailing from Hawaii to Tahiti and back, using ancient Polynesian navigation tradition preserved in songs, proving that travel and migration could have taken place against the prevailing winds and currents of the Pacific. See Ben R. Finney's *Hokule'a, The Way to Tahiti* (Dodd, Mead & Company, New York, 1979). Nonetheless, although the double-canoe experiment proved that Polynesian navigation and naval architecture permitted windward voyaging, some aspects of Polynesian ethnography, history and dating raise questions about the origin, direction and date of the populating of some major islands and island groups. The question of Polynesian origins is not yet settled. It may be exceedingly complex and hold some dramatic surprises. Everybody — both Heyerdahl and his opponents — may be right and wrong at the same time. Easter Island radiocarbon dates and pollen analysis indicate that things are not simple.

4. Zink, David, *The Stones of Atlantis*, Prentice-Hall Canada, Toronto, 1978.

5. This name "Poseidia" does not come from the *Critias* and *Timaeus* dialogues of Plato, but from the numerous psychic readings between 1933 and 1946 in which Edgar Cayce referred to Atlantis during trance regressions.

6. "Beach rock" consists of horizontal deposits of coral or limestone that are often scoured into near-geometric shapes by the action of sand-bearing tidal currents. But beach rock seldom or never exhibits the precisely geometric fissures of the Bimini wall.

7. *The Stones of Atlantis*, page 86.

8. *The Stones of Atlantis*, pages 133-145.

9. *Nexus* magazine, Vol. 4, No. 6, page 56.

10. The famous golden death mask "of Agammenon" was actually discovered by Schliemann in the ruins of Mycenae, not Troy, in 1876. But this is just a quibble because the Trojan War was fought by the Mycenaeans.

11. A Canadian couple, Rand and Rose Flem-Ath, have offered what may be the latest location for Atlantis in their book *When the Sky Fell* (General Publishing, Toronto, 1997). Their book has caused much excitement in certain circles. By rehashing the theories of James Campbell and Charles Hapgood (*Earth's Shifting Crust* and *The Path of the Pole*), the Flem-Aths propose that Atlantis was in

what is now Antarctica. The Flem-Aths stress that (from one point of view, i.e., looking at the Earth from the South Pole) the now ice-covered islands making up Antarctica do occupy a position between the Old World and the New World as Atlantis is supposed to have done. It therefore satisfies Plato's geographic location — or abuses the entire thrust of the Platonic dialogues, depending on one's perspective.

The theories of Campbell and Hapgood regarding crustal shifts that relocate polar zones periodically are the most likely explanation for the so-called and misnamed "Ice Ages." The theory of James Campbell, modified later by Charles Hapgood, was the only theory by anyone else ever endorsed by Albert Einstein. Campbell's crustal shifts not only explain periodic "ice ages" but also explain many prominent geographic features of the planet. It is likely (in my view) that the Campbell-Hapgood construct of crustal shifts does, in fact, explain the Ice Ages more neatly and more probably than the many unlikely explanations proposed by conventional science. There were no Ice Ages, only periodic displacements and relocations of the polar zones — and this must be true because any global reduction of temperature sufficient to form glaciers in Europe would have caused the extinction of several existing tropical species that have slim tolerance for temperature variation (corals and snails).

So we may accept the Campbell-Hapgood theory of crustal shifts as being the most likely explanation for "Ice Age" temperature variations during the past million years or so. Indeed, I argued this in *Chosen People From the Caucasus* (Third World Press, Chicago, 1992, pages 88-114) in an attempt to propose a location for Eden. However, to use the Campbell-Hapgood theory to place Atlantis in Antarctica raises a number of problems that do not seem to bother either the Flem-Aths or their supporters. The most serious of these is that the Campbell-Hapgood theory calls for crustal shifts on the order of about 1,500 miles. While a crustal shift of this magnitude would result in an Antarctica that was partly unglaciated before the end of the last Ice Age, it would still leave all of the unglaciated areas with a severe sub-arctic climate. Even the unglaciated parts would have "enjoyed" (if that's the right word) a climate similar to Baffin Island, Ungava, and the Northwest Territories today. One does not generally think of this sort of climate as nurturing an advanced civilization like Atlantis was supposed to have been. If Atlantis was a worldwide seafaring culture, as the Egyptian priest told Solon (according to Plato), then Atlanteans would doubtless have visited and explored the then unglaciated, but still tundra-like, coasts of current Antarctic islands. Their knowledge of Antarctica could have been, and apparently was, preserved on maps (Piri Re'is, Hadji Ahmed, Oronteus Fineus, and Buache) — but that doesn't mean that the location of Atlantis itself was present-day Antarctica.

But, thankfully for the Flem-Aths' income and for the enthusiasm of their supporters, their theory is much like that proposed in *The Tomb of God* by Richard Andrews and Paul Schellenberger — it cannot be proved or disproved in the near future. Just as proof of *The Tomb of God* requires the removal of several hundred thousand tons of Mount Cardou in southern France, proof of the Flem-Ath theory requires removal of many of the *six million cubic miles* of ice currently covering Antarctica. This is not likely to happen soon — but if it does happen soon, it will be several thousand years before human survivors of the cataclysm regain the literacy to debate the merits of the Flem-Ath theory.

12. Muck, Otto, *Alles uber Atlantis*, Econ Verlag GmbH, Dusseldorf-Wein, 1976.

This book was offered in an English translation by William Collins Sons & Co. (U.K. and U.S.) in 1978 under the title *The Secret of Atlantis*, but it appears to be a condensation of Muck's original German text. *The Secret of Atlantis* features an introduction by PeterTompkins that admits that to "avoid the Scylla of superficiality and the Charybdis of tautology, the American editors of this book have lightly pruned the original text." Also, apparently, some of Muck's arguments and conclusions have been altered to conform more closely to theories held by the editors.

13. It is interesting that the Log of Columbus admits that he had a map of some sort, and that he consulted it during the 1492 voyage. However, Columbus does not claim that he drew this map. It is anybody's guess how Piri Re'is could have obtained a copy of any map possessed by Christopher Columbus — unless Piri Re'is means that he also had a copy *of the same map* that Columbus used. There are no known maps "from before the time of Alexander the Great" except, possibly, some Chinese maps scratched in stone and they depict only the major rivers of China itself.

14. **Centre of the Earth's Land Mass, etc.** This is an important concept and I will explain to the best of my ability. It will be easier to appreciate somewhat better the truly significant placement of the Giza complex.

First, let's consider two squares. One is 100 square units (miles, kilometres, or whatever) in area, the other twice as large, 200 square units in area.

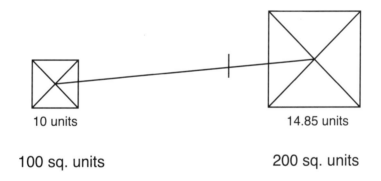

10 units   14.85 units

100 sq. units   200 sq. units

We will find their respective centres by drawing diagonals. Where the diagonals intersect is the centre of each square. Together, these squares represent three units of the largest common denominator — 100 square miles. So we'll draw a line, divided equally into three parts, between the centres of the two squares. Since one square is twice the area of the other, we will mark off two of the three equal parts towards the larger square. This is the centre of their combined areas, given their distance apart. If they were closer together, or further apart, this point would fall elsewhere. Please note that this point is above the centre of the small square but below the centre of the larger one. It is a true geometric centre of the two areas that are separated by this given and arbitrary distance.

It is possible to ascertain the area of an irregular shape, although it is much more difficult to do than using squares.

The largest continent, Eurasia, happens to be about twice the land area of the American continents. These continents are separated by oceans. One can divide the separation into three equal parts, just as above, and find the "centre of these two land masses."

Taking this point, we can calculate Africa into the picture the same way. Africa is about 25% the area of Eurasia and the Americas combined. Therefore, the distance from Africa's geographic centre to the Eurasia-Americas' centre will be divided into five equal parts (i.e. the "4" represented by Eurasia-Americas, and the "1" [25%] represented by Africa's area). Marking off four of these five divisions towards the Eurasia-Americas' centre, since this centre represents a combined land mass four times as large as Africa, will yield a new point, which is the geometric, in this case "geographic," centre of Eurasia-Americas-Africa combined. If we continue this process with the remaining large and small land masses — Antarctica, Australia, Greenland, New Guinea, Java, Sumatra, etc. — we will eventually arrive at a "centre of the earth's land masses." It will be as accurate as our method, plus the arbitrary inclusion of ever smaller islands, will make it.

A meticulous calculation of such a "centre" will result in a point directly on the meridian (longitude) of the Great Pyramid but 6' (minutes) south of the Great Pyramid — but there's only sand in that location. The Giza Plateau is the first solid bedrock on the correct meridian. It is 6' in error from the true centre.

Sixty seconds of 101.3 English feet = 1' (minute) of arc, 6080 feet on the equator = 1 nautical mile, whereas one "common" or "highway" (statute) mile equals 5280 English feet. A nautical "knot" is one nautical mile (6080 English feet) per hour of time; it is a unit of speed measurement, not of static distance.

Sixty minutes = 1 degree of arc, or 60 nautical miles at the equator. The Earth's equatorial circumference contains 360 degrees or 21,600 nautical miles = 24,872.73 common or statute miles.

All this sounds deceptively precise! In fact, of course, standardization of the length of the English foot, and therefore of seconds, minutes and degrees of arc, was not accomplished until the 1750s — and the size of the Earth was not measured correctly at that time. Just as the French Academy made an error in fixing the length of the metre, which was supposed to be one ten-millionth part of the surface distance from the Earth's equator to either pole, because they couldn't measure the Earth accurately, so also the British Admiralty made inaccurate geographic measures. Nonetheless, these measures remain accurate enough for most practical purposes. Nowadays, units of measure are fixed by correlation to electromagnetic wave-lengths. Since 1966, for example, the metre has been fixed as a division of the wave-length of Krypton 86.

A glance at the U.S.A.F. "Azimuthal Equidistant Projection" Map of the world will show that it is centred "near Cairo" — i.e., at the centre of the earth's land masses, as calculated above, and precisely on the meridian of the Great Pyramid — but 36,480 English feet south of the Great Pyramid at the true centre, which falls in an area of sand. A property of Azimuthal Equidistant Projection is that a circle drawn around any given point will have a circumference incorporating points of geography that are truly equidistant from the centre of the circle — the airplane or ship. This is not the case with large-scale maps drawn on the common Mercator projection, which gives accurate longitudes and latitudes of all geography but must distort the polar regions in order to do so. It is also not the case with the Phillips projection, used by the UN, which shows the land area of countries in true proportion to each other but must distort the longitudes and latitudes near the equator in order to do so. These distortions arise from the problem of transferring the curved surface of a spherical Earth onto a flat piece of paper — the best that can be done is to know, and to choose, the kind of distortion that best serves any given need.

The location of the Great Pyramid at the centre of the Earth's land masses, unless it is truly coincidence, implies the following. First, its builders knew the geography and size of the Earth quite accurately because they could not otherwise calculate the correct centre of land masses. Second, they chose Egypt because the centre is there, and this means that Ancient Egyptian civilization may have arisen because of lingering cultural influences as well as because of the supposed advantages conferred by the Nile. Third, the three pyramids of the Giza complex, including the Sphinx, were built by someone other than the Ancient Egyptians — unless we are willing to grant advanced knowledge to them as well — but then we must contend with the various correlations at Giza that all point to 10,500 B.C. as the origin of the Giza complex. Either the three pyramids and the Sphinx were built by an unknown culture long before the beginnings of Ancient Egypt, now dated as about 3200 B.C., or the Egyptians themselves have a much longer history than we think.

15. Pi is the ratio of a circle's diameter to its circumference, 1:3.14 or 7:22. Phi is the ratio of a line divided so that the length of the shorter segment bears the same relationship to the length of the longer segment as the longer segment bears to the whole undivided line, 1:1.618. This "Phi" is sometimes called "The Golden Section" because there's something ineffably pleasing about the ratio. It was used by many Renaissance artists such as Poussin, Michelangelo and da Vinci; it occurs in abstract mathematics, as in the Fibonacci Series of numerical progression; it occurs frequently in nature, for example in the successive length of segments of the chambered nautilus.

16. Actually, the quarry marks were found in what are called "relieving chambers," small spaces stacked above the King's Chamber. Howard Vise was the dubious visitor.

17. Tompkins, Peter, Secrets of the Great Pyramid, Harper & Row, New York, 1978. Tompkins gives an excellent chronological history of scientific expeditions to the monument. Howard Vise was a late "scientific" visitor in this chronology. How did he find quarry marks that others had missed? Tompkins gives a detailed account of thecircumstances.

18. Secrets of the Great Pyramid, page 17.

19. Hancock, Graham, and Bauval, Robert, The Message of the Sphinx, William Heinemann Ltd., London, 1966.

20. Perhaps it should be borne in mind that this lowest precessional declination would also have occurred about 36,500 B.C. — also a time of apparent geological and climate change. This is the date assigned to the so-called Gottweig Interstadial, a temporary warm phase in the last Ice Age, the division between Wurm I and Wurm II according to some climatologists. According to the Campbell-Hapgood theory, this was the time of a relatively minor crustal shift that moved the geography "under the (North) pole" from Canada's Northwest Territories to about the middle of Hudson's Bay. Although a lesser shift and geological disruption than the cataclysm that ended the Wurm Ice Age rather suddenly about 10,500 B.C., this earlier change had definite effects. For example, some anthropologists correlate this time with the emergence, in Europe, of truly modern humanity of the "Cro-Magnon" type (Homo sapiens

sapiens) and the disappearance of the Neanderthals (*Homo sapiens neanderthalensis*). Also, with respect to radiocarbon dates obtained from frozen mammoths, there is a cluster of them around 36,500 B.C. and another grouping around 15,000-12,500 B.C.

The disruption of about 36,500 B.C. may also have something to do with the end of surprisingly advanced human cultures presently unknown (or, at least, not admitted). Some astonishing Paleolithic artistic sketches depict people in coats, hats, and shoes — and apparent horse bridles and bits have been recovered from the European Paleolithic. These cultures may, or may not, be related to "Atlantis" which may have suffered a partial submergence at this earlier time. Therefore, we cannot absolutely rule out the possibility that the alignment of shafts in the King's Chamber may relate to a date of 36, 500 B.C. instead of the last precessional declination at 10,500 B.C.

21. *The Message of the Sphinx*, pages 7-10.
22. *The Message of the Sphinx*, pages 144-152.
23. *The Message of the Sphinx*, pages 15-19.
24. Knight, Christopher, and Lomas, Robert, *The Hiram Key*, Century (Random House), London, 1996, pages 76-78.
25. Stecchini wrote a long appendix on ancient weights and measures for Peter Tompkins's *Secrets of the Great Pyramid*, pages 223-251, in which the inexplicable antiquity of English units is stressed. See also Henry Lincoln's *The Holy Place*, pages 84-90, where he discusses various authorities on the antiquity of English measures and their relation to systems as far removed as Chinese units. As many experts in this obscure field have noted, the interrelation of ancient weights and measures in spite of vast geographic separation suggests a previous and exceedingly ancient unified standard imposed from some unknown source. English weights and measures, especially linear measures, seem to be a sort of "common denominator" for systems from Europe to China and, therefore, to be quite closely related to the original standard.
26. *Histoire de la France*, Vol. 1, References Larousse Histoire, Paris, 1987, pages 70-75.
27. Several newspapers grabbed onto this probably inevitable story title for various articles, of which *The New York Times*, *The Washington Post*, *The Toronto Star*, and Toronto's *Globe and Mail* carried lengthy features. Dr. Daniel Kolos, a professional Egyptologist residing in Orangeville, Ontario (and publisher of Benben Books on Egypt and Egyptology), followed the story as it broke and developed in various publications. He then very kindly sent me an account in November 1997 from which I've taken the major facts — hereinafter "Private correspondence, Kolos."
28. Private correspondence, Kolos.
29. Heyerdahl, Thor, *The Ra Expeditions*, George Allen & Unwin Ltd., London,1971 and *The Tigris Expedition*, Doubleday, New York, 1980, both contain lengthy discussions on the distribution and design of reed boats since these facts were the inspiration for both expeditions.
30. *The Ra Expeditions* is about Heyerdahl's attempt to cross the Atlantic from Morocco to the West Indies in an Egyptian-style reed ship. The first attempt on *Ra I*, built by Baduma tribesmen from Africa's Lake Chad, ended in failure when the reed boat came apart in American waters but only 300 miles from the nearest land. *Ra II*, built by Aymara Indians from South America's Lake Titicaca according to Ancient Egyptian design, successfully completed the crossing without losing a single reed.

31. *The Tigris Expedition* is about Heyerdahl's construction of another reed ship, this time according to ancient Sumerian specifications but also built by the same four Aymara Indians from Bolivia, and his successful navigation of it (against wind and currents on occasion) from Iraq to the island of Bahrain in the Persian Gulf, to Oman on the Arabian peninsula, to the Indus Valley of Pakistan and to the African coast of thenGulf of Aden. Heyerdahl thus travelled to the three major trade destinations mentioned in ancient Sumerian records: Dilmun (Bahrain), Makan (Oman), Meluhha (the Indus Valley civilization of Harappa and Mohenjo-Daro) — and Punt (Somalia) mentioned in both Sumerian and Egyptian records. He therefore showed that open-ocean trade in reed ships, using the Monsoons to cross the Arabian Sea, was possible in very ancient prehistoric times and could explain the undoubted predynastic contacts between Egypt, Sumeria, and the Indus civilizations.

But this contact also presupposes, or at least suggests, a parent civilization once located in some central position. This previous civilization was destroyed, but survivors managed to radiate outwards to seed river civilizations in Mesopotamia, along the Nile and along the Indus. According to our present knowledge, this civilization was described as "Eden" and it disappeared about the same time as Atlantis or a little later. Perhaps Eden was an offshoot or colony of Atlantis, sharing the same general cultural level and religion (sun worship). In *Chosen People from the Caucasus* (1992) I suggested a location for Eden and an expedition to study some apparently above-water parts of it — the Kathiawar peninsula of modern India and Socotra Island. This plan, like Heyerdahl's *Tigris* expedition, ran afoul of contemporary political and religious conflict.

32. Balfour, Michael David, *Stonehenge*, Hutchinson, London, 1979, page 111-113.
33. Severin, Tim, *The Jason Voyage*, Hutchinson, London, 1985, pages 255-257. Severin witnessed modern Georgian tribesmen using a sheep's fleece, stretched and weighted down onto a wooden frame, as a means of collecting gold dust by submerging it in streams flowing from the mineral-rich Caucasus mountains.
34. Hermann, Paul, *Conquest by Man*, Harper & Brothers, New York, 1954, pages 93-105.
35. Henrietta Mertz wrote a short and delightful book about her idea that Jason's voyage had taken him to the Bay of Fundy. I remember reading this book and once owned a copy, but it is not in the Toronto library system. Mertz also wrote an equally enjoyable book, *Pale Ink*, about evidence that Asians discovered America across the Pacific before Columbus.
36. Unfortunately, due to space limitations, I could not illustrate one of these Mexican figurines. However, photos can be found in Pierre Honoré's *In Search of the White God* and also in Thor Heyerdahl's *American Indians in the Pacific*.
37. This passage from Plato very obviously refers to the Mediterranean and, with respect to Atlantis, the context places the lost continent and its associated islands more or less directly westward of Gibraltar. Only by misrepresentation of the only and earliest source for Atlantis can the lost continent be placed anywhere else. The Flem-Ath location of Antarctica can only be bolstered by actual abuse of Plato's clear intent.
38. *Conquest by Man*, pages 28-47.
39. Bradley, Michael, *Chosen People from the Caucasus*, Third World Press, Chicago, 1992, pages 128-135, where various authorities are quoted.
40. Graves, Robert, *The White Goddess*, Faber and Faber Limited, London, 1961.

This book, considered an authority by many, is written in such a convoluted way that no actual page number for a clear statement of Greek-Celtic mythic and literary relations can be given. But the entire book is about Middle Eastern, Greek, and Celtic inter-relations.

41. *Conquest by Man*, pages 82-83.

42. *The Ra Expeditions*, pages 210-212 for a general discussion of the *Guanches*.

43. Severin, Tim, *The Brendan Voyage*, Hutchinson, London, 1978. An account of this two-stage voyage from Ireland to Newfoundland.

44. Pohl, Frederick, *The Lost Discovery*, W.W. Norton & Co., New York, 1952. My favourite compendium of saga references and evidence of Norse voyages to America, including (in my opinion) the best interpretation of Bjarni's sailing directions, which, when reversed, allowed Leif to find Vinland. Bjarni, Leif, Thorfinn Karlsefni, Freydis, and Thorall were all related either by trade or by blood. Frederick Pohl captures the "family" feeling of Norse voyages to North America without sacrificing scholarship.

45. Jones, Gwyn, *The Norse Atlantic Sagas*, Oxford University Press, New York, 1964.

46. *Vinland* means "wineland" ("vineland") if there is no accent on the "i," but means "grassland" ("meadows") if there is an accent. In the sagas, as they were written down some three centuries after the actual voyages were remembered by oral tradition, there are accents sometimes — and sometimes not. It is impossible to prove from the existing written versions what was originally meant, and so there has grown up a scholarly debate over this loophole. Nonetheless, all saga sources state clearly that Leif Eriksson named the place Vineland because his old servant, Tyrker, recognized grape vines in the new land. Grapes do not grow as far north as Norway, Iceland, and Greenland. Leif himself had never seen grapes or grape vines because he had only sailed as far south as the Orkney Isles, but the old servant was named "Tyrker" (i.e., "Turk") because he came originally from a more southerly region — it is impossible to say where. Anything south of Germany was "Tyrker" to the Norse. But Tyrker would have known about grapes and grape vines if he had come from Germany or further to the south. In the sagas, Leif asks, "Are you sure these are grapes, my foster father?" This "foster father" was a term of endearment for the old servant, not the actual truth, for Erik the Red was Leif's actual father and still very much alive. Tyrker answers, "Assuredly these are grape vines, for I come from a country which has no lack of grapes." This dialogue makes no sense if meadows are being referred to — besides, Tyrker was holding a bunch of grapes in both hands, "rolling his eyes in joy and amazement" and "babbling in his southern tongue" according to the sagas.

It is interesting that immediately after this exchange between Leif and his old servant, Leif addresses his crew: "From now on, we have two things to do — will we gather grapes and cut wood as a lading for our ship." The wood would have made Leif a rich man in treeless Greenland, and he probably took the grapes back in the form of juice or sun-dried raisins. It is clear that grapes gave the place its name, and to me the scholarly wrangling is just pedantry.

47. Paul Hermann in *Conquest by Man* (pages 165-215) and Frederick Pohl in *The Lost Discovery* (pages 155 and 261-262) discuss the Norse traditions of this coast.

48. See Hermann and Pohl as above.

49. See Hermann and Pohl as above. The Icelandic annals in Reykjavik were

destroyed by fire in the early fifteenth century. The most important entries were preserved from the memory of a priest who had the annals in his care before the fire. He remembered the entry that in 1347 the "last Markland ship entered Reykjavik harbour."

50. As recently as June 14, 1998, *The Toronto Star* printed a full-page feature entitled "Appalachia's genetic mystery: Who are the Melungeons?" (*Science*, page F8). The black-haired blue-eyed "Melungeons" (or "Melungians") of the Smokey Mountains have previously been considered as poor Irish or Welsh who were there from the earliest colonial times, but now the Melungians themselves have drawn attention to possibly Turkish words in their traditional vocabulary. *Malun can* or *malun djinn* means "accursed soul" in Arabic and it is thought (by some) that Appalachia's Melungians were Turkish slaves who escaped from unknown precolumbian voyages. On the other hand, Melungians of early colonial times were reported to speak an antique kind of Welsh, Gaelic, or English. Still other Melungians introduced themselves to colonists as "Portyghees" — Portuguese — who had been shipwrecked and who had found refuge in the mountains. The fact is that no one really knows who the Melungians are, only that they lived in the Appalachians long before the earliest official colonists. They may be a remnant of several European populations who mixed because of their clear distinction from the American Indians. Indeed, some of them may be descendants of Grail Knights who did not migrate westwards.

51. See the 1977 edition's entry for Azores, page 14.

52. Aside from the Melungians, who may derive from early Moorish or Arabic voyages to the New World before Columbus, we have some other suggestive facts. The American "turkey" of Pilgrim and Thanksgiving fame is, of course, named after something with *Turkish* associations. In Spain, where Columbus supposedly returned with the first known ears of American maize (but there's now proof that the Sinclairs knew of it a century earlier), the plant is rather inexplicably called *turkish corn*.

Chapter 3. Crusades and "The Cross"

1. Bradley, Michael, *The Iceman Inheritance, "prehistoric sources of Western Man's racism, sexism and aggression,"* Dorset Publishing Inc., Toronto, 1978; reprinted in the United States by Warner Books, New York (1979) and by Lushena Books, New York (1992).

2. Worcester, G.R.G., *Sail and Sweep in China,* Her Majesty's Stationery Office, London, 1966, pages 85-86.

3. As this book goes to press, the salmon confrontation on the West Coast remains an explosive issue. My advice is the same as in 1976.

4. As of 1998, there are faint signs that the cod may be starting to recover.

5. Bradley, Michael, *The Black Discovery of America,* Personal Library, Toronto, 1981; reprinted as *Dawn Voyage* by Summerhill Press, Toronto (1987); reprinted under the original title by A & B Books, New York (1992).

6. Michael Bradley, *The Black Discovery of America,* page i.

7. At the time, I thought that *The Black Discovery of America* was the first presentation of an original thesis, and so did the directors of Dalhousie University's Centre for African Studies. Subsequently, we discovered that a similar argument, with roughly similar evidence, had been published by Ivan

van Sertima under the title *They Came Before Columbus*.

8. I have never verified this with Canada Post because it didn't seem very important. I heard this several times from residents of New Ross.

9. Michael Bradley, *Holy Grail Across the Atlantic*, Hounslow Press, Toronto, 1988, pages 45-79, a description of the apparent ruins at New Ross, Nova Scotia.

10. *Holy Grail Across the Atlantic*, page 79.

11. Sinclair, Andrew, *The Sword and the Grail*, Crown Publishers, New York, 1992.

12. Personal correspondence from Claudette Leblanc. I have not verified this assertion.

13. Illustration cut by space restrictions; see page 47 in *Holy Grail Across the Atlantic*.

14. Copies of correspondence between the Nova Scotia Ministry of Culture and me are reprinted on pages 70-72 in *Holy Grail Across the Atlantic*.

15. I am indebted to the Canadian folk singer, the late Stan Rogers, for this information. No one in New Ross mentioned this during my investigations.

16. *The White Goddess*, pages 36-37, where Graves offers a modern English version of the alphabet song "Cad Goddeu" ("The Battle of the Trees") by the medieval Celtic bard Taliesin.

17. *The White Goddess*. Robert Graves also gives a detailed but rambling discussion of the feminine attributes of the willow or osier-tree (mostly on pages 198-250).

18. *The White Goddess*, page 21.

19. Although editions of both encyclopaedias during the 1950s and 1960s carried entries accepting the voyage, more recent editions omit the Sinclair expedition altogether.

20. I was somewhat involved in this replica voyage project as a design consultant on the kind of ship that Sinclair most probably built. In reports to both the Prince Henry Sinclair Society of North America and to Niven Sinclair of London, I suggested that the proper ship would have been a type known as a "cog." Because of time, the replica planners decided to try to construct a more modest "galley of Orkney" for 1998 but even this proved impossible.

21. Joelle Lauriol offloaded a list of *Matthew* sponsors from the Internet: www Matthew.com.

22. Gardner, (Sir) Laurence, *Bloodline of the Holy Grail*, Element Books, Shaftesbury, 1996.

Chapter 4. The Sea Knight

1. Pohl, Frederick, *Prince Henry Sinclair*, Clarkson N. Potter, New York, 1974, page 16.

2. *Prince Henry Sinclair*, page 162.

3. *Prince Henry Sinclair*, page 184.

4. *Prince Henry Sinclair*, page 187.

5. *Prince Henry Sinclair*, page 204.

6. Personal correspondence with Richard Coleman of Guysborough County, Nova Scotia.

7. The *Americana*, while accepting the authenticity of the 1398 voyage did not, however, accept the "fisherman's tale" of an even earlier voyage circa 1350-1370 that supposedly inspired Henry Sinclair.

8. Quoted here from Pohl's *Prince Henry Sinclair*, pages 150-155. But the *Zeno*

Narrative also exists in several very similar English translations from the Italian.
9. *Prince Henry Sinclair*, page 287.
10. Hobbs, William Herbert, "The Fourteenth-Century Discovery of America by Antonio Zeno," *The Scientific Monthly*, Vol. 72 (January, 1951), pages 24-31.
11. *Prince Henry Sinclair*, pages 288-291.
12. Moncrieffe, Sir Iain Sir, *The Highland Clans*, Barrie & Jenkins, London, 1982, page 103.
13. Frederick Pohl gives a detailed discussion of the existing Micmac and Abenaki traditions that mention Glooscap. From this, he reconstructs the routes of Glooscap/Sinclair explorations in Nova Scotia. Along Pohl's suggested routes, this "acadie" suffix occurs repeatedly but not elsewhere in the province. Strangely enough, Pohl himself does not mention this correlation of "acadie" with his own suggested routes of Glooscap/Sinclair explorations. See *Holy Grail Across the Atlantic*, pages 130-140 for a discussion of all this, including maps.
14. As stressed before, no log of Cabot's first voyage (1497) survives. No log of his second voyage survives because he was supposedly lost with his ship somewhere in the Atlantic. This description comes from a letter written by Giovanni Pasqualigo, Venetian ambassador in London, containing an account of what Cabot related to him. A generally similar letter written by Pedro de Ayala, Spain's Ambassador in London, also survives.
15. *Holy Grail Across the Atlantic*, pages 259-269 for an in-depth discussion, including the opinions of Cabot's near-contemporaries Gomera and "Oviedo," and the Juan de la Cosa map of 1500. Also, *The Lost Discovery*, pages 172-180, for a navigator's exposition of "dropping latitude" and westward variation.
16. Hoffman, Bernard G., *Cabot to Cartier*, University of Toronto Press, Toronto, 1961, pages 146-151.
17. Peter Cummings, genealogist of the Prince Henry Society of North America, conducted this research. It was published in the Society's bulletin for 1996. However, my information derives from personal correspondence with Cummings.
18. Colon, Ferdinand, *Life of Colon*, English translation, London, 1812, page 231.

Chapter 5. Le Trésor Maudit

1. *The Holy Place*, page 9.
2. *The Holy Place*, page 72.
3. *The Holy Place*, pages 150-154.
4. *Methuen Historical Atlas*, Methuen, London, 1961, pages 51-63 (map and text).
5. I find it amusing that "advanced Greeks" are always credited with discovering things and then passing on the progress to more primitive neighbouring peoples — when the Greeks themselves stated the opposite! — that they *learned* from the Egyptians, Celts, and North Africans. For example, we know now that the Greeks derived the size of the earth and knowledge of the precession from the Egyptians. On a more general level, Apollo was (more or less) regarded as the "god of science" and "intellection," but the Greeks believed that his earthly abode was not in Greece but in Britain at Stonehenge. Apollo supposedly visited his major temple every nineteen years.
6. *The Holy Place*, page 76.
7. *The Holy Place*, page 77.
8. One statute mile (5280 English feet) equals 1.6 kilometres. This is a ratio of 1:1.6.

9. *Columbia Viking Desk Encyclopedia*, 1968, page 988.

10. Melegari, Vezio, *Hidden Treasures*, Collins, London, 1972, page 64.

11. *Hidden Treasures*, page 64.

12. My own calculation based on the exchange rate in 1898 and estimates of the dollar's buying power in 1898 as opposed to today's currency.

13. Personal correspondence with electronics technician Michael Twose, Faculty of Music, University of Toronto. But see Gardner's *Bloodline of the Holy Grail*, page 259, where it is also stated that the Ark was a powerful electrical condenser. This is a common conclusion among engineers who have studied the Ark's specifications.

14. *Pursuit* (Journal of the Society for the Investigation of the Unexplained), "Blasted Baghdad Batteries!", Vol. 3, No. 4, (Fall, 1970), pages 139-142.

15. *Pursuit*, "Bothersome Beads from Bubastis," Vol. 5, No. 1, (Spring 1972), page 17.

16. The *Harleyan Aids to Studies of the Bible*, page 723, gives a date for the Exodus as about 1250 B.C., but Gardner in *Bloodline of the Holy Grail* equates Moses with the deposed Egyptian pharoah Akhenaten and equates the Exodus with the escape of this monotheistic pharoah and his followers. Akhenaten died outside of Egypt in 1354 B.C. according to conventional Egyptian chronology (*Columbia Viking Desk Encyclopedia*, 1968. page 502).

17. At least, the Ark is not mentioned as being in the Temple after the reign of Manasseh — except in Jeremiah's "retrospective" some fourteen years later.

18. Angebert, Jean-Marie, *The Occult and the Third Reich*, Crown Publishers, New York, 1969, page 53.

19. *Holy Grail Across the Atlantic*, pages 321-323.

20. *The Tomb of God*, pages 103-105.

21. *The Tomb of God*, page 103.

22. Brandreth, Gyles, *The Joy of Lex*, William Morrow and Company, New York, 1980, page 182.

23. De Sede makes no mention of this article in his *Le Trésor Maudit* and, if he had known of it he surely would have mentioned it as additional support for the all-important inscriptions — particularly as the "reference" he chose to cite apparently never existed.

24. *The Holy Place*, page 166.

25. French historian Pierre Vital, author of a fairly obscure book called *Requiem pour une Garonne Défunte* (*"Requiem for a Dead Garonne"*), Editions Wallada, Bordeaux, 1984, reproduces a number of seventeenth- and eighteenth-century maps of the Garonne-Aude waterway. These maps were made by engineering surveyors engaged in planning and building the famous Canal di Midi, which connects the Atlantic near Bordeaux with the Mediterranean near Narbonne and which utilizes the Garonne and Aude rivers. The region of Rennes-le-Château is on tributaries of the Aude and, therefore, appears on some of these surveyors' maps. A collection of such maps published in the memoirs "M. de Viviens," an engineer, dated 1831, is preserved in the archives of the Garonne town of St. Germain but includes maps from the entire canal route along with de Viviens's more modern early nineteenth-century maps of the Canal du Midi.

    Several old maps, plus de Viviens's own surveyor charts of the region of the Blanque and Sal tributaries of the Aude River, show "mines" in the area of our interest. The mine that Joelle noticed near her cross on the Blanque River does not appear on a map of 1721 (but it is a very crude map) but does appear on a map of 1785 (four years after the death of Marie de Blanchefort) and on de Viviens's own considerably more accurate chart of 1817. From this we might cautiously conclude that the mine had not been dug by 1721 (but the chart is so general that the mine might have been overlooked), but had been dug or was being excavated by 1785, a few years after Marie de Blanchfort's grave monuments were carved.

Chapter 6. The Greatest Story Ever Told

1. *Rescuing the Bible from Fundamentalism*, pages 40-65.
2. Birks, Walter, and Gilbert, R.A., *The Treasure of Montsegur*, Thorsons Publishing Group, London, 1987, page 38-42.
3. Naifeh, Steven W., and Smith, Gregory White, *The Mormon Murders*, Weidenfeld & Nicholson, New York, 1988, pages 86-95.
4. *Bloodline of the Holy Grail*, pages 100-12.
5. Esty, Katherine, *Gypsies, Wanderers in Time*, Victor Gollancz, London, 1962, page 124.
6. Baigent, Michael, Richard Leigh and Henry Lincoln, *The Holy Blood and the Holy Grail*, pages 352-353.
7. *Pursuit*, Vol. 6, No. 1, (January 1973) "Yesu of the Druids" by Ivan T. Sanderson, pages18-19. Sanderson, a Cambridge-trained biologist, points out that the Glastonbury Thorn is a specimen of *Crataegus praecox*, the species typical of Palestine, which should not be able to grow in a British climate, and not a specimen of *Crataegus oxyacantha*, the type adapted to North Europe. Also, Sanderson points out that there's not just one Glastonbury Thorn; several small trees have established themselves in the immediate vicinity of Glastonbury, notably along Chalice Road.
8. *The Holy Blood and the Holy Grail*, pages 282-287.
9. There are only four known literary references to Lyonesse. Geoffrey of Monmouth alludes to it as being connected with King Arthur. Chrétien de Troyes, usually acknowledged as the author of the first "Grail Romance" (but his version is incomplete), describes the City of Ys, traditionally the capital of Lyonesse. St.Bresabius of Cardiff offers what may be a completely fanciful king list of Lyonesse, but it is of interest in stating that Arthur's grandfather was a ruler of Lyonesse. St. Columba preaches against the "heretics, witches, idolators and Druids" which continued to thrive in Lyonesse.

   I wrote in the text that Julius Caesar and the Romans did not mention Lyonesse. However, as this book was days from going to press, Joelle Lauriol found a cryptic reference in Caesar's commentaries about a Celtic tribe (the "Rets") that occupied the land "between the estuary of the Loire and the ocean." As written, this makes no sense since there is presently no land "between" the mouth of the Loire and the Atlantic. The Loire flows into the Atlantic.

   However, it is known that some islands once existed off this coast and extended north off the coast of Morbihan. These islands had sunk completely by the fourth century, but the Romans and Celts must have known of them because they were inhabited — and were a part of Lyonesse. If the ocean was considered to begin outside of this fringe of islands to the westward of them, then a tribe could have lived "between the estuary of the Loire and the ocean" — on these islands. Caesar doesn't say more about this tribe. There's no indication that he fought or conquered them.

St. Bresabius, besides giving a dubious king list of Lyonesse, also offers an equally problematical map of the now-vanished island domain. He calls them the "Elder Isles" and stresses that witches, sorcerers, and Druids lived there. Nonetheless, we know that there *were* islands, now lost, in the Bay of Biscay (poetically: "The Cantabrian Gulf") because modern underwater photos have shown both ruins, which look like towns, and also megalithic stones and circles off the coast of France from Ile de Ré ("Island of Ra"?) to Lorient — that is all along the present coast of Poitou and Morbihan. The sunken megalithic structures indicate that this land (or islands) was above water and inhabited as early as 3000 B.C. to judge from non-sunken monuments still existing (and excavated) on the present coast. The largest megalithic assembly known, for example, the astonishing array of giant menhirs at Carnac, is directly opposite the sunken land mass.

In spite of the opinion of modern French archaeology that the megalith tradition began in Provence with the Cardial Culture and merely used larger stones as the culture radiated towards the Atlantic along the Garonne-Aude waterway, it may have been the other way around: the largest and most complex megalithic works may have been on Lyonesse, now sunk, and radiated to the coasts on each side where Carnac and Stonehenge are located. Further from this centre in Lyonesse, the stones became smaller until the modest stone arrangements of the Cardial people near the Mediterranean.

I have mentioned before that the southern Atlantic coast of France would have been an obvious landing place for Atlantean refugees. And, in this context, I find it interesting that Otto Muck attributes the huge mud deposits of the Landes west of the Garonne as being, in fact, floating detritus from Atlantis —buoyant volcanic mud mixed with fine pumice. If Atlantean refugees landed here with some preserved knowledge and a tradition of impressive stoneworking, it might explain the tradition that Lyonesse was the abode of "heretics, witches, idolators and Druids," and might explain why the largest megalithic monuments are opposite lost Lyonesse.

I think this may be worth investigating in much greater detail. As for the story of the Grail, there are definitely asserted associations between Lyonesse and Grail personalities. Other than the tenuous connections already mentioned, it is at least suggestive that both Bresabius and Geoffrey of Monmouth state the original "Avvallon" was a major island of Lyonesse. Presumably, the name "Avallon" was borrowed for the near-insular land around Glastonbury because the two places shared some characteristic similarity. *Avallon* means "apple trees". Perhaps both places had apple orchards. And perhaps the Glastonbury Avallon adopted the name in honour of the Lyonesse island when it sank. The sixth century is known to have been a time in which fairly large-scale reciprocal crustal changes sank the islands called Lyonesse and simultaneously raised the land around Glastonbury.

Aside from the Sinai region, then, and Jesus's supposed link via the Essenes with some ancient Moses/Egyptian/"Atlantean" traditions and knowledge, Lyoness is yet another place where the prechristian elements could have melded with the Christian ones in the Grail Religion. Lyonesse, indeed, may be the key.

10. The Knights of St. John began the practice of applying Roquefort cheese to open wounds. This particular cheese, when it grows mould, harbours a strain of penicillin closely related to that cultured by Sir Alexander Fleming (1928).

There's a suggestion that Fleming, himself a "Knight of Malta," knew of the old Roquefort cheese moulds and tried to culture the same strain under scientific conditions. He found a more powerful kind of penicillin than Roquefort cheese can sustain, and it was not toxic, as were the first antibiotics isolated and cultured by R.J. Dubos of France (1939). Therefore, Sir H.W. Florey (and others) developed Fleming's strain of penicillin for production in commercial quantities (1940).

11. Bowen, Meg, *The Women Troubadours*, W.W. Norton, New York, 1976, pages 37-61.

12. Starbird, Margaret, *The Woman with the Alabaster Jar*, Bear & Company Publishing, Santa Fe (New Mexico), 1993, page 56.

13. Supposedly as a gift for Charles of Luxemburg before he became Emperor of the "Holy Roman Empire" (1346-1378).

14. Sutcliff, Rosemary, *Sword at Sunset*, Hodder and Stoughton, London, 1963, pages 56-69. As an example of Sutcliff's research for a popular historical novel, she contracted the commander of the 1st East Anglian Regiment, Maj. (Sir) J.S. Symington-Smithe, to work out for her the tactics that King Arthur would most probably have used in all the twelve major battle he supposedly fought. She and he also visited the traditional sites of these battles and reconstructed the probable sixth-century terrain and forest cover from paleobotany analysis of pollen.

15. *The Occult and the Third Reich*, page 114.

16. This is merely my opinion based on the demonstrated fact that the Provençal Culture had proved itself capable of incorporating many disparate people, cultures, and religions into a tolerant and vital civilization.

17. Captain Mission's speech:

> "The trading of men can never be agreeable to the eyes of divine justice. No man has the power of the liberty of another, and while those who profess a more enlightened knowledge of the Deity sold men like beasts, they proved that their religion was no more than a grimace...I have not exempted my own men from the galling yoke of slavery and asserted my own liberty, to enslave others. Although these men are distinguished from Europeans by their color, customs or religious rites, they are the work of the same Omnipotent Being and imbued with equal reason. Wherefore I desire that they be treated like free men — for I would banish even the name of slavery from among them."

Thus spake a Libertatia pirate off the coast of West Africa in A.D. 1699, some 166 years before Abraham Lincoln intoned similar words (belatedly) in 1865 — "belatedly" because, by then, all European nations and most South American ones, had outlawed slavery. The United States was the *last*, not the *first*, major nation to make this jump in human conceptions and freedom.

Students of Masonic lore will recognize "code phrases" in Captain Mission's speech, while students of American jurisprudence will recognize both words and concepts echoed in the famous Declaration of Emancipation. But Captain Mission's speech has been preserved in a prosaic source of slim interest to law students or to humanistic thinkers — *Freebooters of the Red Sea* by Hamilton

Cochrane, Bobs-Merrill Publishing, New York, 1965, pages 83-108.

18. Pigafetta, I.F., *Report on the Kingdom of Congo, etc.*, London, 1881, page 137. A member of Magellan's navigating team on the first known voyage around the world in 1519-21, Pigafetta wrote that Magellan had a chart showing the "Straits of Magellan" in advance of discovering them. The chart had been drawn by Martin de Boheme (sometimes spelled "Behaim") and was owned by the King of Portugal. I've quoted Pigafetta's lengthy description in several books but it is not so relevant here. See, for example my *The Columbus Conspiracy* (Hounslow Press, Toronto, 1991, page 150).

19. Hapgood, Charles, *Maps of the Ancient Sea Kings*, Chilton Books, Radnor, 1968, pages 127-135. Hapgood, in association with the Strategic Air Command's cartographic division, analysed many ancient maps (Piri Re'is, Hadji Ahmed, Oronteus Finaeus, Buache, and Zeno) and several hundred portolan charts dating between 1327 and 1489. He came to the conclusion that in many cases the geography depicted was supposedly unknown at the time the maps were made, or that the longitudes and projections were anomalous. His conclusion, endorsed by the Strategic Air Command, was that the maps listed here, and all portolans, derived from maps originally made during the last Ice Age. They resulted from a succession of copies of just one unknown source map that had been in existence in the Middle East up to about A.D. 1200. It depicted the entire world, including both polar regions. All portolans were copies of the Mediterranean section of this source map, while other maps (Hadji Ahmed, Piri Re'is, etc.) showing non-Mediterranean geography were also copies of this one source map. The Arab cartographer Abulfeda claimed to have seen this map in Byzantium in A.D. 1237. The so-called "Franciscan Map" of 1360 may be a complete copy of this ancient source map — or, it may be a fake. Within the next year or two the Franciscan Map will cause a media stir.

Chapter 7. The Newport Tower

1. Leland, Charles G., *Kuloscabe the Master*, Boston, 1881, page 32.
2. *Holy Grail Across the Atlantic*, pages 208-215.
3. For a full discussion of the tower's fourteenth-century architecture, see Pohl's *The Lost Discovery*, pages 176-180.
4. "Peter's pence" is the tithe (or head tax) extracted from each Catholic. But this figure of 6,912 persons for a given year that happens to survive in Norwegian church records may, in the case of Greenland, represent more than one year — but probably not. The actual date of this account is unfortunately lost.
5. *The Lost Discovery*, page 199.
6. *The Hiram Key*, pages 242-251.
7. *The Columbia Viking Desk Encyclopedia*, 1968, page 688.
8. See note No. 46 for Chapter 2.
9. At least, that's the legend from several sources. The three knights were: Sir Hugo, Sir Poy(t)vin, and Sir Pihelha.
10. Henry Lincoln has demonstrated in a new television presentation that the Knights Templar were well established on the Danish island of Björnholm by A.D. 1250. Further, alignments of Templar churches on the island relate to the pentagon of Rennes-le-Château! Björnholm is precisely 1,000 miles from Rennes-le-Château — and both are precisely 2,000 miles from Jerusalem. Björnholm, Jerusalem, and Rennes-le-Château therefore form the three points

of a giant isosceles triangle, but how this figure was surveyed so precisely over such a great distance remains a mystery.

11. *The Lost Discovery*, page 201.

12. *The Lost Discovery*, pages 174-194.

13. *The Lost Discovery*, pages 174-194.

14. Gomera in his *General History of the Indies* (as it is usually called) wrote that da Verrazano ascended "the river of Norumbega" for a distance of twelve miles until he came to a city whose inhabitants were "rich in furs and gold." Esteban Gomez claimed to have attacked Norumbega in 1535 and to have carried some of the surviving inhabitants back to Spain. Although Champlain wrote that Norumbega was a fable, it is one of these mysteries of early North American exploration that will not go away. Norumbega was apparently somewhere in New England, on the coast between Connecticut and Maine. It was apparently a city or settlement. Alison Bishop of the Nova Scotia Ministry of Culture was inclined to the idea that the New Ross ruins were Norumbega since the "castle" is about fourteen miles up the Gold River. Jeanne McKay was of this opinion too. I have no opinion because, aside from the Newport Tower, there are Celtic ruins near Portsmouth, New Hampshire, which could have been Norumbega and also some apparent ruins along the Charles River near Boston. Then, we have the Norse "Hvritmannaland" somewhere along this coast, which could also account for Norumbega.

15. *The Lost Discovery*, page 194.

Chapter 8. The Case of the Acadia Coin

1. *Conquest by Man*, pages 175-179. Here Paul Hermann gives a detailed discussion of the Mandans.

2. Mowat, Farley, *Westviking*, Little, Brown, Boston, 1965.

3. Canadian researcher John Robert Colombo independently came across this reference to Hachila in the Bible. It will apparently figure in his upcoming book.

4. Champlain, Samuel de, *Works*, Vol. 1, pages 255-256.

5. This is quoted in Bourgeois's obituary, printed in a Moncton daily, sent to me by Claudette Leblanc (without exact publication data). I believe the year was 1992.

Chapter 9. The Magog Mill and the Lost Legacy

1. This stone is set into the centre of the brick archway leading to the parking courtyard. The last time I saw it, some vandals had sprayed it with red paint.

2. *The Columbia Viking Desk Encyclopedia*, 1968, page 572.

3. Adair, E.R., "Evolution of Montreal Under the French Regime," *Canadian Historical Review* (Canadian Historical Association Annual Report, 1942), page 26.

4. These sketches are reproduced in *Holy Grail Across the Atlantic*, pages 295-296.

5 Haliburton, Richard, *Seven League Boots*, Dodd, Mead & Co., New York, 1936, page 114.

Chapter 10. The Core of the Matter

1. Lyon, Eugene, *The Search for the Atocha*, Harper & Row, New York, 1979. This account of the famous treasure hunt by a respected historian and associate of the National Geographic Society objectively chronicles a sorry saga of government carelessness, dishonesty, and venality on the part of the State of Florida and the United States.
2. Originally an informal league of north German trading towns from about A.D. 1175, one could say that the "Hanseatic League" came into visible existence in 1241 when Hamburg and Lubeck signed a treaty of mutual protection against pirates. But these two towns were already closely associated with merchants in Wisby, Novgorod, Bergen, Bruges, and London (Merchants of the Steelyard). The League was formally organized in 1358 and by 1370 was powerful enough to force the King of Denmark, Waldemar IV, to grant it an exclusive monopoly on Scandinavian trade in the Baltic and North seas. This monopoly lasted more than a century, but was weakened by the rise of modern nation states (particularly Sweden under Gustavus Adolphus). The League was in decline by the mid-seventeenth century. The name comes from the German word *hansa*, a group, company or consortium.
3. *The Vinland Map and the Tatar Relation*, Yale University Press, New Haven, 1973.
4. *Concordia University News*, May 1989, pages 27-32.
5. Pindera, Loreen, and York, Geoffrey, *People of the Pines*, Little, Brown, Toronto, 1991.
6. *The Columbia Viking Desk Encyclopedia*, 1968, page 521.
7. Bushman, Richard L., *Joseph Smith and the Beginning of Mormonism*, University of Illinois Press, Urbana, 1984, page 5.
8. Brodie, Fawn, *No Man Knows My History*, Knopf, New York, 1971, page 87.
9. *No Man Knows My History*, page 91.
10. Priest, Josiah, *American Antiquities*, Springfield, 1833, page 21.
11. Silverberg, Robert, *The Moundbuilders*, New York Geographic Society, Greenwich (Conn.), 1968.
12. The ancient pit mines on Isle Royal are extensive and reach a depth of sixty feet. The shafts follow veins of pure copper nuggets. Some nuggets were found at the bottom of shafts and pits. It appears that the aboriginal mining came to an abrupt end long before the first known European exploration and colonization. By calculating the volume of all the Isle Royal shafts, pits and tunnels, and then by computing the average amount of copper nuggets in the veins, modern mining engineers contracted by 3M (Minnesota Mining and Manufacturing) have concluded that the ancient miners removed from three million to ten million pounds of copper. Some of these estimates are quoted in Roman Shklanka's *Copper, nickel, lead and zinc deposits of Ontario*, Department of Mines, Government of Ontario Printers, Toronto, 1969, pages 5-13.
13. Robbins, Maurice, and Irving, Mary B., *Amateur Archeologist's Handbook*, Crowell, New York, 1973.
14. Renfrew, Colin, *Before Civilization*, Jonathan Cape, London, 1973, pages 121-153.
15. Personal correspondence with Norman Emerson, 1975.
16. *No Man Knows My History*, page 71.
17. *No Man Knows My History*, page 83.
18. *No Man Knows My History*, page 78.

19. I was told by the current owner of this tablet that it had been part of the original Hill Cumorah collection supposedly discovered by Joseph Smith. It had been given by Smith to Orson Pratt, who arranged and edited the *Book of Mormon* to conform more closely to the Bible. I cannot vouch for the truth of this story or for the authenticity of the tablet itself. Unfortunately, space restrictions prevented me from illustrating this tablet in *Grail Knights of North America*.

20. *Joseph Smith and the Beginning of Mormonism*, pages 35-89.

21. *Joseph Smith and the Beginning of Mormonism*, page 32.

22. All information about Sharon's "Children of Light" comes from a lecture given at the temple. I took notes. Joelle Lauriol also attended this talk, which accompanied a guided tour of Sharon Temple and the supporting farms and houses that have been preserved and now house museums. The writings of David Wilson, some 6,000 pages, are in the process of being edited and published.

23. *Book of Mormon*, concordance ("Topical Guide"), page 97.

24. Vastokas, Joan M., and Romas K., *Sacred Art of the Algonkians*, Hansard Press, Peterborough, 1973.

25. Kelley, David H., "Proto-Tiffinagh and Proto-Teutonic Inscriptions at Peterborough, Ontario", *Review of Archeology*, Fall 1991, page 9.

26. Humber, Charles J., *Allegiance: The Ontario Story*, Heirloom Books, Mississauga, 1991, page 6.

27. Varga, Domokos, *Hungary in Greatness and Decline*, Korvina Kaido, Budapest, 1970, page 18.

28. *Hungary in Greatness and Decline*, page 20.

29. Peguy, Charles, from "La Tapisserie de Sainte Genevieve" in *Oeuvres poétiques completes*, Paris 1957, page 849. This poem was quoted and reproduced in *The Holy Blood and the Holy Grail* but with an inadequate English translation. "Les armes" do not refer to body parts but to weapons. The French word *jamb* means a physical arm. In order to convey the actual sense of the poem, Joelle Lauriol chose a shield for Jesus and a sword for Satan — weapons — but her choice was arbitrary.

Chapter 11. The Niagara Thicket

1. The four-horned depictions of Baphomet have generally been considered a fanciful and imaginary. But there may have been four horned goats. In his *Exotic Zoology* (Bonanza Books, New York, 1987, pages 23-27), Willey Ley devotes a chapter to the artificial alteration of the horns of ruminants. By performing an operation on the horn buds of newly born sheep, goats, and cattle, the number of horns in the adult can be increased or reduced and their placement changed within limits. Four horned goats were created, mostly on Cyprus, as leaders of herds. With cattle, a one-horned or "unicorn" bull seems to be more assertive than normal two-horned bulls. Unicorned bulls were therefore created to lead cattle herds, mostly in Africa and the Middle East. Copying techniques used in the ancient Middle East, Dr. Franklin Dove of Orono, Maine, operated on the horn buds of a bull calf, transplanting the buds to the middle of the calf's forehead. The result was a one-horned bull with a well-developed and perfectly centred horn. Dr. Dove related that his unicorn was very assertive towards other bulls and was able always to intimidate them

(*The Scientific Monthly*, May 1936, pages 9-14).

    I don't think we can rule out the possibility that the Templars may have learned how to perform these operations and created unicorns and four-horned Baphomets for ritual purposes.

2. Or 1957, the date is uncertain.

3. Earlier I promised to give some tips to North American treasure hunters. The Susquehanna and Allegheny rivers would be good places to look for caches of Ancient Celtic or Templar metal. Lake Memphremagog and the Green Mountains are as tempting today as they were in Joseph Smith's time. But, in my opinion, the most likely site of a purposefully hidden collection of Templar or Grail treasure would be between Lake Chatauqua and Lake Erie. For reasons given in the text, I think that may have been the last concentration of Grail Knights population before their dispersal into the far west.

Acknowledgements

Any nonfiction book that has been in preparation for over a decade owes debts to many people. Some people have contributed ideas, bibliographic research and bibliographic discoveries. Others have undertaken the sweat and effort of field investigation with the occasional reward of artefacts or evidence. Still others have contributed the intellectual effort of discussion and correspondence in order to help the author arrange jig-saw pieces of evidence into a potentially coherent picture. And last, but certainly not least, some people contributed *money* that allowed all the foregoing to come together and to result in a book.

All too often, when I've read acknowledgements by other authors, I've seen that those who donated *money*, which permitted the work to go forward, have been the last to receive recognition for their part in books (or other projects) that might expand our knowledge and conceptions. I'd like to reverse this process here and therefore first thank people who put hard cash on the line in order to discover whether a nebulous idea about the European history of North America could be supported by artefacts and evidence.

At the top of this list comes Joelle Lauiol of Ottawa, who answered a cryptically worded advertisement about the Holy Grail. She not only quickly assumed many of the costs of writing this book, a project and expense that she knew would be long and drawn-out because of my physical situation, but (born in France) she turned her attention to the many necessarily French reference sources of this book. She helped not only with "translation," but also with interpretation, basic research, and field trips. *Grail Knights of North America* would not have been written without the financial, intellectual, and emotional support of Joelle Lauriol.

Second comes Peter Flemington, Program Director of VISION TELEVISION of Toronto. At a time when I had just suffered a serious illness, and when he could not have known whether my investigations could ever result in a television presentation for his station, he nonetheless bought the non-exclusive television rights to my then non-existent correlation of my then incomplete research (on the strength of my 45-page script) for several thousand dollars. As I think even he probably suspected, this allowed me to pursue research rather than to produce a finished television program for his station.

Third, Richard and Delayne Coleman, prominent in the Prince Henry Sinclair Society of North America, responded with almost equal generosity as did Peter Flemington, giving me additional funds to pursue my research — and even inviting me to their summer home in Guysborough County, Nova Scotia. There, I had a first-hand opportunity to see the very harbour where Prince Henry Sinclair probably landed, to view the sites that the Colemans had earmarked as monuments to this first known settlement of Europeans in North America (and to meet those artists whom the Colemans had assigned the task of creating the monuments), and there also (fearing that I might not complete the project), I offered Richard Coleman co-authorship of this book. He refused this offer on the grounds that I should complete it myself. Richard's refusal helped me to recover.

Hounslow Press, publisher of *Holy Grail Across the Atlantic* in 1988, and now a division of The Dundurn Group, encouraged the birth of the project with a modest advance.

Rae Thurston of Toronto purchased a film option on a novel (*Vice Royal*) based on some of this research, thereby assisting in further nonfiction research. Although *Vice Royal* could not be written in either fiction or nonfiction guise for reasons explained in the following pages, Rae's enthusiasm and interest were constant inspirations.

I would also like to thank my fellow writer-researcher Winnie Czulinski for her research, discussion, and intellectual support over more than five years; Dr. Gerard Leduc for his fascination with my former book, *Holy Grail Across the Atlantic*, and his undying enthusiasm for finding new evidence of early European visitors in northeastern North America, and his generosity in supplying information and photographs; Dr. David H. Kelley, Professor Emeritus of the University of Calgary, Alberta, for his lack of fear in sharing investigations with "amateurs"; Rob Iveson of Toronto for his attempts to film (or videotape) evidence that was not "politically correct" and that could compromise his career in Canada's uncourageous intellectual environment; Monica Kuehn, art student, whose physical stamina, courage, and clear focus at Peterborough earned her only a bare passing grade in her project to challenge "political correctness" in an academic environment; Don Eckler of Houghton, New York, for his research and field trips and for his making available to me many photographs of artefacts and his carte blanche permission to reproduce them; Bob Williams of Emporium, Pennsylvania, for his discovery of so many anomalous sites in his beloved mountains that may contribute to writing another chapter of North American history; Dr. Dan Kolos, Egyptologist, for supplying me with research and for lively discussions; Claudette Leblanc of Barrie, Ontario, for finding the intriguing sketch of the castle and for much hospitality and fascinating conversations.

Special thanks are due to Michael Twose of Toronto, who accompanied me on many trips to visit sites and artefacts, and who assisted with photography.

Although everyone mentioned above (and many more) contributed to *Grail Knights of North America*, I alone am responsible for errors and the fundamental concept.

I would like to thank the Champlain Society for permission to reproduce maps from the six-volume (plus folio, with maps) *Works of Samuel de Champlain*; the Museum of Antique Art in Rome, the Louvre Museum in Paris, and the Ashmolean Museum at Oxford University for permission to reproduce material in their collections; Chilton Books, for permission to reproduce material from *Maps of the Ancient Sea Kings* by Charles Hapgood; W.W. Norton & Company for permission to reproduce the sketch of the Newport Tower in *The Lost Discovery* by Frederick Pohl.

I would like to extend special thanks to Michael Baigent, co-author of *The Holy Blood and the Holy Grail*, for stimulating correspondence and a fascinating plan to do joint research and writing about Templar cartographers on Majorca. I also appreciate Niven Sinclair's invitation to become involved in the Henry Sinclair replica voyage project, and Peter Cummings's letters and phone conversations from the Prince Henry Sinclair Society of North America. I would like to thank Neil Sinclair, Head of Clan Sinclair in Canada, for his hospitality at his home in Economy, Nova Scotia.